BRADDOCK'S COMPLETE GUIDE TO HORSE-RACE SELECTION AND BETTING

WITH STATISTICAL INFORMATION BY 'TRAINERS RECORD'

Second Edition

PETER BRADDOCK

Longman Group UK Limited,
Longman House, Burnt Mill, Harlow,
Essex CM20 2JE, England
and Associated Companies throughout the world.

© Longman Group Limited 1983

This edition © Longman Group UK Limited 1987

First published 1983
Third impression 1984
Second edition 1987
Second impression 1987

British Library Cataloguing in Publication Data

Braddock, Peter
  Braddock's complete guide to horse-race
  selection and betting: with statistical
  information by Trainers record. – 2nd ed.
  1. Horse race betting – Great Britain
  I. Title
  798.4'01'0941   SF333.G7
  ISBN 0-582-50332-9

Set in 10/11 Linotron Bembo

Printed and Bound in Great Britain
at the Bath Press, Avon

Betting, Backers and Bookmakers

'Never in the field of human endeavour
has so much been given
by so many
to so few'

CONTENTS

FOREWORD

The millions of racing fans who either daily or weekly invest their pounds on the horses come in many shapes and sizes as do their bets. As someone who has lived with the betting ideal for two decades, it is easy to identify the born winners and born losers.

The race-track and the betting shop are a minefield through which the backer must move in order to survive. Either painful lessons are acted upon or the result is penury.

The borderline between the poorhouse and prosperity where gambling is concerned is a thin one. But the serious backer needs to discipline himself to avoid the obvious pitfalls.

I believe that over the years, as the wounds have healed, I have managed an *ad hoc* safety system. Peter Braddock, by contrast, in his *Guide to Horse-Race Selection and Betting*, has systematically laid down rules which he found helpful in his own considerable success as a selector of horses.

The size of the work should not scare the reader. Logic is the thread which runs through these pages; common sense and analytical care the criteria for employing his thoughts.

Only the serious person should apply. Racing success only comes to those willing to work at it. As Fred Hooper, breeder of the year for 1982 in the United States said at the Eclipse Awards in San Francisco in February 1983, 'People say I'm lucky, it's true, I'm very lucky. In fact, the harder I work, the luckier I get.'

I think that speech is the most appropriate sentence or two I could use to apply to Peter Braddock's *magnum opus*. Luck comes to those prepared to work for it. I can guarantee that from the minute I changed my own approach from that of the lazy guesser to the keen form student, the winners began to roll in.

While it might be inappropriate to add my own private coda to someone else's work, I feel I must.

Two rules I always follow. Never bet odds-on, though I realize that a 5–4 on chance with nothing to beat on the Braddock system could for others be a betting proposition *par excellence*.

Second, never be afraid to win too much. I have found that when a horse is a better price than your research tells you it should be, the appropriate action is to increase your bet. If much shorter than you think, either drastically reduce or even abandon it. You will find that even a winner below the expected odds causes little irritation to the disciplined backer.

But now I leave you in the capable hands of Peter Braddock, and also the superb statistical tables of Peter Jones of *Trainer's Record*. They will give you plenty of food for thought, and just the right mixture of awareness and dexterity to win the battle with the bookies.

Good luck, work hard and accept the rewards which will follow.

Tony Stafford
Racing Editor
Daily Telegraph

ACKNOWLEDGEMENTS

We are indebted to the following for permission to use copyright material:

The Jockey Club and Daily Mail for our Figs 4.1, 4.2 and the racecards featured in Chapter 12; The Jockey Club and Racing Post for our Figs 4.5 and 4.6; The Jockey Club and The Sporting Life for our Figs 4.3 and 4.4; Sporting Chronicle Publications Limited and Raceform Limited for our Fig. 4.7; Timeform and Portway Press for our Fig. 4.8 and Ed Byrne, George Selwyn and Alec Russell for the rest of the photographs.

Cover photograph: by kind permission of Sporting Pictures (UK) Ltd.

1 THE SELECTION PROCESS

The aim of this book is simple – to promote the rational process of picking winners. It identifies the factors responsible for producing successful selection results encapsulating these elements in an easy-to-apply selection formula.

The principles of selection are simple, encompassing four basic issues: *Form, Fitness, Class, Conditions*, as a reliable framework to race assessment. The formula promotes the questioning of assumptions, the establishing of facts and encourages a development in the powers of logical reasoning. The book makes no claim to hold the key to an easy or instant fortune from betting. It does, however, provide a reliable framework for the thorough understanding of horse-racing. By this means and by the backer's own application to the task can the book-makers' advantage by nullified. Then, and only then, will a regular profit from horse-racing become a reality.

'To bet or not to bet', is the question facing every backer. Before every betting decision a vital factor – *choice* – distinguishes the attitude of the bettor from that of the punter. He alone decides whether or not to bet, and what, when and how to bet. The punter is oblivious of having a choice.

The bettor bets always with the sole purpose of winning money. It is an activity with a clearly defined and limited aim. Betting is a financial investment of the highest-risk money with the possibility of most lucrative returns. The bettor bets only when in his judgement the chances of winning are most favourable. It is always an act of free will in response to the merits of a situation.

The punter is a victim in the world of gambling. Allured by the prospect of winning money, but depressed, disheartened and disappointed at the actuality of losing, the punter gambles whenever he can no longer resist the temptation. It is never an impassive act, but always a response to retrieve past losses or fulfil a dream of having a big win.

In practice the backer is likely to fluctuate between the two approaches, more easily being drawn into the weak acts of the punter than the strong posture of the bettor.

Betting is a hard struggle in which only the most able survive. And so with this stern warning it must be left to the backer's own counsel to accept the challenge and decide whether 'To bet or not to bet'.

While there may be various methods of non-independently achieving successful selection results (ranging from 'informed tips' to a computerized evaluation of selection), it is intended here to provide the backer with an independent *selection method* that produces successful results. This selection method is encapsulated in a *selection formula*, which incorporates four cardinal principles – *Form, Fitness, Class* and *Conditions*.

FORM

Form is the major consideration in selection, with the other factors serving only as modifying agents. Form is the undisputable record of performance, a record of what a horse has or has not achieved, the sole means of reliably assessing and comparing *ability*. Top-class form is extremely reliable and evokes the statement: 'Form beats everything.' Form is the factor in selection which should never be underestimated.

FITNESS

This is the second principle in the formula and is always likely to have a major influence on form. 'Peak race fitness' must never be assumed without some proof. The most reliable evidence that a horse is 'fit' will be indicated from a race performance within the previous 7 days. A horse should, however, not be automatically considered 'fit' because it has run within the previous 7 days if the quality of that performance is not up to the prescribed standard. Fitness is a balancing factor which can invalidate form.

CLASS

This is the third principle of the formula, and can have a most powerful modifying influence on selection. In terms of horse-racing, class can be defined as the quality of competition a horse races against.

For selection purposes:

- A horse when raised in class has to improve upon its known ability and form.
- A horse in the same class has to reproduce form equivalent at least to what it has shown in that class.
- A horse lowered in class has merely to repeat its normal level of ability as shown in the higher class to have a winning chance.

Class, therefore, in selection assumes a negative, neutral or positive character.

CONDITIONS

This is the fourth and final principle of the selection formula. Conditions will act as an important balancing mechanism in the selection decision when other factors appear equal. The conditions for consideration are: distance; going; weight; penalties; course; draw; jockeyship; sundry factors.

DISTANCE

A horse's ability to stay a distance cannot be accepted until proven by the test of a race. Most horses have only one distance at which they can produce their best form.

GOING

This is the term referring to ground conditions of the race-track. Most horses have a preference for a certain type of going and may be unable to produce their true form on other going.

WEIGHT

The more weight a horse carries the slower it will run – it is the leveller of ability. The handicap weights of horses are constantly being reassessed and changed to correspond to their performances.

Penalties of weight are given to horses after they have won a race. Weight conditions and penalties in a race must always be very seriously considered.

COURSES

Racecourses in the British Isles vary as much in size, shape, sharpness and stiffness in undulation as they do in location, and on National Hunt courses the fences that will be encountered also vary in size and stiffness. The peculiarity of courses produces course-specialists; whether a track suits a horse's style of racing and action may be an important consideration in certain instances.

DRAW

The draw is the position across the racecourse where a horse is placed to start a race. The draw is mainly of significance in sprint races when there are large fields, and one side of the course gives a particular advantage to a horse. *The draw in these instances will be a distinct advantage* to a horse, often to the extent of completely nullifying the chances of a badly drawn horse.

JOCKEYSHIP

The performance of a quality jockey can be the difference between winning and losing a race. Jockeyship at all levels and types of racing is often the margin between victory and defeat.

SUNDRY FACTORS

These include the fitting of blinkers or a visor, which can have a devastating or detrimental effect on a horse's performance. A trainer's record and the stable's current form are also factors to be carefully noted; as are a horse's breeding and ownership.

This selection formula has been designed to make the process of selecting winners a more exact and less hazardous operation. It identifies the constantly important elements which affect the results of races. By careful formulation of the relevant factors and the orderly presentation of this vital information the selector can make logical selection decisions.

2 HORSE-RACING THROUGHOUT THE YEAR

Throughout the British Isles there are two major types of horse-racing: Flat racing and National Hunt racing. Flat racing principally concerns younger horses, and is ostensibly oriented to improve the speed qualities in the thoroughbred horse. National Hunt racing concerns older horses with an emphasis on qualities of strength and endurance as well as speed.

There are separate racing seasons for each type of racing. The Flat race season in the United Kingdom lasts approximately 8 months, beginning in late March and finishing in the early part of November. Meanwhile, the National Hunt season lasts approximately 10 months, starting in the first week in August and ending in the first week in June of the following year.

The Flat race season allows for the younger horses (colts and fillies still in a process of growth and development) and much affected by climatic conditions, to reach their natural physical peak during the more clement weather of late spring, summer and early autumn.

The National Hunt season in contrast, encounters the extremes of climatic conditions; meetings in midwinter may be cancelled due to the harshness of frost, snow or rain, while early in the National Hunt campaign, meetings may be cancelled due to the hard ground and equally dangerous conditions for racing.

FLAT RACING – THE SEASON

There are good-class (valuable) Flat races throughout the season, commencing with the competitive 1m Lincoln Handicap at Doncaster in March in the first week of the season and culminating with the equally competitive 1½m November Handicap in the last week. In between there is a carefully planned programme of racing, highlighted by the three Classic meetings of: the Guineas (at Newmarket in early May);

the Derby (at Epsom in June); and the St Leger (at Doncaster in September). Similar competitive prestigious and valuable race meetings are held at: Ascot (in June) the Royal Meetings; at Goodwood (in July); and the York Festival in August. Many of the leading Flat-race stables focus their training schedule on these events, and are aided in a balanced programme of other races which serve as, and are often recognized as, trials for the major events. Throughout the Flat-race season, there will be opportunities for horses of all classes and preferences to find a race particular to their needs where they should be able to display their true ability.

THE FLAT-RACE HORSE

Flat racing and flat-race horses are essentially concerned with *speed* – speed in races, and a demand for swift physical development, so a horse's abilities at racing may be quickly exploited resulting in many horses being quickly 'burnt out' after a few races and ensuring a short and sharp Flat-race career.

A Flat-race horse's racing life usually begins as a 2 y.o. All thoroughbred racehorses are given an official birthday of 1st January irrespective of what date in the year they are actually foaled – a horse foaled in February and a horse foaled in June will both be officially considered a year old on the 1st January of the following year when one is approximately 10 months old and the other 6 months old.

This can lead to considerable physical disparity in horses in the early part of their lives, especially as 2-year-olds and this imbalance may not be properly resolved until the middle part of their 3-year-old season at racing. A survey of the foaling dates for winning 2 year olds during a recent season shows the advantage that relatively older horses have.

Month foaled in	Winners	Runners		
January	54	439	=	12.3%
February	124	1313	=	9.4%
March	269	2794	=	9.6%
April	248	2991	=	8.3%
May	134	1750	=	7.7%
June	7	101	=	6.9%

Most horses that begin racing as 2-year-olds end their Flat-racing lives by the time they are 5-year-olds. This is either due to injury, complete lack of ability, because they have been retired for breeding purposes (this happens to most fillies, and the best colts will stand as stallions), or more generally because their waning powers of speed means a generation of younger horses supersedes them.

- As a 2 y.o. a horse is physically immature (comparable to a child in human terms).
- As a 3 y.o. its maturity begins (ossification will begin to occur) and it is like a teenager becoming a young adult.
- At 4 years of age a horse is reaching its physical peak – and is usually considered to be at its prime for Flat racing.
- As a 5 y.o. a horse is fully mature – a colt is considered a horse and a filly is considered a mare – there will unlikely be further physical development which would aid a horse's Flat-race career.

Flat racing has a rapidly and constantly changing population in horses as a new crop of 2-year-olds appear every season and replace other and older horses. The fortunes of most Flat-race stables revolve around their yearly intake of new fresh young horses from the sales and private studs. These horses arrive as unbroken yearlings, and each trainer has the often unenviable task of attempting to turn these raw recruits into efficient racing machines. The pressures on a trainer are likely to be high – many of these horses may represent a high financial investment by their owners who will get little or no return on their outlay unless these horses become winners. The risks, therefore, are great, but similarly the rewards to the successful will be enormous for top/good-class Flat-race horses have a considerable value at stud as potential brood mares and stallions.

It will be only the comparative few who are successful and whose future may seem pleasantly assured; the remainder are likely to encounter varying fates. Some will be sold to race abroad in racing of lower standard. Some will be sold out of racing altogether and some will enter a new career as novice National Hunt horses.

NATIONAL HUNT RACING – THE SEASON

The National Hunt season is long and protracted, lasting 10 months and encountering the best and worst extremes of weather conditions. Beginning at the height of summer in the first week of August, it slowly unfolds throughout the autumn, reaching a zenith of activity during the winter months of December, January and February (weather permitting).

The climax of the season comes in March with the 3-day Cheltenham Festival meeting which serves as a championship decider for horses of all types (hurdlers/chasers, novices and experienced horses) over varying distances. Competition is extremely fierce, for not only are the best English horses contesting these most valuable and prestigious races but also the best of Irish horses as well. Irish-bred and trained National Hunt horses for many years have held sway over the British National Hunt scene, and each year they continue to display their influence by capturing a high proportion of races at the Festival meetings. The Aintree (Liverpool) meeting follows a few weeks later and includes the running of the Grand National. This meeting, held similarly over 3 days, signals the progressive slowing down of the National Hunt season during April and its culmination at the end of May.

Throughout the season there should have been opportunities and conditions to suit every type and class of horse, i.e. early and late season provides chances for the more moderate horses and those specializing on firm ground, while the bog-like conditions of winter should allow the heavy-going specialist chances to excel.

The better-class and champion horses will usually not be risked on anything but the best going, and this will certainly be found at some stage during the season. Good-class and valuable races are programmed throughout most of the season, but they tend not to commence until November, when public attention will be focused fully on National Hunt racing, as by this time the Flat season has ended. Many races will serve as trials in the build-up to the Cheltenham Festival, giving the public and trainers ample information upon which to assess ability.

THE NATIONAL HUNT HORSE

National Hunt racing is an extreme test of basic physical qualities in a horse – soundness, endurance and durability. Although speed and jumping ability are essential requirements of any winning perform- ance, these talents will never be fully realized unless a horse is able to withstand the constant rigours inherent in this code of racing. The ever-present unpredictable element posed in a race by obstacles and injury conspires to make National Hunt racing a powerful leveller of horses and men. This ensures it retains its original sporting flavour, attracting its supporters (owners, etc.) from farming and hunting com- munities where there is an appreciation of the difficulties, uncertainties and patience required to bring a National Hunt horse to full racing maturity. Many successful National Hunt horses have been bred and reared by their owners whose sympathetic interest and involvement has made certain the horse be given unhurried consideration to establish a racing career. Success emanating from such an approach cannot be simply bought, and therefore this aspect of the National Hunt horse has no attraction for the business-orientated Flat-race entrepreneur of bloodstock who seeks a fast and assured return on investment.

While the racing life of a Flat-horse is likely to be short, by contrast the National Hunt horse avoiding serious injury may expect five or six seasons, involving a two-part career, first as a hurdler then as a chaser. The length of time a horse spends as a hurdler or chaser will be determined by the age at which it embarked on a National Hunt career and what was considered initially as its possible forte. A hurdler is considered to be at its peak at 6 or 7 years and a chaser is thought normally to be at the height of its powers at 9 or 10 years.

Horses taking part in National Hunt races have come into this type of racing from two different sources: ex-Flat-race horses and those horses bred primarily for National Hunt racing (often called 'store' horses). Ex-Flat horses with any ability at all are usually quickly able to learn the requirements of their new career and develop into efficient hurdlers. However, they tend to lack the physical scope and resilience that is necessary to become top-class chasers. The 'store-type horses' bred on more stoic lines whose long-term objective is to 'make up' into chasers develop more slowly, sometimes being unable to win a hurdle race before they achieve success as chasers. A horse's ability as a chaser may bear no resemblance to its ability as a hurdler (for better or worse) and it is therefore necessary to consider objectively the progress of a novice chaser.

All horses when first entering either mode of National Hunt racing are considered novices, novice hurdlers/novice chasers – and initially for their first season compete in novice events against similar horses. If a horse wins in its first season of National Hunt racing, it will no longer be considered a novice, and will graduate to handicap class in its second season. A horse that does not win can seasonally remain in the novice class until it achieves a success. Similarly, a horse – whether an unsuccessful novice hurdler or an experienced handicap hurdler or a previously unraced National Hunt horse – when tried as a chaser will compete in the novice chase class.

A horse cannot compete in a National Hunt race until the August of its 3-year season, so officially it will be at least 3½ years old (and ossification will have taken place, or will be taking place in its development).

A 3 y.o. can then only compete in juvenile hurdles against horses of the same age until it reaches its official fourth birthday at the turn of the year, midway through its first season. A horse may also not compete in chases until it is 4 years 8 months old (officially). This will occur in the August of its second season of racing.

Horses will vary in capacity and rate of development as National Hunt performers – learning how to jump quickly and accurately and gaining the physical strength necessary to endure the stress of National Hunt racing will be factors comparable with speed in the make-up of a successful National Hunt horse. (This is why horses of moderate Flat-race ability can become stars at the winter race game for it requires different qualities.) National Hunt horses are generally geldings, because entire horses are usually less than inclined to maintain an interest in racing if certain sensitive parts of their anatomy are endangered – this means that a horse's future and value outside racing is limited. (Unsuccessful National Hunt horses will be sold out of racing altogether, as hunters or as potential point-to-point hunter–chasers.)

It is therefore necessary for a National Hunt horse to maintain and/or increase its value entirely from its participation in racing (this will be closely associated with its earning potential as a racehorse) and is best served by the consideration of its long-term rather than short-term future. National Hunt horses will normally be raced on this basis, and it is a factor that should always be carefully considered when making a selection.

3 TYPES OF RACE

To achieve consistently successful results it is necessary that selection be limited to the more easily assessable types of race.

This fundamental consideration places all races into two distinct categories:

1. *Level weight races*. Races where horses carry (basically) the *same* weights.

   These are the more easily assessed and therefore the most favourable type of race for selection.

2. *Handicaps*. Races where horses carry different weights.

   These races are usually more difficult to assess and should be contemplated for selection only by the experienced selector.

THE TYPES OF 'LEVEL WEIGHT' RACE

There are level weight races for horses of all ages, class and distance in both codes of racing (Flat/National Hunt).

There are acceptable variations in the literal interpretation of the term 'level weights'. These are:

1. *Sex allowance* (Flat racing). Colts and horses are expected to give fillies and mares (and sometimes geldings) a 3 lb weight allowance to offset their expected physical superiority. (National Hunt racing.) Colts, horses and geldings give a weight concession of 5 lb to fillies and mares in all chases, hurdles and National Hunt Flat races.
2. *Weight-for-Age allowance* (applies to Flat and National Hunt). Horses of different ages racing against each other are set to carry different weights according to the time of year and distance of the race to take account of the maturity advantage.
3. *Condition races* (Flat/National Hunt). Races where horses are set to carry weights solely in accord to the particular entry conditions of the race.

11

The 'level weight' types of race most favoured for purposes of selection are, in order of preference and reliability:

Flat races
 (i) 2 y.o. and 3 y.o. and condition races
(ii) 2 y.o. and 3 y.o. – maiden races

National Hunt
  (i) Novice hurdles – condition hurdles
 (ii) Condition chases
(iii) Novice chases

FLAT RACES

TWO-YEAR-OLD RACES

There are two types of basically level weight race for 2-year-olds – condition races and maiden races.

Condition races are open to previous race winners with the allocation of weight set in the entry conditions and varying from the strict level weight principle. Maiden races, by contrast, are strictly level weight events except for sex allowance and limited to horses yet to win a race.

Two-year-old condition races which include all the major prizes for the juvenile generation are likely to be the more reliable selection medium with winning form holding a strong influence on the outcome. In the 1985 Flat season 29.2 per cent of 2 y.o. condition races were won by horses who won their previous race. Two-year-old maiden races, although less demanding to win, can be more problematic as many horses have no previous form. In the 1985 Flat season 32.8 per cent of 2 y.o. maiden races were won by horses making their racecourse début.

Two-year-old races are the most reliable type of races in which to make selections, for 2 y.o. horses usually run consistently, and there are few discrepancies in the evolution of form. Table 3.1 suggests that the shorter distance races are the more predictable.

5f races –   contested all season are races demanding pure speed.
6f races –   are contested from mid-May onwards and are similarly focused towards the speed element.
7f races –   are contested from July onwards and while requiring a strong element of speed allow an opportunity for the horse bred to stay middle distances (1m 2f).

TABLE 3.1   Winning favourites in races for 2 y.o. during 1985 Flat season

Distance	Condition WFA* races Winners – races	Maiden races Winners – races	Total Winners – races
5f	50 – 100 = 50%	59 – 156 = 37.8%	109 – 256 = 42.6%
6f	42 – 99 = 42.4%	39 – 115 = 33.9%	81 – 214 = 37.6%
7f	28 – 66 = 42.4%	27 – 81 = 33.3%	55 – 147 = 37.4%
8f	12 – 23 } = 53.8%	9 – 34 } = 28.9%	25 – 64 = 39.1%
9f	2 – 3 }	2 – 4 }	
Total	134 – 291 = 46%	139 – 390 = 34.9%	270 – 681 = 39.7%

* WFA = weight for age.

1m + races – are staged from September onwards. For a 2 y.o., even
those bred to be stayers, 1m can be an extreme distance.
Maiden races for 2 y.o. of 1m are not reliable mediums
for making a selection (see Table 3.1). They are notor-
iously difficult races to assess as most horses competing
have unproven form and are unproven over the distance,
and many are horses which, having proved too slow
over shorter distances, are being run in the final hope
that their lack of speed was the strength of stamina in
disguise.

THREE-YEAR OLD LEVEL WEIGHT RACES

Three-year-old level weight races rival only 2 y.o. races in their reliability as good mediums for selection. Similar to the 2 y.o. level weight
contests there are condition and maiden races. Of the two, 3 y.o.
condition races are the better and will include some of the premier races
in the calendar (e.g. the Classics, their trials, etc.) and range down in
class to races formerly known as maidens at closing. Three-year-old
condition races contested by good horses with proven and winning
form are attractive vehicles for selection.

Maiden races attract horses of less ability. 'Maiden' is the term used to
describe a horse that has not yet won a race. Yet 3 y.o. maiden races are
a reliable type of race for selection. They are races designed for horses
that did not win a race during their 2 y.o. season. The better-class 3 y.o.
maiden races up until the end of July or August are good mediums for
selection (a horse still a maiden after this time, except in special circumstances, is likely to be at best moderate).

These races can involve well-bred and potentially good horses that were backward as 2-year-olds and unable to be given serious race opportunities, but who are likely to develop and display their ability over longer distances as 3-year-olds.

There are two types of 3 y.o. maiden races:

(a) *Maiden races* – limited strictly to horses that have not won a race.
(b) *Stakes races* (formerly referred to as maidens at closing and more properly classified as conditions races) – which allow any horse to run providing it has not won up to a month before the date of the race. These races, therefore, are contested by both maidens and previous winners, allowing winners to continue in maiden company for a short time after winning before graduating to more competitive handicap races.

Overall, 3 y.o. level weight races are second only to 2 y.o. races as reliable mediums for selection. However, some races according to distance are better than others, and the selector is advised to become acquainted with and identify their characteristics (see Table 3.2).

5f, 6f (usually referred to as sprints)

The basic quality necessary to win races over these distances is speed and this is an attribute that is usually readily discernible, especially in condition races, where horses are likely to have prior winning form. It should be noted that the longer a 3 y.o. remains a maiden competing at sprint distances the more moderate it is likely to be. For most horses numerous opportunities occur to win as 2-year-olds over these distances.

7f

This is an in-between distance, neither a pure sprint nor a test of stamina. It is best regarded as a specialist distance and selection should be limited to proven performers in condition races rather than un-proven maidens.

1m

The quality to win a 1m race will be one of some excellence, requiring a horse to have the speed to remain in contention throughout the race yet possess further acceleration within the final 2f to enable it to win. This calls for an almost perfect balance between speed and endurance exemplified in the demands of the first Classic races, the 1,000 and 2,000 Guineas. Mile condition races attracting good-class horses which have these desired qualities offer reliable selection opportunities, while 1m

TABLE 3.2 Winning favourites in races for 3 y.o. during 1985 Flat Season

Distance	Condition WFA races Winners – races		Maiden races Winners – races		Total Winners – races
5f 6f	5 – 11 ⎱ 10 – 26 ⎰	15 – 37 = 40.5%	5 – 15 ⎱ 6 – 18 ⎰	11 – 33 = 33.3%	26 – 70 = 37.1%
7f	15 – 35	= 42.9%	3 – 21	= 14.2%	18 – 56 = 32.1%
8f (1m)	34 – 72	= 47.2%	25 – 68	= 36.8%	59 – 140 = 42.1%
9f (1m 1f) 10f (1m 2f) 11f (1m 3f)	7 – 17 ⎫ 24 – 70 ⎬ 4 – 10 ⎭	35 – 97 = 36.1%	4 – 11 ⎫ 23 – 55 ⎬ 9 – 18 ⎭	36 – 84 = 42.9%	71 – 181 = 39.2%
12f (1m 4f) 13f (1m 5f) 14f (1m 6f) 15f (1m 7f) 16f (2m)	32 – 60 ⎫ 1 – 2 ⎪ 6 – 10 ⎬ 5 – 5 ⎪ 4 – 9 ⎭	48 – 86 = 55.8%	23 – 60 ⎫ 2 – 4 ⎪ 0 – 9 ⎬ 4 – 8 ⎪ 6 – 10 ⎭	35 – 91 = 38%	83 – 177 = 46.9%
Total	147 – 327	= 45%	110 – 297	= 37%	257 – 624 = 41.2%

maiden races attracting unproven performers need to be approached more cautiously. The influence of American breeding on British racing during the 1980s with all four winners of the 2,000 Guineas (1983–86) American bred has produced a general rise in standard of milers, and promises that these races should remain dependable selection mediums.

1m 1f – 1m 3f

The attributes necessary to win races between 1m and 1m 3f (usually referred to as middle distances) are not so readily definable for they are neither a test of pure speed nor a true test of stamina. Although some horses successful at these distances are specialist bred, many more are horses that have failed at other distances (i.e. horses bred for sprinting that have stayed longer distances and potential stayers that have won over shorter distances). As a result these events often prove less predictable and provide some unexpected outcomes.

1m 4f +

These are staying races and require that a horse has stamina to last out the longer distances. This is usually an easily discernible quality, making these reliable mediums for selection, especially in condition races. The extreme distances (1m 6f +) are likely to attract moderate horses who, it is hoped, will finally prove their forte in a test of stamina. These should be approached with caution.

Three-year-old maiden races can therefore be approached on this broad basis of characteristic requirements according to distance.

Races for 3 y.o. maiden fillies are definitely to be approached with caution because fillies with promising 2 y.o. form often fail to 'train on'. Meanwhile many fillies train on at different speeds and consequently their form is not always consistent, resulting in unlikely and unexpected results.

ALL-AGE (3 Y.O. AND UPWARDS) CONDITION RACES – OVER ALL DISTANCES

These range in class from important Group races down to much less prestigious prizes which may give a horse badly treated in handicaps the chance to win a race against inferior horses at basically level weights. They are all suitable races for selection.

NATIONAL HUNT RACES

NOVICE HURDLES

Novice hurdles are always level weight races with concessions only for weight for age (when it applies) sex allowances and penalties for previous winners. Novice hurdles are the most reliable type of National Hunt races to consider for selection. They are usually contested by horses in their first season of National Hunt racing, but remain also open to any horse which had not in a previous season won a hurdle race (see Table 3.3). Although all National Hunt races (except National Hunt Flat races*) require the jumping of obstacles – hurdles are smaller obstacles, the least encumbrant and therefore produce fewer fallers.

Novice hurdles are a reliable selection medium because horses of different and usually easily discernible abilities compete against each other at basically level weights.

All novice hurdles are run over a minimum distance of 2m and range in distance up to 3m approximately. The minimum age for any horse contesting a novice hurdle is as a 3 y.o. at the beginning of the National Hunt season in August, with these juveniles being considered 4-year-olds on their official birthday at the turn of the year midway through the season. There is no maximum age for horses competing in novice hurdles.

In consideration of age and distance for novice hurdles, 3 y.o./4 y.o. (juvenile novice hurdles) and 4 y.o. + (novice hurdles) stand almost on a par with each other in terms of reliability for selection.

Juvenile novice hurdles, broadly speaking, are contested by horses which have recently graduated to National Hunt racing from varyingly successful Flat race campaigns. Their National Hunt form will therefore be quite recent and demand no great scrutiny.

Novice hurdle races for older horses (4-year-olds +) tend to be contested by horses more specifically bred for the winter sport and whose ambitions as hurdlers are likely to be set within the long-term aims of their jumping career. Ex-Flat race horses do sometimes compete in these races after an unsuccessful first season as a juvenile hurdler or as an older ex-Flat-race recruit. The form of novice hurdlers for older horses sometimes appears more complex, as horses with considerable racing experience (albeit Flat race) may meet completely inexperienced newcomers to racing, while previous season novice hurdle form may have to be reconciled with the present season's performances.

Novice hurdle races over a distance of 2m are usually the most readily

---

* Races run on National Hunt courses with the hurdles removed – limited to claiming jockeys and amateur riders and horses that have never competed in any flat races.

TABLE 3.3 Novice hurdles during the 1985–86 National Hunt Season

	Novice hurdle (all age except juvenile) (sellers or novice handicaps not included)				Juvenile novice hurdle (first season – 3–4 y.o. – all distances)	All novice hurdle
	2m to 2m 2f	2m 3f to 2m 5½f	2m 6f to 3m+	Total	Total	Total
Fav.	134	41	15	190 = 38.3%	66 = 43.1%	256 = 39.4%
2nd fav.	66	30	9	105 = 21.2%	29 = 19.0%	134 = 20.6%
3rd fav.	50	14	4	68 = 13.7%	19 = 12.4%	87 = 13.4%
Non-fav.	99	29	5	133 = 26.8%	39 = 25.5%	172 = 26.5%
Total	349	114	33	496	153	649

Condition hurdles during 1985–86 National Hunt Season

	2m to 2m 2f	2m 3f to 2m 5½f	2m 6f to 3m+	Total
Fav.	9	2	4	15 = 39.5%
2nd fav.	6	–	4	10 = 26.3%
3rd fav.	6	1	1	8 = 21.0%
Non-fav.	2	2	1	5 = 13.2%
	23	5	10	38

assessed as the speed element necessary to win them is fairly easy to recognize.

Novice hurdles in excess of 2m but only up to 2½m approximately are similarly reliable selection vehicles although often they take horses into unproven areas in regard to stamina, and thus need to be approached with caution.

NB Four-year-olds competing in 2½m novice hurdle races should be treated with *great caution* as this is an extreme distance for a young horse, who is likely to lack the strength and stamina to cope with twelve flights of hurdles over a distance of 20f, particularly should the ground be soft or heavy. Four-year-old novice hurdlers, however, do improve month by month with age when tackling 2½m hurdles and by the final month of the year and their official fifth birthday are likely to be on a par with older rivals.

2m 6f novice hurdles

This is a specialized distance for any class of horse and presents a number of selection problems. It is not a satisfactory distance for most horses but an intermediary stage for horses moving up from 2½ to 3 miles.

3m novice hurdles

These are likely to be difficult races for selection. There are not many such races in the calendar and the form in those that exist tends to be moderate or unreliable. These races are contested primarily by horses of slow maturing or decidedly moderate ability. It is hoped that the slow maturing types may 'make up' into chasers, but they often lack the technique or speed to be successful as hurdlers. Others, meanwhile, are entered in the vain hope they may have the strength of stamina to compensate for their proven non–ability over shorter distances. Results can therefore be unpredictable and this type of race *must not* be contemplated for the purpose of selection. (It should, however, be noted that horses with ability in these contests are likely to so easily overshadow their rivals that they may win a number or sequence of long–distance hurdles, but usually at increasingly unrewarding odds.)

CONDITION HURDLE RACES UP TO 2½m (4 Y.O. AND UPWARDS)

Basically level weight races with the only concessions being weight-for-age and sex allowance and any particular entry conditions, these type of races for selection purposes are on a par of reliability with novice hurdles. They will include the Champion Hurdle and recognised trials.

Form is consistent, although top-class hurdle races may be competitive and provide a searching test for skilful selection.

CONDITION CHASES UP TO 3½m (5 Y.O. AND UPWARDS)

Basically level weight races with the only concessions being weight-for-age and sex allowance and any particular entry conditions. All chases require a horse to jump the larger obstacles provided in National Hunt racing. The size and concentration of fences can act as formidable hazards and may prevent horses who are jumping at racing speed from completing the course. This has therefore given rise to the assumption that all chases are hazardous ventures which should be avoided for selection purposes. However, this is *not* a fair assessment and experienced good-class horses are extremely reliable jumpers.

Thus condition chases may be considered a good medium for selection.

Horses of unequal ability will race against each other at basically level weights providing the test of selection to be a clear assessment of comparative ability.

The very top-class condition races will include the non-handicap races at the Cheltenham Festival and other races which will serve as trials for these. These races involve top-class experienced horses which are reliable and provide a fair test of the selector's skills (see Table 3.4.)

TABLE 3.4   Condition chases during 1985–86 National Hunt season

	2m–2m 2f	2m 3f–2m 5½f	2m 6f–3m+	Total
Fav.	1	7	7	15 = 44.1%
2nd fav.	1	7	4	12 = 35.3%
3rd fav.	—	1	2	3 = 8.8%
Non-fav.	1	—	3	4 = 11.8%
Total	3	15	16	34

NOVICE CHASES

Novice chases are basically level weight races with the only concessions being weight-for-age and sex allowance and penalties for previous winners. They are restricted to horses which before the start of the National Hunt season had not won a steeplechase. Although contested by horses inexperienced over the more formidable obstacles, in certain instances these are acceptable races in which to make a selection.

Proficient jumping is the essential quality which wins novice chases – a horse that does not complete the course has no possibility of winning the race. The fear of horses falling (which has to be strongly considered) has dissuaded many astute judges from selection in novice chases. This view gains support from the fact that all novice chasers by their nature will be inexperienced jumpers of the larger obstacles and that some will have been put to chasing after their failure in other aspects of racing (Flat racing and hurdling). This type of horse can be clearly identified and *must be avoided*. However, accepting that novice chases are often principally contested by slow and indifferent jumpers, it then becomes obvious that these types of race often take very little ability to win. Therefore a horse of proven hurdling ability (i.e. a good-class handicap hurdler) if 'put to' chasing (providing it has been properly schooled and can adapt its jumping technique to fencing) will have too much speed and ability for the average slow-moving novice chasers.

Handicap hurdlers (of ability) set to chasing are horses that must always be strongly considered in selection of novice chasers.

2m–2½m novice chases

These are usually the more attractive type of novice chase for the purpose of selection. They are contested frequently by horses with proven abilities in other spheres of racing (i.e. a previously successful hurdle or Flat race record) who from the speed aspect are therefore likely to outclass their rivals.

2m 5f+ novice chases

Described as long-distance novice chases, these may be seen as less desirable mediums for selection because they are contested principally by horses of moderate or unproven ability who lack this aspect of speed. The accent in long-distance novice chases is that of stamina, strength and steady, proficient jumping, especially as there are many obstacles to negotiate. These races attract contestants either specifically bred for this task and whose career is focused on their development to become staying chasers, or else horses of mediocre ability whose lack of speed render longer-distance chases as their last hope for redemption. It can therefore often take little ability to win these races, being contested as they are usually by inexperienced or moderate horses. With recent results showing an above-average record for the most favoured horses in long-distance novice chases, this may suggest them to be attractive mediums. However, a closer examination and realization of the nature of these races (i.e. long-distance races, over many large obstacles, often contested in extremes of ground conditions by horses usually without sound credentials of form who are frequently offered at unattractive short odds) show these races in their truer perspective of holding many selection pitfalls and from a long-term betting viewpoint to be uneconomic (see Table 3.5).

TABLE 3.5   Novice chases during the 1985–86 National Hunt season

	2m–2m 2f	2m 3f–2m 5½f	2m 6f–3m+	Total
Fav.	58	41	59	158 = 41.7%
2nd fav.	49	25	29	103 = 27.2%
3rd fav.	24	16	20	60 = 15.8%
Non-fav..	18	20	20	58 = 15.3%
Total	149	102	128	379

HANDICAPS

Handicap races can be full of enigmas and therefore it is usually difficult to predict their outcome.

They should be considered for serious purposes of selection only by the more experienced selector.

It is, however, advisable to examine some of their aspects to gain a wider understanding and realize their context in racing. Handicaps are designed to give horses of different abilities an equal chance of winning the same race by carrying different amounts of weight. Weight is allotted to each horse in accordance with its abilities; the best horse(s) carrying most weight and the worst horse(s) least weight. Handicaps are compiled by an experienced handicapper appointed by the Jockey Club.

Handicap races exist for horses of all types, ages, classes and for all distances, for Flat races and for National Hunt. Official handicappers tend to specialize in either Flat races or National Hunt.

TYPES OF HANDICAP AND PRINCIPLES

Age

Handicap races restricted to 2-year-olds are called nursery handicaps and are staged from July onwards. Older horses compete throughout the whole season in either all-age handicaps or handicaps confined to horses of a certain age group (i.e. for 3-year-olds only; for 4-year-olds and upwards, etc.). In National Hunt races there are handicaps restricted to novices whilst others are unrestricted.

Class

From selling class to horses just below group class. In flat racing selling handicaps are restricted to horses rated 0–25 and the best class handicaps are for horses rated 0–75.

Distance

From a minimum 5f to the marathon 4m 865yd of the Grand National.

Horses become eligible for handicaps under the following conditions:
- Two-year-olds if they have been placed first, second, third, fourth in a race and run three times unless having won a race.
- Other horses – Flat and/or National Hunt – must have run in three races or have won one race. National Hunt horses wishing to run in handicaps, but who have not qualified, are given an automatic top weight.

Initially, a horse is handicapped on the best form which it has shown. To win from that allotted weight a horse must repeat and/or improve upon its best performance. A horse's form is constantly being reassessed by the handicapper, and where and when necessary the horse is rehandicapped, i.e. a horse that has improved on its best form and/or won a race since being originally handicapped is moved up the handicap and given increased weight.

Horses that no longer seem to be able to reproduce their best form from their current weight have their weight reduced and moved down the handicap.

If a horse wins a race and then runs again (in a race where it has been handicapped on its previous best form) it is usually required to carry a winner's weight penalty (appropriate to the value of the race won).

Weight is the greater leveller of the abilities of horses, and this coupled with the change in abilities (improvement and deterioration) contrive to make handicap races the most difficult races to predict confidently. To be confident of winning a handicap requires that a horse is handicapped with a lower weight than is the true reflection of its ability. This situation occurs for a number of reasons:

1. A horse improving with and after every performance, yet can only be rehandicapped on what it has done; therefore it remains ahead of the handicapper.
2. A horse which has improved since its initial handicap assessment, and is better than its current handicap mark.

3. A horse that has been lowered in the handicap from its initial assessment, but has still retained the ability of its appropriate original handicap weight.

These occurrences, especially when a horse is considered remarkably leniently handicapped, are known as a 'blot in the handicap' – they occur very rarely as seldom does the handicapper make serious errors in judgement.

Deliberately losing a horse's form has long been a device used to gain a handicapped horse a winning opportunity. Before the horse is considered 'a good thing' it must be considered that similar conditions of legitimate improvement or malpractice apply equally to other horses in the race.

The consideration of these issues further complicates the difficulties and contrary elements which are present in handicaps.

Horses handicapped for Flat racing are rated by the official Jockey Club handicappers on a scale from 0 (the lowest) to 100 in steps of 1 lb. Thus, a horse rated 70 is thought to be 2 st better than a horse rated 42. Because the normal weight range in Flat handicaps is from 7 st 7 lb to 10 st, i.e. 35 lb, handicap races are graded to confine them to horses of broadly similar ability. A handicap of grade 0 to 35 (0.35) would therefore not be open to horses rated above 35.

The scale of grades for handicaps covering all distances are: 0.25, 0.35, 0.50, 0.60, 0.70, 0.75. As horses improve they may be raised in class in accordance with their rating, and if they deteriorate are then lowered. The range of handicaps allows for a horse rated at 35 to be given top weight in a 0.35 handicap yet a low weight in a top-class (0.70) handicap. A guiding rule to handicaps is – *The best horse on proven form is the top weight.* (If in doubt select the top weight.) Although a horse will not be top weighted without having shown some performances of merit, it is rather too sweeping a statement without consideration of other factors. These include:

1. Is the top weight clearly top weighted, i.e. having to give 7 lb, 14 lb, 21 lb to the second and third weight horses, or is the difference merely 1 lb, 2 lb or 3 lb in which case the difference of ability is likely to be negligible? If the horse is clearly top weighted, are the conditions favourable to concede the weight (its current form, fitness, going, distance and jockey)? It must then be considered how the horse has achieved top weight in the particular handicap.
2. Has the horse been promoted to top weight on the evidence of its most recent performances (i.e. an automatic weight penalty for winning or recent regrading as top weight as the resulting assessment of recent performances)? To defy this newly incurred top weight a horse must be capable of further improvement – only the

horse that is constantly improving and thereby keeping just ahead of the handicapper's rating can overcome the weight burden.

3. Has the horse top weight because it has been lowered in grade (i.e. a horse rated 35 – previously carrying low weights in 0.70 handicaps, dropped in grade 0.35 and required to carry top weight)?

4. The size and conformation of the horse will be a factor, some horses running better with lighter burdens against good-class opponents while others perform better carrying heavy weights against inferior opponents.

5. Ground conditions will similarly have great influence. It is more difficult for horses to carry big weights on soft or heavy ground because the weight has a more telling effect when conditions are testing. Conversely, when the ground is firm weight matters less and top weights are more likely to prevail.

6. If a horse remains top weight (without being downgraded) yet has no recent winning form, the handicapper in this instance still considers there is not enough evidence to constitute a lower rehandicapping of the horse. This may be because the horse has had an absence from racing, but is handicapped on its very best old form and therefore has had no recent opportunity to show whether its current ability still warrants its previously assessed handicap weight. Alternatively the horse may be readily holding its form but not making the necessary improvement to better it. In these circumstances, to gain a winning opportunity, the top weight must have the horses below handicapped to the limit of their ability and capable of no further improvement.

7. To win a handicap a horse must be on a weight level that is most favourable to its current fitness, form and ability.

It may be necessary because of the intricacy of handicap form to specialize in particular handicaps, e.g.

  5f/6f – 3 y.o. – all age
  7f/1m 1f – 3 y.o. – all age
  1m 2f/1m 5f – 3 y.o. – all age
  1m 6f+ 3 y.o. – all age

Similarly, National Hunt racing:

  2m hurdle – 4 y.o. – all age
  2½m hurdle – 2m 7f – 4 y.o. – all age
  3m+ hurdle – all age
  2m chase
  2½m chase
  3m+ chase

The selector will then become familiar with the particular value of form, a task almost impossible to someone trying to understand every type of race.

NURSERY HANDICAPS

Nursery handicaps are handicaps exclusively for the 2 y.o. and are not staged until the middle of July. Form is always recent, the oldest form even by October will not be more than 6 months old. Form of the top-weighted horses tends to work out consistently, although late-season (late October and November) horses that have had a hard season and reached the top of the handicap can become jaded. Opportunities then arise for lighter-weight opponents who appreciate the softer ground conditions.

The success of top-weighted 2-year-olds in nursery and penalized 2-year-olds generally, has given credence to the assumption that all 2-year-olds must be good weight carriers. This has no particular truth, although 2-year-olds (in company with other horses) that win races and gain top weight in handicaps or penalties in stakes races are invariably the fastest, strongest and healthiest. They tend to have the best con-formation, and are thus able to withstand the rigours of racing better than their peers and produce good consistent form.

The 5f–6f nurseries normally see a good display from the top-weighted horses. Races over these distances have been available for contention from the beginning or early season, giving an opportunity to most horses if good enough. The variances occur in races over 7f–1m, these races being staged for the first time later in the season.

Often, horses handicapped on their form over shorter distances are unable to reproduce it over longer distances while other horses improve considerably over longer distances.

HANDICAP CHASES

Like all chases, handicaps are won primarily due to jumping ability. They are seldom run at full racing pace from start to finish and place a prerequisite on fast, accurate jumping; consequently weight is of less account.

The horses who have reached the top of the handicap possess this ability, while the horses lower down the handicap tend to be poor, slow and/or erratic jumpers. Dependable jumping ability always gives a horse a possibility of winning, because if a horse does not complete the course it has no possibility of winning (see Table 3.6).

The best horses are those at the top of the handicap, and in many instances they can be clearly seen to have a winning chance, the mod-ifying factors being:

Current form (does it merit handicap weight?)
Fitness (is there proof of current fitness?)
Going (are conditions favourable – weight is a greater burden to concede on heavy or soft going?)

TABLE 3.6   Handicap chases during the 1985–86 National Hunt season

	2m–2m 2f	2m 3f–2m 5½f	2m 6f–3m+	Total
Fav.	65	49	99	213 = 36.9%
2nd fav.	48	37	61	146 = 25.3%
3rd fav.	26	16	38	80 = 13.9%
Non-fav.	33	40	65	138 = 23.9%
Total	172	148	265	629

SUMMARY OF HANDICAPS

Handicaps are designed to be competitive. The handicapper has sought to nullify the different abilities of horses by allowing each a weight in accordance with its abilities. Horses are then considered to have an equal chance of winning, weight being the great leveller of ability. Sufficient weight will defeat any horse and this constant consideration places a fine balance of judgement in selection and assessment of any handicap.

Handicaps on the Flat and National Hunt racing are popular spectacles, usually providing nail-biting finishes for excited punters, as frantic whip-waving jockeys are seen to drive their horses towards the winning post in a frenzy of action and colour.

Bookmakers often sponsor the more competitive types of handicap quite substantially, gaining business prestige and publicity in the process. Races of such a competitive nature enable the bookmakers to make a 'nice round book' (this means they show a very good profit whoever wins) beguiling the naive punter with generous odds.

The willingness of bookmakers to involve themselves in the sponsorship of handicaps must confirm to the selector that 'Handicaps can't be all good'.

COMMENTS ON VARIOUS TYPES OF RACE

THE CLASSICS (FLAT – LEVEL WEIGHTS + SEX ALLOWANCE)

The Classics are the top races for 3 y.o. colts and fillies. There are five Classic races programmed to take place throughout the season:

2,000★ and 1,000 Guineas, for colts and fillies respectively, run at Newmarket over a distance of 1m in the spring.

Derby★ and Oaks, for colts and fillies respectively, run at Epsom over a distance of 1½m in June.

St Leger, a race open to and regularly contested by both colts and fillies run over a distance of 1¾m at Doncaster in September.

The five Classic races are the Blue Riband events of the Flat race season; they are a stern and true test of ability, the most prestigious and among the most valuable in prize money of any events in the racing calendar. Only the best horses compete in the Classics, they are usually trained by the best trainers and ridden by the best jockeys and are therefore always fiercely competitive races. The challenge to selection in these events is to select the very best from the best – a daunting task – when

- the size of the field may be large;
- most of the runners will have at least a semblance of a chance of winning;
- each horse will be at peak fitness (time in preparation will not be spared).

The main point in favour of selection in such circumstances is that it will be made of top-class horses who reliably hold their form and can consistently reproduce their best performances. A note of caution, however, must be exercised in the consideration of form especially for the first two Classics (1,000 and 2,000 Guineas).

Form for the two early Classics will be based on two sources, the previous seasons 2 y.o. form (which will normally be over distances short of a mile) and the early season Classic trials; both require careful examination because their face value often proves deceptive and unreliable.

2 y.o. form in the consideration of 3 y.o. Classic contenders

Some horses vastly improve from their 2 y.o. days as they gain strength and maturity, while other more precocious individuals fail to develop further. This seems particularly to apply to fillies who were 'flying machines' as 2-year-olds over distances of 5f, 6f or 7f but fail to 'train on' as 3-year-olds and truly stay the distance of 1m.

EARLY SEASON CLASSIC RACE TRIALS

The early season trials in April often involve only partially fit horses on soft going and this form may be reversed as other horses obtain peak

★ It is worth noting that although fillies are eligible they rarely take part.

fitness and race on the normally fast dry ground of Newmarket Heath on Guineas days. Unless an unchallenged contender emerges with outstanding proven form – the first two Classics are likely to produce results which are difficult to forecast.

The Derby and Oaks pose other problems in selection. In June, Flat race form will have begun to be settled and the Classic trials will have produced a number of contenders for the premier Flat race crowns. The two major factors which consistently emerge as being responsible for a horse's failure at Epsom are: (i) its inability to stay the distance; (ii) the inability to act on the gradients and undulations of the course. Horses with the latter characteristic completely fail to negotiate the steep climbs, uphill and downhill gradients and the bends, while horses of speed with unproven stamina tire quickly in the last 2½–3f of the race. Another factor which only to a slightly lesser extent spoils a horse's chances is temperament – a horse becoming upset and overwrought before the race in the preliminaries in response to the noise and size of the crowd (100,000 people) thronging the course and downs.

The Derby and Oaks normally produce winners from among those horses which are considered the leading challengers of form and rarely provide shock outsiders. The English Derby 1974–86 has been won by first or second favourite eleven times. The English Oaks eight times. The winner of these premier Classics will normally be bred in the purple (by a British Classic winner or foreign equivalent) and will need the priceless ability to be able to accelerate almost instantly when asked in the last 2f of the race.

The St Leger can be considered the Classic race which is the most discernible for selection. It is staged in September, and by this time Flat race form at Classic level is well exposed and the abilities, stamina, limitations and requirements of the leading candidate is almost fully exposed. The only shadow to be cast on the consideration of a selection is that some horses who throughout the season may have proven their abilities in hard-fought races over shorter distances may have reached their peak and be unable to withstand the gruelling challenge over this extended distance. This is a factor that should be particularly noted, especially with the failure in recent St Legers of Shergar (1981), Ile de Bourbon (1978), Alleged (1977).

SELLING RACES (FLAT AND NATIONAL HUNT-LEVEL WEIGHTS AND HANDICAPS – FOR 2-YEAR-OLDS AND UPWARDS)

Selling races are contested by horses with the poorest racing ability. *They cannot be recommended* as satisfactory mediums for the purposes of selection. They were designed to give opportunities to horses of the most moderate ability, the winner being offered for sale at public auction after the race (hence 'selling' races) and so providing an owner with the chance to sell slow and unwanted horses for a reasonable price. The conditions of many selling races allows for any horse competing in the race to be claimed afterwards (sold to anyone) for a sum of fixed value in accord with the conditions of entry. These type of races therefore attract the worst type of horses who either have:

1. Little or no racing ability;
2. Are physically and/or temperamentally unsound and who cannot be depended upon to reproduce consistent performances.

In these circumstances there can never be any basis for confident selection and they are races that should normally be avoided.

The only positive factor in favour of selling races for selection or any other purpose is that they are races which require very little ability to win. This has led over the years for them to become a popular medium (especially by trainers and connections) for tilts at the betting ring and led to the adage 'follow the money in selling races'. Some of the less fashionable trainers who struggle to make a living from training alone subsidize their income with carefully planned and concealed coups in selling races. They retain in their stable a horse or two imperceptibly better than selling class who, when skilfully prepared and entered, can be guaranteed to collect the spoils. Such attitudes and approaches further undermine confidence in making selection in selling races, as sudden turnabouts in form can be incomprehensible. While stating that nefarious practices can occur in selling races, most often expectations fail to materialize because of the unreliability of bad horses. Although usually not a suggested medium for selection, the selector occasionally in very rare instances finds a horse of proven ability somehow inexplicably dropped into selling class and is presented with a golden opportunity to take advantage of such fortune.

AUCTION RACES (FLAT-LEVEL WEIGHT SEX ALLOWANCE FOR 2-YEAR-OLDS ONLY)

Auction races are maiden and condition races for 2-year-olds only, and limited to those that were bought at public auction as yearlings for below a prescribed maximum price (usually 10,000 guineas, with the first sale to govern should the horse have been subsequently reauctioned). Auction races are run over all distances from 5f up to 1m and staged throughout the season. They are designed to allow the inexpensively purchased yearling, as a 2 y.o., to race against similar rivals rather than being forced to contest races against very expensively purchased yearlings who would be expected to outclass their humbler opponents. The weight allotted to each horse will vary according to the entry conditions of the race with the provision of each horse receiving a weight in accord with the purchase price – the lower the purchase price the greater the allowance. This gives a good opportunity for unfashionably bred and consequently usually cheaper purchased horses to display their abilities on the race-track by receiving a weight allowance which may not reflect their form (for better or worse). Occasionally maiden auction races can provide a golden opportunity for a bargain–basement horse which has racing ability far in excess of anything expected or reflected by its original purchase price. Auction races can be seen as an interesting and sometimes profitable selection medium.

CLAIMING RACES (FLAT-LEVEL WEIGHTS, SEX ALLOWANCE WITH PENALTIES FOR WINNERS) FOR 2-YEAR-OLDS AND UPWARDS)

Claiming races are basically level weight contests where any horse entered may be claimed (or bought) after the race for the claiming price set in the entry conditions of the race. Claiming races, in class, are a grade or two (depending on the maximum claiming value) above selling races where all winners are offered for sale by auction and other horses may be claimed for a fixed sum. Whereas in selling races horses receive weight strictly according to the handicap, or on a level weights basis in stakes races, in claiming races horses deviate from the level weight principle directly in response to the claiming value placed upon them by their connections. Therefore, from the maximum claiming price, horses receive corresponding weight allowance as their claiming value is lowered – the higher-valued horses carrying most weight the lesser valued ones least. Claiming races can be seen to provide an opportunity for a good horse (perhaps otherwise difficult to place due to its high position in the handicap) to win a less than fiercely competitive race against inferior rivals without fear of the horse being lost at auction for a 'silly' price; or having to be bought back in for a very high price should the stable want to retain it, as is the case when a good horse wins a seller. However, if some buyer should emerge to claim the horse after the race this can only be for the agreed realistic sum set as the claiming price.

Claiming races open to both maidens and previous winners (which are penalized) allow horses often with quite a considerable disparity in their abilities to meet each other at basically level weights with concessions only in regard to their claiming price. In this respect claiming events are often quite easy to assess for selection, holding the possibility of a reasonable profit for the astute backer.

Claiming races have for many years had a high profile on the American horse-racing scene, and now with their popularity growing on this side of the Atlantic promise to assume a greater role here.

APPRENTICE RACES (FLAT-LEVEL WEIGHTS AND HANDICAPS)/CONDITIONAL JOCKEYS RACES (NATIONAL HUNT – LEVEL WEIGHTS AND HANDICAPS)

These races are staged to give young riders experience competing against their peers rather than against the senior and more experienced jockeys. They can be divided into different types:

1. Races limited to apprentices riding only for the stable they are apprenticed to. (This applies only to Flat racing and is designed to give the newest and youngest apprentices an early racecourse riding experience – many apprentices make their début in such races.)
2. *Races limited to apprentices/conditional jockeys* who have not ridden more than a prescribed number of winners.
3. *Non-conditional apprentice/conditional jockeys* – open to all claiming jockeys. These races whatever type, class or distance tend to be won by the most experienced rider competing (especially when there are considerable differences in experience) who is likely to be offered the mount on the horse with the best winning chance.

All these races must be judged on their merits for selection purposes, but conforming strictly to the criteria suggested for race selection – level weights receiving first consideration.

NB. Do not engage in selection in races where inexperienced horses (who may require strong and skilful handling) are ridden by young, equally inexperienced riders.

AMATEUR RACES (FLAT AND NATIONAL HUNT – LEVEL WEIGHTS AND HANDICAPS)

Amateur races, once the almost exclusive preserve of National Hunt racing, have with the introduction of lady riders into the sport become increasingly popular and grown in number in the Flat race calendar.

Amateur races initiating from the hunter chases in the National Hunt programme have spread to include handicap chases, hurdles and novice events, as well as now running the full gamut of distances and types of races in the Flat programme. Amateur races are largely supported by, and provided for, owners who wish to ride their horse(s) in public and by other dedicated and often more proficient enthusiasts who cannot or have no wish to enter the professional riding ranks in racing. Similarly to apprentice races, the most proficient and experienced riders gain the mounts on the best horses, and carefully noting the jockeys in these races often holds the key to selection. The top leading amateur riders (National Hunt) rank with many of their professional counterparts, and many leading professional riders have graduated from the amateur ranks.

Leading amateur riders during recent National Hunt seasons are:

Mr T. Easterby (9 st 7 lb)

Mr T. Thomson-Jones (10 st 2 lb) – Amateur Champion 1985–86

Gee Armytage (9 st) – Ladies' Champion 1985–86

Leading amateur riders during recent Flat race seasons are:

Mr R. Hutchinson (9 st 7 lb)

Amanda Harwood (9 st 0 lb)

Mr T. Thomson-Jones (10 st 2 lb)

Maxine Juster (8 st 7 lb)

Brooke Sanders (8 st 12 lb)

Franca Vittadini (8 st 3 lb)

Amateur races play a useful role and provide variety in racing – amateur races of level weights (Flat and National Hunt) can be an extremely reliable medium for selection.

HUNTER CHASES (NATIONAL HUNT – LEVEL WEIGHTS; DISTANCE 2½m+)

Hunter chases begin the National Hunt programme on 1 February, continuing for the remainder of the season. They are limited to horses that have been certified as hunters during the hunting season and have not taken part in any National Hunt or Flat races after 1 November. These races are supported by the farming/hunting community who provide the backbone to National Hunt racing and are contested by point-to-point horses and ex-racehorses who have been sold out of racing.

(NB. Some professional stables retain horses that have been hunted by their owners during the winter to compete in hunter chases.)

The form of hunter chases normally works out extremely well and they can be recommended as a reliable medium for selection (see Table 3.7).

TABLE 3.7   Hunter chases during the 1985–86 National Hunt season

	2m 4f+	%
Fav.	47 =	52.2
2nd fav.	17 =	18.8
3rd fav.	5 =	5.5
Non-fav.	21 =	23.3
Total	90	

NATIONAL HUNT FLAT RACES

These are limited to horses that have never competed in Flat racing, and are ridden by claiming jockeys and amateur riders only. They are level weights races, with weight-for-age allowances and penalties for previous winners. Distance usually 2m (see Table 3.8).

TABLE 3.8

	2m	%
Fav.	19	43.1
2nd fav.	8	18.6
3rd fav.	6	13.9
Non-fav.	11	25.5
Total	44	

National Hunt Flat races or 'Bumper' races as they are sometimes known have been established to allow purpose-bred National Hunt horses without previous racing experience to gain their first taste of competition against similar opponents. Usually they are programmed as the final event at a National Hunt meeting, being run over the hurdle course with the obstacles removed from the track. The popularity of these races with their growth in entries has meant that a horse is not allowed to compete in more than three such races. Any horse competing in these 'bumper' races will therefore be very inexperienced and usually offer the strict form student little upon which to base a selection. In 1985–86 65% of the winners of National Hunt Flat races won their racecourse debut, with 42.8% starting as favourite, indicating that a strong market move for a horse on its debut may be an omen to follow profitably.

4 TOOLS OF THE TRADE

The successful execution of any trade is subject to three factors – the workmanship, the materials and the use of the best and most appropriate tools.

The trades of selection and betting are no exception to the rule.

DEFINITIONS

WORKMANSHIP

This will be the reflection of the abilities of each selector in such skills as: (i) assessing information; (ii) formulating judgements; (iii) taking calculated action in response to these judgements. Good workmanship demands consistently practising the trade to the highest standard of personal ability and this is particularly aided if enthusiasm can be maintained in the approach to performing the selection/betting skills.

MATERIALS

These are the basic information requirements which make a well-considered selection possible; these will include:

1. Details of race – time, venue, value, distance and going. A list of the declared runners, riders, trainers, owners and weights.
2. Details of the form of each declared runner.
3. Details in a concise biographical account of each runner with particular reference to breeding and conformation.

TOOLS

The *tools of the trade* are the sources from where the essential information is obtained.

1. *Details of race.* Most national daily newspapers or a national daily racing newspaper.
2. *Details of form.* The official Jockey Club form books (supplied in weekly parts), and daily racing newspapers.
3. *Horses' biographies.* Weekly or annual specialized horse racing publications (e.g. Timeform books).

With selection firmly dependent for success upon the quality of the information received it is essential that this information be derived from only the most dependable of sources – these sources if of quality may be considered as being the best tools of the trade.

DETAILS OF THE RACE

A DAILY NEWSPAPER

Although a list of the declared runners, riders, etc. can be found in most of the national daily newspapers, it is a matter of personal choice as to which newspaper is preferred; the factors which have to be considered and offer considerable assistance in selection are: (i) the clarity of the print of the newspaper; (ii) the general layout and presentation of facts; (iii) any unique of features of the newspaper which provides vital information that is not otherwise readily obtainable without more involved investigation. The daily newspaper which is found consistently to fulfil the above requirements in respect of its horse-race coverage is the *Daily Mail*. This is a newspaper of tabloid size, excellently printed with clean, clear lettering thereby giving the reader immediate visual access to information (see Fig. 4.1). Its layout and presentation enable the selector to receive a direct yet comprehensive impression of the race-card at a glance; different race meetings are neatly separated, with races arranged in time order and sequence descending down the length of the page. This allows for relevant information (e.g. trainers' arrangements and jockey engagements) to be quickly recognized. Prestige races are usually given more detailed coverage. A typical example is given in Fig. 4.1. The special and unique feature of the *Racing Mail* is its daytime information (the number of days since a horse last ran) which is represented by a figure after the horse's name. *This is vital information* (a recent race performance is the most positive indication of a horse's present fitness and well-being). Another unique feature of the *Racing*

ROBIN GOODFELLOW		GIMCRACK	
2. 0	Fairway Lady	2. 0	Sameek
2.30	HILTON BROWN (nap)	2.30	MUSIC MACHINE (nap)
3.30 (1)	Dancing Brave	3.30 (1)	Allez Milord
(2)	Bold Arrangement	(2)	Shahrastani
(3)	Mashkour	(3)	Mashkour
4.20	Mailman	4.20	Master Line (n.b.)
4.50	Twice Bold	4.50	Twice Bold
5.20	Shmaireekh (n.b.)	5.20	Swift's Pal

JIMMY LINDLEY'S TV TIPS.—2.0, Sameek, 2.30. Perion. 3.30, Dancing Brave. 4.20, Ballydurrow.

·308 (21) 612610 RACEMAIL (B) 18 (C & D BF) A Tryin 3-8-7 S Cauthen ●78

KEY to all-in-a-line card : Racecard number—draw—six-figure form to ninth place, plus L for last, S—slipped up.. R—refused, F—fell, P—pulled up, C—carried out. Horse's name. (B)—blinkers (H)—hood. (V)—visor. Daytimer is the number of days since horse last ran. C—course winner (different distance). D—distance winner, C & D—course and distance winner, BF (beaten favourite)— trainer—age and weight—Jockey—Form• cast rating (Racemail's private handicap).

FIVE-YEAR RECORD

Jockeys : W. Carson 28, S. Cauthen 25, P. Waldron 20, Pat Eddery 18, P. Cook 10, G. Starkey 10, B. Rouse 9.

Trainers : G. Lewis 26, J. Dunlop 15, R. Hannon 14, H. Cecil 12, I. Balding 9, C. Brittain 9, B. Hills 9.

PRINCIPAL MEETING : Going : Good. TOTE JACKPOT : All six races.
STALLS: Straight course, stands side; Round course, inside.
DRAW ADVANTAGE : High. 5f. and 6f.; Low for 7f. to 1m. 2f.

2.0—(Jackpot Prefix 1) WOOD. COTE STAKES (2-Y.-O.). £6,000 added (£4,643·40). 6f. (7)   C4   Formcast   STALLS

1	(5)	2331 FRENCH TUITION 11 R Hannon 9-0	S Cauthen	66
2	(7)	21 SAMEEK 20 R Armstrong 9-0	W Carson	72
4	(4)	0152 FAIRWAY LADY 11 D Hughes (Ireland) 8-11	M J Kinane	77
5	(3)	122 REGENCY FILLE 14 R J Williams 8-11	R Cochrane	●78
7	(2)	8 DIVINE CHARGER 47 G Lewis 8-9	P Waldron	—
10	(6)	5 PERSIAN STYLE 13 C Brittain 8-9	C McCarron	—
11	(1)	MR EATS P Kelleway 8-6	C Asmussen	—

Probable S.P.: 7-4 Sameek, 5-2 Regency Fille, 5 Fairway Lady, 7 French Tuition, 9 Persian Style, 14 Divine Charger, Mr Eats. FAVOURITES : 0 1 1 1 2 0 0.
1985 : Calixtus, 9-0 (E Legrix) 10-1 R Boss. 8 ran.

2.30—(Prefix 2) NIGHTRIDER HANDICAP. £10,000 added (£7,713). 5f. (16)   C4   STALLS

1	(2)	11120-3 PETROVICH 9 (D5) R Hannon 4-9-10	B Thomson	●78
2	(3)	2830-39 IMPERIAL JADE 9 (D3) A Jarvis 4-9-9	T Ives	71
3	(15)	60-3138 HILTON BROWN (B) 22 (D5) P Cundell 5-9-7	Pat Eddery	71
4	(6)	355830- DURHAM PLACE 348 (D) K Brassey 4-9-4	S Whitworth	60
5	(8)	0-52234 CLANTIME (V) 13 (C&D2 D4) R Whitaker 5-9-0	D McKeown	70
6	(1)	402-122 TYROLLIE 18 (D3) N Vigors 4-8-13	P Cook	71
7	(9)	742L10- AXE VALLEY 258 (D4) P Cole 4-8-12	T Quinn	65
8	(13)	60453-L PERFECT TIMING 13 (D) D Elsworth 4-8-11	S Cauthen	66
9	(4)	14-0242 BOLLIN EMILY 13 (D2) M H Easterby 5-8-11	M Birch	76
10	(5)	L90L8-0 NATIVE SKIER (V) 25 C Austin 4-8-10	C McCarron	—
11	(7)	5-15111 PERION 27 (C&D D4) G Lewis 4-8-9	P Waldron	73
13	(16)	3000-03 CHINA GOLD 5 (D5) Miss L Siddall 7-8-2	C Gosney	69
14	(14)	915-644 MUSIC MACHINE 27 (D2) P Haslam 5-7-8	T Williams	69
15	(12)	44141/4 PRINCESS WENDY 72 (D2) N Callaghan 4-7-8	J Lowe	—
16	(11)	0800L-7 LITTLE STARCHY 27 (C&D2 D2) R Simpson 8-7-7	N Adams	73
17	(10)	4690-62 CELTIC BIRD (D7) A Balding 6-7-7	A Mackay	65

Probable S.P.: 5 Bollin Emily, 6 Tyrollie, 7 Perion, 8 Petrovich, 9 Hilton Brown, 10 Music Machine, Clantime, 12 Imperial Jade. FAVOURITES : — — — — — — 2.
1985 : Chaplins Club, 5-8-12 (W. R. Swinburn), 9-2 jt.-fav. D. Chapman. 12 ran.

FIG. 4.1   Extract from a typical racecard as displayed in the *Daily Mail*.

The big race line-up

KEY—From the left: Racecard number; draw; last six placings; (L= last); horse's name; Daytimer (number of days since it last ran); number of times horse has won over the course (C) or same distance (D) or both (C-D); whether it was beaten favourite (BF) last time out; owner, trainer, weight, rider; Formcast rating (Racemail's private handicap). Second line shows horse's breeding and colours worn by rider.

3.30—**(Prefix 3) EVER READY DERBY STAKES (3-Y.-O. Colts & Fillies). £150,000 added (£239,260). 1m. 4f. (17)** — **STALLS**

ITV — C 4

1	(14)	1-11	**ALLEZ MILORD** 14 (D) (J Brody) G Harwood 9-0 ....C Asmussen 68
			b c Tom Rolfe-Whyme Lord *(Yellow, red sash, black and white hooped sleeves, red cap)*
2	(15)	101-12	**AROKAR** 17 (K Al Said) J De Chevigny (France) 9-0 ....Y St Martin 71
			br c Akarad-Arosa *(Red, white cap, green star)*
4	(13)	32d†-332	**BOLD ARRANGEMENT** 32 (A Richards) C Brittain 9-0 ....C McCarron 71
			ch c Persian Bold-Arrangement *(Black and white, halved horizontally, check cap, yellow sleeves)*
5	(6)	11-11	**DANCING BRAVE** 32 (K Abdulla) G Harwood 9-0 ....G Starkey ●78
			b c Lyphard-Navajo Princess *(Green, pink sash and cap, white sleeves)*
6	(16)	111-21	**FARAWAY DANCER** 27 (P Burrel) H Cecil 9-0 ....W Ryan 71
			br c Far North-Prove Us Royal *(Dark green, white hoops, dark green sleeves, white cap)*
7	(9)	11-15	**FIORAVANTI** 18 (Sheik Mohammed) D O'Brien (Ireland) 9-0 ....C Roche 69
			b c Northern Dancer-Pitasia *(Maroon, white sleeves, white cap, maroon star)*
8	(5)	0111-11	**FLASH OF STEEL** 18 (B Firestone) D Weld (Ireland) 9-0 ......M J Kinane 77
			b c Kris-Spark of Fire *(Emerald green, white diamond frame and diamonds on sleeves, quartered cap)*
9	(4)	21L-	**JAREER** 229 (Maktoum Al Maktoum) M Stoute 9-0 ....B Rouse 60
			b c Northern Dancer-Fabuleux Jane *(Royal blue, white chevron, light blue cap)*
10	(3)	211-311	**MASHKOUR** 25 (D) (Prince A Salman) H Cecil 9-0 ....S Cauthen 71
			ch c Irish River-Sancta Rose *(Yellow, blue diamonds on body, yellow cap, blue spots)*
11	(2)	100-412	**MR JOHN** 18 (J Michael) L Browne (Ireland) 9-0 ....T Ives 75
			ch c Northfields-Ashton Amber *(White, emerald green stars, white sleeves, white cap emerald green spots)*
12	(11)	143-131	**NISNAS** 26 (D) (F Salman) P Cole 9-0 ....P Waldron 60
			ch c Tap On Wood-Suemette *(Dark green, dark green cap, light green spots)*
13	(12)	12-12	**NOMROOD** 21 (D) (F Salman) P Cole 9-0 ....T Quinn 63
			b c Alleged-Sweet Habit *(Dark green)*
14	(10)	2-11	**SHAHRASTANI** 21 (H H Aga Khan) M Stoute 9-0 ....W R Swinburn 71
			ch c Nijinsky-Shademati *(Green, red epaulettes)*
15	(1)	111-843	**SHARROOD** 18 (BF) (Sheik Mohammed) W Hern 9-0 ....W Carson 68
			ro c Caro-Angel Isand *(Maroon, white sleeves, maroon cap, white star)*
16	(17)	23-1323	**SIRK** 21 (Capt M Lemos) C Brittain 9-0 ....P Robinson 66
			ch c Kris-Belle Viking *(Royal Blue, white hoop, striped cap)*
17	(8)	61-1	**THEN AGAIN** 12 (R Shannon) L Cumani 9-0 ....R Guest 58
			b c Jaazeiro-New Light *(Yellow, red epaulettes, red & yellow quartered cap)*
18	(7)	12	**WISE COUNSELLOR** 25 (BF) (S Niarchos) V O'Brien (Ireland) Pat Eddery 63
			b c Alleged-Quarrel *(Dark blue, light blue cross belts, striped sleeves, white cap)*

d†—disqualified from 2nd place.

FAVOURITES : 2 2 1 1 1 0 1.

1985 : Slip Anchor, 9-0 (S. Cauthen) 9-4 fav. H. Cecil. 14 ran.

LATEST BETTING

3 Dancing Brave, 9-2 Shahrastani, 6 Allez Milord, 10 Mashkour, 12 Bold Arrangement, 14 Jareer, Wise Counsellor, 20 Arokar, Nomrood, 33 Flash Of Steel, Faraway Dancer, Fioravanti, 40 Nisnas, Sharrood, Sirk, 50 Then Again, 100 Mr John.

FIG. 4.2 Typical presentation of a more prestigious race as displayed in the *Daily Mail.*

Mail is in its form figures preceding a horse's name, for here up to the first nine placings are recorded as and when a horse finished last, whether it be in a two-runner field or a multi-runner field. Included at the foot of each race is the record of market leaders over the past seven seasons. This is a most important feature, alerting the selector to the likely predictability of the race. These features mean the *Daily Mail* can be highly recommended.

A DAILY RACING NEWSPAPER

While the basic needs for making a selection (i.e. the declared runners and riders) will be accommodated in the daily national newspaper of preference, the selector desiring a wider acquaintance with horse-racing is recommended to obtain a national daily racing newspaper. The *Sporting Life*, maintaining its traditional full-size page, has the space to place the complete card for each meeting, together with the declared runners, riders, weights, etc. on a single page, and the related form information also on that page, or on a following one should there not be enough room.

The *Racing Post* is of tabloid size and therefore, having a restriction on space, has chosen to present each race on a single page, with the related form information directly beneath it. This means that six races, which normally make up the card at a race meeting, are presented on six different pages, though an abridged version of each race meeting is now included for easy reference.

These two newspapers have starkly different design and layout which means that the reader who comes to favour one is likely to be quite disorientated when referring to the other. However, each newspaper does provide a comprehensive coverage of racing. This includes a full description of entry conditions for each race, the prize-money awarded to the first three or four finishers, weight-for-age scale (when appropriate), complete long handicap and the raising of weight (when it applies), plus the draw and stalls location, etc. (in Flat races). Extracts from the *Sporting Life* and *Racing Post* (Figs 4.3 to 4.6) show their typical layouts for a race.

Both newspapers in their contrasting styles have layouts that are clear and concise and present all the relevant information. This includes information on ownership, which is not found in most national daily papers and can be quite an important consideration for the experienced selector conversant with the influential connections and training methods of some trainers. Both papers also identify the racing colours of each owner and this is a most useful aid for the racing fan visiting the racecourse or for those watching on colour television.

The *Sporting Life* which for so long had stood as the major or sole presenter of British racing has responded quickly to meet the challenge of its new rival by sharpening its presentation, lowering its price and

JACKPOT PREFIX No 3

3.30 Ever Ready Derby Stakes (Group 1) C4 ITV 1½m

£150,000 added to stakes; distributed in accordance with Rule 194 (ii)(a); (includes a fourth prize); **for three yrs old, entire colts and fillies**; £800 to enter, £700 ex unless forfeit dec by May 20; £500 ex if dec to run; weights: Colts 9st; fillies 8st 9lb. EVER READY Ltd have sponsored this race, which includes a golden trophy value £4,000 for the winning owner. THERE WILL BE A PARADE FOR THIS RACE. The Stewards of the Jockey Club have modified Rule 121 (ii)(a); for the purpose of this race. (Total ent 261, £800 ft dec for 207, £1,500 ft dec for 36)—Closed Feb 26.

Penalty value: £239,260; 2nd £90,483, 3rd £44,241.50, 4th £20,115.50.

1	1-11	**ALLEZ MILORD(USA)** (Jerome Brody) G Harwood	9	0	C Asmussen	14
2	101-12	**AROKAR(FR)** (K Al-Said) J De Chevigny, in France	9	0	Y Saint -Martin	15
4	22D-332	**BOLD ARRANGEMENT** (A J Richards) C E Brittain	9	0	C McCarron	13
5	11-11	**DANCING BRAVE(USA)** (K Abdulla) G Harwood	9	0	G Starkey	6
6	111-21	**FARAWAY DANCER(USA)** (Peter Burrell) H R A Cecil	9	0	W Ryan	16
7	11-10	**FIORAVANTI(USA)** (Sheikh Mohammed) D V O'Brien, in Ireland	9	0	C Roche	9
8	0111-11	**FLASH OF STEEL** (Bertram R Firestone) D K Weld, in Ireland	9	0	M J Kinane	5
9	210-	**JAREER(USA)** (Maktoum Al Maktoum) M R Stoute	9	0	B Rouse	⸱
10	211-311	**MASHKOUR(USA)** (Prince Ahmed Salman) H R A Cecil	9	0	S Cauthen	3
11	100-412	**MR JOHN** (John Michael) L Browne, in Ireland	9	0	T Ives	2
12	143-131	**NISNAS** (Fahd Salman) P F I Cole	9	0	P Waldron	11
13	12-12	**NOMROOD(USA)** (Fahd Salman) ..P F I Cole	9	0	T Quinn	12
14	2-11	**SHAHRASTANI(USA)** (H H Aga Khan) M R Stoute	9	0	W R Swinburn	10
15	111-043	**SHARROOD(USA)** --btn fav- (Sheikh Mohammed) W R Hern	9	0	W Carson	1
16	23-1323	**SIRK** (Capt M Lemos) C E Brittain	9	0	P Robinson	17
17	01-1	**THEN AGAIN** (R J Shannon) L M Cumani	9	0	R Guest	8
18	-12	**WISE COUNSELLOR(USA)** --btn fav- (S S Niarchos) M V O'Brien, in Ireland	9	0	Pat Eddery	7

Seventeen runners

FORECAST: 3 Dancing Brave, 9-2 Shahrastani, 11-2 Allez Milord, 10 Bold Arrangement, 12 Wise Counsellor, 14 Mashkour, 16 Jareer, Arokar, 25 Nomrood, 33 Flash Of Steel, Faraway Dancer, Fioravanti, 40 Nisnas, Sharrood, Sirk, Then Again, 50 Mr John.

Last Year.—SLIP ANCHOR, 9-0, S Cauthen, 9/4 fav (H Cecil). 14 ran.

1 ALLEZ MILORD(USA) *yellow, red sash, black and white hooped sleeves, red cap*
2 AROKAR(FR) *red, white cap, green diamond*
4 BOLD ARRANGEMENT *black and white, halved horizontally, check cap, yellow sleeves*
5 DANCING BRAVE(USA) *green, pink sash and cap, white sleeves*
6 FARAWAY DANCER(USA) *dark green, white hoops, dark green sleeves, white cap*
7 FIORAVANTI(USA) *maroon, white sleeves, white cap, maroon star*
8 FLASH OF STEEL *emerald green, white diamond frame and diamonds on sleeves, quartered cap*
9 JAREER(USA) *royal blue, white chevron, light blue cap*
10 MASHKOUR(USA) *yellow, blue diamonds on body, yellow cap, blue spots*
11 MR JOHN *white, emerald green stars, white sleeves, white cap, emerald green spots*
12 NISNAS *dark green, dark green cap, light, light green spots*
13 NOMROOD(USA) *dark green*
14 SHAHRASTANI(USA) *green, red epaulets*
15 SHARROOD(USA) *royal blue, white chevron, blue cap, white star*
16 SIRK *royal blue, white hoop on body, striped cap*
17 THEN AGAIN *yellow, red epaulets, red and yellow quartered cap*
18 WISE COUNSELLOR(USA) *dark blue, light blue cross-belts, striped sleeves, white cap*

FIG. 4.3 Extract from a racecard as displayed in *Sporting Life*.

2); 3 Water Cay(USA) (9-0, 2); 9 Ran. 1½l, 2l, ½l, 2l, ½l. 1m 41.21s (a 2.71s). (Following a stewards' inquiry, Bold Arrangement was relegated to fourth position and second place awarded to Nomrood). SR: 73/68/62/60/54/52.

11-11 DANCING BRAVE(USA) (9-0) b c Lyphard(USA) — Navajo Princess by Drone. **1985, 1m firm (Newmarket), 1m good to firm (Sandown); 1986, 1m good (Newmarket), 1m soft (Newmarket). £129,312 (£122,545).**

May 3, Newmarket, 1m (3-y-o), good, £107,145: (Group 1) ; DANCING BRAVE(USA) (9-0 , G Starkey , 3), **held up, progress over 3f out, led over 1f out, quickened clear, impressive** (15 to 8 fav op 2 to 1 tchd 85 to 40); 2 Green Desert(USA) (9-0 , 9); 3 Huntingdale (9-0 , 12); 4 SHARROOD(USA) (9-0 , W Carson , 1), **ran on from 3f out, stayed on final furlong** (14 to 1 tchd 16 to 1); 15 Ran. 3l, 1½l, hd, 1½l, ½l, sht hd. 1m 40s (a 1.1s). SR: 47/38/33/32/27/25.

April 17, Newmarket, 1m (3-y-o), soft, £15,400: (Group 3) 1 DANCING BRAVE(USA) (8-7, G Starkey, 6), **well placed, led over 1f out, not extended** (11 to 8 fav op 5 to 4 tchd 6 to 4); 2 FARAWAY DANCER(USA) (8-7, S Cauthen, 11), **chased leaders, led over 2f out until over 1f out, ran on same pace** (9 to 2 op 7 to 2 tchd 5 to 1); 3 MASHKOUR(USA) (8-7, W Ryan, 9), **good headway over 3f out, every chance from 2f out, not quicken inside final furlong** (14 to 1 op 12 to 1 tchd 16 to 1); 8 SHARROOD(USA) (8-7, W Carson, 10), **well placed until hampered and lost place over 2f out** (11 to 2 op 5 to 1 tchd 6 to 1); 11 Ran. 1l, ½l, 6l, 2l, 6l. 1m 49.96s (a 11.06s). SR: 18/15/13/-/-/-.

Nov 1, Newmarket, 1m (2-y-o), firm, £3,844: 1 DANCING BRAVE(USA) (9-2, G Starkey, 9), **always going well, led two out, pushed clear final furlong** (4 to 9 op 8 to 11); 2 Northern Amethyst (8-9, 11); 3 NISNAS (8-12, T Quinn, 8), **always with leaders, every chance two out, no extra final furlong** (5 to 1 op 3 to 1); 11 Ran. 2½l, ¾l, ½l, 1l, 4l. 1m 40.15s (a 1.25s). SR: 42/27/28/23/17/5.

Oct 14, Sandown, 1m (2-y-o), good to firm, £2,922: 1 DANCING BRAVE(USA) (8-7, G Starkey, 1), **dwelt, smooth progress to lead one out, very easily** (6 to 4 on op evens); 2 Mighty Memory(USA) (9-2, 4); 3 Hubbards Lodge (8-11, bl, 3); 4 Ran. 3l, 5l, 2l. 1m 42.88s (a 1.48s). SR: 59/59/39/38/-/

111-21 FARAWAY DANCER(USA) (9-0) br c Far North(CAN) — Prove Us Royal by Prove It. **1985, 1m good to firm (Sandown), 1m 40yds good to soft (Haydock), 7f good to firm (Goodwood); 1986, 1½m 85yds soft (Chester). £28,474 (£16,960).**

May 8, Chester, 1½m 85yds (3-y-o) listed, soft, £16,960: 1 FARAWAY DANCER(USA) (8-12, S Cauthen, 5), **headway from rear 4f out, led 2f out, pushed clear final furlong** (5 to 4 on tchd evens); 2 Top Guest (8-12, 3); 3 Plaid (9-2, 6); 5 Ran. 5l, 2l, sht hd, 15l. 2m 26.50s (a 15.70s). SR: 55/45/45/40/10/-.

143-131 NISNAS (9-0) ch c Tap On Wood — Suemette by Danseur. **1985, 7f good to firm (Salisbury); 1986, 1½m good to soft (Lingfield), 1m good to soft (Kempton). £7,810 (£6,550).**

May 9, Lingfield, 1½m (3-y-o), good to soft, £2,641: 1 NISNAS (9-4, T Quinn, 6), **progress 4f out, stayed on to lead inside last, ran on well** (12 to 1 op 8 to 1); 2 Verd-Antique (9-4, 3); 3 Mirage Dancer (8-11, 2); 6 Ran. ½l, 15l, nk, 3l, 15l. 2m 41.55s (a 5.85s). SR: 46/45/8/14/1/-.

April 30, Ascot. See MASHKOUR(USA).

April 11, Kempton, 1m (3-y-o), good to soft, £3,908: 1 NISNAS (8-9, T Quinn, 5), **always chasing leaders, effort to lead inside final 2f, ran on well** (7 to 1 op 9 to 2 tchd 8 to 1); 2 Esdale(FR) (8-9, 1); 3 Badarbak (8-9, 3); 5 Ran. ¾l, 12l, 5l, 3l. 1m 44.56s (a 6.86s). SR: 64/62/26/16/2/-.

Nov 1, Newmarket. See DANCING BRAVE(USA).

12-12 NOMROOD(USA) (9-0) b c Alleged — Sweet Habit by Habitat. **1985, 1m good to firm (Newmarket); 1986, 1½m 65yds good to soft (Chester). £25,743 (£21,120).**

May 14, York. See SHAHRASTANI(USA).

May 6, Chester, 1½m 65yds (3-y-o), good to soft, £21,120: (Group 3) 1 NOMROOD(USA) (8-12, T Quinn, 6), **headway 7f out, with leader 4f our, led over 1f out, ran on** (11 to 2 op 4 to 1 tchd 6 to 1); 2 SIRK (8-12, P Robinson, 7), **behind until ran on over 1f out, finished strongly** (28 to 1 op 20 to 1 tchd 33 to 1); 3 Jumbo Hirt(USA) (8-8, 3); 7 Ran. Nk, 1l, 1½l, 5l, 1½l. 2m 46.08s (a 7.88s). SR: 38/37/31/30/24/22.

Oct 26, Doncaster. See BOLD ARRANGEMENT.

Oct 5, Newmarket, 1m (2-y-o) mdn, good to firm, £4,623: 1 NOMROOD(USA) (9-0 , T Quinn , 5), **headway three out, led just inside final furlong, ran on** (16 to 1 tchd 25 to 1); 2 Danishgar (9-0 , 3); 3 White Reef (9-0 , 12); 13 Ran. 1½l, hd, 1l, 1½l, 2l. 1m 41.03s (a 2.13s). SR: 12/7/6/3/-/-.

2-11 SHAHRASTANI(USA) (9-0) ch c Nijinsky — Shademah by Thatch. **1986, 1¼m soft (Sandown), 1½m 110yds good (York). £100,299 (£100,299).**

May 14, York, 1½m 110yds (3-y-o), good, £80,454: (Group 2) 1 SHAHRASTANI(USA) (9-0, W R Swinburn, 4), **soon tracking leader, led 2f out, edged left and ran on, driven out** (11 to 10 on op evens tchd 6 to 5 agst); 2 NOMROOD(USA) (9-0, T Quinn , 2), **always well placed, every chance and ridden on inside 2f out, kept on under pressure** (11 to 2 op 5 to 1 tchd 6 to 1); 3 SIRK (9-0, P Robinson, 1), **waited with, going well, promising effort over 1f out, ran on same pace** (14 to 1 op 10 to 1); 7 Ran. 1½l, 1l, 5l, 2½1, hd. 2m 11.75s (a 2.12s). SR: 84/81/79/69/64/63.

April 26, Sandown, 1¼m (3-y-o), soft, £19,845: (Group 3) 1 SHAHRASTANI(USA) (8-7, W R Swinburn, 1), **2nd until led 2½f out, driven clear, eased final 100yds** (2 to 1 op evens); 2 Bonhomie(USA) (8-12, 3); 3 SIRK (8-7, P Robinson, 2), **last until went**

FIG. 4.4 Extract of horses' previous form as displayed in *Sporting Life*.

Third Race 3.30

The Ever Ready Derby Stakes — 3yo G1 1m4f

Stakes: £150,000 added For: 3yo colts & fillies Allowances: fillies 3lb Entries: 261 Penalty Value 1st £239,260 2nd £90,483 3rd £44,241.50 4th £20,115.50

NO	LAST 6 RACES	HORSE & OWNER (BF Beaten Favourite, C Course Winner, CD Course Distance Winner, D Distance Winner)	TRAINER	AGE	WEIGHT	JOCKEY	DW NO	POST MARK
1	1-11	ALLEZ MILORD (USA) [D] MrJeromeBrody	G.Harwood	3	9-00	C Asmussen	14	83
2	151-12	AROKAR (FR) K.Al-Said	J.DeChevigny (FR)	3	9-00	Y Saint-Martin	15	84
4	324-332	BOLD ARRANGEMENT MrA.J.Richards	C.E.Brittain	3	9-00	C McCarron	13	86
5	11-11	DANCING BRAVE (USA) MrK.Abdullah	G.Harwood	3	9-00	G Starkey	6	96
6	111-21	FARAWAY DANCER (USA) MrPeterBurrell	H.Cecil	3	9-00	W Ryan	16	86
7	11-15	FIORAVANTI (USA) SheikhMohammed	D.V.O'Brien (IRE)	3	9-00	C Roche	9	82
8	9111-11	FLASH OF STEEL MrBertramR.Firestone	D.K.Weld (IRE)	3	9-00	M Kinane	5	86
9	21L-	JAREER (USA) MaktoumAl-Maktoum	M.R.Stoute	3	9-00	B Rouse	4	77
10	211-311	MASHKOUR (USA) [D] PrinceAhmedSalman	H.Cecil	3	9-00	S Cauthen	3	91
11	177-412	MR JOHN MrJ.Michael	L.Browne (IRE)	3	9-00	T Ives	2	85
12	143-131	NISNAS MrFahdSalman	P.F.I.Cole	3	9-00	P Waldron	11	77
13	12-12	NOMROOD (USA) [D] MrFahdSalman	P.F.I.Cole	3	9-00	T Quinn	12	85
14	2-11	SHAHRASTANI (USA) H.H.AgaKhan	M.R.Stoute	3	9-00	W R Swinburn	10	88
15	111-843	SHARROOD (USA) SheikhMohammed	W.R.Hern	3	9-00	W Carson	1	84
16	23-1323	SIRK CaptM.Lemos	C.E.Brittain	3	9-00	P Robinson	17	83
17	61-1	THEN AGAIN MrR.J.Shannon	L.M.Cumani	3	9-00	R Guest	8	72
18	-12	WISE COUNSELLOR (USA) MrS.S.Niarchos	M.V.O'Brien (IRE)	3	9-00	Pat Eddery	7	79

DECLARED RUNNERS 17

LAST YEAR SLIP ANCHOR LordHowardDeWalden | H.Cecil | 3 | 9-00 | S.Cauthen | 3

BETTING FORECAST: 3-1 Dancing Brave, 7-2 Shahrastani, 5-1 Allez Milord, 10-1 Mashkour, 12-1 Bold Arrangement, Wise Counsellor, 14-1 Jareer, 20-1 Arokar, 25-1 Nomrood, 28-1 Faraway Dancer, 33-1 Fioravanti, Flash Of Steel, Sharrood, Sirk, 40-1 Nisnas, Then Again, 50-1 Mr John.

FIG. 4.5 Extract from a raccard displayed in *Racing Post*.

Lingfield 10 May
1m4f GD-SFT **£48573 Group3**
1 Mashkour (USA) 9-00 S.Cauthen3
3rd straight: led well over 1f out: led inside final furlong: driven out
BETTING 7/4
2 Bakharoff (USA) 9-00 .G.Starkey6
3 Tisn't (USA) 9-00 .... T.Quinn1
6 ran DISTANCES ½ 1½ 10 1 6
TIME 2 43.54 (slow by 9.44) PACE slow

Ascot 30 Apr
1m2f GD-SFT **£8402**
1 Mashkour (USA) 9-00 S.Cauthen3
5th straight: led well over 1f out: quickened: easily
BETTING 15/8
2 Mirage Dancer 8-09 .P.Robinson5
3 Nisnas 9-00 .... T.Quinn1
led over 3f out: hard ridden over 1f out: unable to quicken
BETTING 8/1
6 ran DISTANCES 8 ¾ 4 1 30
TIME 2 18.70 (slow by 12.7) PACE avge

Newmarket 17 Apr
see Dancing Brave (USA)

Mr John

White, Emerald green stars, white sleeves, white cap, emerald green spots

Chesnut colt b.1983 by Northfields (USA) - Ashton Amber(by On Your Mark)

RECORD	Raced	1st	2nd	3rd	Earnings
1981/86	8	3	1	1	£28,803
1986	3	1	1	—	£21,270

1986 Phnix 1m L HEAVY
1985 Naas 6f GD-FM
1985 Leop 7f L GD-FM

O progressive Irish colt; acts on any; suited by 1m; not bred to stay 1m4f

---

Curragh 17 May
see Flash of Steel

Phoenix Park 7 May
1m HEAVY **£21270 Listed**
1 Mr John 8-10 .... M.T.Browne5
hdway 4f out: ran on u.p ins fin f: led last stride
BETTING 7/1
2 Weight in Gold 8-07 ... D.Gillespie1
3 Forlaway (USA) 9-09 .... C.Roche2
9 ran DISTANCES sh sh 1½ 2½ 1
TIME 1 50.20

Curragh 26 Apr
see Flash of Steel

Nisnas

Dark green

BETTING 7/1
2 Esdale (FR) 8-09 ....PatEddery1
3 Badarbak 8-09 .... S.Cauthen3
5 ran DISTANCES ¾ 12 5 3
TIME 1 44.56 (slow by 7.06) PACE avge

Newmarket 1 Nov
see Dancing Brave (USA)

Nomrood (USA)

Dark green

Bay colt b.1983 by Alleged (USA) - Sweet Habit(by Habitat)

RECORD	Raced	1st	2nd	3rd	Earnings
1981/86	4	2	2	—	£25,743
1986	2	1	1	—	£21,120

1986 Chstr 1m4f Group3 GD-SFT
1985 Nmkt 8f Mdn GD-FM

O suited by 1m4f; acts on firm and soft surface; on the upgrade

---

York 14 May
see Shahrastani (USA)

Chester 6 May
1m4f GD-SFT **£21120 Group3**
1 Nomrood (USA) 8-12 ...... T.Quinn6
headway over 6f out: 2nd straight: led over 1f out: edged left: ran on
BETTING 11/2
2 Sirk 8-12 .... P.Robinson7
held up and behind: 6th straight: strong run rinal furlong: just failed
BETTING 28/1
3 Jumbo Hirt (USA) 8-08
.... B.Thomson3
7 ran DISTANCES nk 1 ½ 5 1½
TIME 2 46.08 (slow by 8.28) PACE slow

Doncaster 26 Oct
1m GOOD **£43505 G1**
1 Bakharoff (USA) 9-00 .G.Starkey4
2 Nomrood (USA) 9-00 ..... T.Quinn8
lw: hdwy 3f out: disp ld 1 1/2f out: hmpd fnl f: nt qckn: fin 3rd, 2 l: plcd 2
BETTING 5/1
3 Water Cay (USA) 9-00 S.Cauthen2
4 Bold Arrangement 9-00
.... PatEddery9
6th st: led over 2f out: edgd lft dist: hung rt fnl f: fin 2nd, 1 1/2 l: plcd
BETTING 5/1
9 ran DISTANCES 1½ 2 ½ 2 ½
TIME 1 41.21 (slow by 3.61) PACE avge

Shahrastani (USA)

Green, red epaulets

Chesnut colt b.1983 by Nijinsky (CAN) - Shademah(by Thatch (USA))

RECORD	Raced	1st	2nd	3rd	Earnings
1981/86	3	2	1	—	£100,299
1986	2	2	—	—	£100,299

---

3 Sirk 8-07 .... P.Robinson2
3rd straight: no headway final 2f
BETTING 20/1
4 ran DISTANCES 4 5
TIME 2 18.77 (slow by 12.57) PACE avge

Newbury 20 Sept
1m GOOD **£6050**
1 My Ton Ton 8-11 .... P.Robinson3
2 Shahrastani (USA) 8-11
.... W.R.Swinburn17
w'like: scope: shkn up 2f out: str run fnl f: fin wl
BETTING 8/1
3 Mytens (USA) 8-11 C.Asmussen7
18 ran DISTANCES hd 2 sh 2 nk
TIME 1 41.67 (slow by 3.07) PACE fast

Sharrood (USA)

Maroon, white sleeves, maroon cap, white star

Roan colt b.1983 by Caro - Angel Island (USA)(by Cougar II (CHI))

RECORD	Raced	1st	2nd	3rd	Earnings
1981/86	8	4	—	1	£10,923
1986	3	—	—	1	£—

1985 Donc 6f GD-FM
1985 Nbury 7f Hcap0-99 GOOD
1985 Chstr 6f GOOD
1985 Gwood 6f GD-SFT

O useful at 1m; should stay 1m2f; unsuited by heavy but acts on any other

---

Curragh 17 May
see Flash of Steel

Newmarket 3 May
see Dancing Brave (USA)

Newmarket 17 Apr
see Dancing Brave (USA)

Newbury 20 Sept
7f GOOD **£3140 Hcap0-99**
1 Sharrood (USA) 9-09 .W.Carson6
hdwy on ins 2f out: led ins fnl f: rdn out
BETTING 6/4F
2 Highland Chieftain 8-13 ..T.Ives12
3 Normanby Lass 9-02 ....J.Mercer4
12 ran DISTANCES nk 5 nk nk ½
TIME 1 30.20 (slow by 4.70) PACE slow

Sirk

Royal blue, white hoop, striped cap

Chesnut colt b.1983 by Kris - Belle Viking (FR)(by Riverman (USA))

RECORD	Raced	1st	2nd	3rd	Earnings
1981/86	7	1	2	3	£2,680
1986	4	1	1	2	£2,680

FIG. 4.6 Extract of horses' previous form as displayed in *Racing Post*.

generally shaking itself from the lethargy and predictability in which its tradition and monopoly had threatened to engulf it.

The *Racing Post* as the young upstart attempts to bring a fresh and alternative view of racing to the average fan, providing easy access to the most relevant information. The competition engendered by having more than one daily national racing newspaper can only be good for the sport, enlivening the scene, and reminding the racing establishment that in changing times no one can rest on the laurels of past glories for ever.

A national racing newspaper therefore serves as a comprehensive accessory to the basic needs of selection, providing the general news of racing which enables the selector to remain constantly abreast of events in the racing world.

DETAILS OF FORM

In the assessment of form, the serious selector requires the fullest information of form and for this there can be no substitute for the Form Book.

THE FORM BOOK

This is the officially accepted Form Book printed annually in a bound volume, but received by subscribers throughout the season in weekly up-to-date editions. It is called *Raceform Up-to-Date* – there are separate volumes for Flat and National Hunt racing – one referred to as *Flat Racing Season 19–* and the other called *Chaseform*.

The Form Book is the selector's most important and indispensable tool; it is a publication which has a record of every British racehorse's race performance(s) and is indexed and presented as a book. The Form Book contains the result of every race run and/or that was programmed in the British racing calendar. The results recorded always show the first four placed horses in each race and usually the first nine horses (the size of the field permitting, of course). The official distances between the first six finishers is also normally recorded, together with a commentary on their running and any other horse(s) who figured prominently during the race. A page from the Form Book is illustrated in Fig. 4.7. Altogether the Form Book records:

The meeting – the going, the time of the race (and time of the 'off'). The value of the race, and its distance.

The horses competing, in finishing order, with respective trainer and jockey.

```
937    EVER READY DERBY STKS (Gp 1) (3-Y.O.C & F) £239260.00 (£90483.00: £44241.50:
       £20115.50)  1½m                                              3-30 (3-44)

606* Shahrastani (USA) (MRStoute) 3-9-0  WRSwinburn (10) (lw: 4th st: led over 2f
       out: drvn out) ....................................................................... —1
445* Dancing Brave (USA) (Fav) (GHarwood) 3-9-0  GStarkey (6) (lw: wl bhd 9f: plld
       out 3f out: gd hdwy 2f out: str run fnl f: fin fast) ....................... ½.2
553* Mashkour (USA) (HRACecil) 3-9-0  SCauthen (3) (gd hdwy fnl 2f: r.o) ................. 2½.3
512* Faraway Dancer (USA) (HRACecil) 3-9-0  WRyan (16) (2nd st: ev ch wl over 1f
       out: r.o) ................................................................................ hd.4
543* Nisnas (PFICole) 3-9-0  PWaldron (11) (lw: 3rd st: no hdwy fnl 2f) ........................ s.h.5
712a* Flash of Steel (DKWeld) 3-9-0  MKinane (5) (lw: hdwy 3f out: nvr nr to chal) ............. ¾.6
606³ Sirk (CEBrittain) 3-9-0  PRobinson (17) (wl bhd 9f: nvr nrr) ...................................... ¾.7
712a³ Sharrood (USA) (MajorWRHern) 3-9-0  WCarson (1) (a bhd) ................................. 1.8
712a² Mr John (LBrowne) 3-9-0  TIves (2) (unf: s.s) ............................................ hd.9
700* Allez Milord (USA) (GHarwood) 3-9-0  CAsmussen (14) ....................................... ½.10
606² Nomrood (USA) (PFICole) 3-9-0  TQuinn (12) (lw: led over 9f) ........................... hd.11
     Jareer (USA) (MRStoute) 3-9-0  BRouse (4) (lw) .............................................. 1.12
723* Then Again (LMCumani) 3-9-0  RGuest (8) (lw: prom 9f) ................................. 3.13
531a² Bold Arrangement (CEBrittain) 3-9-0  CMcCarron (13) (lw) ............................... 2½.14
714a² Arokar (FR) (JDeChevigny) 3-9-0  YSaintMartin (15) (gd sort: lw: 6th st: wknd
       over 2f out) ........................................................................... s.h.15
712a Fioravanti (USA) (DavidVO'Brien) 3-9-0  CRoche (9) (gd sort: lw) ....................... 10.16
654a² Wise Counsellor (USA) (MVO'Brien) 3-9-0  PatEddery (7) (gd sort: lw: 5th st:
       wknd 3f out) ................................................................................ 17

2/1 Dancing Brave (USA), 11/2 SHAHRASTANI (USA)(4/1—6/1), 8/1 Allez Milord (USA), 12/1 Bold
Arrangement, Mashkour (USA), 16/1 Jareer (USA), 18/1 Arokar (FR), 20/1 Nomrood
(USA), 25/1 Flash of Steel(tchd 40/1), Sharrood (USA), 33/1 Fioravanti (USA), Then Again, Faraway Dancer
(USA), 40/1 Nisnas, 50/1 Ors. CSF £15.168, CT £116.38. Tote £6.10: £2.00 £2.30 £2.30 (£7.00). H.H. Aga
Khan (NEWMARKET) bred by H. H. Aga Khan in USA. 17 Rn                         2m 37.13 (1.13)
                                                                            SF—95/94/89/88/87/85/84
```

FIG. 4.7 Extract from the Form Book.

The weights carried, including overweight and allowances.

The draw (where applicable – Flat), blinkers and hoods.

The winning owner, trainer and breeder.

The race time is also recorded with comparison to standard time and speed figures calculated on these times.

The betting market and starting prices are recorded plus the equivalent Tote prices including the daily double, treble and placepot, etc.

Such detailed coverage of races, which are so clearly marked make the Form Book a trusted asset in the sometimes involved process of form selection.

The *Sporting Life* also produces a form book which serves as a rival to the well-established and officially accepted *Raceform* publication. It appears in two separate annuals covering each code of racing: *Flat Results 19–* and *National Hunt Results 19–*. They are produced in glossy paper-bound covers and contain each season's racing results originating from those printed daily in the newspaper.

These annual form books also contain other features such as a full list of jockeys' weights, trainers' addresses, maps of training establishments and racecourses on the British mainland, a fixture list of the race meetings for the forthcoming season, plus a useful ready reckoner and other records which provide much comprehensive information for the racing fan.

The results of the races themselves are set out in two columns down the page, in date and time sequence, with the title, type of race, prize-money and distance at the top of each race, and beneath, the first nine horses (size of the field permitting) identified in finishing order. By the side of each horse is the weight it carried, its jockey, a close-up commentary of its race performance, plus its starting price and any betting fluctuations. At the foot of each race the margins between the first six finishers are recorded with their corresponding speed rating, and the trainer of the winner. All the English and Irish fixtures in the racing calendar are included plus some of the leading European races. The index at the back of the book contains every horse which raced during the season, its age, pedigree, a full record of the races it contested and who trained it, thus setting off this publication as a useful addition to the armoury of racing information.

Since the 1986 Flat race season the *Sporting Life* has expanded its results service to provide a weekly form booklet obtainable by postal subscription – a challenge to the *Raceform* publication which for so long has held the monopoly.

FORM SHEETS

These are the abbreviated version of the Form Book provided in the national daily racing newspapers. They are not a satisfactory substitute for the more complete information contained within the Form Book, but may in close co-operation serve in the role of an eliminating agent in the initial review of form. In this respect form sheets act as reference points, requiring that the selector undertake a more searching investigation with the aid of the Form Book.

Form sheets present the selector with a useful outline of form, but cannot be confidently accepted as providing the complete picture as often they withhold as much information as they reveal.

A HORSE'S BIOGRAPHY

This is the in-depth information which may finally confirm or deny the impression of a horse's ability that has been developing in the form evaluation process. It will be found most easily and reliably in the specialist racing publications of Timeform – namely the weekly *Black books* and the more detailed *Annuals* (Flat and National Hunt).

The Timeform book contains a brief or detailed account of every horse that has raced, plus some as yet unraced (see Fig. 4.8). There is a brief biography of a horse's breeding, its foaling date and cost if bought at public auction (in the case of 2-year-olds), a description of its con-

SHE

SHEDAR 3 b.f. Owen Anthony 102–Saratoga Maid (Saratoga Skiddy 113) —
(1980 5.3fg 5g 6fg 5f 5g 1981 5d 7d 5v 6g) only poor form, including in sellers;
blinkered last 2 starts. R. Hoad.

SHEER DELIGHT 3 ch.f. Gay Fandango 132–Sheer Joy (Major Portion 129) **92**
(1980 5g 6s³ 6d 7g⁴ 1981 8s 8f* 7fg* 8f⁴ 8fg² 8f) well-made, robust filly;
improved and in June won maiden race at York (ran on well under pressure
and beat Majieda by ½ length) and minor event at Folkestone (by 7 lengths);
gave impression she would have been suited by 1¼m; was well suited by firm
ground; given plenty to do by her apprentice rider fourth start; retired to stud.
B. Hills.

SHEER GRIT 3 b.c. Busted 134–Abettor 103 (Abernant 142) (1980 6g 7g* 8g* **104**
8d³ 1981 7d 10fg⁴ 12g² 12d 12f² 14fg³ 11.1f) rangy, attractive colt; has rather
a round action; smart and genuine as a 2-y-o, winning at Kempton and Doncaster
and finishing excellent third behind Beldale Flutter and Shergar in William Hill
Futurity, also at Doncaster; disappointing in 1981, although was second in
Ladbrokes Derby Trial at Lingfield in May (held up, looked a difficult ride when
going down by 1½ lengths to Riberetto) and 3-runner Churchill Stakes at Ascot
in June (made running but couldn't quicken at all when challenged by Six Mile
Bottom and was beaten ¾ length); never really on terms when about 20 lengths
sixth of 18 behind runaway winner Shergar in Derby on fourth start, best of his
other efforts; stays 1½m; best form with some give in the ground; probably suited
by forcing tactics; said to have jarred a shoulder at Ascot. C. Brittain.

SHELL TOP 3 ch.f. Spitsbergen 103–Mis Tor (Little Cloud 113) (1980 NR —
1981 10.1fg 10.1g) third foal; dam placed over jumps; bought 850 gns Ascot
March Sales; behind in minor event at Windsor in July and maiden race (last of
16) on same course in August; sold 675 gns Ascot November Sales. J. Davies.

SHENOULA 3 ch.f. Sheshoon 132–Yanoula 79 (Nosca) (1980 5d 5s 6d 1981 —
12g 12.2g 12f 13.8f) lengthy filly; soundly beaten in varied company, including
selling; blinkered final start. W. Haigh.

SHERE BEAUTY 4 b.f. Mummy's Pet 125–Mossgo 106 (Vigo 130) (1980 **§§**
7.2fg 8fg 1981 6d 6s) tall, sparely-made filly; moderate (rated 83) at 2 yrs
but has gone the wrong way temperamentally and is best left severely alone;
has worn blinkers. W. Stubbs.

SHERELCO 3 ro.c. Relko 136–Mary D 99 (Vigo 130) (1980 5g 6g 6fg 6g 1981 —
10d) leggy, lengthy, lightly-made colt; little worthwhile form in maiden and
minor events; blinkered fourth outing in 1980; dead. S. Matthews.

SHERGAR 3 b.c. Great Nephew 126–Sharmeen (Val de Loir 133) (1980 8fg* **140**
8d² 1981 10fg* 12.3g* 12d* 12fg* 12fg* 14.6g⁴)
    Who but Shergar could be Europe's 'Horse of the Year' in 1981? There
wasn't a middle-distance performer to stand comparison with him and he built
up an imposing record in some of the most important events for a horse of his
type. Shergar's Derby win was one of the most prodigious in the long history
of the race: he demolished the field by ten lengths, the widest margin of victory
officially recorded in an Epsom Derby. Shergar won the Derby in the manner
of a great racehorse and his exhibition will remain an abiding memory of the
racing year. Until his unexpected defeat in the St Leger, Shergar was unbeaten
as a three-year-old. He won the Guardian Newspaper Classic Trial and the
Chester Vase before Epsom and then took the Irish Sweeps Derby and the
King George VI and Queen Elizabeth Diamond Stakes; in none of these events
did he win by less than four lengths. Alas, Shergar did not contest Europe's
most prestigious and most competitive mile-and-a-half race, the Prix de l'Arc
de Triomphe in October. Although he reportedly worked well at home after
the St Leger and tests carried out in the interim showed him to be in excellent
health—his connections apparently felt there was too much at stake to risk
a repeat of his below-par run at Doncaster. There was never much hope that
the racing public would have the chance to see Shergar as a four-year-old.
Such was the clamour for his services as a stallion that thirty-four shares in
him offered before the King George were quickly taken up at £250,000 each,
representing a valuation of £10,000,000, a record syndication for a stallion to
stand in Europe. Shergar has been retired to his owner's Ballymany Stud
in the Irish Republic.
    Shergar was lightly raced as a two-year-old, having only two outings, in
the Kris Plate at Newbury in September—when he won impressively—and in
the William Hill Futurity at Doncaster in October. He was well fancied for

FIG. 4.8 Extract of a typical page from *Timeform Annual*.

formation – plus an analysis and rating of performance(s) by their experts. The Timeform publications have rightly gained a high reputation for their consistently sound analysis and judgement and will prove extremely useful in providing important background detail for the selector who has little or no visual contact with horse-racing.

TOOLS FOR BETTING

The backer, having made a confident well-chosen selection seeks access to the best facilities to make betting an easy and profitable practice. These are described in Chapter 5.

5 BETTING

The purpose of betting is to win money!

Betting is defined: 'To risk money on the result of an event – to back an opinion with money.'

Betting can be described as the practical act which confirms commitment to a decision.

Betting seeks to exploit for profit a correct opinion. Successful betting is therefore subject to correct selections.

Horse-race selection is subject only to its own process and can exist without betting.

Selection must remain separate from and dictate to, betting. An intrusion of betting considerations in the selection process undermines the selection decision and thereby defeats its purpose.

Betting will only be financially viable if practised as part of a calculated, reasoned act.

TO WIN AT BETTING

The obvious and fundamental necessity is betting on winners. If selections recorded are 100 per cent correct there are no modifying factors that can prevent winning at betting. This is an ideal to be aimed for with selections but is an unlikely practical reality.

THE MODIFYING FACTORS

The factors which prevent winning at betting, are as follows:

1. The percentage of winners to losers;
2. The *odds* of winners backed;
3. The staking method used.

BETTING TECHNIQUE – '*If*' and '*How*' to bet

Betting technique is basically simple; it revolves around one question that must always be asked: 'To bet or not to bet.' Even with a confident reasoned selection decision this question is evoked, because the factor still to be considered that will limit successful betting is 'the odds'.

In the assessment of odds the following should be considered:

- The purpose of betting is to win and the odds place a limit on what can be won.
- The backer has no control in the formation of odds – odds are controlled by the layers (layers of odds bookmakers) who manipulate the odds for the distinct purpose of restricting winnings and limiting their own financial liabilities.
- The backer has only one action to combat this power of fixing the odds that is held by the bookmaker – he has the power of veto.

THE '*IF*'

'Not to bet until the odds be considered fair, reasonable or completely in the favour of the backer is an advantage which must never be surrendered. The bookmaker has to lay odds all the time for each and every race – but the backer can choose if and when to bet.

In assessing the odds the backer, supported by a confident reasoned selection, needs to pose the monetary question: 'What can I win?' Specifically, 'How will the money returned be comparable to the money risked?' Money used for betting is very high risk capital and it is suggested that the minimum acceptable return be at least equal to outlay – 'even money'. *The backer must consider odds of less than evens unacceptable in all circumstances.*

Successful betting is dependent upon the following:

1. *Selecting winners.* Selections formulated without prejudice or enticement to bet, based upon factors of reasoned probability, are selections that hold the most likelihood of winning.
2. *Betting at fair and reasonable odds.* Only betting at odds where gain is appropriate or favourable to the amount of money risked.
3. *Staking system.* One which places no undue emphasis on one particular bet to the detriment or enhancement of the previous betting record.

A successful outcome to betting requires that betting be conducted as a calm reasoned act, paying due regard to these modifying factors. This will mean applying discipline to refrain from betting in unfavourable circumstances and practising only good betting habits.

Selection, odds and staking are theoretically the only factors in the betting process, but in practice there is another all-pervading aspect which can conspire to play a dominant role. This is the *financial consideration*. Although the purpose of betting is to win money, betting entails the risk of losing money. Lucid betting requires the removal of that fear of losing, whether in the form of hard cash, markers, credit or encapsulated ego and pride. The financial involvement, therefore, must be considered, realized and placed in its true perspective.

Money used for betting is high-risk money

It is therefore essential that a bank or pool of money be set aside to be used solely for the purposes of betting. The size of the bank may be large or small, but with the prerequisite that losing the whole or part of the bank places no financial burden on the backer.
- It must be money that the backer can afford to lose.
- It must be money that the backer is not attached to.
- It must be money the backer considers already lost.

A weakening from this rigid viewpoint will serve only to promote the unwelcome influence of the financial consideration. Unchecked, this influence will grow to affect the selection process adversely and thereby undermine the basis upon which successful betting is founded.

THE 'HOW' TO BET

The way

Betting is the simple act of supporting an opinion/selection with money. Placing a bet is an uncomplicated operation – writing instructions on a slip/voucher or verbally giving instructions by telephone.

There are three ways to bet on a single selection: (1) to win; (2) place (only); (3) each way (win and place combine). Single selections may be joined together to form doubles, trebles and accumulators in myriad combinations.

Besides single selection bets there are forecast bets:
- Straight forecast – predicting the first two finishers in correct order.
- Dual forecast – predicting the first two finishers in either order.
- Forecasts can be similarly joined together to form doubles, trebles, etc.
- Tricasts – selecting the first three finishers in correct order in handicap races of 10 or more runners.

SINGLE SELECTION BET

To win   is the simplest and most economic bet. It demands decisive selection.

Place only   is an uneconomic bet; SP and Tote place bets of selections with positive chances of being placed are normally odds-on. It encourages timid and indecisive selection.

Each way   the place part of the bet is uneconomic at one-fifth of the odds. If the selection wins, half the stake has been wasted in an endeavour to protect whole or part of the stake.

Tote odds are not guaranteed for any type of bet.

The single win bet is the best possible way to bet. It is uncomplicated, economically sound and no part of the stake is wasted if the selection is successful. Selection is focused on predicting decisive positive results; its aim is unmistakably understood from the outset.

There are other methods besides single selection bets which include the following. Combined selection bets (doubles, trebles, etc.) designed to give a large return on a small outlay by multiplying the odds together. The increase of odds signifies a decrease in the chances of winning and should be considered an over-ambitious, uneconomic way of betting. Forecasts similarly have the attraction of multiple odds and large possible gain for small outlay, but the inherent weakness of numerous combinations of possible results. Forecasts can only be economically viable when the possibilities of the result are numerically small and the multiplication of odds large (i.e. in small fields of five or less – a combination forecast made of the highest-priced runners. This is a proposition based on mathematical speculation and without any regard necessarily to selection based on reasoned probability).

Single selection bets contain enough unpredictable factors without the further uncertainties introduced when combining selections. It is said that doubles were invented for anyone not satisfied with one loser but preferring two.

STAKING SYSTEMS

The obvious and most simple to operate 'level stakes' is the best method. In level stakes every bet is of the same value, every bet is of equal importance and no particular relevance is attached to any single bet. Therefore, no single selection decision is less or more important than the previous, and one loser places no financial loss out of proportion to other losers.

ODDS (PRICES)

Odds are the degree of probability of winning. Prices are shown as odds *against* the chance of winning. For example with odds of 2–1, one is risked to gain two. Odds are also the means by which the layers of odds make a profit whatever the result. Bookmakers make a book of prices/odds on an event, giving each competitor or runner price or odds against its chances of winning. These prices are carefully mathematically balanced against the money betted, so after settling payment of all winning bets the bookmaker takes a percentage profit on the overall money that has been taken.

The odds are formulated and controlled by the major bookmakers at a race meeting. After an initial write-up or opening 'show' of prices, market forces operate, with prices adjusted to accommodate varying amounts of money wagered. This betting market continues until the start of the race. The starting price odds are the mean average price for each horse calculated by independent assessors, from the lists of the leading bookmakers at the end of trading. They are a fair representation of the amount of money wagered on each horse. In the market exchanges before the start of the race, prices continually fluctuate according to supply and demand and a bet struck during these exchanges will be at a 'board price' which may be more or less than the final or starting price.

THE THREE TYPES OF ODDS

Starting price (SP) odds

The official, independently calculated average odds, that were offered at the close of trading at the start of the race.

Board price odds

The odds laid and taken in the market exchanges before a race. These odds are fixed, guaranteed and not subject to any later market fluctuations.

Tote odds

The odds calculated after the division of the pool of money wagered on a race with the Totalisator Board. These odds are not fixed or guaranteed. They are variable and unpredictable, depending on the size of the pool and how this relates to the number of winning ticket holders (i.e. a large pool with few winning ticket holders pays high odds, a small pool with many winning ticket holders pays low odds).

Tote odds are presented in the form of dividend to a £1 unit staked. For example, £3.50 returned wins £2.50, or odds of 5–2. Tote dividends are the actual amount paid to the backer and are not subject to any further reductions (such as betting tax, rule 4 on withdrawals, etc.) that occur in SP betting.

NB. Many bookmakers no longer accept bets at Tote odds, so the backer can bet with the Tote only when visiting a racecourse, or a Tote-owned betting shop, or as a Tote account customer.

BOOKMAKER'S PERCENTAGE

Bookmakers win in the long run and most backers lose in the long run because the odds available are balanced in favour of the bookmaker. Take the most simple case of all, the two–horse race where both animals are believed to have equal chances of winning. The situation is exactly the same as spinning a coin, heads and tails are both even-money chances. That gives the bookmaker no profit margin, so in a two-horse race if one horse, A, is evens the other, B, will be odds-on say 4–5, to give the bookies their percentage. If the odds-makers have got things exactly right their book on the race may look like this:

£55.55 to win on B at 4–5 – liability £99.99
£50 to win on A at Evens – liability £100.00
Total £105.55

Whichever horse wins, the bookie wins £5.55.

The more runners there are in the race the bigger the bookmaker's percentage can be without it appearing bad value to the backer. On average the bookmakers will have around 30 per cent built into the odds in their favour, but in a two-horse race that would mean odds of approximately 8–15 on both horses which would be completely unacceptable. So they are prepared to accept around 5 per cent on two-horse races but ask for, and get, more than 50 per cent in big fields.

The discerning backer must be able to calculate when the bookmakers' margins are unacceptable and be able to work out the odds. To do this requires a little skill in arithmetic, but it is well worth while practising on a few races.

The odds of each horse must first be worked out in terms of a percentage that it represents towards the bookies' profit. To do this write down the odds of a horse as a fraction, putting the left-hand part of the odds on the bottom and the right-hand part on top. Then add the top part of the fraction into the bottom part, divide it out and show the answer as a percentage. A few examples are shown below:

2–1 is $\frac{1}{2}$ becomes $\frac{1}{1+2} = \frac{1}{3} = 33.3\%$

3–1 is $\frac{1}{3}$ becomes $\frac{1}{1+3} = \frac{1}{4} = 25.0\%$

4–6 is $\frac{6}{4}$ becomes $\frac{6}{4+6} = \frac{6}{10} = 60.0\%$

13–8 is $\frac{8}{13}$ becomes $\frac{8}{8+13} = \frac{8}{21} = 38.1\%$

To calculate the theoretical percentage profit for the bookies in a given race, calculate the percentages for every runner and add them up. The resulting figure is the so-called *overround* figure or the percentage in favour of the bookies. An example taken from the 1985 St Leger is given in Table 5.1.

TABLE 5.1   Bookmaker's percentages

Horse	Starting price			Percentage towards profit
Oh So Sharp	8–11	11/16	=	68.7
Lanfranco	85–40	40/125	=	32.0
Khozdar	15–2	2/17	=	11.7
Phardante	18–1	1/19	=	5.2
Newmain	50–1	1/51	=	1.9
Troy Fair	100–1	1/100	=	0.9
Total				120.4
Percentage in bookmaker's favour			=	20.4

In broad terms the bookmakers are prepared to work on smaller margins in small fields, at big meetings and on the first race at a meeting. They work on big margins in large fields, on bank holidays and in sellers.

It is also important to note that the bookmakers make least out of bets on favourites and short-odds horses and most on long-odds chances. An analysis of the prices of all the horses that ran on the Flat in 1981 is given in Table 5.2.

TABLE 5.2

Prices	Winners	Runners	Profit or loss	Loss percentage
Odds on	223	375	−11	−3
Evens – 2–1	533	1404	−43	−3
9–4 – 5–1	962	4768	−389	−8
11–2 – 9–1	569	5454	−1725	−32
10–1 or more	552	20557	−10951	−53

Odds are the factor which decides how little or how much is returned on the money staked. Winning money demands betting successfully at the right odds.

THE RIGHT ODDS

This can be termed as getting 'value for money', when it is clearly understood to mean obtaining fair and reasonable odds on a well-formulated selection which has a positive reasoned chance of winning. However, value for money often tends to be a term totally misunderstood. Attractive sounding odds are worthless if a horse has no chance of winning.

It is impossible to state categorically what are the right odds without examining the factors particular to any given situation. It can only be left to the personal judgement of the backer to decide what odds in the circumstances are appropriate, always placing supreme importance on two questions: What can I win? and What do I stand to lose? And how these two factors relate to the practical chances of the selection winning.

Before suggesting what may be considered the right odds it can be emphatically stated what can be considered 'bad odds'. 'Odds-on' are bad odds as they are unfair and unreasonable.

They can never favour the backer who stands to lose more than can be gained.

They always favour the bookmaker whose risk is less than his possible gain.

At odds-on the onus is firmly placed on the backer being correct in selection. At 'evens' less than a 50 per cent winning ratio produces financial loss. In such circumstances the only viable response to bad, unfair, restrictive odds is not to bet.

A guide to the 'right odds'

Getting the 'right odds' can be termed as the fine balance of the odds that can be fairly and reasonably demanded by the circumstances and the odds realistically likely to be offered by the bookmakers.

The circumstances reveal and are subject to the following factors

1. The proven quality of the form of the selection.
2. The number of runners, particularly the number with probable chances of winning (i.e. the more competitive the race, the more open should be the betting odds).
3. The type of race (e.g. condition races basically have a reliable predictability value. All types of handicaps are by their nature unpredictable. Chases are similarly laced with drama and surprises that can thwart even the most reasoned of selections).

These prominent factors have to be carefully considered when making a calculated assessment of true, fair, appropriate odds – which may not bear close relationship to the odds offered and calculated solely to favour the layers!

The realistic view of the odds actually offered by the bookmakers is subject to the following:

1. The popular predictability of the selectors (i.e. how strongly have the racing press tipped or ignored the selections).
2. Information/rumour private to bookmakers, of a horse's chances which causes them cautiously to shorten or speculatively lengthen prices.
3. Weight of money wagered before the opening show of prices, which restricts the possibility of a fair price being offered.

After giving due regard to the odds which may be realistically offered; a guide can be suggested upon which to base the 'fair' right odds. This should be constructed on the understanding that 'evens' are the lowest acceptable odds, and that upward price adjustments be made to accommodate competition and conditions.

A 'fair price' for a horse in a race in which there is no foreseeable competition is evens. When betting tax and unforeseen circumstances are taken into consideration there will still remain a good profit for the backer in this situation. Odds-on is not acceptable because the profit for the backer is reduced to unacceptable or non-existent levels.

If there is a serious danger to a selection the backer must look for longer odds to compensate for the additional risk; 2–1 is the least acceptable odds.

Two serious rivals, the backer must look for 3–1 or more; three serious rivals warrants 4–1 or more and so on.

NB. It is considered that a race comprising three or more serious rivals is too competitive to contemplate a selection, and any betting in these circumstances is likely to be most injudicious.

Favourable conditions such as weight, distance and/or going require the reduction of odds by a fraction of a point. Similarly, if these and/or other elements are to the disadvantage of a selection, then fractions of a point should be added.

By this method the backer can calculate odds that are fair and equivalent to the practical elements influencing the winning chances of a selection. The backer with this formed and detached assessment of the odds can readily make a reasoned comparison with the actual odds offered by the bookmaker, and not be unknowingly beguiled to accepting less than a fair value. The value offered to backers does vary considerably from course to course according to the strength of the market.

BETTING VALUE HINTS

Every backer knows how difficult it is to beat the bookie because the satchel man fixes the odds. Ask a bookmaker if you can have a bet on the toss of a coin and he will offer you 4–5 for each of the two so he can make his profit.

What few backers realize is that the bookie's profit margin varies from race to race and that the off-course bookmaker and backer is in the hands of the on-course bookmaker who fixes the prices.

The backer can obtain a vital edge by knowing when the odds are in his favour and avoiding betting on races when the bookies' take is high.

A survey was made of flat races run in 1981 and, using a computer to make the many thousands of calculations involved, it produced the following results. The average mark-up was just over 20 per cent which gives the odds fixers a reasonable profit. However, in some races the mark-up went to over 60 per cent and in many it was less than 10 per cent.

By and large, the more runners there are in a race the bigger the bookies' margin becomes. In our coin-tossing example, the layers would have to go to 4–6 heads and tails to get their average 20 per cent margin and who would bet at those odds? It can be seen from Table 5.3 that betting in fields of 5 runners or less is a much better proposition than betting in fields of 16 or more runners.

TABLE 5.3

Size of field	% Mark-up
5 and under	9.4
6–15	21.0
16 and over	43.0
All races	20.1

The other major factor is the strength and make-up of the on-course market. In this survey, Salisbury gave the backers the worst value and Lingfield the best. But when we take into account the number of runners in the races concerned, the position changes and we get the *Backers value table*:

Very Good	Ascot, Brighton, Catterick, Kempton, Leicester, York
Good	Epsom, Lingfield, Newbury, Ripon, Sandown, Warwick
Average	Beverley, Chester, Folkestone, Goodwood, Nottingham, Pontefract, Thirsk, Wolverhampton
Poor	Bath, Doncaster, Haydock, Newcastle, Newmarket, Redcar, Yarmouth

Very poor   Ayr, Carlisle, Chepstow, Edinburgh, Hamilton, Salisbury, Windsor

The Tote is changing its methods of collecting dividends so often we do not know where we stand. But it should be worth while betting on the Tote at the poor value meetings and on the book elsewhere.

TOTE ODDS

These are not guaranteed and can always be subject to very unpredictable elements; they are not usually considered a professional or reliable way to bet. Tote punters tend to be small stakes, fun punters who dislike the atmosphere of the bookmakers' betting ring and prefer the more respectable demure approach of the Tote officials. Few serious backers will ever bet on the Tote because the risks are unknown. Tote dividends are calculated on the basis of the number of winning tickets on the successful animal and the backer cannot know in advance what the pay-out will be. The backer, therefore, gambles twice – once on the outcome of the race and then again on the dividend.

Because the Tote take-out is constant there are occasions when on average it will pay to bet on the Tote rather than with bookmakers. This is when the bookmaker's percentage is known to be high in big fields, outsiders, bank holidays, sellers, etc.

Never back on the Tote in small fields, on favourites or on fashionable jockeys. The dividends in these circumstances are invariably disappointing. Tote backers by and large bet names, numbers, fashionable jockeys, trainers, and famous horses, and herein lies the essence of predicting Tote odds.

Fashionable jockeys, trainers (or ones with good records at a course particularly the provincial ones). Well-tipped horses	Pay bad odds (i.e. odds that are invariably worse than SP)
Untipped horses, from unfashionable stables with little-known jockeys (i.e. unfashionable ones, new apprentices or inexperienced amateurs)	Pay good odds (i.e. odds invariably considerably better than SP)

STAKING

Stakes

The amount of money bet is of equal importance and fully complementary to odds. Winning money is the outcome of developing a successful betting technique, and this will only be established by maintaining a disciplined staking method. Although many staking plans abound, the best, most efficient, obvious and simplest to practice is *level stakes betting*. Level stakes ensures every bet is treated with equal importance.

The size of the stake

This essentially must be left to the personal consideration of each backer. For practical guidance it is recommended that a bank of money (set aside for betting purposes) be divided into 20 equal parts to represent 20 bets at level stakes. Such an approach enables the betting to commence without any financial pressure or looming insolvency.

Level stakes may appear a cautious, mundane method of betting – but results testify to its effectiveness and sound economic basis.

Favourable odds

When odds are offered that are well above their real value (e.g. 5–1 is offered for a selection whose realistic odds should be 2–1) such favourable odds demand an increase of the stake. The amount of increase can only be left to the personal judgement of the backer; the guiding factor being: 'the greater the value the greater the increase in the stake'.

The occasions when bookmakers generously err in the odds offered is extremely rare – they do exist – but only enforce the wisdom of maintaining level stakes at most times. Real over the odds value from bookmakers is comparable to 'solid gold' watches being sold cheaply – it is a situation to be viewed with great scepticism.

In the fluctuations of the betting market, drifting odds can become favourable odds if they reach well above a level thought to represent fair value. This situation justifies making another bet, if one had already been struck at lower odds, or increasing the stake if a bet has yet to be made.

In the charged atmosphere of the betting ring the drifting or lengthening of odds are the bookmakers' only method of attracting money to balance their 'book'. The drifting of the odds of any carefully formulated selection should not cause the backer to lose nerve but rather to take full advantage of the opportunity to obtain extra value by increasing the stake.

Shortening odds are unfavourable odds

If odds shorten no attempt must be made to increase stake to compensate for loss of the price value. If a bet was not made at the fair 'right odds' a bet must not be made later at shorter odds (especially when there is a temptation to increase stakes).

An increase of stakes to offset shortening of odds is at best an extreme method of buying money, which if habitually practised will quickly lead to betting bankruptcy.

ACCUMULATIVE STAKING (BASED ON THE LEVEL STAKES PRINCIPLE)

Level staking makes no immediate use of winnings.

Accumulative staking seeks to make full use of winnings by immediate reinvestment to produce further profit.

The bank – divided into 20 equal units representing 20 equal bets – allows for 20 consecutive losers before the bank is lost completely. The profit from winnings is added to the bank, which is divided immediately to raise the level of stakes of the remaining bets.

If the first bet is a winner, e.g. 2 pts profit:

2 pts + bank 20 pts = 22 pts
22 pts ÷ 20 (bets) = 1.1 pts (20 remaining bets)

If the first bet was a loser and the second bet a winner, e.g. 2 pts profit:

2 pts + (remaining bank) 19 pts = 21 pts
21 pts ÷ 19 (remaining bets) = 1.105 pts (19 remaining bets)

If it were desired to keep the bank intact in the second instance, then:

21 pts ÷ 20 (original no. of bets) = 1.05 pts (20 bets)

NB. The rate of increase in stakes is subject to the odds and consistency of winning selections.

SUMMARY OF BETTING

A guide to successful betting may be summarized in the following formula:

S	O	S
Selection	Odds	Stakes

These alone are the three factors which govern betting.

Selection

This is the first and fundamental element. Selection is the *means* – without winning selections there is no possibility of achieving successful betting results.

Odds

These are a modifying element, secondary to selection. Odds are the modality which impose a limit on how much can be won. Objectively they must evoke the question: 'Is the reward worth the risk?'

Stakes

These are the other modifying element – complementary to both odds and selection. Stakes are the method which serves to apply the means. Stakes raise the question: 'How much should be risked?' Stakes are the vital monetary aspect whose inconsistent or ordered application will frustrate or promote the successful outcome of betting.

The outcome of successful betting is to win money. This objective can only be consistently achieved by supporting successful selections at the 'right odds' with a rational system of stakes.

BETTING AND BOOKMAKERS

BOOKMAKING

This is the making of a book (set) of odds on the outcome of an event. The odds are mathematically calculated to provide the maker of the book with a percentage profit on turnover irrespective of the outcome of the event.

BOOKMAKERS

These are the layers of odds – they form the betting market which they endeavour to control and manipulate to maintain an advantage over the betting public. The layer of odds seeks to obtain the minimum of liability (pay-out) coupled with the maximum of income from betting stakes. This therefore makes odds-on the most attractive and favourable bet to the bookmaker and the most unfavourable bet to anyone taking those odds.

Bookmakers operate through the British Isles 'on' and 'off' the course, some are strictly on-course or off-course bookmakers, while others combine and are both kinds. The betting market, however, is formed and controlled solely at the racecourse (except for ante-post betting) by the on-course bookmakers.

Types of on-course bookmakers

There are three separate groups of on-course bookmakers who can be immediately recognized from the position where they trade on the racecourse: (i) the 'rails' bookmakers; (ii) the 'Tatts' bookmakers; (iii) the Silver Ring (or public enclosure) bookmakers.

The 'rails' bookmakers – stand on the railings dividing the members' enclosure from the Tattersalls Ring. In the foreground a principal of one firm is receiving instructions via cellular telephone while his clerk looks down their ledger of bets taken on the race. Meanwhile to the right a principal of another firm answers an enquiry of a client from the members' enclosure, as in the background a tic-tac man frantically relays market moves to other bookmakers.

The 'Tatts' bookmakers display on blackboards the price on offer for each horse, which can vary between bookmakers.

Bookmakers
A scene overlooking the frantic action of the betting rings. In the foreground the 'Tatts' bookmakers conduct business, their prices for each horse marked up in chalk on boards. In the background the credit-oriented 'Rails' bookmakers line the members enclosure, taking bets from clients in both rings. Between the two lies the area known as 'no man's land' where a 'tic-tac' man stands high on wooden crates expertly relaying the latest market moves. Beneath him men called 'bookies runners' await to rush and 'lay-off' bets taken by the 'rail bookmakers' with other bookmakers in the 'Tatts' ring, who may be showing that horse at a higher price.

The 'rails' bookmakers

These are the foremost and, at most race meetings, the group of bookmakers which holds a commanding influence in the betting market. They take their position on the racecourse lining the railings which divide the members' enclosure from the Tattersalls enclosure. They are the senior, longest established and largest firms of bookmakers, wielding considerable power in the trading activities of the betting market. Betting transactions are made verbally with them and recorded on large boarded sheets of paper which give them an immediate visual indication of their commitments. Business is conducted almost entirely on credit, and therefore only with clients that have been vetted and are of a reliable standing; these include other bookmakers, professional racing people who often bet in larger sums than the average 'Tatts' bookmaker can or wishes to lay, and racing stables who, when they place their commissions on course, prefer the credit facilities offered by the 'rails' bookmakers.

The 'rails' bookmakers do not visually display the odds they have on offer and it is necessary to ask or listen to their exalted barker-like calls to discover what odds they are prepared to lay. These odds will be subject to market fluctuations and therefore change in response to the on-course betting activities conveyed to the 'rails' bookmakers by strategically placed and frantically signalling 'tic-tac' men. Off-course betting developments are conveyed to the 'rails' bookmakers with equal swiftness and efficiency via the 'blower' (the racecourse–off-course direct telephone link) and will produce an appropriate response in odds.

The 'rails' bookmakers with their off-course betting links and their facility to lay the larger on-course bets command the most powerful and dominating influence in the betting market. Significant market activity which permeates through to affect prices in the other betting rings is sure to have emanated from trading moves of the 'rails' bookmakers (i.e. 'laying off' money – the bookmaker's method of limiting liability by placing whole or part of an accepted commission with other bookmakers). Such moves which bring a volume of money suddenly into trading activities causes an immediate depression of prices as money chases odds and the market forces of supply and demand are intensified.

As the betting market closes at the 'off', it is from the 'mean' or average prices laid by the 'rails' and leading 'Tatts' bookmakers that independent assessors who have observed and recorded the foregoing market trading compile the SP odds.

The 'Tatts' bookmakers

The 'Tatts' bookmakers usually form the majority of bookmakers to be found on the racecourse; they are located in the Tattersalls Ring which is the focal point of betting at a racecourse. The Tattersalls area represents the medium-priced entrance fee for racecourse enclosures, attracting the racing enthusiast who is non-professional and whose principal interest is likely to be a moderate flutter (i.e. betting in sums from £5 to £10 up to perhaps a maximum of £100). The Tattersalls bookmakers exist principally to accommodate these punters, offering 'cash-only' betting and visually displaying the prices they have on offer on boards.

'Tatts' bookmakers form the cornerstone of bookmakers in the betting market, they offer odds which are competitive among themselves and often with those on offer by the 'rails' bookmakers. It is necessary for them to be (as their well-earned reputation confirms), sharp in their dealings and forever vigilant of the constant change of currents in market trends which unheeded would quickly swamp them. 'Tatts' bookmakers have for long provided colour to the racecourse betting scene epitomized in the caricature of 'Honest Joe' standing beside a board of prices, with a satchel heavily laden with the money of losing punters.

The Silver Ring bookmakers

The Silver Ring bookmakers are the least influential of bookmakers found at a racecourse, they are located and operate in the Silver Ring or public enclosures (the cheapest entry admissions on a racecourse). They provide a betting service for the amateur racegoer more likely interested in a day's outing in the open air than any hearty ventures into betting. Silver Ring bookmakers like their 'Tatts' counterparts insist on cash-only bets, and being at the lower end of the market take only the smaller bets. They compensate for this lower turnover by usually offering undervalue odds (prices that are lower than what is on offer in the other betting ring).

Silver Ring bookmakers play no influential role in the betting market, and will be given a wide berth by the more experienced racegoers and backers. Their role is to serve the needs of the amateur, inexperienced and indiscriminate backers, the prices offered by the Silver Ring bookmakers have no influence on the eventual SP odds.

The on-course betting market

The on-course betting market except for the larger prestigious races and meetings (Flat and National Hunt) tends to be extremely sensitive and quite unable to withstand any sizeable bets without a violent depression of odds. This is because without strong market activity (a considerable flow of money), the aim of bookmaking (making a rounded book of prices, with money proportionally evenly spread to show a percentage profit whatever the result) is challenged and threatened.

In such circumstances any large influx of money in an inactive market will be met with the counterbalancing response of an immediate reduction in the odds. If the influx of money is too great for even this guarded response, the bookmakers will enforce their strongest weapon: 'We maintain the right to refuse a part or whole of any commission.' In other words they will choose what bets, and what size of bets they are prepared to lay – usually refusing whole or part of sizeable bets at odds which are attractive to the backer.

The bookmaking fraternity are extremely nervous when faced with the possibility of accepting – or even worse of having already accepted – sizeable bets at long odds on a horse with a real winning chance. Such fears by bookmakers have forced any determined backers who want sizeable bets at less than derisory odds to find undetectable methods of 'getting on'.

On-course or off-course, large single bets at long odds will just not be taken by bookmakers except in the most competitive of races and where there is an extremely large and strong market (i.e. Derby, Grand National, or popular handicaps where there is ante-post betting). Large bets for other races at best will usually only be accepted in part and then only at reduced odds; occasionally bookmakers will accept them whole or in part at SP (if they have sufficient time to 'lay off' the bet). This will result in a sweeping depression of the SP as the bookmaker quickly lays off the bet and in the process gains free trading points profit.

Laying the bet off will immediately reduce the SP to lowly odds as money floods in one direction in a weak market. The SP returning perhaps at evens when as the money was laid off (spread with a number of other bookmakers) the odds may have varied in this process from 5–1 to 2–1, giving the original bookmaker who laid the bet off 2, 3 or 4 points profit on a winning bet.

The only hope any intrepid backer has to defeat such ploys is to get the bet laid without the bookmakers being aware of its real size. It will mean 'spreading the money'. This can be achieved on-course or off-course, but will require careful planning and skilful execution. On-course it will require a team of people simultaneously to place small bets (in total equivalent to the large bet) and having them accepted at prices before the significance of such prices on the market is realized. Off-course money may be spread over a wide area in small amounts and with the hope of a reasonable SP as the market activity on-course will be uneventful.

The off-course bookmakers

There are two types of off-course bookmakers representing cash or credit business, although some do combine both.

Cash bookmaking

This is the dominant feature of off-course bookmaking and is represented by betting shops/offices which cater for the needs of the majority of the betting population. Business which is strictly 'cash only' is conducted in a casino-like atmosphere where some events for betting (i.e. horse-racing or greyhound racing) are normally occurring every 10 to 15 minutes throughout the late morning and afternoon. Commentaries of races may be interspersed with, and are supplemented by, betting shows conspiring to engulf the betting-shop customer in constant action and excitement. In 1986 liberalization of the law allowed bookmakers who so desired to turn their erstwhile Spartan premises into more comfortable surroundings, with live television coverage of racing and other events and the serving of non-alcoholic drinks, etc. The backer, however, should be under no illusion as to the purpose of this new public image – to extract the punter's money!

Bets of almost any size from a nominal minimum to a fairly high maximum will be accepted in betting offices, and there is no discrimination between the large or the small backer. The smaller backers are in fact encouraged to bet small stakes in myriad combinations which if successful at good/long odds would produce a considerable return on a small investment (a possibility which to the dismay of the punter and the expectation of the bookmaker seldom happens).

The cash bookmakers involved with betting offices play no significant role in the on-course betting market, although themselves always subject to the results of its trading in the SP. Occasional large bets taken in the offices may be phoned through to be 'laid off' on-course to depress the SP; or similarly threatening commitments from the final leg of a successful but incomplete accumulative bet may warrant the same response and have an influence in the on-course market. Normally, betting offices passively lay the Board prices shown which represent the 'on-course' market trading and rely completely on the SP to settle all other bets.

Off-course bookmakers are therefore very vulnerable to any coup in on-course trading which could inflate starting prices, and have to remain extremely alert in preventing such situations from arising.

Betting offices, the only legal places for off-course cash betting, have become social institutions providing warmth and a meeting-place for those of like mind and disposition among the betting classes.

Credit bookmaking

Although smaller in volume this is normally of greater significance than off-course cash betting and bookmaking. Credit bookmaking is usually conducted by telephone, with backers conveying their instructions verbally and betting in larger amounts than the normal cash customer. The larger credit bookmaker is likely to have as clients professional racing interests (trainers, owners, etc.) whose betting habits are likely to be a specific indication of a horse's real chances of winning. The value of such information to a bookmaker amply compensates the retaining of these possibly regular winning accounts which would otherwise not be tolerated because of their unsound economic basis. Precise reliable information from these sources will prompt bookmakers to anticipate market trends and act accordingly, being ready to hold or lay off bets as the situation demands. All the larger credit bookmakers have, or have access to, course representztives with whom they will be in constant contact, entrusting them to initiate or regulate market activity with the aim always of limiting the bookmaker's liability.

Credit clients are only accepted by bookmakers from reliable personal references or after scrutiny of financial references as to their credit-worthiness. Transactions of often such a delicate financial nature require goodwill and trust by both parties, of which bookmakers with their years of experience have designed safeguard systems which seldom give rise to any disputes over bets. Credit accounts work well and provide excellent service to the backer; accounts are rendered for settlement weekly or fortnightly and they can be recommended as the easy comfortable way of betting for all except the impulsive, and uncontrollable gambler.

Ante-post betting

Ante-post betting is the betting that takes place on an event some time before it actually occurs – any time from 24 hours up to a year or more before the event. All the large races (i.e. Derby, Guineas, Classics, Grand National, etc.) have an ante-post betting market and they are constantly engendered by bookmakers to create betting activity at all times. The rule of ante-post betting is that all bets stand whether a horse runs in the event or not. Horses entered a long time in advance for a race may become injured, ill or prove inadequate and be withdrawn from the race.

All bets on these horses are lost, and herein lies the weakness and uncertainty of ante-post betting. The only attraction to ante-post betting is the chance of obtaining good odds and the possibility of holding a winning voucher on a 20–1 chance whose starting price is returned at possibly 4–1 or 5–1. Ante-post betting to be successful usually requires professional racing knowledge as to a horse's aims and more than a fair share of luck. It cannot be recommended to the amateur who will lose out more often than not with the horse failing to run.

There are some concessionary ante-post bets on the morning of a race which offer possible longer than SP odds without risk of losing the stake if the horse be withdrawn. These cannot normally be recommended as a good betting medium. Ante-post betting can fairly be said to be designed by bookmakers solely for their self-development and publicity.

Cash ante-post bets where bookmakers have the backer's money a considerable time before settling day must appear an extremely attractive proposition to bookmakers and be a conclusive argument against this form of betting.

6 THE SELECTION FORMULA ANALYSED: FORM

Form is the first and foremost constituent in the selection formula.

Form is the record of a horse's race performances and the factual evidence of racing ability.

Form is therefore the primary consideration in race analysis and the fundamental element upon which to base selection.

In the evaluation of form it is necessary to ask: 'What horses has the horse beaten?' or, 'What horses have finished behind it?' The only satisfactory answer is previous and/or subsequent winners. Such confirmation establishes the form as of value. It means a horse has finished in front of horses which have previously or subsequently beaten many other horses. It is the best and most reliable criterion of form, the soundest foundation upon which to base selection and is applicable to races of all types and class.

PROOF OF FORM

Assessment relying on factors of proven ability is the most reasoned approach to form analysis and the surest foundation upon which to base selection. Proven ability can only be assessed from past performances.

Proven positive ability

This is ability proven by race performances. It is where a horse produces a race performance of definable positive value (i.e. winning or being placed, etc.).

The more race experience a horse has, the more information there is upon which to judge ability; patterns in performance become established from which a horse will make only discernible and probable deviations (i.e. its racing style will be determined).

Proven positive ability is only what a horse has achieved in race performance, it is exposed ability, and it can be identified in horses of all types, ages and class.

Unproven ability

This is ability that is unexposed and can be said to exist where the evidence from race performance is insufficient. It applies to inexperienced horses, some of which display potential ability, and to horses that have not previously raced. The less experienced a horse, the less opportunity it has had, and the less information there is upon which to assess ability. In these circumstances it is judicial to consider a horse's ability as unproven.

Potential ability and supposed abilities emanating from off-course reputation all remain unproven until confirmed in race performance; this applies to horses of all types, ages and class.

Proven non-ability

This is where a horse of experience has shown no ability in its race performances, or at best moderate ability which shows no sign of improvement. In such instances the horse can be considered to have proven non-ability, this also applies to horses of all types, ages and class.

DATE OF FORM

Form is a record of past performances, and by its very nature it is always past form. This can be considered and graded as: (i) recent form; (ii) less recent form; (iii) older past form. As can be seen from Table 6.1 the value of form decays progressively as it grows older.

TABLE 6.1

Days since last ran	1985 Flat			1985–86 National Hunt		
	Winners	Runners	%	Winners	Runners	%
1 – 14	1027 – 9680 =		10.6	1029 – 9386 =		11.0
15 – 28	870 – 8684 =		10.1	625 – 6274 =		10.0
29+	453 – 5969 =		7.6	460 – 6349 =		7.2
Seasonal debut	571 – 8551 =		6.7	445 – 6760 =		6.6

Recent form (1–14 days)

This is the first grade; it is the most reliable indication of whether or not a horse is likely to reproduce its proven abilities. Recent form undeniably reflects a horse's current form, fitness and general well-being. The time scale for considering form as current is *as recent as possible* but allowing up to 14 days.

Less recent form (15–28 days)

This is of second grade in value and likely to be slightly less reliable as an indication of a horse's current ability. It can however be appropriate when considering the form of 2 y.o. Flat race horses and National Hunt chasers – who often need a longer time to recover from the demands of racing. Less recent form can only be relied upon when 'top class' (i.e. Classics, group races or their National Hunt equivalent). Any time from 22 to 28+ days can be considered less recent form.

Older past form (29+ days)

This is the lowest grade in value; it can be termed 'old form'. The older form becomes, the less relevant it is likely to be to the present.

Distant past form is a record of what a horse is capable of, while recent form reflects its present abilities. A comparison of the two will indicate whether a horse has maintained its form, improved or deteriorated. If distant past form is top class it can never be completely disregarded, as a horse with proven ability may always reproduce it. However, a horse which has lost its form is unlikely to suddenly return to form without prior indication.

Distant past form can be considered as 91 days+ for 2-year-olds, 140 days+ for 3-year-olds, 182 days+ or previous season's form for older Flat horses and all National Hunt.

WINNING FORM

Simply said: the **best form** is **winning form** and **losing form** the **worst form**.

Such a statement may appear obvious, but in analysing form and making a selection this most basic approach is frequently overlooked. Unless the entry conditions of race preclude previous winners, previous winning form always demands the closest attention and is the area where the selector should immediately focus interest.

TABLE 6.2

| Days since last ran as a winner | 1985 Flat | | | | | | 1985–86 National Hunt | | | | | |
| | 2 y.o. | | | 3 y.o.+ | | | Hurdles | | | Chases | | |
	Winners	Runners	%	Winners	Runners	%	Winners	Runners	%	Winners	Runners	%
1 – 7	67 –	634 =	10.6	244 –	2262 =	10.8	199 –	1923 =	10.3	152 –	1290 =	11.8
8 – 14	213 –	1750 =	12.2	503 –	5034 =	10.0	348 –	3514 =	9.9	330 –	2659 =	12.4
15 – 28	151 –	1375 =	11.0	368 –	3915 =	9.4	212 –	2427 =	8.7	204 –	1640 =	12.4
22 – 28	103 –	931 =	11.1	248 –	2465 =	10.1	121 –	1370 =	8.8	88 –	837 =	10.5
29+	139 –	1905 =	7.3	314 –	4064 =	7.7	245 –	4215 =	5.8	215 –	2134 =	10.1
Seasonal debut	212 –	3188 =	6.6	359 –	5363 =	6.7	244 –	4626 =	5.3	201 –	2134 =	9.4

Winning form means that a horse has previously shown it has the ability to win a race and beat other horses in the competitive atmosphere of a racetrack. Horses often grow in confidence from the experience of a victory which can lead to future triumphs if other factors such as class, going, course, etc. are similar.

Winners in horse-racing as in other walks of life are likely to win again.

In practical terms a winning racehorse is likely to receive that extra attention and encouragement when it returns home to its yard that a loser will not. Everybody in the stable will be affected as morale is lifted and hopes for the future raised. A horse, if only a winner of a minor prize, will for a short time get star treatment and be the focus of attention, and an interest in its future has been created. The stable lad who looks after the horse, having constant close contact with the animal (feeding it, riding it, grooming it and being aware of its health and moods) will be instrumental in lavishing renewed praise and care. This lad will be able to stand tall with peers who may not have had such recent success, bathing in the kudos and freshened by the optimism to carry out the routine tasks of stable duties, which are often arduous, with renewed vigour. The spice of victory will also be felt from the financial angle if the lad had backed this winner or received a present from a grateful owner. In contrast the frequent losers will get none of these benefits.

CHANGING FORM

Also involved in the assessment of merit are previously unmentioned elements of: **consistency**; **inconsistency**; **deterioration**; **improvement**. These have to be carefully considered when interpreting form. Their existence can be established by examination and comparison of recent with past form.

Consistency is shown by form which contains performances of constant equal merit.

Inconsistency is displayed in form where performances are unpredictable and of varying merit.

Horses of top-class ability are usually consistent in performance. Horses of moderate ability tend to be unreliable and inconsistent in performance.

Deterioration is form that is worsening and displays present performances which are inferior to past performances. It can be apparent in horses of all types, ages and class (but it is especially found in National Hunt horses who fail to recapture their previous form after injury, in younger horses (Flat and National Hunt) who suffered from physical ailments, and in horses whose enthusiasm for racing has been soured).

Improvement is form which shows that a horse's performance has become better. It applies to horses of all types and class, and is a particular prominent feature in the assessment and interpretation of the form of younger inexperienced horses. Improvement can be positively established and calculated in respect of past performances, but its existence in the present and future is purely speculation. It is this assessment of its future development which pose the imponderable issues. The issues to be considered are as follows:

1. Is further improvement necessary?
2. Is further improvement likely to continue or has a peak been reached?
3. If further improvement is likely or possible then by what degree?

1. Is further improvement necessary?   Improvement is essential for horses that carry a weight penalty, and for horses raised in class. In both instances they must better their previous performance to have a winning chance.

Constant improvement is essential for all inexperienced horses if they are to maintain their status with their peers. This applies to 2-year-olds – many show early season promise but as the season progresses they fail to maintain it. Consistency alone in these events is likely to be inadequate (e.g. the form figures 33232 may reveal admirable consistency but insufficient improvement to win without a lowering in class).

The criterion for improvement being a necessity, applies to all horses (3–4 y.o. maidens, novice hurdlers, novice chasers – and even handicappers) if they are to maintain their status. It is, however, more particularly apparent when applied to 2-year-olds where rapid growth and improvement exist as very dynamic factors. The only time improvement is not a required necessity is when it is applied to a current proven champion (i.e. Classic champions, sprinters, milers, middle-distance horses, stayers and their National Hunt equivalents) where if challenged at equal conditions (weight – distance – going) it is the challenger who must improve – and the consistent reproducing of proven ability will be enough for the champion to win.

2. Is further improvement likely?   The likelihood of improvement will be indicated in the previous performance and will depend on three factors:

(a) *Manner of performance.* A horse that has not won may be judged as having to improve to win. A horse that has won displays proven ability which can be assessed for further development.

Form is the undisputed record of a horse's race performance. The smaller the margin of victory or defeat the more possible a reversal of form. The greater the margin of victory or defeat the less likely a reversal of form.

An example of a close margin finish. The official margin between first, second and third was a short-head and a neck.

An example of a wide margin finish. The official winning distance was 6 lengths, with a short-head dividing the second and third.

Close-up showing the proximity of horses – typical of a close margin finish.

Close-up showing distance between horses – typical of a wide margin finish.

Horses can gain a vital advantage by jumping fences and hurdles accurately and quickly.

While horses may brush through hurdles and only lose impetus . . .

. . . horses that hit the much sturdier fences in chases are likely to pay the higher price of falling.

The guiding principle in a horse improving upon its performance is the ease with which it wins. A horse that wins 'easily', 'unchallenged', can do no more – if an inexperienced horse (e.g. 2 y.o.) running for the first time this is a highly commendable performance which suggests in all probability it will improve. Although particular to 2-year-olds first time out, any horse winning easily suggests further improvement. The more hard fought the victory, the less obvious scope in ability a horse has for improvement.

(b) *Physical fitness* at the time of performance.

A horse that wins easily when not at peak race fitness can be almost guaranteed to improve.

A horse that wins in a hard-fought race when unfit is also very likely to improve as it obtains peak fitness.

A horse that wins easily when fit can still improve, especially if inexperienced.

A horse that wins in a hard-fought race when at peak fitness is less likely to improve.

The modifying factor here will be the scope for further physical development in the horse. This is not a factor that can be satisfactorily judged from form; it can only be assessed by seeing the horse and observing its physical conformation.

(c) *The methods and ability of the trainer.* Improvement is always subject to training methods. It is noticeable that some trainers in their racing preparation of inexperienced and experienced horses allow themselves an area in which to improve a horse i.e. racing it initially short of peak race fitness, allowing weaker horses (2-year-olds that are growing) time to recover from races and gain strength, and generally allowing a horse to fulfil its physical potentiality.

Other trainers run their horses 'fully wound-up' (peak race fit), have less scope to improve them, and in fact will in some instances 'burn out' a horse (especially 2-year-olds).

Improvement is dependent upon the skill, method and, in some instances, patience of the trainer.

3. Degree or rate of improvement If a horse is likely to improve, what degree of improvement could be expected? This is an almost unanswerable question. Improvement will be strongly influenced by:

(a) The horse's physical scope (allowing for the possibility of any rapid or slow development).

(b) The trainer's method, which may be to allow the horse to mature slowly and not be rushed (i.e. in the case of 2 y.o. who is bred to stay as a 3 y.o., or a backward National Hunt horse which is considered primarily as a staying chaser and is allowed as much as two seasons to develop).

Improvement can be compared to growth or learning; it is a gradual process that occurs in stages. There will be phases of progress and of consolidation.

The degree of improvement is not one of improbable and incomprehensible leaps.

- The improvement to winning form is normally from progressively better performances (this is not always apparent from mere abbreviated form figures – closer analysis may be required to establish this fact).
- The improvement on winning form often originates from the impetus of winning. (The experience of winning gives added confidence.)

The rate of improvement will be closely linked with the type of horse (i.e. Flat or National Hunt, sprinter, stayer, 2m hurdler, 3m chaser) and whether the horse is precocious or slow maturing.

As a rule, the shorter the distance the faster maturing the horse is likely to be, and the longer the distance the slower maturing the horse will be. Sprinters 'come to hand' quicker than potential stayers, and are likely to be trained with a short-term viewpoint. Stayers (especially National Hunt 3m chasers) are trained with a long-term viewpoint. Between the extremes there are numerous rates of progress.

Once a horse (of whatever type) begins improving, its rate and range should not be underestimated. For example, early season 2 y.o. 'sharp types', often run up a sequence of wins over the minimum 5f distance in the first month of the Flat season. Similarly, 2-year-olds without previous experience, or with moderate form over shorter distances suddenly improve extensively and rapidly when running over a distance 7f–1m (late season). Three-year-old maidens can, during their second season, improve quickly and considerably when racing at longer distances, although sometimes not developing until late in their 3 y.o. season. Novice hurdlers usually learn quickly after a few races, but some may take a whole season.

Whatever its type, once a horse shows improvement, its *rate* of improvement will be closely attached to its *degree* of improvement and its abilities must then be considered carefully.

The misuse and misunderstanding of the term 'improvement'. Improvement is always a speculative judgement, and only exists as a proven fact when it is a comparison of past and recent form. The misuse and misunderstanding of the term 'improvement' often emanates from journalistic copy which has presented opinion as fact.

'Has improved' is a statement of fact that can be disputed or verified by examination of form. Correctly understood, this statement provides concisely defined information upon which to make a judgement.

'Has improved', however, can have the unfortunate connotation of implying more than it can represent, arousing speculation and exceeding the limit of accurate definition.

'Will improve' – 'sure to improve' – 'can only improve' have become commonly used and accepted terms in horse-racing parlance, but from the objective viewpoint are meaningless. They insinuate proven fact, but are and can only ever be subjective opinion.

'Is improving' is another misleading term from any objective viewpoint of form. It has been confused with and often mistakenly used instead of the term 'has improved' which is an observed comparison of past and recent form. 'Is improving' is an unproven assertion of no value to objective form selection, and can only be assumed as meaningful when it can be attributed to a trainer who has witnessed improvement in its ability since the horse last raced.

FORM COMMENTARIES

The form of a horse is the record of its race performances.

To assess form correctly the selector will need to read the records and fully understand how the real live flesh-and-blood issues of horse-racing relate to the abstract figures and words in the Form Book. Unfortunately, most racing fans fail to achieve even a basic skill in this. Video-recorders have given the racing fan an opportunity to recall live action at the flick of a switch, but this still demands reference to the Form Book for factual details.

To obtain the required skill it is necessary to interpret the language of the commentaries found in the Form Book. As abbreviated terms they are explained at the beginning of the form, and are largely self-explanatory. The facts such as weight, age, jockey, trainer, going, prize-money, etc. are relatively uncomplicated, but sometimes with a deep significance that will only be understood with experience.

The commentaries of a horse's running in a race can be divided into two parts. The first part gives an indication of how active a role a horse took throughout the race, or its position at different stages (e.g. 3rd st: led wl over 1f out). The second part states how the horse finished the race (e.g. r.o.wl.)

The Form Book may also have opening comment describing a horse's pre-race physical condition (e.g. l.w. – looked well – meaning looking very fit; or adversely BWD – backward – meaning the horse looked decidedly lacking in peak fitness). These observations may therefore explain how a horse subsequently ran in the race, thus modifying conclusions about its earlier form.

Although it is necessary to understand the whole of the form commentary, it is particularly important to focus attention on how a horse finished. In broad terms the better a horse's performance in the closing stages of a race the greater the value its form is likely to be.

The positive comments which denote a good performance at the finish of a race are:

r.o. = ran on – means the horse was running on or finishing in the closing stages;

r.o.wl. = ran on well – means running on well in the closing stages;

comf. = comfortably;

drew clr. = drew clear;

easily = easily;

qckned clr. = quickened clear;

unchal. qcknd. = unchallenged quickened.

The negative comments (especially if they are a consistent feature in a horse's form commentaries) which denote unsatisfactory performances at the end of a race are:

one pce = one pace: means a horse being unable to find extra acceleration from the one speed;

a.bhd. = always behind: means always behind – a most unfavourable comment;

sn.btn. = soon beaten: means a horse's challenge was soon beaten off;

sn.wknd. = soon weakened: means a horse's challenge soon petered out.

Numerous other comments from the form commentary are much less concrete and open to varying interpretations. These comments, while not necessarily negative, would need to be interpreted in an extremely imaginative way to be considered very positive. Referring to winners they include:

all out – meaning the horse was all out to win;

driven out – meaning the horse had to be driven out to win;

pushed out – meaning the horse had to be pushed out to win;

rdn. out – meaning the horse had to be ridden out to win.

The latter two observations suggest the horse may have had more to give if asked – while the former suggest the horse was at full stretch and this may bode less favourably for the future.

Two other comments that fit in this neutral category seldom apply to winners:

kpt on = kept on: meaning the horse kept on with its challenge;

styd on = stayed on: meaning the horse stayed on ('saw out') the distance of the race.

Both these commentaries can be interpreted in a positive or negative light:

kept on – can mean that the horse kept on with its challenge and although not showing any marked acceleration produced a good performance; alternatively it may be viewed that by keeping on without showing any acceleration the horse displayed its deficiencies and demonstrated it was not good enough;

stayed on – means a horse lasted out the distance of the race well. This bodes well for the future if the horse faces a similar or greater test of stamina. However, a horse that merely stayed on may have shown that it lacks the vital quality of acceleration, and again may not be good enough.

Other comments from the form commentary can be placed in this neutral category because although they have a negative prefix they can also be understood to have a more favourable interpretation:

no ex. = no extra – meaning a horse had no extra (effort, acceleration) to give;

nt. qkn. = not quicken – meaning a horse could not quicken or accelerate;

no imp. = no impression – meaning a horse made no impression on winning rivals or was not close enough to challenge the winner or leading horses;

nvr. nrr. = never nearer – meaning a horse was never nearer winning than its finishing position;

wknd. = weakened – meaning a horse weakened at a particular distance during the race;

no extra: means a horse on the day was not good enough and had no extra to meet the challenge of the winner. More favourably viewed it could be because the horse was short of race fitness (i.e. making seasonal début or a reappearance after recovering from illness, injury, etc.) or due to the distance of the race, stiffness of track or testing going;

not quicken: this may be an observation that identifies a horse as one-paced. In its most negative aspect this is a damning accusation of a horse's lack of ability. More favourably, however, it may be explained as due to a horse being unfit and/or inexperienced (especially in the case of 2 y.o., 3 y.o. maidens, etc.) and therefore without the fitness or experience to respond at the crucial time in a race when the pace suddenly quickens.

no impression: means a horse made no impression in challenging the winner and on the day was certainly not good enough. However, there may be extenuating circumstances explained in the other part of the commentary (National Hunt: mistakes, blundered. Flat: started slowly) which give reasons for this and allows the performance to be seen more favourably. Sometimes it is also due to horse not quite staying the distance of the race;

never nearer – means a horse never being in a closer position than its finishing position which is some margin from the winner and leading horses. On that performance the horse is certainly not good enough. However, the extenuating circumstances here may imply a 'non-trier'. Horses are sometimes schooled in public (which is against the rules of racing and could result in a trainer losing his licence), but blatant disregard of the rule has to be tempered with the fact that backward and inexperienced horses may need an educational race or two to learn the business of racing, after which they often improve.

The unacceptable side of this is where a horse's true ability is deliberately being concealed to provide connections of that horse with the ammunition for a future betting coup;

weakened – means the horse weakened at a certain stage in the race and obviously was not good enough. However, there may be other reasonable excuses for this performance that demand the form be given some consideration. A horse may 'weaken' due to lack of fitness, the burden of weight, 'greenness' – in the case of inexperienced horses, being raised in class and tackling a better-class opponent, or the most frequent case, racing over the wrong distance (usually one that is too far).

These later form commentaries demonstrate a variety of interpretation and sometimes explain why the unexpected does occur.

FORM FOR AGE (FLAT RACING)

Some basic observations can be made about the form of Flat-race horses of different age groups.

Two-year-old form is in essence about speed. The race distances are short. The longer distance races do not take place until late in the season (1m races commence in September and those of 7f not before late June or early July). Therefore, early season races will be essentially contests of pure speed. Later in the season racing experience and a horse's ability to learn quickly are of advantage. For example FAYRUZ (1985) made its racecourse début at Newmarket on 16 April and finished unplaced, yet by 17 May had won six consecutive races.

Three-year-old form is in essence about improvement. The longer distances which horses may now be tackling give opportunities for the slower-maturing type of animal to show its worth. In handicaps especially early in the season when the going rides soft, over distances in excess of 1¼m, some lower-weighted horses often show a considerable improvement upon their 2 y.o. form, where in races over shorter distances they were not able to show their true ability. In contrast, previous winners as 2 y.o.'s are unlikely to be viewed lightly by the official handicapper, so in the early part of the season, until rehandicapped, they can be at a disadvantage with lighter-weighted rivals, who may have been underestimated.

Horses previously maidens as 2-year-olds usually compete in suitable maiden races as 3-year-olds with winners often graduating to stakes races before tackling handicap company. Three-year-olds often continue to improve and are the most difficult type of horse to assess accurately. As more and more handicaps from June onwards become open to horses of all ages the more difficult it can be to assess a 3 y.o. against older rivals. Three-year-olds on the upgrade who are skilfully placed by their trainers can often run up a sequence of victories before the handicapper catches up with them. For example, PERKIN WARBECK (1985) after being placed fourth in its racecourse début in a stakes race at Newmarket in early May, won a maiden race in its next race and then proceeded to win a sequence of a further five races, one of which was a 0.70 graded handicap in August carrying top weight, 9 st 12 lb.

Four-year-old form is in essence about horses confirming what they are known to be capable of. Horses at this stage of their lives are subject to less sudden, or rapid rates of improvement. Occasionally older horses chalk up an unexpected sequence of wins as when a new trainer may perhaps discover and exploit their abilities. For example, in 1985 AL TRUI as a 5 y.o. won six races – including the most competitive Steward's Cup at Goodwood (6f), and CHAPLINS CLUB as a 5 y.o. won nine races – both in the first season with new trainers. However, these are the exceptions. Both were sprinters, 5/6f specialists, are the type of horse that sometimes only really get their act together with age, learning by experience to explode from the starting stalls and how to time their final finishing spurt to a nicety. Older horses in general tend only to confirm rather than improve upon the abilities they have previously shown, and sometimes even these strengths will be swept aside by the talent of the rising stars of the younger generation.

NATIONAL HUNT FORM

The longer distances and the obstacles to be jumped in National Hunt racing means that the finishing margins between horses will be wider than in Flat racing. In a 3m chase the margin between the winner and the last horse to finish is commonly 30–40 lengths, while a competitive 5f sprint handicap on a fast down course like Epsom may see only 10–15 lengths between first and last horse.

National Hunt form cannot be observed in terms of age-groups. Horses are intended to have a longer career than their Flat-race counterparts. A National Hunt horse usually has a dual career beginning first as a hurdler at the age of 4 or 5 years, and then progressing from the age of 6/7 years to become a chaser.

Hurdle form

This is principally about speed; similar in some ways to longer distance Flat races, the technique for jumping hurdles is different from that of fences. Horses need to be faster and hurdlers usually jump flatter than chasers, often brushing through the top of the hurdle without necessarily finding great hindrance to their progress.

Chase form

This is principally about safely negotiating the fences. Unless a horse is able to jump fences efficiently and therefore complete the course it will have no chance of winning. Horses have to jump higher in chases than in hurdles and horses which do not jump cleanly will pay the price either of falling or at least of having their progress impeded.

Novice hurdles

These are basically level weight races open to horses which before the beginning of the season had not won a hurdle run. They can be contested by horses of all ages (4 y.o. and upwards) although some have conditions of entry limiting them to horses of a prescribed age – and in the autumn as the season commences there are juvenile hurdles – races confined to 3-year-olds. Therefore, novice hurdlers tend to be younger horses. This is the beginning stage in a horse's National Hunt career. Theoretically, older horses can compete in novice hurdles provided they have not won a hurdle race in previous seasons. Occasionally the strange occurrence is witnessed when an older experienced handicap chaser who had never won a hurdle race is sometimes put back to hurdling in a novice event to regain lost confidence after a series of falls or injury. However, such horses usually will not have the necessary speed to succeed over hurdles.

Speed and quickly gaining a technique to jump hurdles will be an essential requirement to win a novice hurdle. Ex-Flat-race horses with racing experience often adapt more quickly to these requirements, but usually have less scope for development for a further National Hunt career as chasers. Novice hurdlers, therefore, improve at varying rates. Some need a whole season of experience in novice contests and only show their ability in their second season as a novice hurdler. Others show good form quickly and win in their first season before graduating into handicap hurdle company in their second season. After a season's experience in novice hurdles gaining in strength and maturity, horses can sometimes become transformed performers in their second season. For example, TEN PLUS (1985/86) the devastating winner of the Sun Alliance 2½m Novice Hurdle at the Cheltenham Festival and unbeaten in its three prior races – failed to win and was placed only once in three races as a novice in the previous 1984/85 season.

Handicap hurdle races

These are the contests novice hurdlers graduate to – usually in the second season of their National Hunt career after winning a novice event in their first season. While novice hurdlers can and sometimes do compete in handicap hurdles, these races are principally contested by more experienced hurdlers. Handicap hurdlers are performers who have usually developed a most effective hurdle technique, such races usually being determined by a horse's ability to accelerate in the final stages on the run-in to the winning post. Handicap hurdles are often competitive and sometimes not easy to predict, but broadly speaking in races of approximately 2m the best horses, with the speed to win, will be those at the top of the handicap. Their ability will not be easily negated by the burden of weight.

Longer-distance handicaps (2m 6f+ and 3m+ handicap hurdles) can be much more gruelling contests of stamina where even the fastest horses at the top of the handicap may be worn down by weight, especially on heavy or soft going. Handicap hurdles are essentially won by experienced horses, and therefore horses with winning form can never be discounted from selection calculations.

Novice chases

These are races where horses are required to carry basically level weights and are confined to horses which, at the beginning of the current season, have not won a chase. They constitute the second stage of a horse's National Hunt career and are contested by: (i) horses whose racing ambitions have always been to 'make up' into being chasers; (ii) horses whose powers as hurdlers are flagging; (iii) horses who failed completely as hurdlers and are being put to chasing as a last hope.

Horses contesting novice chases will obviously be inexperienced at jumping the larger obstacles, and the essential requirement to win a novice chase will be to negotiate the fences and complete the course. A ride on a novice chaser who is an erratic jumper is a most hair-raising and unwelcome engagement for any National Hunt jockey.

Jumping ability is the foremost quality necessary to win any novice chase.

Horses who successfully 'take' to novice chasing can sometimes set up a sequence of victories, as they have speed and jumping techniques which put rivals in the shade. Novice chases can be won (especially in very poor class events) simply by a horse surviving to complete the course. In the 1984/85 National Hunt season more than half the runners failed to complete the course in 50 per cent of these races.

Handicap chases

These denote the final stage in a horse's career. All specifically bred National Hunt horses are expected to graduate successfully to this level at the zenith of their racing careers. Novice chasers will usually compete in handicap races after prior success in novice chases. This will usually mean that they spend a season gaining experience competing in novice chases against similar rivals.

Handicap chases are therefore contested only by more experienced horses. The speed element, while never to be discounted, will always be tempered by jumping ability. Therefore, horses promoted to the top weights in handicap chases will be those who are the best jumpers and whose superior abilities in this sphere may not be easily thwarted by the weight burden. This is because, as a rule, handicap chases are not run at a breakneck pace from start to finish. Instead, especially in the longer-distance races (3m+) there is a gradual build-up of momentum as the race progresses, with horses reaching their peak of speed in the final third of a race. It is at this point, as the pace dramatically quickens, that the poor jumpers can ruin their chances with fencing errors, as the better jumpers and consequently top-weighted horses may be able to maximize their abilities.

HANDICAP FORM

The basic approach for someone contemplating making a selection in a handicap is to realize that most of the work in assessing the varying abilities of the competitors has already been done by the handicapper (who is constantly in the closest contact with racing, carefully watching how horses perform and assessing them accordingly). On all known form the fastest horse will be those at the top of the handicap and the slowest ones those at the bottom. From this simplistic viewpoint and by using the judgement of a truly expert professional – the handicapper – selection in handicaps can be made much less complex.

The best horses in a race will be in the upper part of a handicap and usually they will be the ones which have previously won at least one race. That means they will have that vital power of acceleration in the final stages of a race that winners usually possess. Although the better horses in a handicap will be burdened with greater weight, in middle-distance races (7f–1m 2f) their winning speed of acceleration will not be countered easily. This is the case on tight-turning racetracks (i.e. Chester, Catterick, Folkestone, Kempton, etc.) for the speed horses can travel round bends is less than on unrelenting straight courses. Therefore, races develop into a competition essentially decided by final acceleration, in which they are proven superior.

Therefore, when making a selection in a handicap, the selector will best be served by beginning at the top of the list of runners, eliminating those thought not to have the right credentials, and working down through the handicap until the one is reached which appears to have winning prospects. Sometimes the selection choice will be made very quickly, and stop at the very top weight or second or third top-weighted horse. However, once the suitable selection candidate has been arrived at by eliminating horses in weight order the selection process can stop, because the handicapper has already done the rest of the work, rating the horses beneath the selection choice as inferior. This simple approach is an effective yet uncomplicated method by which to tackle the problems posed when making a selection in handicaps.

It applies on the Flat or National Hunt – the more favoured Flat races have been explained, National Hunt races are similar although jumping obstacles safely and quickly is an added factor for horses reaching the upper part of handicaps.

COLLATERAL FORM

If there is no immediately obvious comparison of form (i.e. horses have either not run against each other and there is no disparity in class), form evaluation may be made by comparison through *collateral form*. This is form of two horses (A and B) which have not competed against each other, but have commonly raced against a third horse (C). It is by comparison of their separate performances with the third horse (C) that the abilities of *A and B* can be assessed.

To be reliable collateral form requires that:

1. The third horse is a consistent performer;
2. The conditions of the two races are similar (i.e. distance, going, jockey, course);
3. The conditions of weight can be clearly calculated.

Collateral form is most reliable when applied to top-class horses and cannot be confidently applied to moderate horses. If after the examination of collateral form the differences between horses appear indefinably balanced it is suggested (except in the case of the very top-class horses★) that no evaluation be undertaken and the selector refrains from betting.

★ Top-class horses usually produce extremely consistent performances and it may therefore be possible to conclude an evaluation from a careful balancing of the pertaining modifying factors (fitness and conditions).

TIME FORM

Time. This means race time and is the time taken to run a race. As a general rule, the faster the time of a race, the better the value of form. It can be expected that race times will be faster on firmer going and slower on softer going – this consideration, and weather conditions, must always be fully taken into account.

A fast time invariably represents form of value – a race in such a time will have been a true and searching test; the winner will have had to provide a noteworthy performance, as would other horses who finished within close proximity.

A slow time usually represents form of little or no value – it does not require a noteworthy performance to win and may suggest that the race was falsely run and not a true test over the distance, and therefore any margins between horses are likely to be misleading.

The actual time of the race. (NB. Only the times of Flat races are official times.) In reading of form, the actual time of the race is recorded, next to which will be its comparison to the average or standard time for the race: (b0.0) represents below average time in seconds and tenths of a second; (a0.0) represents above average time in seconds and tenths of a second; (eq) indicates equally average time.

Below average time is always a fast time – and of the highest value in assessing form.

Equal average time is a good time, but its exact value can only be ascertained by comparison with other times on the day and consideration of the going (i.e. it is not of much value when the going is firm/hard and the times of other races at the meeting are below average).

Above average time is of least value; however, the degree of such time must be considered, as well as comparison with other race times on the day and the state of the going.

Race time applies both to Flat and National Hunt racing – good form in both codes is usually in faster comparable times. Time has been thought to be more applicable to Flat racing where the emphasis is purely on speed, there are no obstacles to contend with and ground conditions tend to be more consistent during the summer. A fast time, however, is a fast time, and the merits of a fast-run race cannot be disputed under either code of racing.

Race time is a most reliable guide to assessing the value of recent unproven form. This applies especially to 2 y.o. races of whatever class and value, for unless they are run in 'good' (fast) time the value of form is likely to be suspect. GOOD 2 y.o. form demands fast, truly run races, placing emphasis on race fitness and a horse being in a forward physical condition to compete throughout the race. On the Flat where times are most important the last furlong of true run races is completed in around 12 seconds, thus in 1 second a horse travels approximately 18yd or 6 lengths. Time can therefore be translated into weight using the following scales:

5–6f	1 sec	=	18 lb	=	6 lengths
7–8f	1 sec	=	15 lb	=	6 lengths
9–11f	1 sec	=	12 lb	=	6 lengths
12–14f	1 sec	=	9 lb	=	6 lengths
15f+	1 sec	=	6 lb	=	6 lengths

A comparison of race times for horses of different ages over the same distance on the same day (similarly handicaps with non-handicaps, etc.) give a reliable indication in the assessment of form.

A major factor affecting time is the going. A selling plater can run a faster time on firm ground than a top-class horse can return when the going is heavy. Before the value of a time can be assessed the nature of the going must be known and the time adjusted accordingly. As a rough guide the following can be used:

Firm	Add 0.2 sec per furlong to recorded time
Good	Subtract 0.2 sec per furlong from recorded time
Soft	Subtract 0.8 sec per furlong from recorded time
Heavy	Subtract 1.2 secs per furlong from recorded time

For example, a horse that runs 6f in 70 seconds on firm ground may take 76 seconds on soft ground and 72.4 seconds on good ground. Really firm ground does not make for faster times because few horses stride out freely when the ground becomes hard.

Horses racing on the same race programme but in different races can be compared from their finishing positions in the race and the corresponding race time. In novice hurdles, which usually open and end the programme at a race meeting, in heavy/soft going the earlier divisions are likely to be faster than the later divisions as the course becomes more ploughed-up with horses racing on it. This consideration is of paramount importance in the comparison of time.

Other points to consider in respect of time. Shorter races, i.e. sprints 5–6f and races up to 1m (Flat) and 2m hurdles (National Hunt)), are invariably run in faster comparable times (i.e. to standard) than longer races. Shorter races are less contests of race tactics (i.e. making sure a horse gets the trip) and more tests of pure speed. Longer races are often subject to smaller fields, muddle pace, 'cat and mouse' tactics and the resulting slower times.

The more fiercely contested races (conditions and 'going' allowing) produce fast times. This can be observed by examination of the times of top-class races (i.e. the Classics, group races), races at Ascot and other top meetings, the Cheltenham Festival (usually soft ground) and the Aintree Festival (going usually good) which produce races of below-average times.

SPEED

SPEED is the factor responsible for producing winning form, particularly in the latter stages of a race. Here the main challenge is shown by rivals and a horse has to produce that something extra to win.

This speed is a horse's ability to 'quicken' or accelerate in the final 2f of a Flat race, or from the final two obstacles in a National Hunt race.

It is the speed when a horse finds an 'extra gear' in the closing stages of a race which separates winners from losers and applies to all classes of races and distances.

All great horses have possessed this quality of speed to a marked degree, having an electric burst of pace that left rivals trailing in their wake, demonstrated in the Classic successes of SIR IVOR (1968), NIJINSKY (1970), MILL REEF (1971) and more recently TROY (1979), SHERGAR (1981) and fillies ALL ALONG (1983 – Prix de l'Arc de Triomphe), PEBBLES (1985 – Champion Stakes), the triple crown success of OH SO SHARP (1985) and the triumphs of DANCING BRAVE (1986). Champion hurdlers such as BULA, SEA PIGEON and MONKSFIELD also exemplified this quality of speed.

In contrast, horses without the ability to 'quicken' consistently end up losing, and can be seen regularly among the beaten horses in the Form Book with the ominous race commentary 'one paced'. Only in stamina – sapping long-distance Flat races (i.e. 2m and further) and long-distance hurdles and chases (3m+) especially when the ground conditions become extremely testing (soft to heavy) may the merely one-paced horse succeed over rivals with a greater turn of speed as the contest becomes essentially one of tenacity, courage and endurance.

FORM RATINGS

It is sought throughout this guide to give the enthusiast the necessary information to make reasoned independent selection decisions. Yet it is also realized that some racing fans will shy from this daunting task because of the time and skill demanded. For those without these necessary qualities it is advisable to seek some protection by following the ratings of a racing expert. Ratings information is regularly found in the racing pages of newspapers, or more private ratings can be obtainable from reputable tipping services.

It is recommended that whichever rating service the backer chooses to follow (and this has to be a personal choice) they do so consistently. Otherwise what will, and does frequently happen, by flitting from one to another they miss any purple patches of success that may be enjoyed, and end up catching losers. Each daily newspaper has its experts providing ratings, some using up-to-date computer technology to reach their findings, while others follow more traditional methods. Each tries their best but are faced with an almost impossible task of trying to pick winners for every race on the card to fulfil the whims of the ever capricious punter. It will be therefore necessary for the racing fan to concentrate on the less competitive races and gain more reliable guidance and the prospect of winning by following their mentor only on these occasions.

The most desirable ratings will be when one horse is rated well ahead of its rivals, for when the ratings of horses are similar then the value of the top-rated horse is likely to be more problematic. Ratings are private handicapping by the expert with emphasis on different aspects of form. Some focus on weight, some on time (the latter usually identified as speed ratings).

Any 'nap' rating demands close inspection as it will be considered the best advice and to have received special consideration. Ratings give the selector easy access to a well-informed viewpoint that can still be subjected to objective appraisal by the other elements contained in the selection formula.

FAVOURITES' FORM

Although not in the strictest sense within the bounds of assessment of form, a very helpful aid in the form selection process is for a careful note to be taken of the statistical record of favourites in a certain race over a number of seasons. It is more within the realms of betting than selection, but is a meeting-point of the two which will show the selector how the expectations of form (usually reflected by the market) have been upheld over a period of time.

Two examples which vividly demonstrate these extremes:
Doncaster Cup (Group III) 2¼m Doncaster.
from 1974 to 1986 was won by ten favourites, one 2nd fav., one 3rd fav. and one outsider
While in contrast:
Cambridgeshire Handicap 1m 1f, Newmarket
from 1974 to 1986 was won by 13 outsiders whose prices ranged from 10–1 to 50–1.

The first example showing how more predictable form elements held sway while the second seems mainly open to the whims of chance. The selector who becomes acquainted with such information can often focus form assessment into more fruitful pastures and avoid the unrewarding incomprehensible character that some races hold.

SUMMARY OF FORM

1. Form is the record of past performance; it is the most reliable indication of ability.
2. Recent winning form is the most positive guide to assessing current ability.
3. Good top-class form is extremely reliable.
   Form of lower class is generally unreliable.

7 THE SELECTION FORMULA ANALYSED: FITNESS

Fitness is the second constituent in the selection formula and the major modifying factor to form. Unless a horse is fully race fit it is unlikely to produce its true or best race form.

Fitness can never be absolutely assured – a degree of fitness has to be left to trust (i.e. to the good judgement of the trainer) yet it must not be assumed just because a horse is declared to race that it is fully fit to reproduce its best form. The fact that a horse is competing in a race is not alone proof of its race fitness, and must not ever be arbitrarily accepted as such.

A horse competing in a race should have no physical ailments, be sound of eye, wind, heart and limb, but if it has not raced for a time its race fitness is not assured and cannot be assumed. This applies particularly to inexperienced horses (2 y.o., 3 y.o., maiden novice hurdlers, novice chasers), for until they have proved themselves on the racecourse, the trainer has little information upon which to assess what constitutes fitness in an individual horse, and off-course preparation is problematic.

Physical and race fitness, although closely related and dependent upon one another must not be regarded as the same. A horse's fitness on the day of the race will depend on its natural health (well-being) and the training preparation it has received prior to the race. Race fitness may be defined as peak physical fitness which gives a horse (if good enough) a positive chance of winning, as opposed to fitness which enables a horse merely to complete the race without physical injury.

The general term 'race fitness' from the selector's viewpoint should be understood as *peak race fitness*.

Although there can be many imponderables surrounding the race fitness of a horse, surprisingly, much unquestioning trust is placed on a horse being in peak physical condition when there is no evidence to support this assumption (a horse making its racecourse début, or reappearance after a lengthy absence, are in fact indications to the contrary – though some horses do show their best form on these occasions when 'fresh').

A horse will usually have to be at peak race fitness if it is to have a real chance of winning a race. The most reliable indication of a horse's fitness is a recent race performance.

This horse, photographed in the paddock prior to winning a race is instantly recognizable as being fit by the well-defined and developed lines of muscle running down its hindquarters and the lack of fatness around its girth and ribs. The skin is clear and healthy and this is borne out by the diamond pattern that is glowing across the top of its hindquarters, evidence that the horse has been well groomed as part of its pre-race preparation.

This horse, photographed prior to finishing well beaten in its race, can be instantly recognized as still having to reach peak fitness. While appearing as a strong robust horse, there is a lack of well-defined and developed muscle on its hindquarters and an excess condition around its girth and ribs. The markings on the coat, however, are where the horse has been trace clipped, a common feature on many National Hunt horses once they have grown their winter coats.

The most reliable evidence of a horse being 'race fit' is proof from a recent race performance. 'Recent' is the operative word – within the previous 7 days is the most favourable.

In this recent race performance a horse must have figured prominently at some stage. This will indicate that peak fitness has, or is about to be, reached. Applying the above stipulations can almost guarantee that a horse is at or will have gained peak race fitness. This is not private or inspired information but public to anyone prepared to examine recent form.

SEVEN-DAY RACE FITNESS

A horse racing twice within seven days is the fine tuning that can put a very keen edge on a horse's performance. It is a most reliable confirmation of peak race fitness. It applies where a winner, or narrowly beaten horse, races quickly again, ready to exploit proven form; or where an unfit horse is given a 'pipe-opener' to put it right for its next immediate engagement.

Whilst many of the highly successful and leading stables seldom practise this method of getting their horses fit, having their horses generally well prepared and in good race condition when they run, even their horses can be defeated by the peak race fitness of horses from less well known yards which have raced more recently (i.e. within the last 7 days).

Seven-day race fitness has a particularly dominating influence upon:
(a) Flat 3 y.o. + who stand up well to racing;
(b) National Hunt in the first and last month of the season, where peak fitness holds the key over less prepared rivals;
(c) all horses that have just struck the top of their form.

Seven days may appear an arbitrary time. It is, however, a well-tried and tested indicator of race fitness.

The essential quality of race fitness is that it is the peak of physical condition and therefore it allows the full expression of racing ability. It is, however, a transitory state which can only be maintained for a short time – 7 days is that approximate time. In practice, this means a horse will remain (without further training preparation) in physical peak condition for about a week.

An obvious qualifying factor with regard to racing again within 7 days is that the horse must have suffered no injury during its previous race. This factor can only be left to trust on the reasonable assumption that a trainer would not race a horse again so quickly if it had suffered any injury.

Similarly, races in quick succession may not be suitable for (i) horses of a weak constitution or wayward temperament who require a longer interval between races, (ii) those who have suffered from the effects of long-distance travel (travelling can blunt a horse's vitality as much as hard races).

In all of these instances, after paying due regard to the facts available, the selector must trust that the trainer's judgement to race the horse is the correct decision.

The general guiding rule to race fitness is the more recently a horse has run, the more likely it is to be race fit. The longer the time since a horse last raced, the less likely it is to be in peak condition.

On a time-scale:

1–7 days – is that special fine tuning sometimes necessary for less than top-class horses to succeed in keenly matched contests, where peak form and fitness just 'carries the day'. Most appropriate for 3-year-olds + (Flat) and hurdles (National Hunt). In the 1985–86 National Hunt season 30.7 per cent of hurdle race winners who raced again within a 7-day period won – while similarly Flat 1985 24.8 per cent of 3-year-olds + winners also won their subsequent race.

8–14 days – up to 14 days is a most assured confirmation of a horse's race fitness, and this slightly longer time is appropriate to all types of horses, but particularly any who benefit from a less than immediate return to racing. (This is most appropriate for chasers who need, while maintaining their peak form and fitness, a little longer to recover from their race exertions.)

In the 1985–86 National Hunt season 30.2 per cent of chaser winners won again when subsequently raced within 8–14 days.

15–21 days – although shedding some uncertainty on peak fitness this is a most suitable time-span for horses less able to withstand frequent races. Therefore it is most appropriate for 2-year-olds whose lack of physical maturity often demands a longer recovery between races.

In the 1985 Flat season 26.4 per cent of 2 y.o. winners won again when subsequently raced within 15–21 days.

22–28 days – a length of time that sheds doubt on a horse's peak fitness, and in many instances may be a signal that a horse has just gone 'off the boil'. Appropriate, however, to all top-class horses whose next most appropriate racing engagement may fit into this time-scale.

29 days+ – in most instances this is too long a period, and a horse's fitness cannot be accepted without an acquaintance with a trainer's methods or the special requirements of a particular horse.

It appears that only chase winners can be expected to retain a fair degree of fitness over an absence from racing of longer than 28 days.

In the 1985–86 National Hunt season 21.7 per cent of chase winners won again after an absence of 29 days + from racing. Similarly, 9.4 per cent of chasers won on their seasonal reappearance on a racecourse as opposed to 5.3 per cent of hurdlers and 6.7 per cent of Flat horses. This is further reinforced by the statistics given for both the Flat and National Hunt in Table 7.1.

The statistics of recent winners in Tables 7.2–7.5 suggest that the shorter the time-span in which a winner races again, the greater its winning chances.

The exceptions to this rule are the particular methods employed by certain trainers (the leading ones especially) who have the staff, the skill and facilities to prepare horses off-course, on home gallops. It applies particularly in the cases of top-class horses of experience (Flat and National Hunt) which may have an advance programme of races marked out for them at the beginning of a season, and time and effort will not be spared in these preparations.

In cases of inexperienced horses and of trainers without the staff, facilities or abilities, recent race fitness is the determining factor in the consideration of a horse's fitness and must never be lightly overlooked.

Proven fitness is the most dominating factor when considering a horse's chances of winning – and in this sphere there can be no substitute for 7-day race fitness which may finely tune a horse's performance to give it a winning edge.

While a short time between races is the ideal proof of a horse's fitness, there is often a factor which subjects a horse's next racecourse appearance to be of a longer time-span. This is the programming of race meetings and the accommodation of a suitable race for a horse. Early and late season, under both codes of racing, meetings are less frequent and so allow fewer opportunities for a horse to reappear and contest a similar type of race. Only at the height of the summer and winter seasons do race meetings abound, giving horses a greater chance of races, and the opportunity to race again within a short time – their fitness proven. So at many times during the season the selector may be presented with the dilemma of a horse having worthy form credentials, yet less than the desired guarantee of peak fitness. The most important consideration in this instance is to remember that **form** is the major element in the selection formula. Good form can beat everything and fitness is the factor which can only modify form. (A slow horse, however fit it is, is still unlikely to beat a faster one that is less fit.) Another factor in these instances is that similar conditions often apply to every horse in the race, placing none at a particular disadvantage.

The value of form can also be more satisfactorily established when

TABLE 7.1 Winners (horses with proven fitness) racing again

Days since last ran	1985 Flat						1985–86 National Hunt					
	2 y.o.			3 y.o.			Hurdles			Chases		
	Winners	Runners	%	Winners	Runners	%	Winners	Runners	%	Winners	Runners	%
1–7	11 –	64 =	17.2	60 –	242 =	24.8	59 –	192 =	30.7	21 –	144 =	14.6
8–14	43 –	174 =	24.7	97 –	485 =	20.0	79 –	341 =	23.2	105 –	348 =	30.2
15–21	39 –	148 =	26.4	84 –	442 =	19.0	42 –	229 =	18.3	59 –	248 =	23.8
22–28	31 –	134 =	23.1	58 –	287 =	20.2	29 –	124 =	23.4	18 –	99 =	18.2
29+	19 –	140 =	13.8	37 –	272 =	13.6	39 –	288 =	13.5	40 –	184 =	21.7
Seasonal debut	212 –	3188 =	6.6	359 –	5363 =	6.7	244 –	4626 =	5.3	201 –	2134 =	9.4

the time-span between races is longer and other horses who competed in the race will have contested other prizes to endorse or deny their worth.

Races such as group races are the most obvious examples of the programming of similar races of a longer rather than a shorter time-scale, being placed at strategic points throughout the season.

Of the 102 pattern or group races during the 1985 Flat season only one winner ran within the previous 7 days. (This was FREE GUEST 4 y.o. filly who won two group race prizes within a week during her autumn campaign.)

Fifty-five per cent of the races were won by winners who last raced 8–28 days previously.

Races (Flat and National Hunt) early in the season will, due to their position in the fixture calendar, be won by horses making their seasonal/racecourse débuts, underlining the problematic fitness consid-erations facing selection on these occasions. A trainer's record for producing horses 'fit' early in the season must be the main guide here. Some National Hunt horses are given a 'pipe-opener' on the Flat before re-embarking on a career over obstacles – especially hurdlers suited by firm 'going', which usually prevails in the opening weeks of the season.

Some horses excel early in the season, running their best races while fresh, and their later performance tails off as the season progresses. The fitness aspect in these instances does not readily submit to statistical analysis, and can be assessed only by the racing fan who goes to the race-track judging a horse's fitness by how it looks.

'FITNESS' BY LOOKS

Assessing a horse's fitness by how it looks, although outside the realms of the 'stay-at-home' racing fan and not subject to strict objective appraisal of statistics, is one of the best ways for an experienced judge to gauge a horse's fitness. Television helps to convey some of the correct impressions, but nothing beats being at the racecourse and the close presence of the horses, when a paddock inspection of the runners will quickly reveal the state of their fitness. The visual signs to notice denoting both a very fit and an unfit horse may be seen from the two photographs on page 111.

A fit horse will have its muscle well defined, have little or no loose flesh, with a hint of its ribs being able to be seen. Its coat is likely to be shiny, having a gleam of well-being. (Darker coloured horses, black, brown or dark bays stand out prominently in this aspect, while grey-coloured horses are the most difficult to assess confidently from the look of their coats.)

A horse's behaviour in the paddock before a race can range from being very calm, as is common with older horses who may be experienced campaigners, to quite nervously excited, highly strung individuals, as often is the case with younger inexperienced horses. The calmer horses are likely to liven up and the more excitable ones calm down once they have been mounted and led out on to the racecourse to canter to the start.

A horse sweating up badly before a race (i.e. sweat pouring from its body and/or neck) is not a good sign as it shows signs of distress, for whatever reason, and it has wasted some of its energy before the race even starts. Weather conditions have to be taken into account as even the most placid horse may sweat at the height of summer when the temperature is high. Also it is not unusual to see a horse break out in a mild sweat between the hind legs (this is called a kidney sweat) and usually merely indicates that it is just winding up ready to spring into action once the race begins.

While not wishing to see a horse over-excited in the pre-race formalities, it is not encouraging either to see a horse so calm or disinterested that it looks half asleep and completely lacking energy. This latter impression may be dispelled once the horse leaves the parade paddocks and canters to the start, and many older horses only come to life then.

The most encouraging signs to see from a horse cantering to the post is one taking a firm hold of its bit (without pulling the jockey's arms 'out') and having a co-ordinated stride, an athletic action exuding power and energy. This is particularly important for inexperienced horses, especially 2-year-olds, who may as yet not know how to physically 'use themselves'.

This last observation is a most subjective one, yet is most important, as it quickly identifies the latent power within a horse, and therefore available to be used, sometimes with devastating effect in the race.

The racing fan who regularly goes racing will become acquainted with these illuminating insights as to a horse's fitness and then may be able to adopt, as the situation demands, a more liberal interpretation of the fitness factor than is laid down by the strict statistical terms of the selection formula.

Date of last run tables

Tables show the days since a horse last ran; the finishing position (whether first, second, third or unplaced) and the record of winners to runners on a time-scale. Also how much a single point staked on every runner produced a profit or a loss is stated in the column headed 'Take'.

At the foot of each table the number of horses making their first appearance of the season is shown.

1985 Flat – Horse wins/date of last run comparison, 6,590 runs examined – 2-year-olds

| Days elapsed since the horse last ran | On horse's last outing: | | | | | | | | | | | |
| | Came 1st | | | Came 2nd | | | Came 3rd | | | Unplaced | | |
	Wins	Runs	Take	Wins	Runs	Take	Wins	Runs	Take	Wins	Runs	Take
1	1	2	0	0	0	0	0	0	0	0	0	0
2	0	2	-2	0	2	-2	1	2	6	1	13	-8
3	0	2	-2	2	6	0	0	5	-5	0	26	-26
4	2	8	-4	0	8	-8	2	4	1	6	56	-14
5	4	14	-5	2	14	-2	3	15	-2	6	85	-37
6	1	15	-12	3	13	-4	2	19	-4	7	79	-4
7	3	21	-15	6	28	-7	3	35	-28	12	160	-77
8	5	19	3	6	26	-3	4	23	5	12	128	-17
9	7	23	3	5	33	-12	8	24	19	14	163	-27
10	4	19	-9	6	21	8	6	30	-5	16	191	-56
11	5	27	-4	5	16	0	4	38	-21	10	145	-64
12	8	32	-7	9	39	3	5	32	-1	10	194	-100
13	6	22	-2	6	28	-5	3	23	-10	14	156	54
14	8	32	8	10	42	3	6	33	1	11	191	-69
15 to 21	39	148	-4	28	155	-36	28	153	-14	56	917	-562
22 to 28	31	134	-5	16	92	-17	10	76	-36	46	626	-307
29 to 35	10	55	-19	5	48	-31	11	50	13	29	426	-189
36 to 42	1	20	-16	4	32	7	2	20	-12	9	296	-235
43 to 63	7	43	-1	4	35	-21	6	49	-8	27	406	-123
64 to 91	1	15	-12	2	15	-3	1	16	-6	11	217	-99
Over 91	0	7	-7	3	13	-1	2	12	-4	4	130	-102

Total number of first season runners: 3,188
1st Places: 212; 2nd Places: 215; 3rd Places: 231; Unplaced: 2,530; Winnings: -1,585

1985 Flat – horse wins/date of last run comparison, 17,740 runs examined – 3-year-olds+

| Days elapsed since the horse last ran | On horse's last outing: | | | | | | | | | | | |
| | Came 1st | | | Came 2nd | | | Came 3rd | | | Unplaced | | |
	Wins	Runs	Take	Wins	Runs	Take	Wins	Runs	Take	Wins	Runs	Take
1	1	1	3	0	3	−3	0	2	−2	2	11	6
2	5	10	5	2	11	−3	4	9	6	1	39	−35
3	6	19	7	4	13	10	2	11	−2	7	94	−28
4	8	23	12	4	21	−8	2	25	−14	17	181	−10
5	8	43	−1	7	38	8	6	36	13	20	263	−53
6	16	63	−1	8	59	−26	8	49	−6	23	354	−134
7	16	83	−13	21	109	−25	10	95	−43	36	597	−242
8	15	57	28	9	69	−22	7	61	−15	28	394	−159
9	11	66	−10	14	75	−9	11	77	−25	31	478	−145
10	18	66	10	14	85	−22	11	84	0	39	514	−108
11	15	70	−10	17	89	−22	10	88	−45	32	513	−198
12	14	83	−18	10	83	−42	12	72	6	28	478	−235
13	8	59	−32	13	67	−23	13	66	12	34	412	−105
14	16	84	−32	21	100	−13	14	108	−1	38	636	−355
15 to 21	84	442	−122	72	420	−49	48	408	−122	164	2,645	−1,010
22 to 28	58	287	17	27	200	−67	28	216	−66	135	1,762	−483
29 to 35	14	110	−64	17	109	−23	16	92	7	62	974	−336
36 to 42	8	62	−29	8	45	23	8	70	−41	39	556	−221
43 to 63	10	53	−13	12	69	−20	11	87	9	59	875	−351
64 to 91	3	26	−12	5	35	−22	6	46	−7	13	428	−333
Over 91	2	21	−5	3	25	−15	1	20	−16	17	361	−205

Total number of first season runners: 5,363
1st Places: 359; 2nd Places: 364; 3rd Places: 365; Unplaced: 4,275; Winnings: −2,061

1985–86 National Hunt (hurdles) horse wins/date of last run comparison, 13,439 runs examined

On horse's last outing:

Days elapsed since the horse last ran	Came 1st			Came 2nd			Came 3rd			Unplaced		
	Wins	Runs	Take	Wins	Runs	Take	Wins	Runs	Take	Wins	Runs	Take
1	0	2	−2	0	3	−3	0	1	−1	2	11	−5
2	5	14	0	2	10	−6	0	11	−11	4	71	−21
3	3	11	−2	1	8	−5	2	9	7	7	114	−29
4	9	25	4	2	22	−9	2	22	8	13	150	−63
5	10	36	4	9	34	−1	2	32	−18	13	250	−67
6	13	50	1	6	42	−15	5	31	−4	24	319	−8
7	19	54	12	8	58	−19	11	56	12	27	467	−237
8	16	50	32	14	47	31	7	41	−8	18	339	−108
9	12	46	1	11	40	12	7	59	−16	32	357	−58
10	11	46	−14	12	44	1	8	57	−2	18	349	−181
11	8	40	−22	8	47	−12	5	49	−25	21	349	−193
12	16	64	−7	7	44	−15	10	48	9	23	385	−191
13	7	38	−4	5	42	−22	8	46	2	21	307	−188
14	9	57	−22	11	66	−23	7	60	−18	16	397	−266
15 to 21	42	229	−31	46	246	−62	28	221	−38	96	1,731	−938
22 to 28	29	124	−13	18	110	5	16	103	−2	58	1,033	−382
29 to 35	9	79	−43	10	62	−16	9	76	12	35	686	−339
36 to 42	10	55	−8	4	43	−27	7	38	−12	24	506	−236
43 to 63	14	87	61	9	76	−50	4	65	8	49	1,002	−533
64 to 91	3	33	−21	4	38	−14	4	52	−32	30	586	−184
Over 91	3	34	−20	2	31	−24	0	35	−35	15	631	−435

Total number of first season runners: 4,626
1st Places: 244; 2nd Places: 248; 3rd places: 248; Unplaced: 3,860; Winnings: −2,421

1985–86 National Hunt (chase) horse wins/date of last run comparison, 8,560 runs examined

Days elapsed since the horse last ran	On horse's last outing:											
	Came 1st			Came 2nd			Came 3rd			Unplaced		
	Wins	Runs	Take	Wins	Runs	Take	Wins	Runs	Take	Wins	Runs	Take
1	0	1	-1	0	1	-1	0	0	0	1	10	-8
2	1	3	0	2	3	4	0	4	-4	7	57	13
3	0	8	-8	2	9	5	1	7	-4	6	49	-26
4	1	13	-9	3	14	0	3	18	2	11	112	-36
5	5	34	-21	6	24	3	3	27	-15	9	152	-64
6	3	29	-12	10	40	-7	4	36	-20	15	187	-61
7	11	56	-23	14	56	-5	6	60	-36	28	280	-50
8	15	47	0	11	44	-5	11	44	16	11	214	-133
9	7	49	-18	5	36	-18	6	47	0	14	234	-151
10	18	40	15	11	54	-11	6	45	-19	15	217	-136
11	15	46	-8	9	61	-31	3	41	-18	13	215	-95
12	14	54	-9	13	65	29	3	57	-5	16	235	-107
13	14	43	8	13	42	0	1	36	-29	19	224	-71
14	22	69	11	15	71	-14	9	54	21	18	275	-176
15 to 21	59	248	-35	43	210	-47	26	172	5	76	1,010	-388
22 to 28	18	99	-44	12	97	-46	19	99	0	39	542	-220
29 to 35	13	55	6	8	57	-10	6	50	1	26	337	-129
36 to 42	8	38	-9	7	36	-17	5	47	-23	24	245	-95
43 to 63	9	48	-12	9	57	0	2	55	-46	33	493	-237
64 to 91	8	26	14	0	14	-14	2	25	-15	20	232	-76
Over 91	2	17	-13	4	16	2	4	35	2	13	251	-170

Total number of first season runners: 2,134
1st places: 201;   2nd places: 179;   3rd places: 197;   winnings: -635

8 THE SELECTION FORMULA ANALYSED: CLASS

Class is the third constituent in the selection formula and an important modifying factor.

Class in the racing sense means the quality of opposition a horse has competed against. In respect of quality this can range from the very best – 'top class', the Classics, Group Races (Flat) and the National Hunt equivalent – Champion Hurdle, Gold Cup – down to selling races which have been designed for the worst horses.

A 'class' horse, or 'class' in the colloquial sense accurately used means the very best horses (type and age applying).

A horse can be raised or lowered in class or compete in the same (similar) class.

A horse raised in class must improve to have a winning chance.

A horse lowered in class has only to reproduce its known form to win.

A horse in the same class may have either to improve upon or simply reproduce its best run form, depending on the evaluation of that form.

The most favourable situation, for consideration in selection is when a horse with consistent proven ability is lowered (dropped) in class.

A horse must never be considered to have a winning chance just because it has been dropped in class. It must have discernible positive ability in the higher class.

The extreme example is when a horse raced initially well above its class (e.g. maiden 3 y.o. competes in the Derby to fulfil the wishes of an ever-optimistic owner and finishes tailed off behind the rest of the field) fails or struggles when dropped in class to a modest maiden race later in the season. It is therefore necessary to examine carefully all the facts of form before making any judgements.

The evaluation of class plays a dominating role in the evaluation of form, and while differences are easily definable at the extreme ends, differences are less distinguishable in the middle range of class. Prize-money and the grade of course (Group I, II, III or IV according to Jockey Club ruling) provide the obvious indications of class.

One of the easiest and perhaps obvious methods of defining the class

Class is the quality or type of race contested by a horse. Top-class horses usually have the conformation and looks to match their ability while slower, moderate horses are correspondingly lacking in these features.

Champion sprinter LOCHNAGER who can be clearly seen as a strong imposing horse with a muscular athletic appearance – he is well proportioned and of good conformation.

A very fit and top class horse in action. DANCING BRAVE at Ascot, European champion 1986.

111

of races, horses and their form is by identification and comparison of racecourses. A graded list of racecourses is given in Table 8.1. It has been compiled in respect of the quality value of the form of most of the races contested in accord with the level of allocated prize-money (i.e. the greater the level of prize-money, the more competitive are the races, the better are the horses and therefore the higher the value of form). This list is closely based on the Jockey Club's own grading of racecourses in regard to the amount of prize-money and subsidies allotted to each course, but also with special consideration placed on experience of form selection.

The Flat racecourses have been divided into five grades and the National Hunt courses into four grades. It may be seen that while there is a clear-cut distinction between the top and bottom grades of courses, this distinction can become much less clear in assessing the value of form between two of the lower grades of courses. It will, however, serve as a basic and most reliable guide.

The most valuable races, fiercely competitive on the most testing courses, can be considered top class. The lowest prized races on the smaller, easier racecourses which attract the same regular group of contestants can be considered the lowest class. Class plays an important role in the selection formula as it is the factor which may require form improvement as a necessity or in other cases no more than a reproducing of known ability.

The old adage suggested to racehorse owners: 'Run your horse in the worst company and keep yourself in the best company', applies with equal wisdom to those seeking selections from horses lowered in class.

TABLE 8.1 Grading of racecourses

	Flat	National Hunt	
Grade I	Ascot, Goodwood, Newbury, Newmarket, Sandown, York	Ascot, Cheltenham, Doncaster, Haydock, Kempton, Liverpool, Newbury, Sandown	**Grade I**
Grade II	Ayr, Chester, Doncaster, Epsom, Haydock, Kempton, Newcastle	Ayr, Chepstow, Lingfield, Newcastle, Nottingham, Wetherby, Wincanton	**Grade II**
Grade III	Bath, Brighton, Leicester, Lingfield, Nottingham, Redcar, Ripon, Salisbury, Yarmouth	Carlisle, Catterick, Folkestone, Huntingdon, Leicester, Market Rasen, Newton Abbot, Stratford, Towcester, Warwick, Windsor, Wolverhampton, Worcester	**Grade III**
Grade IV	Beverley, Chepstow, Pontefract, Thirsk, Windsor, Wolverhampton	Bangor, Cartmel, Devon and Exeter, Fakenham, Fontwell, Hereford, Hexham, Kelso, Ludlow, Perth, Plumpton, Sedgefield, Southwell, Utoxeter, Taunton	**Grade IV**
Grade V	Carlisle, Catterick, Edinburgh, Folkestone, Hamilton, Warwick		

9 THE SELECTION FORMULA ANALYSED: CONDITIONS

Conditions are the fourth constituent in the selection formula, they are modifying factors which may act as the vital balancing role in forming the selection decision.

If these modifying factors are of proven positive value, they can only act as an endorsement to a decision. If they contain the negative aspect, they may serve as the eliminating element in the balance of decision-making. Occasionally these modifying elements may assume the role of the salient factor in the forming of a selection decision.

The conditions affecting the reproducing of form are in order of importance:

1. Distance (the distance of a race).
2. Going (the ground conditions on which the horse must race).
3. Weight (the weight carried, and whether it involves penalties or allowances).
4. Courses/draw (the variation of courses, and the fixed starting positions in Flat racing).
5. Jockeyship (the quality).
6. Sundry factors (i.e. blinkers – breeding – trainer – owner).

DISTANCE

Distance is the distance of a race in which a horse competes. A horse can only be considered *proven* over the distance by winning at that distance, or showing form of proven value at the distance. A change of a horse's distance from its proven distance(s) places it in the area of the unknown – for the horse is unproven at that distance.

Most horses specialize and perform best at only one distance (i.e. sprinters may be only 5f horses or be equally proficient at 5f and 6f). Milers may only act best at 1m or may act equally well between 7f and 1m 1f. Middle-distance horses, similarly, may only race well at 1¼m or

Most horses, whether Flat or National Hunt, produce their best form over one particular distance. A change in distance often produces a change in form.

These two photographs, looking up the July Course at Newmarket, clearly show the difference in distance between 1f and 2f. In the top picture the disc on the rails to the right is the 2f marker from the winning-post while in the bottom picture the disc to the right is the 1f marker from the winning-post.

be versatile between 1m 1f and 1m 4f. Stayers also may need 1½m, 1¾m, 2m or 2m+ or may act over a range of extreme distances. National Hunt horses have equal speed and stamina restrictions, ranging from 2m hurdlers to 3½m+ chasers.

Distance can and does alter performances. This may apply particularly to maiden horses (Flat and National Hunt) which may suddenly improve when they find their best distance. Change of distance is one of the fundamental reasons for reversals in form, and improvement of form when the correct one is found.

NB. All maiden 2-year-olds and 3-year-olds – novice hurdlers and chasers who show considerable improvement when raced over a different distance (normally a longer one).

Experienced racehorses are often given a 'pipe-opener' over a shorter distance than they need to bring them to peak race fitness with a race to obscure the value of their form. The oldest and easiest ploy to disguise a horse's true form and ability is to race it over its wrong distance. In the case of many maidens, however, often to the frustration of a trainer, and to confound all laws of breeding, a horse's best distance is only discovered by trial and error from racing it over various distances.

Breeding is likely to be the strongest indication of a horse's most suitable distance, but is only an assumption that cannot be accepted as fact. Breeding is not an exact science, but by examining the records of leading sires given in Table 10.1 (pages 162–3) it is possible to identify the characteristics and influences inherited by a sire's racing stock.

Distance is a most important factor in the consideration of form.

GOING

Going, on a level par with distance, is often the culprit responsible for reversals in form. A horse can only be considered to act on going if proven from the racecourse test. Similar going or slight variations are unlikely to affect a horse, but extreme changes which have not been previously encountered can have devastating effects (e.g. changes from good to heavy or good to hard).

It has been said that a 'good horse' will act on any going, and while there is a certain truth in this remark, it must strongly be stated that most horses have strong preferences and act best on particular ground. A horse's action and physique will allow it to perform better and with greater ease on certain going, and this allows some horses to display specialist capabilities on extremes of going (e.g. the soft ground specialist who revels in the mud in heavy ground and cannot act and may even get jarred up on other going; or the other type of specialist who only acts on ground when hoofs can be heard to rattle). Breeding often

Variations in going can have a vital influence on form.

Typical going that is encountered during the summer months – officially described as firm.

Going officially described as soft with clods of turf being visibly kicked up.

THE SELECTION FORMULA ANALYSED: CONDITIONS

produces characteristics such as these passed down from one generation to the next (i.e. some sires, themselves soft ground specialists produce stock of similar tendency, other sires who preferred good or firm ground pass on this characteristic and have offspring only able to act on this type of surface). Although breeding will give strong indications of a horse's likely preferences, each horse is an individual, whose requirements can only be confirmed by test on the racecourse.

In extremes of going – going can be the salient factor to affect form.

WEIGHT

Weight is the weight a horse has been set to carry in the entry conditions of a race. This weight includes a fully clothed jockey plus the saddle and number cloth. A jockey is weighed out before the race and weighed in after the race by the clerk of the scales in the weighing-room. If the jockey and equipment are too light to make the prescribed weight the difference is made up by thin pieces of lead which are placed in pockets in the saddlecloth. A jockey must weigh in at the same weight as he

A comparison between a 1 lb saddle (left) and a 5 lb saddle (right) to illustrate part of the dead weight which a horse has to carry.

Weight is a major factor which can produce a reversal of form and can defeat even the best horse. Burdened with enough weight even a fast horse can be beaten by a normally slower rival who is carrying less weight.

weighed out, and anyone failing to make the correct weight at the weigh-in will be disqualified.

Weight is the great leveller of ability. It applies to all types of horse and in all classes of race. Enough weight given to even the very best horses will stop them from winning. At level weights a race is a contest only of comparative ability and fitness, but as differences occur (weight penalties or concessions) a more involved consideration begins to dominate the assessment process.

The changes in conditions of the weight carried bring about changes in form, as revealed by handicaps and the myriad questions posed by the unequal distribution of weight. The effect weight has is exemplified in the principle of handicapping by weight, where the best horse, in the opinion of the handicapper, is given the most weight and the worst horse the least. The object is to burden the faster horses with enough weight to bring them down to the speed of the slower horses. Herein lies the key to understanding the effect of weight:

A burden of **weight** can make a **fast horse** run **slower** but even a very light **weight cannot** make a **slow horse** run **faster**!

The consideration of weight always creates certain imponderables and it is necessary as part of the selection analysis to be acquainted with the conditions of weight and their influence in the outcome of a race.

Races where horses carry level weight (within certain prescribed limits) are more readily assessed. The weight variations within this basic criterion are as follows:

1. Sex allowances (Flat racing). Colts giving a weight concession of 3lb to fillies and geldings. Sex allowances were extended to National Hunt racing from 1983–84. Colts, horses and geldings giving a weight concession of 5lb to fillies and mares in all chases, hurdles and National Hunt Flat races.
2. Weight-for-age (Flat and National Hunt). Horses of different ages giving or receiving weight according to an official scale.
3. Weight penalties (incurred for winning and/or differing according to the value of the race won).
4. Weight allowances (Flat and National Hunt for maidens at starting). A special allowance (Flat only) for horses which have previously not run.

Sex allowance

A weight allowance of 3lb is given by colts to fillies (and often to geldings); this was introduced to counterbalance the basic differences of physical strength and development between the sexes. Colts are normally more robust and faster maturing than fillies or geldings, and would without this compulsory weight concession hold initially an unfair advantage in races.

The effect of the sex allowance in practice is therefore to resolve the physical imbalance and give equal opportunity to colts, fillies and geldings racing against each other.

NB. The sex weight allowance at certain times may, however, not represent the true differences between colts and fillies and therefore be to the positive advantage of one or the other:

1. Early in the season 2 y.o. colts with racing experience have a distinct physical advantage over fillies which is likely to be more than 3 lb sex allowance.

2. In the summer of their 3 y.o. careers (late July and throughout August and September) fillies tend to develop considerably physically, to the extent that suddenly they reach a par with colts. The 3 lb weight concession then is to their advantage and it is noticeable at these times how the rapidly improving fillies defeat colts in maiden races and condition races.

Weight for age (Flat and National Hunt)

Weight for age is an official scale of weights formulated by the Jockey Club to give horses of different ages racing against each other equal opportunity, by apportioning them varying weights. On the Flat it applies to 2–4-year-olds (older horses considered equal), and in National Hunt to 3–5-year-olds (older horses considered equal) and pays due regard to the varying distances (5f–2½m Flat, 2m–3m National Hunt). The scale changes throughout the season to accommodate the normal rate of maturity of younger horses (i.e. in March/April Flat racing a 4 y.o. would be expected over 5f to give a 3 y.o. 12–13 lb and a 3 y.o. to give a 2 y.o. 31–32 lb, but by October the scale would have fallen – the 4 y.o. gives a 3 y.o. 0–1 lb and the 3 y.o. gives a 2 y.o. 16–17 lb – similarly weight changes apply to National Hunt racing). Tables 9.1 and 9.2 give the scale of weight for age for Flat and National Hunt respectively.

Although the Jockey Club have an official weight-for-age (WFA) Scale this serves only as a guide to the clerks of courses who can frame the conditions of their races differently. It is therefore advisable to examine the conditions of WFA races and note whether conditions would seem to favour one age rather than another or if the race conforms strictly to the Jockey Club Scale.

Note well the conditions of all races where WFA applies, particularly *novice* hurdlers, where, especially in heavy going, a weight concession can be a decisive factor.

Weight penalties (Flat and National Hunt)

Weight penalties are incurred by all horses that win except if the conditions of the race preclude them.

TABLE 9.1 Scale of weight-for-age for Flat races

	Age (yrs)	Mar & Apr 1-15	Apr 16-30	May 1-15	May 16-31	June 1-15	June 16-30	July 1-15	July 16-31	Aug 1-15	Aug 16-31	Sep 1-15	Sep 16-30	Oct 1-15	Oct 16-31	Nov 16-31
5f	2	32	31	29	27	26	25	25	23	21	20	19	18	17	16	15
	3	13	12	11	10	9	8	7	6	5	4	3	2	1	—	—
6f	2	—	—	30	29	29	28	27	26	26	24	22	21	21	20	18
	3	15	14	13	12	11	10	9	8	7	6	5	4	3	2	1
7f	2	—	—	—	—	—	—	—	—	—	—	24	23	23	22	21
	3	16	15	14	13	12	11	10	9	8	7	6	5	4	3	2
1m	2	—	—	—	—	—	—	—	—	—	—	27	27	26	25	24
	3	18	17	16	15	14	13	12	11	10	9	8	7	6	5	4
9f	3	18	17	16	15	14	13	12	11	10	9	8	7	6	5	4
1¼m	3	19	18	17	16	15	14	13	12	11	10	9	8	7	6	5
11f	3	20	19	18	17	16	15	14	13	12	11	10	9	8	7	6
1½m	3	20	19	18	17	16	15	14	13	12	11	10	9	8	7	6
13f	3	21	20	19	18	17	16	15	14	13	12	11	10	9	8	7
1¾m	3	21	20	19	18	17	16	15	14	13	12	11	10	9	8	7
15f	3	22	21	20	19	18	17	16	15	14	13	12	11	10	9	8
2m	3	22	21	20	19	18	17	16	15	14	13	12	11	10	9	8
2¼m	3	23	22	21	20	19	18	17	16	15	14	13	12	11	10	9
2½m	3	25	24	23	22	21	20	19	18	17	16	15	14	13	12	11

Note: Allowance assessed in lb which: 3 y.o. will receive from 4 y.o., 2 y.o. will receive from 3 y.o.

TABLE 9.2 Scale of weight-for-age (jumping)

The Stewards of the Jockey Club recommend the following revised scale of weight-for-age should, on and after 1st January 1985, be used as a guide.

Hurdle races

Allowance, assessed in lb, which 3 years old and 4 years old will receive from 5 years old and upwards

		Jan	Feb	Mar	Apr	May	June	July	Aug	Sept	Oct	Nov	Dec
2m	3	12	10	8	6	5	5	20	20	18	17	16	14
	4							3	3	2	1	—	—
2½m	3	13	11	9	7	6	6	21	21	19	18	17	15
	4							3	3	2	1	—	—
3m	3	14	12	10	8	7	7	23	23	21	19	18	16
	4							4	4	3	2	1	—

Steeplechases

Allowance, assessed in lb, which 4 years old and 5 years old will receive from 6 years old and upwards

		Jan	Feb	Mar	Apr	May	June	July	Aug	Sept	Oct	Nov	Dec
2m	4	10	9	8	7	6	6	15	15	14	13	12	11
	5							3	3	2	1	—	—
2½m	4	11	10	9	8	7	7	16	16	15	14	13	12
	5							4	4	3	2	1	—
3m	4	12	11	10	9	8	8	17	17	16	15	14	13
	5							5	5	4	3	2	1

Weight penalties are incurred by all horses that win except if the conditions of the race preclude them.

Weight penalties apply particularly to maidens at closing Flat, all novice hurdlers and novice chasers, National Hunt. A horse with a penalty must be considered handicapped by this extra burden of weight – it will mean that whatever performance has been achieved, the horse is likely to have to improve further to overcome this new handicap of weight.

Individual penalties range from 3 lb to 10 lb (Flat) and 5 lb–10 lb (National Hunt). These are often cumulative in novice hurdlers and chasers or may be 7 lb for one race and 10 lb for two races won; similarly, the conditions of some races (both National Hunt and Flat) require varying weight penalties according to the value of the races won.

TABLE 9.3   The weight scale applied to the handicapping of horses

Flat		National Hunt	
5–6f	3 lb per length	2m	2 lb per length
7–8f	2½ lb per length	2½m	1½ lb per length
9–11f	2 lb per length	3m	1 lb per length
12–14f	1½ lb per length	3m+	½ lb per length
15f+	1 lb per length		

The penalty scales given in Table 9.3 are those most widely applied.

On fast ground the allowances need to be increased, and on soft ground decreased. For example, some judges believe that 4 lb represents a length over 5f on firm ground, and ½ lb a length may be the best yardstick over 2m on soft going. The selector should use his own judgement within the broad guidelines. While weight seeks to eliminate the advantage of a faster horse it can do nothing to help a slow horse run faster than it can run already. On testing courses, especially over long distances, the burden of carrying weight can wear a faster horse down to the level of inferior rivals. However, on easy, tight-turning courses where horses cannot really race at top speed until they enter the straight (especially middle-distance races 7f–1m 2f) the weight concession by faster horses (who are the ones with that vital acceleration in the final stages of a race) will not be of any great disadvantage.

Flat racing handicaps
In flat racing handicaps the weight penalty for previous winners is usually set according to the distance of the race. A smaller penalty (usually up to 5 lb) in longer distance races (14 furlongs +), where the burden of weight is greatest; and a larger penalty (e.g. 6 lb +) in shorter distance races (sprints 5f/6f), where the burden of weight is felt least.

In the 1985 flat racing season the record of horses defying a penalty in handicaps over sprints and longer distances was:

	5/6 furlongs			mile 6 furlongs +		
	Winners	Runners		Winners	Runners	
up to 5 lb	2	25	= 8.0%	9	70	= 12.9%
6 lb+	34	173	= 19.7%	2	16	= 12.5%
	36	198	= 17.2%	11	86	= 12.8%

These findings show that the longer the distance of a race the greater is the effect of weight. A horse can more easily defy a large penalty over a short distance.

A further survey for the first part of the 1986 flat racing season revealed that 18.3% of all horses in handicaps who carried a penalty were able to defy it and win again.

In respect of distances:

	Winners	Runners	
5/6 furlongs	32	163	= 19.6%
7/9 furlongs	26	166	= 15.7%
10 furlongs	39	201	= 19.4%
	97	530	= 18.3%

whilst in terms of the penalty carried:

	Winners	Runners	
3–5 lb	47	247	= 19.0%
6 lb	14	74	= 18.9%
7 lb	26	154	= 16.9%
8–9 lb	5	38	= 12.8%
10 lb	5	16	= 31.3%
	97	530	

This again clearly shows that the greater the size of penalty the more likely will a horse be defeated by it. A surprising exception comes in the instance of the very highest penalty, 10 lb, where the ratio of winners was a surprising 31.3%. This suggests that any horse set to defy such a burden is good enough to be considered favourably.

To discover the reasons for this we need to examine the intentions of trainers who allow a horse with a penalty to compete in a handicap.

The most positive reason is because the horse is considered 'well-in' at the weights. The handicapper, having already reassessed the horse for future handicap races, has raised its weight even more, and so, by comparison, even whilst carrying this penalty, the horse is still ahead of the handicapper. This is a situation which arises mainly in younger horses who suddenly improve. In the survey, of the five winners defying the 10 lb penalty, three were 3 year olds who made the rapid improvement of which second season campaigners are often capable.

By contrast, for a more negative reason, a trainer may run a horse in a handicap with a penalty to show the handicapper that the ability of the animal is strictly limited, and any reassessment of its handicap rating should be on the side of leniency.

A third reason why a horse may be allowed to carry its penalty in a handicap is simply because it has hit peak form and so might as well be allowed to strike again quickly whilst the 'iron is hot'. The average handicapper will probably have a limited choice of future engagements anyway, be less likely of great further improvement, and have the best chance of another victory by exploiting current top form and fitness.

Many situations demand the practical consideration of penalties and the likelihood of a horse defying a penalty can be said to depend on:
1. The form of a winner;
2. The size of penalty;
3. The scope it has to make the necessary improvement.

1. Form;
The form of some winners in non-handicap races is so superior to rivals that a penalty of the largest size is no inconvenience. The form of other winners may be less superior and ability to defy a penalty will depend on its size.

2. The size of the penalty;
3 lb–5 lb The lowest and easiest penalties for a horse to overcome – many horses can improve the necessary amount to overcome these low penalties, for example simply by winning a race. Early season 2-year-olds would normally develop this amount from a winning experience.
7 lb This requires greater improvement and is likely to defeat less than better class horses, or those dropped in class.
10 lb and 10 lb+ This requires considerable improvement and will defeat all but the very best or rapidly improving horses.

3. Scope for improvement;
This is essentially bound to the horse's physical constitution and scope for development; this information can hardly be gleaned from examination of form but requires experienced observation of the horse.

Scope for improvement will also be indicated from the manner of the horse's winning performance (i.e. the ease or difficulty of winning). A horse that wins easily can hardly do more and is likely to improve upon that performance, while a horse that wins 'all out' suggests that it is unlikely to improve.

Weight allowances

Weight allowances are normally framed in the conditions of race as a concession to lack of achievement (due to inability or inexperience), i.e. maiden allowance for horses that have not won a race; a weight allowance for horses which have not run previously; a weight allowance for horses that have not won a race since a certain date or a race of a prescribed value.

COURSES

There are over 50 racecourses spread throughout Britain, some specializing in Flat or National Hunt racing while others can accommodate both types. These courses can vary as much in size, shape and gradient as they do in location.

Courses range in extremes from a sharp flat track at Chester which is approximately 1m in circumference to the wide-open galloping expanses at Newmarket where there is a course a straight mile long. This variation of courses can and does strongly influence a racehorse's performance, so that some horses become course specialists. These horses only seem able to produce their best form under the conditions prevailing on a certain course, and at other tracks produce below-par performances.

The variation of courses is as wide for National Hunt racing as for Flat racing. Extremes exemplified at one end of the spectrum by figure-of-eight-shaped circuits at Fontwell and Windsor and at the other by wide galloping tracks at Aintree and Haydock. The former two tracks have easy fences while the latter have large awesome fences which, having a drop on the landing side of the fences, are negotiated only by the safest of jumpers.

These differences combine to endorse the maxim 'horses for courses' especially where the course is of extreme character. *Flat*: Chester – small circuit with tight bends; Epsom, Brighton – rolling gradients; Newmarket – straightness and openness; Windsor – figure-of-eight shape. *National Hunt*: Fontwell, Windsor – figure of eights; Newton Abbot – tight flat track 1m circumference; Haydock, Aintree – big fences, galloping courses; Cheltenham – tough fences, large circuit, stamina-sapping gradients.

Some courses are right-handed, others left-handed, some suit front

The different characteristics on race-tracks can have an effect on a horse's performance. British racecourses vary as much in their shape, size and undulation as they do in location.

These photographs illustrate the two extremes. The top one is looking down the July Course at Newmarket – a wide, straight galloping track, while the bottom one shows Chester which is a tight round track of approximately 1m circumference.

runners, others benefit long-striding horses who need a galloping course to be seen to best advantage. The variety of racecourses in Britain is one of the intriguing and attractive features of British racing, allowing a horse to keep its own characteristic individuality and not necessarily have to conform to the stereotyped conditions of racing that exist elsewhere. Therefore, it is always necessary when assessing a horse's chances to pay attention to the special features and requirements of the course. The characteristics of both Flat and National Hunt racecourses in the UK are given below.

FLAT RACING

ASCOT (RH)	Round course 1m 6f with a run-in 2½f. It is a galloping-type course. Straight course 1m is undulating with a stiff 3f, uphill finish.
AYR (LH)	Round course 1m 4f with a run-in 4f. Straight course 6f.
BATH (LH)	Round course 1m 4f with a run-in 4f. It is a galloping-type course. Straight course 5f 167yd and uphill.
BEVERLEY (RH)	Round course 1m 4f with a run-in 3½f and stiff uphill finish. Straight course 5f.
BRIGHTON (LH)	U-shaped course 1m 4f with a run-in 3½f. It is an undulating course.
CARLISLE (RH)	Pear-shaped course 1m 5f that is undulating with a run-in 3½f uphill. Straight course 6f.
CATTERICK (LH)	Oval course 1m 2f with a run-in 3f. It is a sharp course. Straight course 5f that is downhill most of the way.
CHEPSTOW (LH)	Oval course 2m with a run-in 5f. It is an undulating course. Straight course 1m.
CHESTER (LH)	Tight, round-shaped course of 1m with a run-in 2f. Spring races are run on the round course.
DONCASTER (LH)	Round course almost 2m with a run-in 4½f. It is a galloping course. Straight course 1m.
EDINBURGH (RH)	Oval course 1m 2f with a run-in 4f. It is a flat, sharp course. Straight course 5f.
EPSOM (LH)	U-shaped course 1m 4f with a run-in 4f. It is an undulating course. Straight course 5f downhill and very fast.
FOLKESTONE (RH)	Pear-shaped course 1m 3f with a run-in 3f. It is a sharp course. Straight course 6f.
GOODWOOD (RH)	Is a loop-shaped course that allows races up to 2m 5f to be run, run-in 4f. Straight course 6f. It is a sharp, fast course.

HAMILTON (RH)	Loop-shaped course allowing for races up to 1m 5f, run-in approximately 5f. Straight course 6f. It is an undulating course.
HAYDOCK (LH)	Round course 1m 5f with a run-in 4f. It is a galloping course. Straight course 5f.
KEMPTON (RH)	Triangular-shaped course 1m 5f with a run-in 3½f, plus a dog-leg-shaped course 10f (Jubilee Course). Separate straight 6f across in the centre of the course. It is a flat course.
LEICESTER (RH)	Oval course 2m with a run-in 5f. It is a galloping course. Straight mile which is downhill at first.
LINGFIELD (LH)	Round course 1m 4f with a run-in 3f. It is an undulating course. Straight course 7f 140yd.
NEWBURY (LH)	Oval course 1m 7f with a run-in 5f. It is a galloping course. Straight course 1m.
NEWCASTLE (LH)	Oval course 1m 6f with a run-in 4f. It is a galloping, testing course. Straight course 7f.
NEWMARKET (RH)	*Rowley Course.* Long course of 2m 2f with a gentle bend into the straight in 1m 2f from finish. It is a wide, galloping course.
(RH)	*July Course* – is of similar shape with a gentle bend into its straight 1m from the finish. It is slightly more undulating.
NOTTINGHAM (LH)	Round course 1m 4f with a run-in 4f. It is a flat course. Straight course 7f.
PONTEFRACT (LH)	Pear-shaped course 1m 4f with a run-in 2f. It is a sharp, undulating course. There is no separate straight course.
REDCAR (LH)	Round course 1m 6f with a run-in 5f. It is galloping course. Straight course is 1m.
RIPON (RH)	Round course 1m 5f with a run-in 5f. It is a sharp course. Straight course 6f.
SALISBURY (RH)	Loop-shaped course with races up to 1m 6f with a run-in 7f. Straight course approximately 1m. Last 4f are uphill and provide a stiff test. It is a galloping course.
SANDOWN (RH)	Round course 1m 5f with a run-in 4f. Stiff galloping course. Separate straight course 5f in the centre of the course and steadily rising throughout.
THIRSK (LH)	Round course 1m 2f with a run-in 4f. It is sharpish course. Straight course 6f.
WARWICK (LH)	Circular course 1m 6f with a run-in 3f. It is a sharp course. The 5f course bends left with the junction of the round course.

WINDSOR (RH)   Shaped as a figure of eight. Flat races bend right-handed. Has almost straight 6–6f courses.

WOLVERHAMPTON (LH)   Triangular course 1m 4f with a run–in 4½f. Straight course 5f.

YARMOUTH (LH)   Oval course 13f with a run–in 5f. It is a flat course. Straight course 1m.

YORK (LH)   U–shaped course 2m with a run–in 5f. It is a galloping course. Straight course 6f.

National hunt

	Circumference	Run-in (from final fence) (yd)	Type of course		Fences
ASCOT (RH)	1m 6f	160 (uphill)		Testing	Stiff
AYR (LH)	1m 4f	210	Flat	Average	
BANGOR (LH)	1m 2f	325	Flat	Sharp	
CARLISLE (RH)	1m 5f	250	Undulating	Stiff	
CARTMEL (LH)	1m	800	Undulating	Easy	
CATTERICK (LH)	1m 2f	240	Undulating	Sharp	
CHELTENHAM (LH)	1m 4f	350 (uphill)		Testing	Stiff
CHEPSTOW (LH)	2m	240	Undulating		
DEVON & EXETER (RH)	2m	250	Hilly	Sharp	
DONCASTER (LH)	2m	250	Flat	Galloping	
FAKENHAM (LH)	1m	220	Undulating	Sharp	
FOLKESTONE (RH)	1m 3f	220	Undulating	Easy	
FONTWELL					
(Chases – figure of eight)	1m	220	Flat	Tricky	
(HURDLES) (LH)	1m	220	Flat	Easy	
HAYDOCK (LH)	1m 5f	440	Flat	Testing	Stiff
HEREFORD (RH)	1m 4f	300	Flat	Easy	
HEXHAM (LH)	1m 4f	250 (uphill)	Undulating	Stiff finish	
HUNTINGDON (RH)	1m 4f	200	Flat	Galloping	
KELSO (LH)	1m 3f	490	Flat	Average	
KEMPTON (RH)	1m 5f	200	Flat	Easy	Stiff
LEICESTER (RH)	1m 6f	250	Undulating	Sharp	
LINGFIELD (LH)	1m 2f	200	Undulating	Stiff	
LIVERPOOL (LH)					
Grand National Course	2m 2f	494	Flat	Galloping	Stiff
Mildmay Course	1m 2f	260	Flat	Sharp	
LUDLOW (RH)	1m 4f	450	Flat	Stiff	
MARKET RASEN (RH)	1m 2f	220	Flat	Sharp	
NEWCASTLE (LH)	1m 6f	220	Undulating	Stiff	
NEWBURY (LH)	2m (approx.)	255	Flat	Galloping	Stiff
NEWTON ABBOT (LH)	1m	300	Flat	Sharp	
NOTTINGHAM (LH)	1m 4f	240	Flat	Galloping	
PERTH (RH)	1m 2f	450	Flat	Average	
PLUMPTON (LH)	1m 1f	200	Undulating	Sharp	
SANDOWN (RH)	1m 5f	300 (uphill)		Stiff	Stiff
SEDGEFIELD (LH)	1m 2f	525	Undulating	Sharp	
SOUTHWELL (LH)	1m 2f	250	Flat	Sharp	
STRATFORD (LH)	1m 3f	200	Flat	Sharp	
TAUNTON (RH)	1m 2f	150	Flat	Average	
TOWCESTER (RH)	1m 6f	300	Undulating	Stiff	
UTTOXETER (LH)	1m 2f	300	Flat	Galloping	
WARWICK (LH)	1m 6f	240	Flat	Sharp	
WETHERBY (LH)	1m 4f	190	Flat	Galloping	
WINCANTON (RH)	1m 3f	200	Flat	Galloping	
WINDSOR (figure of eight)	1m 4f	200	Flat	Average	
WOLVERHAMPTON (LH)	1m 4f	220	Flat	Average	
WORCESTER (LH)	1m 5f	220	Flat	Average	

A mammoth fence at Aintree (Liverpool).

An open ditch at Sandown Park.

The usual type of plain fence encountered on a park course.

The type of hurdle encountered on National Hunt courses.

TYPES OF FENCE

In National Hunt racing there are two types of obstacle – fences in steeplechase races (chases) and hurdles in hurdle races. In chases there are three different types of fence – plain fence, open ditch and water jump. On National Hunt steeplechase courses there is only one water jump, one or two open ditches, the remaining fences being plain fences. A water jump has a fence not more than 3 feet in height preceding it and an expanse of water not less than 12 feet in width. An open ditch consists of a fence not less than 4 feet 6 inches in height with a ditch not less than 6 feet in width on the take-off side of the fence. All plain fences are sturdily built non-movable structures made of firmly packed birch and trimmed gorse and are not less than 4 feet 6 inches in height.

Hurdles are portable structures consisting of two-bar wooden frames covered with gorse and are staked to the ground. They are not less than 3 feet 6 inches in height from the bottom to the top bar. The stiffness and type of fences can vary from course to course.

THE DRAW (APPLIES ONLY TO FLAT RACING)

This is the position across the course from where a horse must start, whether placed in a starting stall or lining up behind a barrier (tape) or by flag.

It is really only a significant factor in races up to 1m with perhaps the Derby, Cambridgeshire Handicap (where there are large fields) and some longer races at Chester the exception. The draw is of particular importance in the shorter distance races of up to 1m where ground advantage lost at the start cannot be regained. The draw plays a more important role on some courses more than others, and in certain prevailing ground conditions more than others.

In considering the draw a number of factors must be taken into account:

1. The use or non-use of starting stalls. Stalls are used on most occasions (when stalls are not used, especially in races for 2-year-olds, it is essential that a jockey be experienced and competent).
2. The positioning of starting stalls. The position of the starting stalls may be moved from their normal position close to the rails, to a position either to the far side or middle of the course and thus the advantage of the draw can be radically affected. (The movement of stalls occurs usually only in emergency situations, but the effect can be dramatic.)

3. Change of going. While under normal going conditions certain numbers (high, low, middle) will be favoured by the draw, a change of going could nullify and/or reverse this advantage. For example, at Ayr the high numbers, on the stand side, are normally favoured in 5–6f races, but on very soft or heavy going the advantage reverses to the low numbers on the opposite side.
4. The size of the field. In a small field of 5 or 6 runners the runners will not be spread across the course so there is little advantage from the draw, but in fields of 16 or more runners with horses spread across the course, favourably drawn horses have a distinct advantage.

Form books, guides and newspapers regularly carry the information regarding the considered favoured draw positions on each course and this needs careful consideration when assessing the chances of a horse.

Course	Draw	Distance	Going
ASCOT	No Advantage	(round course)	
	Low numbers	5f–1m straight course	
AYR	High numbers	5f, 6f	
	Low numbers	5f, 6f	Soft
	Low numbers	7f upwards	
BATH	Low numbers	Up to 1m	
BEVERLEY	High numbers	5f and 1m	
BRIGHTON	Low numbers	5f, 6f	
CARLISLE	High numbers	Up to 1m	
CATTERICK	Low numbers	5f, 6f, 7f	
CHEPSTOW	High numbers	5f–1m	
	Low numbers (straight course)	5f–1m	Soft
CHESTER	Low numbers	All distances	
DONCASTER	High numbers (straight course)	5f–1m	
	Low numbers (round course)	1m	
EDINBURGH	Low numbers	5f	
EPSOM	High numbers	5–6f	
	Low numbers	7–8f	
FOLKESTONE	Low numbers	5f, 6f	Soft
GOODWOOD	High numbers	5f, 6f	
HAMILTON	High numbers	5f, 6f	
HAYDOCK	High numbers	5f	
	Low numbers	6–8f	
KEMPTON	No advantage	5f, 6f	
LEICESTER	Low numbers	5f, 6f	
LINGFIELD	High numbers	5f–7f 40yd	
	Low numbers	5f–7f 40 yd (particularly heavy)	Heavy

Course	Draw	Distance	Going
NEWBURY	High numbers (straight course)	5f–1m	
NEWCASTLE	High numbers	5–7f	
	Low numbers	5f–7f	Heavy
NEWMARKET (Rowley, July courses)	Variable	5f–1m	
NOTTINGHAM	High numbers (but variable as stall positions alter)	5f, 6f	
PONTEFRACT	Low numbers	5f, 6f	
REDCAR	High numbers	5–8f	
RIPON	Low numbers	5f, 6f	
	High numbers	8f	
SALISBURY	High numbers	5–8f	
SANDOWN	High numbers	5f	
	High numbers	7f, 8f	
THIRSK	High numbers	5f, 6f	
	Low numbers	7f, 8f	
WARWICK	High numbers	5f	
WINDSOR	No advantage	5f, 6f	
WOLVERHAMPTON	Low numbers	5f	Soft
YARMOUTH	High numbers	5–8f	
YORK	Low numbers	5–6f	

The draw affects only the distances stated and can be assumed to be of no advantage at other distances.

However, the most thoughtful analysis of the draw over recent seasons has been made by John Whitley in his book *Computer Racing Form*, an annual publication which diligently covers many aspects of Flat racing.

The effect of the draw can vary slightly from season to season in response to changes in the placement of the stalls across the race-track and improved drainage, etc., so it is suggested that the more dedicated refer to Whitley's latest edition for the most up-to-date information (*Computer Racing Form*, Racing Research, 226 Wakefield Road, Light-cliffe, Halifax, HX3 8TP).

JOCKEYSHIP

'Fear runs down the reins' – this statement proclaims the importance of good jockeyship. Jockeyship can be the marginal difference between winning and losing in evenly balanced contests, and only when a horse is vastly superior will it overcome the disadvantage of poor handling. Good jockeys cannot win without a good horse underneath them, but bad jockeyship will certainly ruin a horse's chances of winning.

The draw applies only to Flat racing and the position of the draw can have a significant influence in sprint races where an advantage at the start may never be overcome at a later stage of the race.

Horses are usually started from stalls in Flat racing.

The tape barrier start used in National Hunt racing allows a jockey to pick his starting position. The horses are started as far as possible in a straight line and at a reasonable distance from the tape.

A jockey needs certain qualities:

(a) to be competent and reliable in ability and judgement;
(b) to be honest in application;
(c) to have tactical ability (independently to devise a strategy for a race, or to carry out proficiently the instructions given by the trainer, and yet be adept to improvise should the situation demand);
(d) to control and impose authority on a horse while encouraging it to give of its best.

The first two qualities mentioned can be said to be the basic requirements common to all the leading riders. It is in the varying degrees of development of the other two qualities, plus character and ambitious purpose, which determine the great from the merely good riders.

The aspect of a jockey's integrity requires close examination. It is usual to hear disgruntled punters loudly claim that a jockey's dishonesty was responsible for a horse's defeat when seldom is there anything further from the truth. A jockey, it must be understood, has his first allegiance to whoever engages him to ride (i.e. the trainer/owner) and it will be expected that the race instructions he is given be followed whether or not they comply strictly to the rules of racing. While making this declaration, it must be stated unequivocally that the advantages for winning far outweigh the considerations for deliberately losing a race.

A horse that a trainer may condone not winning a race, will usually not have on the day more than an extremely tenuous chance of winning. For example, in the case of a proposed future betting coup the horse is unlikely to be fully fit, and the conditions of the race – going, distance, weight – are likely to be equally unfavourable. And an inexperienced horse is likely to lack the physical maturity or racing 'know-how' at this stage in its career. Instances of trainers stopping a horse with a real winning chance from trying to win are most unusual, for most have learned from experience that a certain winner today (at any odds) is better than risking waiting for an uncertainty in the future.

For a jockey the financial rewards in the long term and sometimes in the short term of successful honest endeavour so outweigh the benefits of malpractice that such acts are a most unattractive proposition. The close-knit racing community demands a code of loyalty and integrity which once broken immediately deems a jockey unemployable.

The basic qualities of jockeyship apply to both Flat and National Hunt riders with, however, defined and distinct physical characteristics which reflect the particular demands of each code of racing.

Flat racing is a manifestation of speed, the maximum racing distance is 2m 6f and the maximum weight carried by a horse is normally 10 st. National Hunt racing is a combination of speed, strength and endurance, the minimum distance is 2m with eight flights of hurdles to jump and the minimum allotted weight is 10 st. Flat race jockeys are therefore small, of light weight (approx. 8 st) and rely on speed of thought and reflex to practise their skill. *National Hunt* jockeys are of normal average height, with a riding weight of 10 st (approx.). Strength, courage, durability and clear understanding are essential elements in their make-up.

The riding lifetime of National Hunt jockeys is a short one; while not gaining the full physical strength to fulfil their full potential until their mid-twenties, within a decade the effects of falls and the rigours of race riding will signal their retirement. Meanwhile Flat race jockeys not subject to the continuous effects from the hazards of injury improve with age and experience, often reaching a plateau of maturity in their thirties which they are able to exploit with notable effect.

Good National Hunt jockeys need the full complement of skills in horsemanship and race riding possessed by their Flat race counterparts with some additional ones as well:

1. The jockey's skill in keeping position during a race and bringing the horse with a well-timed challenge at the end of the race.
2. The horseman's skill in placing a horse well at its fences so that it may jump them in the easiest and most efficient way.
3. The physical courage to keep a horse racing even after it may have made bad errors in jumping – this confidence by example being transferred to the horse.
4. A strong physical constitution, to withstand the rigours of riding long distances, and crushing falls, with a resilience to make fast and complete recovery from injury and the health to resist normal winter ailments, such as colds and flu.

JOCKEYS (FLAT RACING)

In the cause of brevity it is quite impractical here to analyse every good jockey riding in the British Isles. A concise list of jockeys has been compiled composed of those riders which have ridden an English or Irish Classic winner or a race of equivalent stature. An omission of any jockey from this list is not an intended slur on his ability, but a present lack to meet the qualifying requirement.

All good jockeys are a combination of horseman and race rider:

Race riding requires the skill of judging pace, tactical awareness and ablity to anticipate situations, plus the drive and power to ride a horse in a finish.

Horsemanship is command, control and empathy with a horse. Balancing a horse, enabling it to maintain its stride pattern, settling and imparting confidence in a nervous and/or free-running horse, galvanizing and/or inspiring a faint-hearted or ungenerous one.

The many skills a Flat race jockey needs to develop means that many jockeys only reach the height of their powers with maturity. A fact exemplified by the success of the more senior jockeys.

'Great riders are born not made' is a statement inspired by observing the empathy great jockeys have with a horse, a oneness in action and of purpose. Great jockeys, although not immune from making errors of judgement, make far fewer and less vital ones than the average rider. It is also an ability to extricate themselves from difficult or potentially difficult situations that separates the great jockeys from the others. The startling difference that divides great jockeys from the others is captured in the statement: 'Great jockeys win races they had no right to win, while other jockeys lose races they had no right to lose.'

Willie Carson (*riding weight 7 st 10 lb*)   Willie Carson's youthful appearance and attitude belies the fact that he is one of the senior jockeys still riding, gaining his first success in 1962. This should leave no one in any doubt that this experienced professional is anything less than a formidable battling opponent. A serious riding accident at the York Festival of 1981 for a time threatened to curtail his career, but after a lengthy convalescence Willie Carson bounced back in his inimitable way to regain the champion jockey's crown in 1983.

William Hunter Carson, the first Scottish-born champion Flat race jockey, has won the title on five occasions in 1972, 1973, 1976, 1980 and 1983; and although now entering the autumn rather than the spring of his career, he is always the rival that other jockeys have to be at their best to defeat. The partnership forged with Major Hern's prestigious West Isley stable since the 1970s has always been a most successful one, with many Classic and major race victories regularly gained. The 1985 season was probably the leanest one since the association began due to the yard being stricken with the dreaded 'virus' among its inmates, and Dick Hern himself suffering from the injuries of a hunting accident. However, the stable still managed over 50 winners during the season, with PETOSKI's victory in the King George and Queen Elizabeth Stakes at Ascot being the obvious highlight. The Carson–Hern partnership which has produced two English Derby winners, TROY (1979) and HENBIT (1980), three Oaks winners DUNFERMILINE (1977), BIREME (1980) and SUN PRINCESS (1983) plus an Irish Derby and three Irish Oaks winners, an Ascot Gold Cup, Eclipse Stakes, King George and Queen Elizabeth Stakes and York's Benson and Hedges Cup is certainly never one to be disregarded or taken lightly.

Willie Carson's famous 'push-push' style as a jockey, where he sits behind a horse and vigorously drives it into action, has seemed to overshadow any appreciation of his numerous other skills. He is a most tactically astute jockey, frequently able to seize the initiative during a race from lesser opponents; a superb horseman particularly able at keeping his horses well balanced throughout a race, but especially at

Action photographs of 4 of the leading Flat race jockeys.

Willie Carson

Steve Cauthen

Pat Eddery

Walter Swinburn

'holding together' a tired or inexperienced horse in the closing stages where there is the tendency to wander under pressure. Willie Carson also is a fine judge of pace, either by riding a well-judged race from the front or else coming with a blistering late challenge to collect the spoils. Although Willie Carson is not known for over-use of the whip (he may give a horse a couple of smacks to set it running) he lacks nothing for effectiveness in a finish, preferring to employ his all-action, head-down pushing technique that still rouses any horse to give its all without vigorous punishment from the whip. His forthright and honest appraisal of his horses and corresponding post-race reviews make him an ideal booking for any handlers seeking to know whether their charges are 'swans' or only 'geese'.

Many famous big race victories, coupled with his open engaging personality to public interview, have made Willie Carson a very popular figure among racing fans. He is always likely to bring a joyfulness and light-heartedness to any race or important occasion. Willie Carson in his association with many good and a few great horses has risen from humble beginnings to earn himself a niche in racing's hall of fame among the best jockeys. Despite a loosening of his hold on the jockey's crown over the past couple of seasons, Willie Carson still possesses that tenacious will to win which means he should never be disregarded. He has always been the gamest of triers, often coming to win a race like a shining white knight to rescue 'Joe Public' from a seemingly lost cause. The cries of 'Come on Willie' echo around the racecourse as similar calls did in an earlier era for two other heroes, Steve Donoghue and Gordon Richards, ensuring that the spirit of Willie Carson will always hold lasting memories for every racing fan.

Steve Cauthen (*riding weight 8 st 8 lb*)   Having arrived on these shores for the first time in 1979, Steve Cauthen has emerged from being thought of initially as perhaps a young American upstart with an overblown reputation, to becoming champion jockey and winning a place of special affection in many British hearts. His championship tally of 195 winners in the 1985 season was the highest total since the time of Sir Gordon Richards some three decades earlier, and sealed a highly successful first-season partnership as retained jockey to Henry Cecil's all-conquering Newmarket stable. Steve Cauthen gained his second and consecutive champion rider's crown while Henry Cecil became champion trainer for the sixth time, winning a record of almost £1½ million in prize-money, and the pair sharing four English Classic victories.

Steve Cauthen gained his first English Derby success on SLIP ANCHOR and then experienced the very rare triple crown glory due to the exploits of the amazing filly OH SO SHARP who won the 1000 Guineas, Oaks and St Leger. The association with such horses and his contract with Henry Cecil's all-powerful establishment has placed Steve in the position where he is the rider all other jockeys must fear. Although having adjusted his style of riding from the influence of his American origins to suit European and particularly English conditions, he still retains his essential cool and stillness which has been his trade mark and gives his riding a quality of authority and purpose. He loses nothing, however, in a finish, where he has developed a more powerful and persuasive technique, yet ensuring that his mounts always remain well balanced in the final drive to the finishing post.

Steve Cauthen is a master of pace (a throwback from the demands of his apprenticeship on the very time-orientated American race-tracks) and can be guaranteed to have his horse in the best position at the right time throughout a race, either racing from the front or else coming with a late challenge. Usually his horses are placed in a prominent position during a race, giving them every chance to grab the spoils if they are good enough. The young American has a style which is slightly more upright in appearance than some of his rivals, but wants nothing in its effectiveness and he has the priceless asset of keeping his mounts nicely balanced at all stages during a race. Such abilities emphasize Steve Cauthen's qualities as a natural horseman who is quickly able to gain a rapport and empathy with all his mounts, making him an almost perfect jockey for any trainer to engage, in the certainty that his post-race comments are likely to be most perceptive and practical.

Steve Cauthen has received some unwelcome and over-dramatic media coverage regarding some personal problems which beset him during the 1985 season when he regained his champion's crown. This should not be allowed to overshadow or detract from this modest young man's outstanding skills. Steve Cauthen in triumph or defeat conducts himself with a dignity that can only be a shining example to other more temperamental media personalities, and ensures that these events will soon be forgotten and seen in their true perspective as but a brief chapter in a career which will scale ever greater heights.

Pat Eddery (*riding weight 8 st 4 lb*)   Pat Eddery, from being champion apprentice in 1971, assumes the mantle of now being one of the most experienced riders in the British Isles and one of the most sought-after jockeys world-wide. His rise to this international status is in no small way due to his association with the legendary Vincent O'Brien's Irish stable, and their domination in the early 1980s of the European racing scene. Champions such as EL GRAN SENOR, GOLDEN FLEECE, ASSERT, SADLER'S WELLS, SOLFORD and KING'S LAKE, to mention only the leading stars, have emerged during this period from the Ballydole yard and helped to place Pat Eddery at the forefront of the international racing scene. When we add to this list the successes Pat Eddery achieved in the golden autumn of 1985 on PEBBLES (who so impressively trounced a field of European stars in the Champion Stakes at Newmarket before her later triumph in the United States), plus RAINBOW QUEST's eventual victory in the Prix de l'Arc de Triomphe and DANCING BRAVE's win in 1986, it is no wonder that this Irish-born rider can be considered to have reached the very highest plateau on the world jockey stage.

Pat Eddery physically is almost of perfect size for a modern international jockey and he has refined a full complement of riding skills to match this attribute. He has a riding style which is as pleasing to the eye as it is effective and exudes a rare power and precision in execution. The 12 seasons since he gained his first champion jockey crown in 1974 have seen him grow steadily in stature as a rider, until now he can immediately stamp his authority on a race and seize the initiative from less decisive rivals. As events during a race gradually unfold, Pat Eddery is a jockey almost guaranteed to have his mount in the right spot, invariably giving little ground away and coming the shortest route home. He is the jockey (upon the retirement of the old maestro Lester Piggott) who is the strongest rider in the finish, excelling at these moments, when he brings his awesome persuasive powers to bear.

He is an excellent judge of pace, either controlling things at the head of his field or sitting just off the pace, ready to pounce with a characteristic late challenge. If the horse is good enough Pat can be expected to produce it at just the right moment at the business end of the race, swooping inside the final furlong to capture the victory spoils. Such devastating riding skills ensure that Pat Eddery's services are in constant demand by all the leading trainers without a retained jockey, and he always has a healthy total of winners at the season's end. Only the fact that his loyalties were divided between riding in England most of the week and in Ireland at the weekends for his principal retainer, has stopped Pat Eddery regaining the champion jockey crown which he so majestically wore, winning four titles in consecutive seasons 1974–77. Pat Eddery's new contract to ride for Khalid Abdullah promises to promote him to world-wide stardom.

Walter Swinburn (*riding weight 8 st 5 lb*)   Owing to his association with the brilliant and later ill-fated horse SHERGAR, Walter Swinburn rose from being just a promising young rider to achieving star status almost overnight. In June 1981 and 2 months before his twentieth birthday Walter Swinburn rode his first Derby winner and received the world-wide acclaim which accompanies such a success. From this meteoric rise to prominence this young man with the beguiling choir-boy looks and manner has developed into one of the most accomplished English jockeys riding, quite able to hold his place with distinction alongside the mighty trio of Carson, Cauthen and Eddery. Walter Swinburn's career since his initial Derby success has been one of steady and consolidated progress, bridging the difficult gap between star apprentice and full professional rider with consummate ease and forging a successful partnership with Michael Stoute's powerful Newmarket stable which also has grown in distinction during their association.

Horses such as MARWELL, SHAREEF DANCER, SHADEED (most recent Epsom Derby winner), SHAHARISTANI and SONIC LADY plus lesser stars DALSAAN, ELECTRIC, ROYAL HEROINE and SHADARI have given Walter Swinburn the vital experience and confidence necessary for any young jockey seeking to throw down a serious challenge for the title crown.

Nothing seems to epitomize Walter Swinburn more than his disarming ability to meet each new challenge so calmly yet so successfully. He appears to take things so coolly in his stride, taking advantage regularly of what opportunities may befall him whether it be from an opponent's error on the race-track or a rival's misfortune off the course. Nothing more aptly illustrates this than his second Derby success on SHAHARISTANI where he was able to accept the hospitality of fortune and take full advantage of another jockey's mistake, and when he gained the ride on Mr Daniel Wildenstein's ALL ALONG in autumn 1983. The latter incident occurred after a dispute between the owner and a certain jockey called L. Piggott, resulting in Walter Swinburn being engaged, and the combination of a young English jockey and a brilliant French filly capturing three top international races, (Prix de l'Arc de Triumph, Washington DC International and US Turf Classic), within the space of a few weeks in the autumn of 1983. Such prestigious victories do not pass unnoticed and they immediately placed Walter Swinburn in the international arena as a jockey with many future opportunities likely to be offered to him.

The result of these successes is completely mirrored in his riding style which is one of a cool measured confidence reinforced by an uncanny instinct consistently to do the right thing at the right time. Walter Swinburn's riding has also been influenced by his partnership with such an intelligent and thoughtful trainer as Michael Stoute and this has made Walter into very much a thinking jockey; a rider able to plan and assess races beforehand, yet always having common sense and retaining enough spontaneity to respond to the unpredictable should it occur as events unfold.

Walter Swinburn is a superb horseman whose calm approach is immediately transmitted to his mount, coaxing and quietening a headstrong individual while readily able to galvanize the fainter-hearted ones. His style is undemonstrative, with him often appearing to glide unseen into a finishing position at the right moment during a race rather than with any frantic last-ditch or belated challenge. With experienced horses Walter Swinburn will normally have them in a prominent position from a fair distance out, giving them every chance should they be up to the task, although he is still able to rouse a horse in a close-fought finish when the need arises. Walter Swinburn with his concise and honest appraisal of a horse is a jockey any trainer would welcome to employ knowing their charge can be trusted to his expert care and riding skills.

It can only be expected that this young man will achieve even greater glories in the many years which lay ahead of him as a top jockey.

R. Cochrane (*riding weight 8 st 1 lb*)   Ray Cochrane is a young jockey who has gained wide public acclaim due to his success on MIDWAY LADY in 1986, the English 1,000 Guineas and the Oaks. This partnership, so effectively established, aptly demonstrates how the ability to seize opportunities which unexpectedly arise can play an important role in establishing a young jockey's racing career. Ray Cochrane only gained the mount on this filly after two other star jockeys were forced at a late hour to change their riding plans.

Ray Cochrane's rise to prominence has been the overnight success story which has taken 12 years to happen. He rode his first winner as an apprentice in 1974, but due to rising weight and lack of opportunities was forced to pursue a National Hunt career for a short time in the late 1970s, riding eight winners, before a serious fall coincidentally helped resolve the weight problem and persuaded him to relaunch his Flat race career.

Serving out his time as an apprentice under the guidance of Ron Sheather at Newmarket, a loyal association was formed and rewarded both in 1984 with the brilliant exploits of that grand horse CHIEF SINGER, who won the July Cup and Sussex Stakes, having previously made EL GRAN SENOR fight all the way for its English 2,000 Guineas victory.

The battling qualities and brilliance shown by CHIEF SINGER on these occasions epitomizes Ray Cochrane's riding style which is brave, resourceful and extremely powerful in a finish. He is a determined jockey who has forged a place for himself alongside the very top riders, showing he is overawed by no one nor intimidated by any challenge on the race-track. The sweet fruits of success that Ray Cochrane has only just recently tasted are the result of much hard work and dedication, and ensure that this Irish-born rider will not easily be swept aside but will remain for many years a feared opponent with greater ambitions still to fulfil. In 1987 he is contracted to ride for L. Cumani's stable.

P. Cook (*riding weight 8 st 1 lb*)   Paul Cook is a very dependable senior jockey who has been riding for over the past 20 years, having been champion apprentice in the mid-1960s and gaining his first Classic success in the 1966 1,000 Guineas on GLAD RAGS. In common with many young jockeys who as claiming riders achieve considerable success, Paul Cook found the transition to establishing himself in the top category of the non-claiming ranks a difficult and protracted affair. It was not until after his second Classic victory on TOUCHING WOOD in the 1982 St Leger (some 16 years after his first) could it be said that he had finally arrived and set himself among the very leading riders.

Paul Cook is nothing if not determined, and this feature of his character is reflected in his riding style which is one of a neat effective persuasiveness, rhythmically driving out his mounts in a run to the finishing post. The unassuming manner which Paul Cook emits should not persuade anyone they are dealing with anyone less than a reliable experienced professional who still retains the ambition to scale the heights and grab the big race successes which promised to become a regular feature in his early career.

T. Ives (*riding weight 8 st 3 lb*) Tony Ives is an Englisy jockey who after a thorough grounding on the less glamorous northern race-tracks of Britain has made the breakthrough from this unfashionable background to be accepted as one of the leading riders of the mid-1980s. After having ridden his first winner in 1971, Tony Ives quite quickly established the reputation of being a dependable and proficient rider but without the essential connections with top-class horses which does wonders to boost a jockey's confidence and self-esteem, and help to turn the merely good jockeys into great ones.

However, within the racing fraternity Tony Ives's talents had not gone unrecognized and his contact with better-class horses was established when he accepted the retainer with W. O'Gorman's Newmarket-based stable and moved to the centre of British racing. Although considerable success was achieved during this partnership, particularly with the sprinters for which the stable is renowned, it was not until Tony Ives's successes with that famous horse TELEPROMPTER that he received the acclaim his abilities deserved. The international success of Lord Derby's gelding in the Arlington Milion race in Chicago has brought Tony Ives great public fame and has meant his services as a jockey are regularly sought by numerous leading stables in some of the prestigious races.

Since his association with Bill O'Gorman's stable Tony Ives has been acknowledged as a specialist rider of sprinters, at which he excels, but this should not overshadow his other appreciable skills. He is strong in a finish, a good judge of pace, who is likely always to have his mounts prominently placed (an essential point in winning sprints) and always likely to seize the initiative from rivals in a final flourish to the winning-post.

Tony Ives, having made the vital breakthrough to the higher echelons in the jockey's league, has now gained the special confidence success brings, to remain one of the leading challengers for racing honours, and in 1987 is contracted to ride for Ian Balding.

A. Murray (*riding weight 8 st 4 lb*) Tony Murray, after a successful early career in England, first as a star apprentice then as a top-class senior rider, spent about 6 years in the late 1970s and 1980s riding in France and Ireland before returning to these shores in 1982. A constant battle over his weight, which also produced a health problem, caused him to contemplate announcing his retirement from riding in the autumn of 1983. However, the condition was resolved during the close season and Tony Murray returned to begin the 1984 Flat racing season clearly demonstrating he was every bit as good if not a better jockey than he had ever been.

His retainer to H. Thomson-Jones's superbly run Newmarket stable with its host of well-bred and often expensively purchased Arab-owned inmates have seen Tony Murray's own ambitions revitalized and him riding with a renewed vigour. This was highlighted by the partnership established with AL BAHATHRI who was narrowly defeated in the English 1,000 Guineas (1985) but gained compensation by winning the Irish 1,000 Guineas and would be rightly claimed as the best miler of her sex and generation if not for the presence of the brilliant and versatile OH SO SHARP in the same year.

Tony Murray is a strong resourceful rider equal to anyone in a finish and who combines the attributes of both a very good horseman and jockey, having a wealth of race-riding experience to call on at the highest level. He rode his first Classic winner in the English Oaks on GINEVRA in 1972 and his second on BRUNI who had a facile victory in the 1975 St Leger, and has had Irish Classic victories on DICKENS HILL (1979) and WASSL (1983) in the 2,000 Guineas, plus 1,000 Guineas success on CAIRN ROUGE (1980) and an Irish Derby victory on TYRNAVOS (1980).

Recently nothing has exemplified Tony Murray's dedication and will to win than his determined victory on KAYUDEE in the 1985 Cesarewitch where he nursed home this battle-scarred campaigner after spending the previous week diligently wasting, to ride at a featherweight for him of 8 st 1 lb. Such sacrifice was justly rewarded by a famous victory although he has since announced his retirement for the second time due to his problem of riding weight.

W. Newnes (*riding weight 8 st 0 lb*)   Billy Newnes is a young jockey who, after most ably seizing his chances and building such a successful partnership with that brilliant filly TIME CHARTER in winning the 1982 Epsom Oaks and Champion Stakes, had within a year received even greater public attention. However, this unfortunately was due to notoriety and resulted in 1984 in Billy Newnes being suspended for 3 years by the Jockey Club. This sentence was reduced later on appeal and the young rider, who throughout his ordeal had been totally supported by his former governor Henry Candy, was regranted a jockey's licence from the beginning of July 1986. It can only be hoped that this most public punishment with its accompanying stigma does not harm the future of a young man who was just climbing the first rung of what promised to be a most successful career in racing. The character he has shown since the ban, which immediately and drastically affected his livelihood, but which he refused to respond to or profit from in tempting and financially rewarding public interviews, should stand him in good stead as he sets about rebuilding his future.

J. Reid (*riding weight 8 st 4 lb*)   John Reid is one of the unsung heroes among the senior jockeys whose talents seem to be largely unnoticed and therefore unappreciated by the racing public at large. Irish-born John Reid is an experienced jockey who rode his first winner in 1973 and gained his first Classic race success in the 1982 1,000 Guineas, riding ON THE HOUSE. His first big race victories had come some years earlier when partnering ILE DE BOURBON to win the King George VI and Queen Elizabeth Stakes (1978) and then capturing the Coronation Cup of the following year on the same horse. Besides these successes John Reid has had group race victories on DOUBLE FORM, TATIBAH and KHAIRPOUR and more recently on those two fast sprinters PRIMO DOMIR and PRINCE SABO. However, even with these noticeable successes John Reid has been unable to capture the imagination of the general racing fan, perhaps because there are no histrionics in his riding style.

This is characterized by the manner in which he often seems to ghost into a challenging position before swiftly laying his seal on a race. He is therefore a rider with fine judgement, good at 'sitting off the pace'. A calm and collected jockey, he rides with a longer length of leather than some other jockeys but lacks nothing in a finish for this; rather, he gains an extra grip which keeps a horse better balanced. Such qualities mentioned illustrate both his jockeyship and horsemanship and make him an ideal booking to ride an inexperienced horse, especially a 2 y.o. who will respond to patient handling rather than a thorough rousting.

John Reid is a reliable, very professional rider who has yet to receive the regular support his abilities deserve and it can only be hoped that a new association with a top-class horse, or partnership with a leading stable, places him in the limelight, allowing to him opportunities to display his undoubted skills as a top class jockey.

P. Robinson (*riding weight 7 st 9 lb*)   Philip Robinson, son of a famous jockey (the late Peter Robinson) represents the new younger generation of riders who have emerged during the 1980s as successors to the old brigade, a number of whom have recently retired. Since riding his first winner in 1978 and becoming champion apprentice in 1979 and 1980, Philip Robinson has quite successfully made the awkward transition to being accepted as a senior jockey after a difficult initial stage at the end of his apprenticeship. Any loss of confidence he may have suffered during this time was quickly restored when he had his first English Classic success on PEBBLES in the 1984 1,000 Guineas, which was followed shortly by a sparkling victory on KATIES in the Irish equivalent race. These victories, beside completely restoring his morale also brought him into the public eye, elevating him to a status where he must be considered one of the most promising riders of his generation.

His style as a rider is neat and compact, undemonstrative in appearance, yet lacking nothing in effectiveness, particularly in a finish, where he keeps his horses well balanced as he rhythmically drives them to the winning-post. He is most adept at holding a horse up to come with a well-timed late challenge inside the final furlong, and which seldom fails to 'deliver the goods' providing the horse is good enough. Philip Robinson is an ambitious young jockey who has shown he has the capability when given the opportunity, as he clearly demonstrated on his group race victory in the early part of 1986 season on SUPREME LEADER.

Trainers and connections tend to choose the most experienced riders with a proven track record when it comes to engaging a jockey for the most prestigious races, and this continues to limit Philip Robinson's opportunities – as with many jockeys in the initial stages of their career. However, from his handy weight mark and with consideration of the sound record of successes he has already attained, Philip Robinson should be able to make the most of the chances which are bound to present themselves to a young jockey with his considerable ability.

B. Rouse (*riding weight 8 st 0 lb*)   Brian Rouse is one of the most senior jockeys riding, having ridden his first winner as an apprentice in 1956. For some time he drifted out of racing during the 1960s to return during the 1970s where his career has since been one of continuous progress. Although a late developer in terms of riding successes, Brian Rouse has shown, in common with many Flat race riders before him, that age is no bar but rather an asset, as maturity and experience can be most helpful tools in the execution of judgement in practising a jockey's craft. Epsom-based Brian had initially ridden for mainly local trainers, but as his reputation has grown he is often engaged by leading trainers when they seek experienced expertise, particularly in prestigious races where the occasion can become daunting for less experienced riders. Such instances have given Brian Rouse the chance to seize the opportunity to demonstrate his skills, none more so than when gaining his first Classic victory on QUICK AS LIGHTNING in the 1980 1,000 Guineas and the partnership he established with that brilliant mare STANERRA who won the International Japan Cup in autumn 1983.

Brian Rouse is a very cool determined jockey who has experienced the highs and the lows of racing, but whose skills have brought him through to the top, and he therefore holds no illusions about the horse-racing business. With this knowledge and approach he is an excellent jockey for a trainer to engage, able to give accurate and concise post-race verdicts as to a horse's performance, without the misguided optimism which surrounds some jockey's opinions. He rides well to instruction but has the experience to improvise should the situation demand and is not overawed or intimidated by situations on or off the race-track.

Brian Rouse is a thoroughly professional jockey, a brave rider, a good judge of pace, strong and resolute in a finish, with a cool commanding manner on or off a horse. He is a jockey who continues to improve with age and experience, who will make the most of the future favourable circumstances that are likely to befall him.

G. Starkey (*riding weight 8 st 5 lb*)   Greville Starkey, on the retirement of Lester Piggott and Joe Mercer, fills the position of being the most senior jockey among the leading riders still practising their craft. Having ridden his first winner in 1956 and becoming champion apprentice in 1958, like many Flatrace jockeys he did not really achieve the successes that his early career promised until reaching the maturity of his mid-thirties and claiming a famed and international success by winning the 1975 Prix de l'Arc de Triomphe on STAR APPEAL. This marked the beginning of a rise in Greville's fortunes that was to be followed by notable unique double victories on SHIRLEY HEIGHTS and FAIR SALINIA in the English and Irish Derbys and Oaks in 1978.

Newmarket-based Greville Starkey, following this, signed a retainer with Guy Harwood's ambitious Sussex stable in what has proved to be a most rewarding and successful association for both. A victory on TO-AGORI-MOU in the 1981 English 2,000 Guineas was their largest early British success, to be followed by victories for KALAGLOW in Sandown's Eclipse Stakes and Ascot's King George and Queen Elizabeth Stakes of 1982 which helped to bind the partnership. When other stars such as ROUSILLON, champion miler 1985, RECITATION, French 2,000 Guineas 1981, top-class sprinter INDIAN KING (1982) plus good class 2-year-olds ALPHABATIM (1983), BAKHAROF (1985), LEARFAN (1983) and KAFU (1982) are added to the list of achievements the successes have been most impressive. Add the jewel in the crown to these in the shape of an emphatic 1986 2,000 Guineas winner DANCING BRAVE and it can be seen what a formidable partnership has been established.

Greville Starkey is a strong resourceful jockey, powerful in a finish and renowned for a late pouncing challenge which can be quite devastating to rivals. The wealth of experience from which he can draw means he is a tactically astute jockey, quickly able to assess any situation that might arise and to respond accordingly, often seizing the initiative from less aware opponents. The memorable victories Greville Starkey has achieved, supported by the Pulborough racing machine, has given him a wonderful confidence characterized by his famous looking across or around at toiling rivals as he cruises past them in the final stages of a race. Having really come of age in his mature years and being such a shrewd judge of a horse's capabilities, he is a jockey any backer would rather have riding for them than in opposition. Although now entering the latter stages of his career, Greville Starkey is still a jockey likely to gain even more big race prizes.

B. Thomson (*riding weight 8 st*)   Brent Thomson is a New Zealand-born rider who after a visit a year earlier returned to these shores in 1985 to take up the retainer with Robert Sangster and Barry Hill's stable, left vacant when Steve Cauthen moved on to be first jockey at the Warren Place stable of Henry Cecil. After serving his apprenticeship in New Zealand where he rode his first winner in 1973, and was champion apprentice on two occasions, Brent Thomson then moved to Australia where in Melbourne he became champion jockey three times. Following in the footsteps of fellow antipodeans of an earlier generation such as Scobie Breasley, Ron Hutchinson, Bill Williamson and others, Brent Thomson tried his luck in the northern hemisphere and made a very successful transition to English racing. He has quickly adapted to this new environment with its constant need to travel almost daily from meeting to meeting and has become in a short time a popular and respected jockey on the racing circuit. In England his most famous victory has been in the Ascot Gold Cup in 1985 when he partnered GILDORAN to a gallant pillar-to-post victory and second consecutive win in the event.

Brent Thomson has a style of riding characteristic of what has become expected of jockeys from the Southern Continent, in that he is quiet, often seemingly effortless, and always in sympathetic rhythm with the horse. He is a good judge of pace, able to control a race by leading throughout and setting his own pace, or more frequently appearing to glide into a prominent position at the furlong marker to deliver his challenge in the final stages of a race.

In common with jockeys of international status Brent Thomson is a thoughtful intelligent rider able to accept instruction or be trusted to rely upon his own devices and to have post-race comments that are likely to be most instructive to any trainer who engages him. Now that he has established himself as a leading rider on the British racing scene it cannot be long before Brent Thomson supplements his victories in the top Australian races with equally prestigious victories in England and the European continent.

NATIONAL HUNT JOCKEYS

A list of top National Hunt jockeys has been compiled covering the leading riders of the 1985–86 season. Comments have been made as to their particular abilities, noting which jockeys have been champions yet refraining from categorizing them into degrees of excellence, but allowing their past record and current form to be sufficient testimony.

National Hunt racing is nothing if not a test of fate, and the jockey who is a hero and victor one day in one race can just as swiftly be cast in the role of an accident victim the following day or the next race. Fitness and durability are therefore two essential qualities needed by any National Hunt jockeys who hardly expect to sustain their riding career for as long as their Flat counterparts. In these circumstances it is hardly surprising that opportunities constantly present themselves to aspiring riders, and no jockey can rule absolutely supreme.

Peter Scudamore (*riding weight 10 st*)   The 1985–86 National Hunt season has seen Peter Scudamore strive to fill the gap left at the head of the National Hunt jockey's league on the retirement of the erstwhile champion, and possibly greatest post-war National Hunt rider, John Francome. Having shared the title while injured in the 1982–83 season due to the sporting gesture of Francome (who also stopped riding for the remainder of the season when he drew level with his rival), Peter Scudamore emerged from the shadows to win the crown for the first time outright in 1986. While rising to the top of his profession, Peter Scudamore has yet to form a partnership with a really great horse or one that captures the public's imagination. He did, however, in the cold spring of 1986 break his Cheltenham hoodoo and ride his first two winners at the festival meeting after some frustrating near misses in previous seasons.

Peter Scudamore's riding has a cool studied air about it and, coupled with his vigorous determination, makes him a most formidable opponent whether placing a horse at its fences or hurdles, or powering a horse from the final obstacle to the winning-post. His style has gained a polish and effectiveness as he has grown in maturity and his concise and accurate appraisal of a horse and its form must make him the ideal jockey that every trainer wishes to engage. This is an opinion obviously shared by eight-times champion trainer Fred Winter (himself an ex-champion jockey) who retained Peter Scudamore as first jockey for his powerful Lambourne stable for the 1986–87 National Hunt campaign. Such a partnership should provide Peter Scudamore with the continuous and consistent quality of rides which in the past he has not always enjoyed, and thereby enable him to maintain a most determined challenge for the National Hunt's most prestigious races and the champion jockey's crown.

Hywel Davies (*riding weight 10 st 4 lb*)   Having risen from the wreckage of a horrifying fall in the spring of 1984 when he almost died, Hywel Davies a year later gained the attention of a world-wide audience with his immaculate performance on that wily old character LAST SUSPECT when winning the 1985 Aintree Grand National. Although this victory brought instant public fame, the average racing fan was already well acquainted with the impressive talents of this young Welshman Hywel Davies as first jockey to Tim Forster's chaser-orientated stable. His abilities as a horseman were regularly brought to the fore without any loss to his skill or competitiveness as a jockey. A superb rider of chasers with the ability to get them jumping fast and accurately throughout a race, Hywel Davies is able to impart a determination and will to win which gets that extra response from a tired horse in the

Peter Scudamore

Hywel Davies

Steve Smith-Eccles

Richard Dunwoody

closing stages of a race, which makes him always a feared opponent. Hywel Davies is established as one of the leading National Hunt jockeys of the 1980s, guaranteed to give a horse a good ride whatever the circumstances and but one step away from reaching for the highest honour of champion jockey.

Steve Smith-Eccles (*riding weight 10 st 2 lb*)   Steve Smith-Eccles is now one of the senior riders on the National Hunt scene. Having risen gradually through the ranks during the 1970s he is rightfully regarded as one of the leading riders of the 1980s. His association with dual champion hurdle winner SEE YOU THEN has brought his name to the forefront for a wide racing public, and is evidence of how the quick seizing of opportunities, which sometimes fortunately arise, play such a large part in forging a National Hunt rider's career. Steve Smith-Eccles's forceful no-nonsense approach to race riding makes him a very formidable opponent where no quarter is asked or given. Experience and maturity have harnessed an eagerness which earlier often threatened to curtail his career before it was established. Yet Steve has lost nothing of his original enthusiasm, retaining the same cavalier approach traditional among National Hunt jockeys which unfortunately has been lost in most other sports. Steve Smith-Eccles has shown that such a spirit need not in any way undermine professionalism and demonstrates that the fun aspects can still be retained in what is a most challenging profession.

Richard Dunwoody (*riding weight 10 st*)   Richard Dunwoody is a young jockey who has quickly made his mark on the National Hunt scene, and from having ridden his first winner in only May 1983 his name received world-wide attention with his masterly 1986 Grand National victory on WEST TIP. In this short space of time the average racing fan has quickly witnessed this young man's continued and rapid rise to prominence until he now stands among the leaders in a most competitive sport. Richard Dunwoody's approach exudes a cool studied confidence far in excess of someone of his tender experience and years. He is arguably the most stylish National Hunt jockey riding, comparable to a great stylist such as David Mould from a decade earlier, yet this pleasing appearance lacks nothing in drive or effectiveness. Anyone who witnessed his Grand National victory on WEST TIP would have also seen what an equally superb horseman he was, placing his horse perfectly at its fences in a manner reminiscent of the retired champion John Francome whose shoes this heir apparent must some time surely fill.

Simon Sherwood (*riding weight 10 st 2 lb*)   Having won the amateur jockey's crown of the 1984–85 season, Simon Sherwood was forced by his proficiency either to join the professional riding ranks or to have his amateur mounts restricted to a limited number each season. At an older age than most aspiring professionals, Simon Sherwood elected to join the fee-paid corps and immediately established himself as a jockey of some repute in these most competitive circles. Bridging the gap between the two camps with remarkable ease, Simon Sherwood set off from the start of the 1985–86 season with a great flurry of winners, establishing a clear lead over his rivals until after the midwinter freeze-up and the abandonment of fixtures in February 1986.

He has shown himself to be a most stylish jockey, displaying great poise and dash, as proficient at riding over hurdles as he is over fences, and with his services being sought by many leading trainers. Such a successful transition to the professional ranks should have cemented this experienced Corinthian's confidence, giving him the know-how to remain one of the leading riders as long as he retains the enthusiasm for this tough unrelenting winter sport, where the professional is subject to many unglamorous hazards and where disaster may be only just one obstacle away.

Simon Sherwood

10 THE SELECTION FORMULA ANALYSED: SUNDRY POINTS TO NOTE REGARDING CONDITIONS

BLINKERS AND VISORS

Blinkers are stiffened eye screens attached to a cloth hood which restrict a horse's vision to looking forward. The overnight declaration of blinkers or visors is compulsory for Flat racing and National Hunt racing.

They are fitted to a horse for the purpose of inducing it to run faster. It is therefore of particular significance to establish when a horse wears them for the first time, as it is on this occasion that they are likely to have their most dynamic effect. When blinkers are fitted to a horse its field of vision is reduced, thereby forcing it to direct its attention forward and hopefully concentrate its efforts into running faster. Visors are modified blinkers, with a hole that allows side-on vision.

In practice fitting for the first time can have three effects:

1. They may encourage a horse to concentrate its energies and run faster.
2. They may discourage a horse so much that it does not want to race at all and therefore goes slower.
3. They may over-excite a horse to run too quickly in the early part of a race and so it exhausts itself before the finish.

The effect when fitted for the first time in a race is always problematic and the outcome can never be guaranteed. An indication of the outcome may be drawn from observing a horse's behaviour after they have been fitted and the manner in which it cantered to the start. The questions to consider are as follows:

1. Did the fitting appear to markedly affect the horse's attitude and behaviour?
2. Did they appear to over-excite the horse, causing it to break out in sweat and become disturbed?
3. Did the horse canter to the post in an uncontrolled manner, was it pulling too hard or was it reluctant to canter at all?

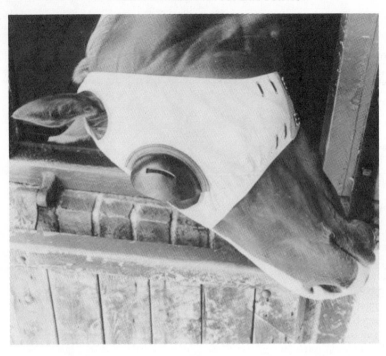

Visor A horse fitted with a visor – showing how, as opposed to blinkers, the eye screens on a visor have a hole in them which allows a horse some side-on vision.

Blinkers restrict a horse's area of vision. They are fitted with the desire to concentrate a horse's attention forward and thereby induce it to run faster.

Those are the negative aspects. However, if the horse appears galvanized by their application (i.e. gently on its 'toes', excited without undue nervousness) and canters to the start keenly, taking a firm hold of its bit, these are the indications that it is responding favourably and likely to improve its performance.

Of nearly 32,000 runners on the Flat in 1981, 3,306 wore blinkers. Of these only 6 per cent won their respective races compared with over 10 per cent for horses without blinkers. *Winning favourite* statistics of horses that wore blinkers is dismally only 22 per cent – a survey of horses winning who wore blinkers for the first time produced statistics that were even worse. The conclusion from this survey is to beware of all horses wearing blinkers or visors unless they have previously won when so equipped and wear them on a regular basis. Horses wearing them for the first time should be viewed with caution as an extra element has been introduced which cannot be calculated in advance.

BREEDING

Breeding is a factor to consider usually when some of the more fundamental elements in the selection process (such as form or fitness) need clarification or endorsement.

Breeding is an inexact science that often throws up quirks which seem to defy all reason, but usually it can give a fair indication of what will be a horse's best racing distance and sometimes what 'going' preferences it may have. It is information that can be used when considering previously unraced horses, and may at least eliminate the more unlikely candidates from consideration. Horses tend to pass on their particular strengths, weaknesses and preferences to their immediate offspring, and an acquaintance with the breeding record can be a helpful guide.

The successful outcome of matings can never be confidently predicted as numerous breeders have found to their cost, and the only comforting adage is 'Breed the best with the best and hope for the best'. Even if this mating does not produce the desired champion a consoling thought is that 'Blood will out' – meaning that bloodlines of proven quality often reproduce their influence in subsequent generations. Even the less successful representatives of a line, when mated themselves, often produce offspring better than themselves, thus continuing the quality of the line.

Horses who were absolute champions can seldom produce an immediate offspring as good or better than themselves. For example BRIGADIER GERARD (1968), a champion beaten only once during three seasons of racing has produced no horses to rival his achievements. In

TABLE 10.1   Characteristics of leading sires of Flat horses

Year of birth	Sire	Sire's sire	Average 2 y.o. wins in England/ Ire.	Best dist. for 3 y.o.	Sires winning distances minimum – maximum
75	Absalom	by Abwah	9	6–8f	5–7f
75	Ahonoora	by Lorenzaccio	10	8f	5–6f
74	Alleged★	by Hoist The Flag (USA)	4	10–12f	7–12f
72	Auction Ring	by Bold Bidder	12	7–8f	5–6f
71	Bay Express	by Polyfoto	7	5f	5–6f
74	Be My Guest (USA)	by Northern Dancer	8	8–10f	6–8f
66	Blakeney	by Hethersett	3	10f+	7–13f
74	Blushing Groom (Fr.)★	by Red God	7	8f+	5½–8f
64	Bold Lad (Ire.)	by Bold Ruler	6	5–8f	5–7f
63	Busted	by Crepello	2	10f+	10–12f
71	Bustino	by Busted	5	10f+	10–14½f
75	Camden Town	by Derring-Do	5	8f+	6–8f
68	Comedy Star (USA)	by Tom Fool	7	5–8f	6–8f
72	Dominion	by Derring-Do	13	8–12f	8f
75	Dom Racine (Fr.)★	by Kalamoun	3	8f	9–10f
75	Formidable	by Forli (Arg.)	9	7–10f	6–8f
73	Free State	by Hotfoot	5	8–12f	6–8f
76	General Assembly (USA)	by Secretariat (USA)	8	8–12f	5½–10f
74	Godswalk★	by Dancer's Image (USA)	15	6–7f	5–6f
72	Grundy★	by Great Nephew	—	10f+	6–12f
73	Gunner B★	by Royal Gunner	3	8f+	5–12f
66	Habitat	by Sir Gaylord	10	6–10f	8f
74	He Loves Me★	by Sovereign Path	5	Various	5–7⅓f
66	High Line	by High Hat	2	10f+	7–16f
69	High Top	by Derring-Do	5	8–12f	5–8f
69	Home Guard (USA)★	by Forli (Arg.)	6	7–8f	5–7f
75	Homing	by Habitat	6	10f	6–10f
76	Kris	by Sharpen Up	10	8f+	5–8f
72	Lochnager	by Dumbarnie	8	5–7f	5–6f
65	Lord Gayle (USA)	by Sir Gaylord	6	10–12f	7–10f
69	Lyphard (USA)★	by Northern Dancer	4	8–10f	7½–10½f

Year of birth	Sire	Sire's sire	Average 2 y.o. wins in England/ Ire.	Best dist. for 3 y.o.	Sires winning distances minimum – maximum
73	Malinowski (USA)★	by Sir Ivor	5	Various	6–8f
69	Martinmas	by Silly Season	6	6–8f	6–8f
76	Miami Springs	by Northfields	6	Various	6f
68	Mill Reef (USA)	by Never Bend	7	8f+	5–12f
72	Monsanto (Fr.)	by Breton	5	8f	8–10f
70	Mr Prospector (USA)★	by Raise A Native	6	7–10f	6–7f
68	Mummy's Pet	by Sing Sing	18	5–6f	5–6½f
73	Music Boy	by Jukebox	10	5–6f	5–6f
67	Nijinsky (Can.)★	by Northern Dancer	4	8f+	6–14½f
76	Niniski	by Nijinsky	6	12f	8–15½f
61	Northern Dancer★	by Nearctic	6	7–12f	6–10f
68	Northfields (USA)★	by Northern Dancer	7	7–12f	5½–9f
75	Persian Bold	by Bold Lad (Ire.)	14	8f+	6–7f
67	Prince Tenderfoot (USA)	by Blue Prince II	8	7–10f	5–6f
72	Raga Navarro (Ity.)	by Reform	10	12f+	5–8f
72	Record Token★	by Jukebox	7	Various	6–8f
73	Relkino	by Relko	3	8–12f	6–10½f
69	Riverman (USA)★	by Never Bend	4	8f	5–9.2f
69	Sallust	by Pall Mall	10	6–8f	5–8½f
69	Sharpen Up★	by Atan	—	5–8f	5–6f
75	Shirley Heights	by Mill Reef	6	10–12f	7–12f
70	Star Appeal	by Appiani II	4	8–12f	6–12f
76	Tap On Wood★	by Sallust	7	7–10f	5–8f
75	Thatching	by Thatch (USA)	9	6–8f	6–9f
74	The Minstrel (Can.)★	by Northern Dancer	9	7–12f	6–12f
75	Try My Best (USA)	by Northern Dancer	7	8f	5–7f
64	Tumble Wind (USA)	by Restless Wind	9	6–8f	5–10f
66	Welsh Pageant	by Tudor Melody	5	8f+	6–8½f
73	Wolverlife	by Wolver Hollow	6	7–8f	5–7f
76	Young Generation	by Balidar	9	6–8f	5–9f

★ Stands abroad.

contrast horses who may have competed yet failed at the very top echelons of racing, can often produce champions better than themselves. For example GREAT NEPHEW (1963) was just below the very best of his generation but has been responsible for two Derby winners, GRUNDY (1975) and SHERGAR (1981), who were champions of their generation.

It is important for breeders of mares seeking success to have them mated with tried and tested stallions whose breeding influence has been proven. It compares 'to drilling for oil where it is known to have already been found'.

TRAINERS

The skill of racehorse trainers may be most fairly judged by their record of success from the resources at their disposal. While it should not be difficult for almost anyone with 100 horses in their care to win 50 races in a season, it would be a remarkable achievement for a stable having only 25 horses to win 50 races. Almost all trainers begin their training career with limited means (some of the most famous established names had quite lowly beginnings) and it is from the adept handling of moderate horses that a reputation is gained. Then they graduate to training better horses in higher-class races.

Although a proven ability to produce winners consistently should firmly establish a trainer within the top ranks of the profession, to reach the highest echelons, particularly in Flat racing, it will also be necessary to attract the patronage of the wealthiest owners. Only the richest owners can afford the quality of horse any trainer must have to challenge for the Classic races and other top-class prizes. And to attract and maintain this patronage a trainer may also need to be successful in climbing a rung or two up the social ladder. Barriers of class may have been broken in other spheres of British society, but in horse-racing a person's background and class are still of fundamental consideration. A failure by a trainer to enter, or be favoured by, the most privileged or fashionable circles will mean having to settle for less wealthy patronage, with correspondingly less expensive, and usually moderate horses.

The first stage in training racehorses is obtaining the horses to train. This is usually achieved by a trainer buying horses at public auction or privately, although occasionally an owner with a horse will send it on to a trainer. This is the vital beginning of the training process, where judgement, luck and available finance are the elements that control a trainer's fortunes for the following years. The results of this initial venture will be judged in the light of forthcoming success or failure on the racecourse. Skilful or fortunate buying will mean horses performing well and withstanding the rigours of racing and training. Less successful purchases will mean a trainer struggling with moderate and often unsound horses that are difficult to train and not good enough to win a race.

Each season trainers replenish their stock of horses. Flat race trainers with a new intake of yearlings, from the autumn or late summer sales, who will make into 2 y.o. of the following season. National Hunt trainers take in new recruits (which are always older horses) at more varied times throughout the year. (Ex-Flat-race horses in the autumn; unraced or lightly raced National Hunt bred horses probably from the spring or summer sales.) At these sales a trainer either buys a horse personally or through a bloodstock agency, either because their advice has been sought or to hide the identity of the prospective buyer during the auction. Leaving aside the trainer's method of purchase, the sales they attend will be strictly governed by the size of the budget available, and the commissions in hand. This applies both to Flat and National Hunt racing, but most particularly to Flat racing where the auction price of the most prized lots at the premier sales in the United States, England and Ireland can reach vast proportions. A trainer with a small budget would not be able to reach a fraction of this value and would in most instances hardly bother to attend such sales. All trainers have to cut their coat according to their cloth!

Even the 'wealthiest' patronized trainers have only so much to spend, and although the most expensive and choicely bred lots may leave the sale ring supreme, the real test of horses and man eventually takes place on the race-track. This is the leveller that even the richest owners in the world have to submit to, as many have found to their cost. For example, SNAFFI DANCER, the most expensively priced yearling at auction in 1983 failed even to make an appearance on the race-track. On the other hand the humbly bred filly SOBA (1983) won the Group III King George Stakes at Goodwood, to keep hope alive for the less wealthy people connected with racing. Wealth, while influential in racing, certainly cannot guarantee success, or prevent exceptional training skills or ability from making their mark.

It can often be noticed by the racing fan who attends race meetings, or even those who watch on television, how many of the leading trainers have horses in their charge which seem to conform to a certain type in appearance. An established trainer is likely to take on the training of a racehorse basically because he likes the look of it. It may be due also to pedigree, which causes a trainer to favour a certain sire's stock, or to experience with other members from the same family (i.e. brothers and sisters) or because they had trained the dam, etc. These factors coupled with a trainer's preference sometimes for certain colouring in a horse (some like browns and bays, and distrust chestnuts or horses with any flashy markings) plus actual training methods (feeding, grooming and general preparation) and especially combined with the type of racing tack used (bridles, nosebands, etc.) contrive to mark out horses as almost from a particular mould. H. Cecil's horses invariably have a similar look about them, as do G. Harwood's, W. Hern's, I. Balding's, and M. Stoute's animals, while W. O'Gorman's sprinters (usually bought by his brother R. O'Gorman) also have a certain similar look.

Racing fans who acquaint themselves with the practices of the leading trainers at least, will often be in the favourable position to read and understand the form of their runners.

Training methods vary from trainer to trainer and are likely to be a reflection of the varying practices encountered by a trainer during an apprenticeship of gaining training experience.

The older trainers can be expected to be found practising the well-tried and tested methods of preparing racehorses (i.e. using only established food products and feeding habit patterns, having a prescribed amount of work and method of exercising horses in preparation and using only conventional methods of treating injuries). Newer and/or younger trainers may be more inclined to innovation and prepared to experiment in their training methods (i.e. new or different foodstuff, varying exercise in training with perhaps bouts of swimming for horses, seeking and being aware of other treatments to cure illnesses and heal injuries).

With so many possible ways of training a horse it is hardly surprising that there can be no strict uniformity of training methods. Individual methods can only be judged by the results they produce which will be subject to certain factors – but especially to the character and ability of the trainer himself (limited by the facilities and staff at his disposal and restricted by the type, quality and physical constitution of the horses in his care).

These considerations will be fundamental in establishing whether a horse will receive a careful, thorough off-course preparation to be brought to peak race fitness or whether it will only achieve its peak fitness by running in races. Some trainers are noted for having their horses always extremely well prepared before they are raced, ensuring that their horses are fully race fit for their seasonal racecourse reappearance or on their racing début.

Leading Flat race trainers

Henry Cecil, *Newmarket*. Born 11 January 1943, first licence 1969. His professed driving ambition each season is to be champion trainer and, while he has already outstripped his stepfather, Sir Cecil Boyd-Rochfort, he has some way to go before matching father-in-law Sir Noel Murless's tally of nine. This is an outstanding stable to follow with a ratio of winners to runners regularly better than one in three. At close to 40 per cent the record at Newbury is more impressive than higher ones at the less competitive tracks. Runners at the Berkshire course and winning débutants are perhaps the Warren Place specialities which should be for the shrewd backer.

Luca Cumani, *Newmarket*. Born 7 April 1949, first licence 1976. Took his first Classic with COMMANCHE RUN and has established himself as one of the country's leading trainers, getting a boost from the patronage of Sheikh Mohammed. The stable usually starts the season slowly but comes into its own in midsummer, with improving 3-year-olds taking more than their fair share of handicaps. Giving horses time to mature is a general policy, and 2-year-olds should be treated cautiously. An overall strike rate hovering around 20 per cent means that with just a little selectivity the stable can be successfully followed.

Michael Dickinson, *Manton, Wiltshire*. Born 3 February 1950, first licence 1986. Now established in the 2,300 acres which make up the Manton House Estate, Michael Dickinson has the credentials to become the English Vincent O'Brien. Like him, he has the total backing and trust of Robert Sangster and an impeccable past as a trainer of jumpers. During his winter campaigns a third of Michael's runners won when they went to post, and early indications are that frivolous or sporting entries are to be a rarity. With facilities for a maximum of 60 boxes Michael will be hard pressed to match his record score of 120 jumping winners achieved during the 1982–83 season. Quality not quantity will be the keynote for the most exciting recruit to Flat racing for many years.

John Dunlop, *Arundel, Sussex*. Born 10 July 1939, first licence 1966. No longer is such a patient policy played with the juveniles who are considerably sharper than they used to be. Still, John Dunlop is never one to rush a horse unduly, and if an inexperienced horse arrives in the top class the tip should be taken. With a lower strike rate than the other major stables, selectivity is required for a profitable return. Course statistics are worth attention: at more than 30 per cent York is impressive, and from smaller numbers Thirsk's record means you can almost back all runners blind.

Guy Harwood, *Pulborough, Sussex*. Born 10 June 1939, first licence 1966. Khalid Abdullah's speedy DANCING BRAVE gave this top stable its second Classic win in 1986 2,000 Guineas, following TO-AGORI-MOU's victory in the same race 5 years earlier. As Guy Harwood's overall percentage rises, the main problem for the backer is the bookmakers' habitual lack of generosity. Concentration is best kept to 3-year-olds who regularly pick up more than half the team's score, although late season juvenile Classic aspirants always play a part. Runners at Folkestone traditionally find the opposition easy prey; at a more competitive level those at Goodwood are worth close attention.

Dick Hern, *West Isley, Berks*. Born 20 January 1921, first licence 1957. Where Classic success is concerned only the acknowledged maestro

Vincent O'Brien has outstripped Dick Hern in the last decade. An Epsom double with BIREME and HENBIT in 1980 ranks as the highlight of his illustrious career to date. Hern frequently makes a slow start and winning representatives before July are the exception to the rule. A master of gallops preparation, the stable's first-time-out record with older horses is excellent. Hern's hunger for big race success has resulted in his record at most of the major courses being relatively good, but it is runners at Wolverhampton that are particularly significant with a 50 per cent strike rate.

Barry Hills, *Lambourn*. Born 2 April 1937, first licence 1969.
Many top-class horses have been handled by Barry Hills since his early training successes with HICKLETON, bought out of a seller back in 1968. The most famous was RHEINGOLD, the Prix de l'Arc de Triomphe winner in 1973. Despite that victory and the later successes of GILDORAN and SURE BLADE, Hills is most highly regarded for his training of fillies. His association with Robert Sangster and, more recently with numerous Arab owners, has certainly brought a cosmopolitan flavour to the Lambourn yard. However, the trainer's overall strike rate continues to average around 13 per cent, only rising significantly at the minor northern courses, making it a difficult stable to follow and one whose representatives are best judged on their individual merits.

Lester Piggott, *Newmarket*. Born 5 November 1935, first licence 1986.
Reluctantly decided to give up riding and turn his attention to training at the end of the 1985 season. He certainly has the right contacts, and judging by the way in which he has started his career, winning the Group III Coventry Stakes (1986) with CUTTING BLADE, his first runner at Royal Ascot, many more big race successes should come his way.

Michael Stoute, *Newmarket*. Born 22 October 1945, first licence 1972.
None can boast a pattern race record to compare with that of Michael Stoute in recent seasons. The quality of his large string is maintained by a continual influx of well-bred, often expensive juveniles as a result of powerful support from the Aga Khan and a number of wealthy Arab owners. It is to Stoute's credit that they are rarely given more than a couple of chances in group class. Consequently, his record in handicaps is also excellent, although success here is restricted almost entirely to 3-year-olds. While strike rates at the major courses are obviously impressive, it is at less fashionable tracks such as Redcar and Newcastle that representatives are of particular note.

Leading National Hunt trainers

Mrs M. Dickinson, *Harewood, Yorkshire*. Born 19 September 1924, first licence 1984.
Monica Dickinson took over the family licence after her son, Michael,

Leading Flat race trainers of the 1980s.

Henry Cecil

Luca Cumani

Michael Dickinson

John Dunlop

Guy Harwood

Dick Hern

Barry Hills

Michael Stoute

made his much-publicized switch to training on the Flat in 1984. The stable, however, maintains one of the best strike rates around and their team of chasers, which in the past has consisted of horses like GAY SPARTAN, SILVER BUCK, BREGAWN and BADSWORTH BOY, continues to be the envy of many. The hurdlers in the yard tend to attract slightly less attention, although the novices are usually cleverly placed around the smaller tracks to earn their keep. Southern raiders are worth keeping an eye on, although starting prices tend to be cramped.

M. H. (Peter) Easterby, *Great Habton, Malton, Yorkshire.* Born 3 August 1929, first licence 1950.

While Peter Easterby rose to stardom in the National Hunt arena as a result of victories by the likes of SEA PIGEON, NIGHT NURSE and LITTLE OWL, it is his less experienced campaigners that form the punter's closest ally. Peter's novice chasers regularly return annual strike rates in excess of 40 per cent and invariably a level stakes profit. Recent seasons have seen their success reach outstanding levels on selected northern tracks, Catterick and Wetherby being of particular interest. Southern raids also remain significant, especially visits to Ascot.

Jimmy FitzGerald, *Malton, Yorkshire.* Born 22 May 1935, first licence 1969.

Has proved himself to be one of the shrewdest big race trainers in the business, with his handling of 1985 Gold Cup winner FORGIVE'N FORGET and the same year's Hennessy hero GALWAY BLAZE bringing him to the focus of public attention. The chasers, with a one-in-four strike rate, have emerged as the mainstay of the string, although well-supported representatives over the smaller obstacles should not be overlooked. Numerically December has proved a good month for winners, although April and May often show better returns to a level stake following.

Tim Forster, *Wantage, Oxon.* Born 27 February 1934, first licence 1962.

One of the most consistent outfits in the game, the yard has built its foundation on the success of the chasers, and with Grand National victories for WELL TO DO, BEN NEVIS and LAST SUSPECT Forster boasts one of the finest records in the world's greatest steeplechase. The young hurdlers are in no way rushed and usually need an outing or two before showing their best. The middle months of the season are the best time of the year to follow the stable and, once it hits form, winners tend to come thick and fast.

Josh Gifford, *Findon, Sussex.* Born 3 August 1941, first licence 1970.

Former champion jockey, Josh Gifford became a household name after the fairytale victory of ALDANITI in the 1981 Grand National. The Findon horses, however, tend to be a little below top class and do better around the smaller tracks such as Fontwell and Huntingdon, although northern raiders at Wetherby should be kept an eye on. The trainer's strike rate is generally below 20 per cent which makes level stake

Leading National Hunt trainers of the 1980s.

Monica Dickinson

M. H. (Peter) Easterby

Jimmy Fitzgerald

Josh Gifford

Nicky Henderson

Jenny Pitman

Fulke Walwyn

Fred Winter

betting unprofitable. Stable runners are usually at their best in the first half of the season.

Nicky Henderson, *Lambourn*. Born 10 December 1950, first licence 1978.

A Cheltenham double in 1985's Champion and Triumph Hurdles, followed by a virtual repetition with victories in the Champion and Sun Alliance Hurdles of 1986 stamped Nicky Henderson as one of the best big race trainers in the game. Unfortunately his domination of the festival in recent seasons is in marked contrast to the yard's overall performance. Henderson's annual strike rate hovers around 15 per cent with Nottingham being his most successful course; yet returning only 20 per cent winners, the stable generally makes a substantial level stakes loss. Support then, should be restricted to representatives in better-class events with particular attention being paid to the hurdlers.

John Jenkins, *Epsom*. Born 10 October 1947, first licence 1979.

In placing his charges to win the maximum number of races rather than selecting lucrative prizes as their main objectives, John Jenkins has perfected what can only be regarded as an alternative approach to racehorse training. An intrinsic part of this strategy is the necessity for an intense early season campaign when competition is reduced and pickings, despite being poor, are easy. Strike rates during August and September are around 30 per cent and handsome level stakes profits during this period make Jenkins one of the punter's best friends. Newton Abbot is a particularly popular haunt and representatives in sellers remain worthy of the utmost respect.

Martin Pipe, *Wellington, Somerset*. Born 29 May 1945, first licence 1977.

A rise from relative obscurity to a position as one of jump racing's top three winner-producing trainers in 8 years, make Martin Pipe the most improved National Hunt handler in the last decade. Pipe's success has been based almost entirely on the performance of a useful string of hurdlers, with over 90 per cent of the yard's victories coming in this sphere. Martin Pipe has wisely ploughed much of his earnings back into the operation, resulting in a continual improvement in facilities which include equine swimming-pools, solariums and all-weather gallops. Hence, winners come all year round and at a gradually improving strike rate. Level stakes profits in many areas make him a trainer to follow.

Mrs J. Pitman, *Lambourn*. First licence 1975.

Another trainer who came to the public's attention with the handling of her steeplechasers. With horses such as BUECHE GIOROD, CORBIERE and BURROUGH HILL LAD, Jenny Pitman has picked up most of chasing's major prizes, including a Gold Cup and a Grand National. In recent seasons the string has become more balanced with the novice hurdlers, in particular, worth following after an initial run; stable charges in National Hunt Flat races also do well. November and December are traditionally fruitful months for the yard to be followed.

Fulke Walwyn, *Lambourn*. Born 8 November 1910, first licence 1939. Now in the autumn of his career Fulke Walwyn remains one of the outstanding personalities in National Hunt racing. The stable's big race successes over the years are too numerous to mention and recognition here is restricted to two races that are becoming Walwyn specialities – The Whitbread Gold Cup and the Stayers Hurdle at Cheltenham. Both events come at the back end of the season, a period which forms one of the yard's notorious purple patches. The secret of success seems to be to jump on the bandwagon at the beginning of just such a period – the Cheltenham Festival often marks an appropriate starting date.

Fred Winter, *Lambourn*. Born 20 September 1926, first licence 1963. Following a long career as a jump jockey, including a hat-trick of champion jockey titles in the mid-1950s, Fred Winter has enjoyed equal success in the training sphere. A stream of top-class animals have been through his hands including Champion Hurdle winners BULA and LANZAROTE, and the 1978 Gold Cup winner MIDNIGHT COURT. Winter's runners are dangerous in any company but especially so in the big handicap chases, and first-time-out runners are generally fit enough to do themselves justice. Stable runners at Chepstow, Towcester and Wincanton are worth noting.

The trainers portrayed above are a selection of those who besides producing a large number of winners each season have had and usually have many of the best horses that compete in the most prestigious races. The selector will gain a fully comprehensive understanding of the many trainers in British horse-racing by referring to the publication *Trainers Record* from which two annuals are produced – *Flat Race Edition* and *National Hunt Edition*.

TRAINERS' RECORDS

For a racehorse trainer, producing winners can be described as a two-fold process. Firstly consisting of the art of training a horse to attain physical and peak race fitness, and secondly involving the often under-estimated skill of successfully 'placing' a horse (deciding the when and where to run it) so that it may have more than a hopeful chance of winning.

A trainer's record is a testimony of the methods he employs and provides a further factor for consideration in the selection process. A trainer's record portrays how he races his horses, and it is useful to be acquainted with the training records of the leading trainers (Flat and National Hunt), establishing the following:

1. The racecourses where they are most successful (i.e. where they are the leading trainers or figure prominently as one of the leading trainers):

(a) Courses where a trainer has a high percentage of winners to runners. This may be where Newmarket horses are sent by their stables for rare but successful visits to minor courses – or vice versa – northern stables visiting southern courses.

NB This may apply particularly in National Hunt racing where the standard of racing throughout the country is more evenly balanced and some northern stables have a particularly high ratio of winners to runners at courses such as Ascot, Newbury, Kempton and Sandown.

(b) Conversely there are courses where trainers have a very high ratio of runners to winners – and no particular importance can be placed on their horses running there. For example, Newmarket-based horses racing at Newmarket; Lambourn-based horses racing at Newbury; northern (Malton)-based horses racing at York/ Doncaster (invariably 2-year-olds, inexperienced 3-year-olds, novice hurdlers, etc. are given introductory races at these meetings close to their base).

2. The times of the season a trainer has most winners. Trainers often have the major proportion of their winners at a certain time in the season – early, mid-season or late.

A disposition for a trainer to produce winners at certain times in the season may be by circumstance or design or by a combination of the two. For example, southern trainers based at Epsom and on the south coast have a reputation of producing winners in the early part of the Flat season, being favoured by the supposed more clement winter weather conditions. Yet certain northern trainers not blessed with the supposed milder weather conditions of their southern counterparts, have a reputation for similarly producing early season winners.

Design then appears to have an equal role with circumstance, a fact which is borne out by the number of trainers who are mid-season specialists focusing their training schedule to have their horses in top condition in mid-season (Flat – July and August; National Hunt – January, February and March) when the racing fixtures are heaviest and prizes on average more valuable.

Similarly, some trainers avoid the strong competition of mid-season and concentrate early or late in the campaign. For example National Hunt trainers with the more moderate horses are seen regularly to contest prizes at the lower grade courses at the seasons opening in August, September, October or at its close in April and May.

The leading trainers, however, usually manage to have winners constantly throughout the season, yet with particular months when their crop of winners reaches a height.

Circumstance and design merged when stables stricken by the virus (which has blighted a number of Flat race stables) were forced to readjust their training programmes and make the most of their opportunities whenever possible.

3. Meetings at which a trainer is consistently successful. Certain meetings hold a particular significance for some trainers. The most important of these are (Flat) Newmarket, Newbury meetings, Epsom's Derby and spring and bank holiday meetings, Royal Ascot, the Goodwood Festival, the York Festival in August. (National Hunt) the bank holiday meetings – Christmas, Easter, Whitsun, summer – Cheltenham Festival, Aintree meeting.

A trainer may have established a good winning record at these meetings, and having discovered the specific requirements for winning a race, is then often able to seasonally reproduce that success. The runners from such a stable at these meetings are therefore always especially well prepared and always give a good account of themselves, even if they fail to win.

The significance of these races to trainers may have arisen due to other than purely racing considerations. Owners who pay the bills may demand to see and be seen watching their horses run at certain meetings and the trainer is therefore forced to accede to their wishes (e.g. H. Cecil and M. V. O'Brien are trainers with horses particularly prepared for Royal Ascot and other major meetings).

The four bank holidays provide a feast of National Hunt races – and without a generally high standard of quality opponents in so many races, allows great opportunity for the well-placed, well-prepared horse. Some trainers who realize the value of having horses 'ready' at these meetings are rewarded with multiple winners on the day – three, four or even five winners. Trainers such as F. Winter, J. Gifford, S. Mellor, M. Dickinson, M. H. Easterby and M. Rimell have good records on these occasions. These may be one of the few occasions when their sporting working owners have the opportunity to watch their horses run and see them win.

Other meetings may be of significance in understanding a trainer's record, not because of the initial success that is obtained but because these meetings serve as preparation races for later successes. These meetings will be essentially before the trainer has his horses completely prepared, but serve as an indicator of the progress still to be made and act as introductory race for 2-year-olds (Flat) and novices (National Hunt).

All the horses of trainers which run at a meeting where he regularly has success should always be seriously considered and their form thoroughly examined. Similar consideration can be given to the runners of a trainer who has a particularly good record in a particular race; whether it is a top-class competitive race like the Derby – where M. V. O'Brien has an enviable record – or the Grand National – where T. Forster reigned supreme – or a particular handicap at a small meeting that one trainer wins regularly.

4. Significant travelling. The significance of a horse being sent a long distance to compete in a race should not be underestimated for there is little point in a trainer going to such time and effort if the horse has not got a winning chance. The strongest indications will be as follows:

(a) When the trainer sends only one horse to the meeting – engaging a top jockey who travels a similar distance for this one ride of the day.

(b) When it is unusual for a top trainer to have a horse or horses travelling such a journey to such a meeting.

When the trainer sends a team of horses it is unlikely they all have an equal chance of winning – one probably has a real chance and the rest may be there to fill up the horse-box. This is not always so, but is generally the case. Exceptions to this are leading trainers who send better-class horses to a lower-grade meeting, often with successful doubles or trebles the outcome of such ventures.

A trainer may also be just sending a horse a long way because the owner wishes to see it run there (i.e. the owner may be a steward at the meeting, live near the course or be on holiday close by). There can be many reasons why a horse is sent a long journey to race; it is a significant factor if it is solely a calculated decision by the trainer to give a horse a positive chance of winning; it assumes less importance if made for other reasons.

5. Jockey engagement. The engaging of a top jockey to ride a horse will be for two reasons:

1. If the horse has some hint of form that it can win the race, the jockey will be engaged for that purpose.

2. If the horse has no form and/or is inexperienced it is likely the jockey is being engaged to obtain a professional opinion of the horse's racing potential and to give it an education.

It is often a significant move when successful apprentices (Flat) and claimers (National Hunt) are engaged by a trainer especially in handicaps where the reduction of a few pounds of weight gives a horse a winning edge.

The engaging of a top jockey or otherwise cannot alone make a horse win, but coupled with other factors gleaned from a trainer's record and methods is a further indication which may assist in the assessment of a horse's chances. Reference to *Trainers Record* publications will provide this indispensable information.

The successful training of racehorses depends upon a large percentage of work and preparation and a final ingredient of inspiration or intuition, and it is this certain element which separates the great from the merely competent trainers.

OWNERS

To complement the manner and methods employed by trainers in the way they race their horses, it will be enlightening for the selector to have some knowledge and understanding of racehorse owners.

The owner of the horse as understood from the race-card is the person(s) or business officially registered with the Jockey Club as the owner(s). The owner will have bought or leased the horse and be responsible for training fees (that include the additional variables of veterinary bills, entry and jockey fees), but have the privilege of seeing their colours worn on the race-track.

The owner with such a considerable financial commitment can be seen as the cornerstone of the racing industry, creating and maintaining employment for trainers and their staff by providing the product (i.e. horses) that enable racing to function. Owners may come from any class in society and with the advent of horse syndication (up to 12 partners are allowed to hold shares) even from modest backgrounds, but the high cost required to own and train a horse ensures that principally owners come from the wealthiest echelons. The two different types of racing tend to produce two differing breeds of owners. Flat racing with its ever increasing outlay in new young bloodstock yet with equally its amazingly high potential reward for the most successful, attracts basically the richest and most class-conscious patrons. National Hunt racing, meanwhile, which is less prestigious, without unbounded reward for the most successful and with the prospect of disaster and injury ever looming tends to attract the more sporting enthusiast and die-hard type of owner.

This being a basic classification of the types of owner it will be useful for the selector seeking a greater comprehension of racing to become familiar with the names of leading owners and to recognize their involvement in racing and motives for ownership. Such comprehension will often give the final process of selection confirmation or further indication of a horse's chance.

Owners, whether they be seen as misguided philanthropists ever supporting the horse-racing and betting industry, mere exhibitionists with inflated egos seeking public limelight or perhaps a peculiar mixture of these two extremes, all live with the constant hope and dream of seeing their horse in the winner's enclosure. Having a winner to any owner is vindication of their decision to become owners, it is the reward for their months or maybe years of hope, disappointment and expense. It will serve as the proof to silence the doubters, the mocking critics and act as a rebuff to personal enemies. The racecourse then becomes the place where owners may flaunt their success, respectably exhibiting their possessions and power in the guise of expensive thoroughbred horseflesh. Ownership may become a means of obtaining fame, possibly fortune and self-advancement simply by association, deriving the benefits from the effort, struggle and skills of others (i.e. horse, trainer and jockey).

Ownership with its hands tightly affixed around the purse-strings of racing can be seen to hold the seat of considerable power and influence. In consideration of these observations it will assist the selector to become acquainted with the 'who's who' of racing (reference to the *Directory of the Turf* will be most informative) and acknowledge how trainers will often direct their efforts to produce winners on particular occasions for their most favoured or prestigious patrons, for instance:

1. An owner who is a racing steward will take particular pleasure from seeing his horse win at the meeting where he is an official.
2. A prospective royal winner(s) will often be indicated by the presence of members of the royal family at the racecourse when they have horses as runners.
3. An owner surrounded by a large party of friends and relatives, all especially invited to the racecourse, is usually expecting or hoping for an occasion to celebrate success.
4. A foreign owner in the country on a business or pleasure visit, will without doubt find their stay enhanced at the prospect of witnessing their horse(s) win. Such pleasing memories will in their absence from British racing serve to appease for some time any past or future lack of success that they may encounter.

These examples illustrate (while no owner has the power of guaranteed success) that when trainers focus their efforts on achieving particular aims, the selector who realizes these ambitions is in a most favourable position to recognize what may be the salient factors regarding selection in that instance.

11 THE PRACTICAL APPROACH TO MAKING A SELECTION

The approach to selection must always be in a controlled, reasoned manner, with sufficient time allowed for the unprejudiced examination of the relevant facts of form before coming to a selection decision.

SELECTION OF THE RACE

1. Decide which race(s) are suitable for selection. Those easiest to assess are likely to be non-handicaps and non-selling races with a recommended maximum of 12 runners.
2. Having chosen the race(s), check the starting time(s), and be sure to allow enough time for thorough, unhurried assessment and analysis. If there is insufficient time do not even begin assessment.

ASSESSMENT OF THE RACE

1. Consider the type of race – Flat or National Hunt – the ease or stiffness of the course and/or fences and what is required for winning, e.g. speed in sprints, stamina in long-distance races and jumping ability in National Hunt racing.

2. Read the conditions that apply to the race:
(a) The prize-money (the higher the value of prize-money, the better the class of race and often the more competitive).
(b) The distance.
(c) The entry conditions (maidens, novices, etc.).
(d) The weight conditions (sex allowances, weight-for-age allowances, etc.).

Note the 'going' – this must always be given particular attention. Due regard should be given to sudden extreme changes of going which can engineer reversals of form. Extremes of going often allow certain horses, who can only produce their best form under such conditions, to reign supreme.

3. Analyse the form of each runner. In practice form analysis consists of:

1. The systematic assessment of the form of each runner;
2. The elimination of the improbables and no-hopers;
3. The formation of a concluding short list of probables.

4. Final selection. If the form analysis should reveal only one probable, the final selection decision can be considered complete – awaiting only final verification from the modifying factors in the formula.

Should form analysis produce more than one probable, a selection is made by comparing the corresponding graded factors of each probable as revealed in the selection formula. The horse(s) with the lowest merit grade rating will be eliminated leaving the remaining probable as the selection choice.

The most desirable situation is for the selection choice to be a probable which has top merit rating in each section of the selection formula.

In practice this total positive confirmation of all factors occurs only on rare occasions.

NB. It does occur and the selector who is discriminating and disciplined enough to wait only for these pristine opportunities is likely to be rewarded with an almost 100 per cent success rate. The one failing of such selections is that the odds offered on them tend to be very short, and this makes betting uneconomic on these alone.

Therefore, it becomes necessary to balance skilfully all the factors in the formula to provide reliable selections.

USING THE SELECTION FORMULA

The selection formula must be realized as containing two parts, of different degrees of importance.

$$F - F : C : C$$

Form is the dominating first part – the *keynote* in importance. Proven form is the undeniable proof of what has or has not been achieved in performance.

Fitness/Class/Conditions are the modifying factors of the second part: they can only qualify the likelihood of reproducing proven form.

The selection formula is based upon the skilful analysis of form with the assessment of the value of that form the keynote to selection.

Each section of the formula should be separated, each element divided into its key factors which are graded in an order of merit.

FORM – THE KEYNOTE

Form can be divided into four categories:

Rating	Abbreviation		
★★★	P	Proven Form	This is of the highest value – it means a horse has proven form better than rivals. It 'holds them' on form.
★★	Prom	Promising Form	This is of the second highest value. It means a horse has form of value, but is not emphatically proven as the best (i.e. there may be no means of reliable comparison with other form).
★	Imp	Improving Form	This is of the third highest value. A horse has shown improved form (i.e. has beaten horses that it had previously been beaten by). The true merit of its form is difficult to assess positively, because once a horse improves, it is difficult to judge its further capacity for improvement.
—	Hti	Has to improve	This is worthy of noting, but not of a merit rating – there are indications of abilities that have still to be realized. It means a horse would have to improve to the maximum degree to have a winning chance.

Form is the keynote – its value cannot be stated too forcibly.

THE MODALITIES: FITNESS, CLASS, CONDITIONS

FITNESS

An element of the fitness factor always has to be taken on trust, but the best indication of a horse's race fitness is by a recent racecourse performance.

Fitness can therefore also be graded into four categories:

Rating	Days since last race	
★★★	Up to 14 days	The most assured indication of a horse being at peak fitness (a horse without further preparation can hold its peak fitness after a race for about 7 days).
★★	15–21 days	Similar to 14-day fitness – but of a slightly lower order in confirming fitness – a horse can be falling from its peak by this time – but it is appropriate for 2-year-olds to have this slightly longer period between races.
★	22–28 days	After 21 days' fitness, confirmed peak fitness is suspect – a horse is likely to be past its peak without careful preparation – it will depend on the trainer's methods. *NB*. It is often appropriate for top-class horses whose race engagements fit this pattern.
—	after 29+ days	After a month, or longer absence from racing, a horse's fitness has to be taken entirely on trust. The selector will need to be well acquainted with a trainer's methods to have confidence in the horse being race fit. A 29-day+ absence from racing indicates that a horse has met with a training setback (illness or injury) or has been 'let down' for a rest.

NB. Whatever the value of previous form, it is most unwise to consider a 2 y.o. for selection who has had an absence from racing of 42 days (6 weeks) or more because it is likely that due to illness or injury that the horse has suffered a reversal in its training programme. As the season progresses 2 y.o. form becomes subject to constant re-evaluation.

CLASS

This means a horse is competing against better, worse or the same quality of opposition.

Abbreviation
dr   Drop in class – is the most favourable indication. A horse has less to do.

—   In the same class – requires a horse to repeat its known performances.

up   Up in class – means a horse must improve upon its best performance to have a winning chance.

CONDITIONS

The final, and the important balancing factors which sometimes hold sway in forming a selection decision.

Distance. Change of distance can be of crucial consequence. Most horses are suited to a particular distance and are not so effective over a longer or shorter trip.

Proven/suited   *Unproven and/or untried*
D√   D?   If a horse is untried or unproven at a distance, the indications on whether it will be suited can only be estimated from its breeding and the manner it has been performing over shorter or longer distances (i.e. r.o. over shorter distances, weakening over longer distances).

NB. Experienced horses of proven ability will often more readily be successful when reverting to shorter distances than when attempting longer distances where their stamina rather than their speed will be put to the test. Recently MOORESTYLE (1981 – 7f) successfully reverted to sprint distances, ARDROSS (1981 – 2½m Gold Cup) won at 1m 5f and ARTAIUS (1977 – 1¼m Eclipse) won the 1m Sussex Stakes in the same year. COMMANCHE RUN (1984 St Leger – 1m 6f) the following season won races at 1m 2f.

Going. Can the horse act on the ground conditions? Horses have varying actions and conformations which make it possible for them to produce their best form only on specific ground conditions.

Proven   *Unproven*
G√   G?   Changed but similar going (i.e. good, good to firm, good to soft, soft) are likely to prove no measurable encumbrance to a horse. It is the extremes of going that produce the ground 'specialists' (heavy, very soft, fast). Breeding and conformation (action) are the indications to how a horse will adapt to the going.

Weight. The first consideration is *weight*. Weight is the leveller of ability. Weight allowance (lb) is positively favourable; weight concession (lb) is a disadvantage. The amount of weight allowed or conceded is the issue. It is always a matter of personal opinion to judge in each instance how much will be the deciding amount. Up to 5 lb in penalties is negligible; 7 lb+ must be given thoughtful consideration. Due regard must be given to 'going' – obviously weight is a greater burden in 'heavy' going.

Course. Will the horse act on the track, especially if of an extreme character?

Further factors that influence conditions

Jockeyship
Jockeyship essentially resolves to personal opinion. It can be stated that while there are only slight differences in competence and ability among the leading riders, there is a considerable difference in ability between the top-class jockey and the average jockey.

Draw
The draw is applicable only to Flat racing. Its significance is dependent on:
1. The race-track;
2. The distance of the race;
3. The size of the field.

Blinkers/Visors
These are mainly of importance in Flat racing. They become of particular interest when worn by a horse for the first time.

In the context of the formula, merit ratings for the form and fitness sections have been symbolized in degree by stars, a three-star rating representing the highest value and one star the lowest.

The other sections of the formula have been symbolized as positive, negative or passive value for class (by dr, up or —); and for conditions by indicating if there is a weight allowance, e.g. 4 lb pen.) and by a tick and question-mark system.

In symbols a six-star rating: ★★★ form + ★★★ fitness would be the top rating, the ideal and desired choice for selection.

As the ideal situation seldom presents itself, a reliable minimum standard must be established which adheres to the principles of the selection formula. *It is recommended that a four-star rating, where there are no negative or unproven factors influencing, become the minimum standard for selection.* Passive factors will only serve as neutral influences, while positive factors give endorsement to such a selection.

A four-star rating guarantees that a selection is based on reasonable proven elements of form and fitness. Less than four-star rating is below the standard necessary for reliable selection.

Final selection is made by the comparison of the merits of each probable drawn from form analysis. These merits are more easily identified and evaluated when clearly marked in visual symbols. An example is given below:

Meeting (course) **Going** **Time**

Type of race **Value** **Distance** **Number of runners**

Name of probable **Trainer** **Age** **Weight** **Jockey**
  (A)

F. **F.** **C.** **C.**
P (5) — 10 lb pen
★★★ ★★★

Name of probable **Trainer** **Age** **Weight** **Jockey**
  (B)
F. **F.** **C.** **C.**
Imp (14) up 10 lb pen
★ ★★

NB. (Have a maximum of only three probables. If form analysis has produced more than three, a selection must not be contemplated.)

The formula credentials of each probable can be quickly compared, the one(s) with the lowest merit rating eliminated, leaving the remaining probable as the selection choice.

In the above theoretical example probable (B) would automatically be eliminated with a rating below the minimum standard, and probable (A) which has a rating above minimum standard becomes the selection.

If the final probables have identical merit ratings they are too finely balanced to allow a selection decision to be made.

SUMMARY OF STAR RATINGS

Rating			Betting odds comment
6 star –	with all the modifying factors favourable	THE IDEAL RATING	Normally odds on
–	with a balance of positive and negative factors	MOST DESIRABLE RATING	Normally best odds – evens
5 star –	with all modifying factors positive	GOOD practical VALUE	Likely to be viable betting odds
–	with a balance of modifying factors	GOOD practical VALUE	Viable odds
4 star –	with all modifying factors positive	The MINIMUM requirement. (The most commonly encountered selection rating, lacks absolute quality, but skilful selection will be well served by selection of this merit rating)	Good economic betting

The less positive and proven factors a selection has to support it, the longer the odds should be against it winning.

For practical guidance it can be stated that a five-star selection which is not overburdened by negative condition factors is likely consistently to produce winning selections at economic odds.

12 PRACTICAL EXAMPLES OF THE SELECTION FORMULA AS APPLIED TO ACTUAL RACES

The key to successful selection is the correct interpretation of form. So often the evidence necessary to assess the value of form is non-existent, contradictory or incomplete. Therefore, however tightly structured the selection formula is, the analysis and assessment of form depends on the experience and judgement of each selector. This aspect allows selectors to bring their initiative, skill and understanding to bear while submitting the final decision to the completely objective elements of the selection formula.

The races included as examples were all analysed and a final decision made before the races were run and the *result known*. They are a sample taken from many types of race to demonstrate how the principles in the selection formula apply despite the constantly changing facets of horse-racing.

Analysis of the majority of races reveals that the most favourable factors stipulated in the selection formula and star rating system only infrequently exist. This means that the selector must discriminately wait for only the most advantageous selection opportunities or else warily lower the highest standards prescribed in the formula.

In response to these ever present practical realities, races filling both the above categories have been included as examples. Also races ranging from the premier in the calendar to more obscure races which may be seen to conform more reliably to the highest standard desired in the selection formula.

FLAT RACE SEASON 1986

Form Book No. 232 *BEVERLEY 12 April 1986 (soft)*

4.45—ERIC SMITH BREAKFAST STAKES. **£1,700 added**
(£1,555·20). 1m. 4f. (16)

1	(8)	40000-0	WELSH SPY (B) 19 J P Smith 5-9-8	I Johnson	64
2	(2)	800/000-	PORTER 168 E Carter 7-9-7	Wendy Carter (7)	—
4	(10)	002206-	COLONEL JAMES 340 Mrs S Oliver 4-9-6	R Cochrane	—
5	(11)	1	JACK'S LUCK 23 M Tompkins 5-9-6	M Rimmer	●78
7	(4)	002020/	WHAT WILL I WEAR (B) 542 J Glover 8-9-6	M Brennan	—
8	(3)	25406/0	WINNING STAR 22 A Bailey 5-9-6	P Bloomfield	—
9	(15)	0021/6	WISE CRACKER 22 (D) G Richards 5-9-5	J Carroll (7)	—
11	(9)	90	ARDOON PRINCE 17 K Stone 4-9-2	C Dwyer	—
12	(14)	32-	CASTIGLIONE 187 J Francome 4-9-2	S Keightley	76
13	(7)	32	CHRISTO (BF) 1 R Simpson 4-9-2	S Whitworth	77
14	(6)	0887-	FAR TO GO 296 M Chapman 4-9-2	G Carter (5)	—
15	(1)	600877/	GO LISSAVA (B) 1704 R E Peacock 8-9-2	J Lowe	—
16	(5)	05/000-0	HARBOUR BAZAAR (V) 23 M Chapman 6-9-2	J Williams	—
17	(16)	4444-0	MOUNT ARGUS 12 M McCourt 4-9-2	R Wernham	—
21	(12)	378/640-	ELECTRIFIED 226 J Leigh 5-8-13	J Reid	74
22	(13)		FILL ABUMPER R Hollinshead 4-8-13	S Perks	—

Probable S.P. : 7-4 Jack's Luck, 7-2 Colonel James, 9-2 Christo, 7 Castiglione, **8** Electrified, 12 Wise Cracker.

FAVOURITES : 1 — — 1 — 0 1.
1985 : Khaelan. 3-8-4 (J. Lowe). 4-9 fav. S. Norton. 12 ran.

4.45 —ERIC SMITH BREAKFAST STAKES 1½m (£1,555)

-32 CHRISTO(CAN) (4-9-2) ch c Halo — Slight Deception by Northern Dancer.
Ran second here yesterday (4.15). March 22, Doncaster, 1¾m 127yds mdn, good, £959: 1 Mr Quick (7-8-11, 3*, 5); 2 Artesium (4-9-0, 10); 3 CHRISTO (CAN) (4-9-0, S Whitworth, 4), **improved under pressure 5f out, hard ridden 2f out, ran on final furlong** (5 to 1 op 7 to 1 tchd 9 to 2). 17 ran. 1l, 3l, 2l, 3l, nk. 3m 21.88s (a 15.38s).

552205- COLONEL JAMES (4-9-6) br c Captain James — Faraday Girl by Frigid Aire. 1985, 1m good to soft (Navan). £1,104 (—).
Oct 5, Phoenix Park, 1m 1f h'cap, good to soft, £7,800: 1 Altos De Chavon (3-8-4 , 3*); 2 Dochas (4-8-13); 3 Acclamation (4-8-0 , 5*); 5 COLONEL JAMES (3-8-6 , S Craine), (14 to 1); 10 Ran. 1l, hd, 2½l, 3l, 3l. 1m 56.8s (a 5.8s). SR: 49/52/43/31/27/17.
Sept 14, Curragh, 1m h'cap (listed), good to soft, £12,571: 1 National Form (4-9-9); 2 Point Of Order (3-8-3, inc 1lb ow , bl); 3 More Votes (5-7-3, inc 3lb ow , 7*, bl); 10 COLONEL JAMES (3-8-11 , A J Nolan , 5*), (10 to 1); 24 Ran. Sht hd, ½l, nk, 2l, sht hd. 1m 44.8s (a 6.8s). SR: 31/10/-/7/4/19.
Aug 27, Tralee, 1m h'cap, , £2,760: 1 Acclamation (3-8-3 , 5*); 2 COLONEL JAMES (3-8-5 , C F Swan , 5*), (3 to 1 fav); 3 Whatyawant (3-8-11); 10 Ran. Nk, 6l, 4l, 3l. 8l. 2m 5.9s

-1 JACK'S LUCK (5-9-6) b g Lucky Wednesday — Miss Deed by David Jack. 1986, 1½m 50yds good to firm (Doncaster). £959 (£959).
March 20, Doncaster, 1½m 50yds mdn, good to firm, £959: 1 JACK'S LUCK (5-9-0 , M Rimmer , 3), **not clear run over 3f out, weaved through last**
2f, led under pressure near line (25 to 1 op 20 to 1); 2 Careen (5-9-0 , 17); 3 Coral Harbour (4-9-0 , 2); 9 ARDOON PRINCE (4-9-0 , C Dwyer , 4), **mid-division, no impression on leaders over 2f out** (25 to 1 op 20 to 1); 0 HARBOUR BAZAAR (6-9-0 , J Williams , bl, 22), (33 to 1); 30 Ran. ½l, 1l, 7l, hd, 3l. 2m 20.42s (a 11.92s). SR: 52/51/49/32/31/25.

194

Probables

(4) COLONEL JAMES – Mrs S. Oliver 4-9.6 R. Cochrane

F.	F.	C.	C.
Prom	(340)	dr	D?
	(8 days)		
★★	N. Hunt		G√
	★★★		4 lb pen

(5) JACK'S LUCK – M. Tompkins 5-9.6 M. Rimmer

F.	F.	C.	C.
Prom	(23)	—	D?
★★	★		G?
			4 lb pen

(13) CHRISTO – R. Simpson 4-9.2 S. Whitworth

F.	F.	C.	C.
Prom	(1)	—	D?
★★	★★★		G√

This is an example of an early season condition stakes race for older horses (4-year-olds +) who, before 23 March, had not won a race value £1,500. It was a basically level weights contest for horses of varying abilities where a previous winner was penalized by a weight penalty of 1 lb for each £200 first place prize-money they had earlier won.

With many horses of obvious proven non-ability in the race form analysis revealed three probables, COLONEL JAMES, JACK'S LUCK and CHRISTO.

JACK'S LUCK was a late maturing type who had not made his Flat race début until a 5 y.o., winning, first time out, a maiden race over 1¼m at Doncaster's opening meeting some 23 days earlier. Of the two other probables CHRISTO (who had been pursuing a novice hurdle campaign during the winter), had shown promise without being able to win in two prior Flat races, one, only the day previously in a 2m maiden event over the Pontefract course. COLONEL JAMES was an ex-Irish horse who had also pursued a winter National Hunt campaign in some very high-class novice hurdle events while previously having run in some good-class handicaps in Ireland during the summer.

Applying the selection formula JACK'S LUCK was eliminated due to not meeting the desired standard – and the choice was left between COLONEL JAMES and CHRISTO, both having the same star rating if it be accepted that COLONEL JAMES's race 8 days previously over hurdles at Aintree was proof of its fitness.

The difference then resolved to the conditions and class sections of the formula, with COLONEL JAMES definitely now experiencing a lowering in grade from the competition met in Irish racing, yet had the question mark over his stamina, having not raced on the Flat beyond 1m 1f (although racing over 2m in the National Hunt campaign) and also conceding 4 lb to CHRISTO. CHRISTO was racing in a similar class to its two previous Flat race ventures but now over a shorter distance. The unproven nature of the two horses over this distance seemed to nullify each other, leaving as balancing factors the lowering in class and the weight concession of a proven winner first time out the previous season, which favoured COLONEL JAMES, who was made the selection choice.

Result: 1st COLONEL JAMES (5–2) won by ¾ length.

Form Book No. 261 *NEWMARKET 16 April 1986 (good to soft)*

4.10—(Prefix 5) ABERNANT STAKES. £10,000
added (£7,609). 6f. (9)   STALLS

1	(5)	63520-6	CRAGSIDE (B) 7♥(C&D) G Lewis 4-9-12	P Waldron	69
2	(1)	8361-11	GREY DESIRE 16 (C&D D6) M Brittain 6-9-12	K Darley ●78
3	(9)	131213-	OROJOYA 178 (D3) J Hindley 4-9-12	M Hills	74
6	(6)	333592-	PRINCE REYMO 158 (D2) R Armstrong 6-9-12	W Carson	70
11	(2)	95455-3	QUE SYMPATICA 25 R Boss 4-9-6	M Miller	69
12	(3)	11/2-	HOMO SAPIEN 198 (D2) H Cecil 4-9-2	S Cauthen	74
13	(4)	142736-	POLYKRATIS 194 (D) M E Francis 4-9-2	Pat Eddery	71
14	(8)	200200-	ATOKA 182 Lord J FitzGerald 4-8-13	—	—
15	(7)	221-	BLUE EYED BOY 172 (D) M Stoute 3-8-2	B Rouse	63

Probable S.P. : 2 Grey Desire, 3 Orojoya, 9-2 Prince Reymo, 6 Homo Sapien, 10 Blue Eyed Boy, 14 Que Sympatica.
FAVOURITES : 1 3 0 2 3 0 1.
1985 : Grey Desire, 5-9-12 (Pat Eddery) 9-4 fav., M. Brittain. 9 ran.

4.10   Conditions 3-y-o and up 6f

0361-11 GREY DESIRE (6-9-12) gr h Habat — Noddy Time by Gratitude. 1982, 5f firm (Redcar), 5f good (Edinburgh), 5f good to firm (Beverley); 1984, 6f good (Thirsk), 6f good to firm (Thirsk), 7f good to firm (Newmarket); 1985, 6f good (Newmarket), 6f heavy (Kempton), 6f soft (Doncaster), 7f 40yds good (Haydock); 1986, 6f good (Doncaster), 6f soft (Kempton). £67,013 (£13,438).

March 31, Kempton, 6f soft, £4,604: 1 GREY DESIRE (6-9-10, K Darley, 7), **headway 2f out, led and quickened 1f out, soon clear, comfortably** (11 to 8 on op 11 to 10 on); 2 Amigo Loco (5-9-5, bl, 5); 3 Sharp Romance(USA) (4-9-10, 4); 15 Ran. 3l, nk, ½l, 2½l, nk, 2l, 4l. 1m 19s (a 7s). SR: 90/73/77/62/42/64.

March 22, Doncaster, 6f (listed), good, £8,834: 1 GREY DESIRE (6-9-10 , K Darley , 5), **strong run inside last 2f, quickened to lead near finish** (7 to 4 fav op 2 to 1); 2 Sharp Romance(USA) (4-9-7 , 4); 3 QUE SYMPATICA (4-9-4 , M Miller , 10), **ran on well over 2f out, not quicken well inside final furlong** (11 to 2 op 5 to 1 tchd 7 to 1); 13 Ran. 1½l, 3l, 1l, 1l, 2l, 1l, ¾l. 1m 18.27s (a 5.67s). SR: 80/71/64/58/48/27.

Nov 9, Doncaster, 6f soft, £5,435: 1 GREY DESIRE (5-9-7, K Darley, 5), **behind until headway under pressure two out, switched left entering final furlong, stayed on gamely to lead close home** (9 to 2 op 4 to 1 tchd 5 to 1); 2 PRINCE REYMO (5-9-4, S Cauthen, 7), **close up, led halfway, headed one furlong out, stayed on** (7 to 4 fav op 11 to 10 tchd 2 to 1); 3 John Patrick (4-9-4, 6); 14 Ran. ½l, 1l, 2l, 1l, 1l. 1m 18.54s (a 19.94s). SR: 90/85/81/76/62/65.

Sept 30, Goodwood. See HOMO SAPIEN.

11/2- HOMO SAPIEN (4-9-2) b c Lord Gayle — Bold Caress by Bold Lad(IRE). 1984, 6f firm (Nottingham), 6f good to firm (Leicester). £5,550 (—).

Sept 30, Goodwood, 7f listed, good to firm, £9,692: 1 Efisio (3-8-4 , 5); 2 HOMO SAPIEN (3-8-6, inc 2lb ow , S Cauthen , 5), **good headway three furlongs out, strong run over a furlong out, every chance inside last, ran on** (9 to 1 op 5 to 1 tchd 10 to 1); 3 Sarab (4-8-12 , 8); 8 GREY DESIRE (5-8-12 , P Robinson , 3), **never troubled leaders** (14 to 1 op 10 to 1); 11 Ran. ¾l, hd, 1l, ¾l, hd, nk, 3l, ¾l. 1m 27.63s (a 1.03s). SR: 75/75/82/74/71/77.

Probables

(2) GREY DESIRE – M. Brittain 6-9.12 K. Darley

F.	F.	C.	C.
Prom	(16)	—	D√
★★	★★		C√
			G√
			10 lb pen

(12) HOMO SAPIEN – H. Cecil 4-9.2 S. Cauthen

F.	F.	C.	C.
Proven	(198)	—	D√
★★★	—		C√
			G?

Trainer record for first time out winners.

This is an example of a conditions stakes race over 6f for 3-year-olds and older horses early in the season and is testimony to how well top-class form stands up to inspection even when there is a quite long time-lapse since it occurred. This prestigious spring race graded under the prefix of 'listed race' was for good-class sprinters, some of whom would be expected to graduate to group race competition as the season progressed. On analysis it resolved to two probables GREY DESIRE and HOMO SAPIEN.

GREY DESIRE was a popular hardy old campaigner who had shown it was already in great form by winning its two previous races already this season and was attempting to win the Abernant Stakes for the second consecutive time. HOMO SAPIEN in contrast was a very lightly raced horse having had only three previous races in the 2 years of its racing life. However, for such an inexperienced horse it had already shown its mettle, winning its only two contests as a 2 y.o. and finishing second in its only outing as a 3 y.o. In this latter encounter it had beaten GREY DESIRE by just over 2 lengths receiving 6 lb, and today was now in receipt of 10 lb.

Strictly applying the selection formula HOMO SAPIEN, without a prior race that season and therefore unproven in terms of fitness, should be immediately eliminated, but as the element of unproven fitness applied to two-thirds of the runners it was felt appropriate to waive this feature in the circumstances, especially as the trainer of HOMO SAPIEN has an enviable record of producing horses to win first time out (36.7 per cent of 4-year-olds 1981–85 won first time out).

Form then appeared to be the dominant issue, and with HOMO SAPIEN having already (first time out in its 3 y.o. campaign) defeated GREY DESIRE at less advantageous weight terms, there seemed no reason why this form should not be confirmed.

The balancing factors to consider in the conditions part of the formula were (i) the distance, which both horses had won over, and which was now perhaps GREY DESIRE's best distance; (ii) the going which also definitely suited GREY DESIRE, but was not extreme enough to be considered a disadvantage to HOMO SAPIEN, who had previously raced on faster ground; (iii) the course, which GREY DESIRE was proven over, yet which was the home base of HOMO SAPIEN, although still to run a race over this Newmarket track. GREY DESIRE was set to concede 10 lb to HOMO SAPIEN. With **form** being the prevalent issue, which always has to be considered most carefully, HOMO SAPIEN was made the selection choice.

Result: 1st HOMO SAPIEN (7–1) won by ½ length

Form Book No. 370 *SANDOWN 26 April 1986 (soft)*

3.40 **(Prefix 4)—WESTBURY EBF STAKES £30,000**
added 1m. 2f (9)

1	(3)	4853L-1 SUPREME LEADER 10 (C) C Brittain 4-8-12 ...P Robinson ●78
2	(6)	85112-4 ENGLISH SPRING 10 I Balding 4-8-9 ....S Cauthen 75
3	(7)	2211-6 BIG REEF 10 J Dunlop 4-8-8 ....W Carson 65
4	(2)	34023-5 CHAUMIERE (V) 7 (D3) R J Williams 5-8-8 ......R Cochrane 56
5	(5)	226111- IROKO 225 (C & D D3) M Stoute 4-8-8 ....W Swinburn 66
6	(8)	L090-15 K-BATTERY 10 (D4) W C Elsey 4-8-8 ....——— 66
7	(4)	032273- SEVERN BORE 247 F Durr 4-8-8 ....G Starkey 63
8	(1)	22D-011 RAMICH JOHN 21 (D2) L Browne (Ireland) 4-8-5 .....——— 67
9	(9)	144/36L- THALESTRIA 290 C Austin 4-8-5 ....M Roberts 40

Probable S.P.: 4-5 Supreme Leader, 5 Iroko, 6 English Spring, 8 Ramich John,
12 Big Reef. **FAVOURITES : 1 2 1 3 1 0 0.**
1985 : Elegant Air 4-8-8 (J. Matthias), 8-1 I. Balding. 12 ran.

3.40 Conditions (Gr. 3) 1¼m £21,600

40530-1 SUPREME LEADER (4-8-12) b c Bustino — Princess Zena by Habitat. 1985, 1m good (Sandown); 1986, 1m 1f good to soft (Newmarket). £25,653 (£22,794).

April 16, Newmarket, 1m 1f good to soft, £22,794: (Group 3) 1 SUPREME LEADER (4-8-10, P Robinson, 2), **not clear run from over 3f out, switched right 2f out, led inside final furlong, pushed clear** (7 to 2 op 5 to 2 tchd 4 to 1); 2 Field Hand (4-8-10, 5); 3 Damister(USA) (4-9-1, 7); **4 ENGLISH SPRING**(USA) (4-8-10, S Cauthen, 1), **effort from rear 3f out, no impression on leaders final 2f** (8 to 1 op 5 to 1 tchd 9 to 1); 5 K-BATTERY (5-8-10, T Ives, 4), **well in touch, no progress 2f out** (16 to 1 op 14 to 1 tchd 20 to 1); 6 **BIG REEF** (4-8-10, G Duffield, 10), **changed positions from over 3f out, ridden and weakened 2f out** (20 to 1); 10 Ran. 3l, 6l, ¾l, hd, nk. 1m 59.02s (a 6.22s). SR: 66/60/53/46/45/44.

Oct 19, Newmarket, 1½m good to firm, £87,200: (Group 1) 1 Pebbles (4-9-0 , 8); 2 Slip Anchor (3-8-10 , 4); 3

Palace Music(USA) (4-9-3 , 3); 10 SUPREME LEADER (3-8-10 , P Robinson , 1), **close up for seven furlongs, soon beaten** (66 to 1 op 50 to 1); 10 Ran. 3l, hd, 1½l, 5l, 1¼l. 2m 4.79s (b 1.21s). SR: 102/92/98/85/78/72.

Sept 6, Kempton, 1m 3f 30yds good, £17,300: (Group 3) 1 Shernazar (4-9-2 , 4); 2 Slip Anchor (3-8-11 , 3); 3 SUPREME LEADER (3-8-4 , P Robinson , 1), **never reached leaders** (11 to 1 op 8 to 1 tchd 12 to 1); 5 Ran. ¾l, 15l, 6l, 12l. 2m 16.20s (b 3.90s). SR: 103/97/60/62/31/-.

Probable

(1) SUPREME LEADER – C. Brittain 4-8.12 P. Robinson

F.	F.	C.	C.	
Proven	(10)	—	D	
★★★	★★★		C	
			G	
			4 lb pen	

This is an example of a conditions race for 4-year-olds and upwards over a distance of 1m 2f and staged early in the flat race season. The Westbury Stakes is a Group III race for the older generation of middle-distance performers, who after an encouraging performance here will be hoping to progress to even grander pattern race prizes as the season unfolds.

This example serves to show how proven superior form of good-class horses is almost guaranteed to be upheld.

Analysis revealed only one probable, SUPREME LEADER, a horse who had promised much in its 3 y.o. career, finishing fourth in the English Derby, and third in the 2,000 Guineas, but who had only just begun fulfilling its obvious potential by winning the Earl of Sefton Stakes (Group III) on its seasonal début as a 4 y.o. 10 days earlier at Newmarket. It had already comprehensively beaten three opponents in today's race in this prior encounter, while of the five remaining rivals, all were experiencing a rise in class and three were making their seasonal début. The value of the Newmarket form had been healthily endorsed by the second FIELD HAND's commanding victory in the Group III Trusthouse Forte 1m race the previous day.

Applying the formula, where the rating was of the highest grade, SUPREME LEADER was made the selection choice.

Result: 1st SUPREME LEADER (1–2 fav.) won by a neck.

Form Book No. 413 *ASCOT 30 April 1986 (good to soft)*

3.40—(Prefix 4) WHITE ROSE STAKES (3-Y.-O.).
£10,000 added (£8,402). 1m. 2f. (6) STALLS

2	(2)	3211L-3 SIT THIS ONE OUT 21 D Laing 9-7	W Carson	63
4	(3)	2211-3 MASHKOUR 13 H Cecil 9-0	...S Cauthen	●78
5	(6)	143-1 NISNAS 19 P Cole 9-0	T Quinn	69
9	(1)	22- DANISHGAR 207 M Stoute 8-9	W R Swinburn	52
12	(5)	5254-6 MIRAGE DANCER 32 R Smyth 8-9	P Robinson	54
13	(4)	23- SHIP OF STATE 253 I Balding 8-9	Pat Eddery	52

Probable S.P. : 5-4 Mashkour, 2 Danishgar, 6 Nisnas, 12 Ship Of State, 16 Sit This One Out, 25 Mirage Dancer. **FAVOURITES : 1 0 1 1 — 0 2.**

3.40 Conditions 3-y-o 1¼m (£8,402)

2211-3 MASHKOUR(USA) (9-0) ch c Irish River(FR) — Sancta Rose by Karabas. 1985, 1m good to firm (Goodwood), 7f good (Yarmouth). £5,409 (—).

April 17, Newmarket, 1m (3-y-o), soft, £15,400: (Group 3) 1 Dancing Brave(USA) (8-7, 6); 2 Faraway Dancer(USA) (8-7, 11); 3 MASHKOUR-(USA) (8-7, W Ryan, 9), **good headway over 3f out, every chance from 2f out, not quicken inside final furlong** (14 to 1 op 12 to 1 tchd 16 to 1); 11 Ran. 1l, ¾l, 6l, 2l, 6l. 1m 49.96s (a 11.06s). SR: 18/15/13/-/-/-.

Sept 14, Goodwood, 1m (2-y-o), good to firm, £4,467: 1 MASHKOUR-(USA) (8-11, Paul Eddery , 2), **always in touch, led two our, ridden out** (8 to 11 op 4 to 7 tchd 4 to 5); 2 Sirk (8-11 , 6); 3 Emerald Point (8-11 , 7); 7 Ran. 2½l, 3l, 1l, sht hd, 10l. 1m 44.11s (a 5.11s). SR: 38/30/21/18/17/-.

Aug 22, Yarmouth, 7f (2-y-o) mdn, good, £941: 1 MASHKOUR(USA) (9-0 , Paul Eddery , 1), **in touch, led two furlongs out, well clear final furlong** (11 to 10 fav op 4 to 5 tchd 4 to 7); 2 Misaaff (9-0 , 2); 3 Shibil (8-9 , 5*, 8); 13 Ran. 10l, ¾l, hd, sht hd, 1½l. 1m 28.4s (a 3.4s). SR: 70/40/38/37/36/34.

23- SHIP OF STATE (8-9) b c Troy — Sea Venture by Diatome.

Aug 20, York, 7f (2-y-o) listed, good to soft, £8,363: 1 Native Wizard(USA) (8-11 , 2); 2 Huntingdale (8-11 , 8); 3 SHIP OF STATE (8-11 , Pat Eddery , 7), **chased leaders, hard ridden to challenge two furlongs out, beaten when eased closing stages** (11 to 8 fav tchd 9 to 4); 8 Ran. ¾l, 1¼l, 1l, 12l, ¾l. 1m 29.09s (a 5.39s). SR: 59/57/52/56/10/8.

July 20, Newbury, 7f (2-y-o), good, £5,344: 1 Water Cay(USA) (9-2 , 6); 2 SHIP OF STATE (8-7 , Pat Eddery , 1), **headway 3f out, chased winner final 2f, not quicken** (4 to 1 op 2 to 1); 3 Mashhur (8-11 , 3); 6 Ran. 6l, 3l, 1½, 4l, 2½l. 1m 30.58s (a 4.98s). SR: 69/42/37/35/16/12.

143-1 NISNAS (9-0) ch c Tap On Wood — Suemette by Danseur. 1985, 7f good to firm (Salisbury); 1986, 1m good to soft (Kempton). £5,168 (£3,908).

April 11, Kempton, 1m (3-y-o), good to soft, £3,908: 1 NISNAS (8-9, T Quinn, 5), **always chasing leaders, effort to lead inside final 2f, ran on well** (7 to 1 op 9 to 2 tchd 8 to 1); 2 Esdale(FR) (8-9, 1); 3 Badarbak (8-9, 3); 5 Ran. ¾l, 12l, 5l, 3l. 1m 44.56s (a 6.86s). SR: 64/62/26/16/2/-.

Nov 1, Newmarket, 1m (2-y-o), firm, £3,844: 1 Dancing Brave(USA) (9-2, 9); 2 Northern Amethyst (8-9, 11); 3 NISNAS (8-12, T Quinn, 8), **always with leaders, every chance two out, no extra final furlong** (5 to 1 op 3 to 1); 11 Ran. 2½l, ¾l, 1l, 1l, 4l. 1m 40.15s (a 1.25s). SR: 42/27/28/23/17/5.

Oct 4, Newmarket, 7f (2-y-o), good, £10,971: 1 Truely Nureyev(USA) (8-8 , 11); 2 Huntingdale (8-8 , 5); 3 Badarbak (8-11 , 10); 4 NISNAS (8-11 , T Quinn , 1), **leading group , every chance two out, not quicken approaching final furlong** (8 to 1 op 5 to 1); 11 Ran. 1l, 2l, 1¼l, hd, sht hd, sht hd. 1m 25.93s (b 0.17s). SR: 71/68/65/60/64/63.

Probables

(4) MASHKOUR – H. Cecil 9.0 S. Cauthen

F.	F.	C.	C.
Proven	(13)	dr	D?
★★★	★★★		G√

(5) NISNAS – P. Cole 9.0 T. Quinn

F.	F.	C.	C.
Prom	(19)	up	D?
★★	★★		G√

(13) SHIP OF STATE – I. Balding 8.9 Pat Eddery

F.	F.	C.	C.
Prom	(253) —	D?	
★★	—	G√	

5 lb allowance + for maiden

This is an example of 3 y.o. conditions stakes over 1¼m, with this particular race, the White Rose Stakes (formerly a Group III race in the pattern race system) often serving as a useful Classic race trial to sort out the real contenders from the mere pretenders.

In a compact field of six runners, analysis revealed three probables, MASHKOUR, NISNAS and SHIP OF STATE.

MASHKOUR had already made its seasonal reappearance in another Classic race trial in the Group III Craven Stakes and finished third, while NISNAS had won a conditions stakes race at Kempton on its seasonal reappearance. SHIP OF STATE in contrast was making its seasonal début here, but having run such a good race in finishing close behind HUNTINGDALE (one of the leading 2-year-olds of 1985) in its second and final race of its first season had to be considered a serious candidate if reproducing that sort of form.

Form comparison between NISNAS and SHIP OF STATE as 2-year-olds through HUNTINGDALE made these two horses of almost equal ability, while a collateral form line between MASHKOUR and NISNAS through the erstwhile favourite for the English 2,000 Guineas DANCING BRAVE (MASHKOUR beaten 1 length at level weights by DANCING BRAVE – NISNAS beaten 3¼ lengths receiving 4 lb by DANCING BRAVE) made MASHKOUR the superior.

Applying the selection formula NISNAS and SHIP OF STATE were eliminated leaving MASHKOUR, with a top rating, the selection choice.

Result: 1st MASHKOUR (9–4) won by 8 lengths.

Form Book No. 445 *NEWMARKET 3 May 1986 (Good)*

3.0 (Prefix 3) — **GENERAL ACCIDENT 2000 GUINEAS** (3-Y.-O.). £75,000 added (£107,145). 1m. (15) £75,000 STALLS

1 (14) 211- **ALSHINFARAH** 246 Thomson Jones 9-0 ....A Murray 40
bc Great Nephew—Scintillate. *(Royal blue, white epaulets, stripped cap)*

2 (3) 11-1 **DANCING BRAVE** 16 (C & D 2) G Harwood 9-0 G Starkey ●78
bc Lyphard—Navajo Princess. *(Green, pink sash and cap, white sleeves)*

3 (13) 327-13 **EXOTIC RIVER** 27 P Biancone (France) 9-0 ....G Mosse 65
ch c Irish River—Exotic Age. *(Light blue and red stripes)*

4 (8) 57-5L **FARNCOMBE** 24 C Brittain 9-0 ....P Robinson 48
bc Moorestyle—Thalassa. *(Black & white, halved horizontally, check cap, yellow sleeves)*

5 (11) 11112-1 **FAUSTUS** 14 H Cecil 9-0 ....S Cauthen 70
bc Robellino—B F's Sailingal. *(Dark blue, light blue cross-belts, striped sleeves, white cap)*

6 (9) 21214-1 **GREEN DESERT** 17 (C) M Stoute 9-0 .... W R Swinburn 74
bc Danzig—Foreign Courier. *(Royal blue, white chevon, light blue cap)*

7 (7) 12 **HAIL TO ROBERTO** 13 (D) G Mikhalides (France) 9-0
C Asmussen 62
chc Roberto—Singing Rain. *(Green, red armlets and cap)*

8 (15) 11111-3 **HALLGATE** 14 Miss S Hall 9-0 ....K Hodgson 70
bc Vaigly Great—Beloved Mistress. *(ark blue and white diamonds, dark blue sleeves, white cap)*

9 (12) 221- **HUNTINGDALE** 197 (C) J Hindley 9-0 .... M Hills 77
ch c Double Form—Abbeydale. *(Flame, gold striped sleeves, hooped cap)*

10 (4) 4-114 **JAZETAS** 16 (D2) N Callaghan 9-0 ....R Cochrane 63
ch c Jaazeiro—Pesetas. *(Light grey, dark green sleeves, lilac sash and cap)*

13 (1) 01111-8 **SHARROOD** 16 W Hern 9-0 ....W Carson 62
ro c Caro—Angel Island. *(Maroon, white sleeves, maroon cap, white star)*

15 (6) 1113-1 **SURE BLADE** 14 (CD) B Hills 9-0 ....B Thomson 75
bc Kris—Double Lock. *(Maroon, white sleeves, maroon cap, white star)*

16 (10) 011-3 **TATE GALLERY** 21 (BF) V O'Brien (Ireland) 9-0 ..T Ives 65
bc Northern Dancer—Fairy Bridge. *(Dark blue, light blue cross-belts, striped sleeves, white cap)*

17 (5) 11-1 **TOCA MADERA** 14 L Browne (Ireland) 9-0 ....S Craine 70
bc Taufan—Genesis. *(Red, pink diamonds and sleeves, white cap)*

18 (2) 31102-6 **VAINGLORIOUS** 14 H Candy 9-0 ....R Curant 57
bc Vaigly Great—Princess Blanco. *(Dark blue, brown 'V' yellow sleeves and cap)*

Probable S.P.: 7-4 Dancing Brave. 6 Sure Blade, 9 Huntingdale, 10 Toca Madera, Tate Gallery. 12 Green Desert, 16 Faustus, Sharrood, 25 Hallgate.
1985 : Shadeed 9-0 (L Piggott) 4-5 fav. M Stoute. 14 ran. **FAVOURITES:** 0 0 1 3 01 1

3.00 2,000 Guineas (Group 1) (3-y-o) 1m (£107,145)

11-1 DANCING BRAVE(USA) (9-0) b c Lyphard(USA) — Navajo Princess by Drone. 1985, 1m firm (Newmarket), 1m good to firm (Sandown); 1986, 1m soft (Newmarket). £22,167 (£15,400).

April 17, Newmarket, 1m (3-y-o), soft, £15,400: (Group 3) 1 DANCING BRAVE(USA) (8-7, G Starkey, 6), **well placed, led over 1f out, not extended** (11 to 8 fav op 5 to 4 tchd 6 to 4): 2 Faraway Dancer(USA) (8-7, 11); 3 Mashkour(USA) (8-7, 9); 4 JAZETAS (8-7, Pat Eddery, 3), **headway over 2f out, ridden and no extra over 1f out** (25 to 1 op 20 to 1); 8 SHARROOD-(USA) (8-7, W Carson, 10), **well placed until hampered and lost place over 2f out** (11 to 2 op 5 to 1 tchd 6 to 1); 11 Ran. 1l, ¾l, 6l, 2l, 6l. 1m 49.96s (a 11.06s). SR: 18/15/13/-/-/-.

Nov 1, Newmarket, 1m (2-y-o), firm, £3,844: 1 DANCING BRAVE(USA) (9-2, G Starkey, 9), **always going well, led two out, pushed clear final furlong** (4 to 9 op 8 to 11); 2 Northern Amethyst (8-9, 11); 3 Nisnas (8-12, 8); 4 JAZETAS (8-9, R Cochrane, 3), **ran on from two out, no chance with winner** (33 to 1); 11 Ran. 2½l, ¾l, ¼l, 1l, 4l. 1m 40.15s (a 1.25s). SR: 42/27/28/23/17/5.

Oct 14, Sandown, 1m (2-y-o), good to firm, £2,922: 1 DANCING BRAVE(USA) (8-7, G Starkey, 1), **dwelt, smooth progress to lead one out, very easily** (6 to 4 on op evens); 2 Mighty Memory(USA) (9-2, 4); 3 Hubbards Lodge (8-11, bl, 3); 4 Ran. 3l, 5l, 2l. 1m 42.88s (a 1.48s). SR: 59/59/39/38/-/-.

011-3 TATE GALLERY(USA) (9-0) b c Northern Dancer — Fairy Bridge by Bold Reason. 1985, 7f good to soft (Curragh), 7f soft (Curragh). £67,375 (---).

April 12, Curragh, 7f listed, yielding, £3,906: 1 Lidhame (4-9-11); 2 Air Display(USA) (3-8-6); 3 TATE GALLERY(USA) (3-8-12, Pat Eddery), (7 to 2 on); 6 Ran. ¾l, 2l, ¾l, 2l, 1½l. 1m 30.1s (a 5.4s). SR: 82/61/61/69/66/55.

Sept 14, Curragh, 7f (2-y-o), good to soft, £65,650: (Group 1) 1 TATE GALLERY(USA) (9-0 , C Asmussen), (4 to 6 fav); 2 Nashamaa (9-0); 3 Sweet Adelaide(USA) (8-11); 9 Ran. 1½l, 1½l, 1½l, 5l, 1½l. 1m 28.8s (a 4.1s). SR: 64/59/51/49/34/29.

Aug 31, Curragh, 7f (2-y-o) mdn, soft, £1,725: 1 TATE GALLERY(USA) (9-0 , Pat Eddery), (7 to 4 on); 2 Hungry Giant (9-0); 3 Mario Sivieri (9-0); 20 Ran. 2½l, 1½l, 2l, 4l, 1l. 1m 29.3s SR: 70/62/57/51/39/36.

Probables

(2) DANCING BRAVE – G. Harwood 3-9.0 G. Starkey

F.	F.	C.	C.
Prom	(16)	up	D√
★★	★★		C√
			G√

(16) TATE GALLERY – V. O'Brien (Ire.) 3-9.0 (T. Ives)

F.	F.	C.	C.
Prom	(21)	—	D√
★★	★★		G√

This is an example of a 3 y.o. conditions stakes race restricted to colts and fillies over a distance of 1m. The 2,000 Guineas is a Group I event and the premier race for 3-year-olds whose optimum distance will be 1m. It has been included here to show how the selection formula and analysis technique may be successfully applied to what is usually regarded as a most competitive race but which has wide popular appeal.

As befits such a prestigious race which attracts great public interest the form of the runners beforehand receives expert and detailed scrutiny, so a horse promoted to favourite does not gain this role lightly and therefore demands special attention. The record of the favourites in the 2,000 Guineas show this, with four favourites winning (1974–85), while six non-favourites have been successful in this time, suggesting that the expectations of form are either reliably upheld or surprisingly confounded. This was therefore an important consideration to be borne in mind and an objective assessment of the form of each runner was accordingly undertaken:

(1)	ALSHINFARAH	having first run of the season, a considerable handicap for a horse to overcome, and although having form including a 6f Group II success in Germany considered unlikely to be good enough.
(3)	EXOTIC RIVER	a French challenger, winner of a maiden race at Longchamp after unsuccessfully contesting group races as a 2 y.o. – not good enough.
(4)	FARNCOMBE	a maiden still – not good enough.
(5)	FAUSTUS	a gallant winner of the Greenham Stakes 7f at Newbury. A useful 2,000 Guineas trial, but on form on a par with HUNTINGDALE and SURE BLADE and with three horses so closely rated unlikely to be good enough.
(6)	GREEN DESERT	a good winner of the 2 y.o. Free Handicap, but usually such a horse proves to be just below the very highest grade needed to win this contest.
(7)	HAIL TO ROBERTO	experiencing a huge rise in class after winning a maiden race at Longchamp in its previous race.
(8)	HALLGATE	a sprinter rather than a miler who ran a cracking race to finish only a head and short head behind FAUSTUS in the Greenham Stakes, if lasting out the extra furlong, it should finish close to that horse.
(9)	HUNTINGDALE	ended 2 y.o. career winning the prestigious Group I Dewhurst Stakes 7f over the same Newmarket course as today's race while still a maiden. However, in recent years the winners of this prestigious race subsequently only continued to disappoint. Would need to be a shining exception to defy this curse, especially as this race was its seasonal reappearance.

(10) JAZETAS	would have to improve 7½ lengths to reverse form with DANCING BRAVE over the course and distance.
(13) SHARROOD	would have to improve over 15½ lengths to reverse form with DANCING BRAVE.
(15) SURE BLADE	a top-class 2 y.o. easily won on its seasonal reappearance, a 1m stakes race at Thirsk 14 days earlier. Closely banded with HUNTING-DALE and FAUSTUS. On previous form unlikely to be good enough.
(17) TOCA MADERA	an improving Irish horse who had won a Group III race at Phoenix Park on very heavy going and was unbeaten but now experiencing a huge elevation in class.
(18) VAINGLORIOUS	beaten over 6 lengths by FAUSTUS in the Greenham Stakes; would not be good enough.

Eliminating these runners left two probables – the unbeaten DANCING BRAVE, who was an impressive course and distance winner on its seasonal reappearance 16 days earlier, and Vincent O'Brien's (who had to be respected) Irish challenger TATE GALLERY, who won a Group I race over 7f as a 2 y.o. at the Curragh but who had disappointed somewhat in its reappearance as a 3 y.o., being beaten by another 3 y.o. who was no more than handicap class.

Applying the selection formula there was little to choose between these two probables on the star rating system. However, by completely subjective assessment of form, DANCING BRAVE's performance in the Craven Stakes had received endorsement when the third, MASHKOUR, had a subsequent facile win in the White Rose Stakes at Ascot.

DANCING BRAVE was made the selection choice.

Result: 1st DANCING BRAVE (15–8 fav.) won by 3 lengths.

Form Book No. 518 *SALISBURY 7 May 1986 (soft)*

3.30—SALISBURY STAKES (2-Y.-O.). £4,000 **a d d e d**
(£2,765·40). 5f. (5)   STALLS

1	(1)	121 QUEL ESPRIT 5 (D2) M McCormack 9-4	.........R Wernham	●78
2	(5)	51 DIAMOND FLIGHT 15 (D) R Hannon 9-1	.........A McGlone	65
3	(4)	1 ENCHANTED TIMES 26 (D) C Horgan 9-1	.............T Quinn	75
7	(2)	MILLPOND BOY C Hill 8-11	....................Doubtful	
9	(3)	43 QUICK SNAP (B) 11 A Ingham 8-11	.................R Curant	68

Probable S.P.: 11-10 Quel Esprit, 7-4 Enchanted Times, 11-2 Diamond Flight, 12 Quick Snap.   FAVOURITES : 2 1 3 1 2 1 3.
1985 : Websters Feast, 9-1 (R. Cochrane), 4-1, M. McCormack. 5 ran.

3.30 🐑🐑🐑 | Conditions
2-y-o 5f
(£2,765)

121 QUEL ESPRIT (Feb 17, 10,000gns)
(9-4) b c What A Guest — Les Sylphides
by Kashmir II. 1986, 5f good (Doncaster), 5f good (Newmarket). £4,237.

May 2, Newmarket, 5f (2-y-o), good,
£3,074: 1 QUEL ESPRIT (9-0 , S
Cauthen , 1), **made virtually all, kept
on well inside final furlong** (100 to 30
op 5 to 2 tchd 3 to 1 and 7 to 2); 2
Mister Majestic (9-4 , 6); 3 Alkadi (8-11
, 3); 7 Ran. ¾l, 2½l, 4l, 2l, nk. 1m 3.33s (a
3.53s). SR: 30/32/15/-/-/-.

April 8, Ayr, 5f (2-y-o), good to soft,
£959: 1 Gallic Times (9-4, 4); 2 QUEL
ESPRIT (9-4, R Cochrane, 3), **led till
well inside last, no extra** (2 to 1 on op
7 to 4 on tchd 13 to 8 on); 3 Scottish
Fling (8-4, 7*, 2); 4 Ran. ¾l, 1½l, 25l. 1m
4.83s (a 6.23s). SR: 50/48/35/-/-/-.

1 ENCHANTED TIMES (Feb 18,
7,400gns) (9-1) b c Enchantment — Miss
Times by Major Portion. 1986, 5f good
to soft (Kempton). £1,944.

April 11, Kempton, 5f (2-y-o) mdn,
good to soft, £1,944: 1 ENCHANTED
TIMES (9-0, Pat Eddery, 7), **chased
leader till went on inside final furlong, ran on well** (9 to 2 op 6 to 4 tchd
5 to 1); 2 French Tuition (9-0, 9); 3
Micro Love (9-0, 4); 4 QUICK SNAP
(9-0, J Reid, 5), **pressed leaders 3f out,
no headway** (4 to 1 tchd 8 to 1); 9
Ran. ¾l, 6l, 1l, ¾l, ¾l. 1m 6.07s (a 6.67s).
SR: 8/5/-/-/-/-.

Probables

(1) QUEL ESPRIT – M. McCormack 2-9.4 R. Wernham

F.	F.	C.	C.
Prom	(5)	—	D√
★★	★★★		G?
			7 lb pen

(3) ENCHANTED TIMES – C. Horgan 2-9.1 T. Quinn

F.	F.	C.	C.
Prom	(26)	up	D
★★	★		G
			4 lb pen

Non-runner: MILLPOND BOY

This is an example of a 2 y.o. conditions race over 5f and highlights how in small fields where all the runners have their form exposed 2 y.o. stakes races can be considered as a most reliable medium for the backer.

This small field of four runners resolved to two probables QUEL ESPRIT and ENCHANTED TIMES. QUEL ESPRIT, the most experienced runner in the field, had three prior races winning two of these and just being beaten in the other; while ENCHANTED TIMES won a maiden race at Kempton in its only start. On a line of form between QUEL ESPRIT's vanquished rival at Newmarket, MISTER MAJESTIC, who had previously beaten a horse called FRENCH TUITION by 4½ lengths (at level weights) while ENCHANTED TIMES only beat FRENCH TUITION by ¾ length (at level weights) on their racecourse débuts, QUEL ESPRIT was the superior of ENCHANTED TIMES and applying the formula made the selection choice.

Result: 1st QUEL ESPRIT (evens fav.) won by 4 lengths.

Form Book No. 606 *YORK 14 May 1986 (good)*

3.40 — **(Prefix 4)** **MECCA - DANTE STAKES**
(3-Y.-O.). **£50,000 added (£80,454).**
1m. 2f. 110yd. (7) **STALLS**

1	(7)	2 ALL HASTE 13 H Cecil 9-0	S Cauthen	51
2	(6)	37130-2 DANCING ZETO (V) 21 (C) P Kelleway 9-0	P Cook	65
3	(5)	1152-15 FLYING TRIO 8 L Cumani 9-0	Pat Eddery	75
6	(2)	12-1 NOMROOD 8 P Cole 9-0	T Quinn	74
8	(4)	2-1 SHAHRASTANI 18 (D) M Stoute 9-0	W R Swinburn ●78
9	(1)	423-132 SIRK 8 (D) C Brittain 9-0	P Robinson	73
11	(3)	134-5 TOP RULER 28 (C) R Armstrong 9-0	T Ives	58

Probable S.P.: 4-5 Shahrastani, 4 All Haste, 6 Nomrood, 8 Flying Trio, 12 Sirk, 33 Dancing Zeta, Top Ruler.
FAVOURITES 2 3 0 1 1 1 0.
1985: Damister, 9-0 (Pat Eddery), 5-1. J. Tree. 5 ran.

3.40 Stakes (Group 2) 3-y-o 1m 2½f (£80,454)

2-1 SHAHRASTANI(USA) (9-0) ch c Nijinsky — Shademah by Thatch. 1986, 1¼m soft (Sandown). £19,845 (£19,845).

April 26, Sandown, 1¼m (3-y-o), soft, £19,845: (Group 3) 1 SHAHRASTANI(USA) (8-7, W R Swinburn, 1),

2nd until led 2 ½f out, driven clear, eased final 100yds (2 to 1 op evens); 2 Bonhomie(USA) (8-12, 3); 3 SIRK (8-7, P Robinson, 2), **last until went 3rd 5f out, stayed on** (20 to 1 op 14 to 1 tchd 33 to 1); 4 Ran. 4l, 5l, dist. 2m 18.77s (a 13.27s). SR: 55/52/37/-/-/-.

Sept 20, Newbury, 1m (2-y-o), good, £6,050: 1 My Ton Ton (8-11 . 3); 2 SHAHRASTANI(USA) (8-11 . W R Swinburn , 17), **good headway over 1f out, finished well** (8 to 1 op 4 to 1); 3 Mytens(USA) (8-11 , 7); 18 Ran. Hd, 2l, sht hd, 2l, nk. 1m 41.67s (a 2.97s). SR: 52/51/45/44/33/37.

Probable

(8) SHAHRASTANI – M. Stoute 9.0 W. Swinburn

F.	F.	C.	C.
Proven	(18)	—	D√
★★★	★★		G√

This is an example of a top-class conditions stakes race for 3-year-olds of 1m 2½f. It is the Dante Stakes, a Group II race which serves as one of the important trials for the English Derby. The 1986 contest, in common with races in previous years, attracted a moderately sized field of horses hoping to become contenders for the Epsom Classic.

Form analysis quickly revealed that the race really only resolved to one probable, SHAHRASTANI. The other runners were eliminated for the following reasons. ALL HASTE was a lightly raced horse who was still a maiden, yet meeting here experienced horses with winning form on equal terms. DANCING ZETA was a horse easily beaten in a listed race on its seasonal reappearance as a 3 y.o. by BELDALE STAR who in its next race (at level weights) had been beaten by just over 8 lengths by NOMROOD, a challenger in today's race. NOMROOD had only just beaten SIRK, by a neck at level weights, in this race; with FLYING TRIO, another challenger in today's contest, a further 6½ lengths behind in fifth place.

SHAHRASTANI, in contrast, in its first race of the season, the Classic Trial (Group III) Sandown, had beaten SIRK (at level weights) with consummate ease by 9 lengths, and therefore on these collateral form lines had the beating of four of its six rivals here. TOP RULER, the only other runner to be considered, was a horse tackling this higher grade and longer distance for the first time and was considered unsuited to both. Applying the formula to the one probable, SHAHRASTANI was made the selection choice.

Result: 1st SHAHRASTANI (10–11 fav.) won by 1½ lengths.

Form Book No. 710 *GOODWOOD 22 May 1986 (soft)*

5.10 (PREFIX 6) — EBF HALNAKER STAKES (2-Y.-O.)
£3,500 added (£3,297·50). 6f. (9) STALLS

2	(2)	L12 JONLEAT 10 (BF) L Piggott 9-2	Pat Eddery	62
3	(5)	1 OLORE MALLE 29 R Hannon 9-2	R Wernham	60
6	(4)	BAUMANIERE H Beasley 8-11	D McKay	—
8	(9)	CAMBRIDGE REBEL C Brittain 8-11	S Cauthen	—
9	(1)	CEE-EN-CEE M McCourt 8-11	J Reid	—
10	(7)	52 GULF KING 8 P Kelleway 8-11	C Asmussen	●78
11	(8)	LORD WESTGATE M Usher 8-11	B Thomson	—
12	(3)	76 MAKIN MISCHIEF 7 D Laing 8-11	S Whitworth	—
13	(6)	TOUGH N GENTLE L Piggott 8-11	W R Swinburn	—

Probable S.P.: 13-8 Olore Malle, 3 Jonleat, 4 Gulf King, 6 Cambridge Rebel, 10 Tough N'Gentle, 12 Lord Westgate. FAVOURITES : 1 — 1 1 3 0 1.

5.10 | Conditions
2-y-o colts
and geldings
6f £3,297

52 GULF KING (March 28, IR£26,000)
(8-11) ch c Kings Lake — Pearl Star by
Gulf Pearl.

May 14, York, 6f (2-y-o), good,
£3,340: 1 Quel Esprit (9-3, 8); 2 GULF
KING (8-11, P Cook, 15), **slowly into
stride, headway half-way, strong run
final 2f, finished well** (6 to 1 op 4 to
1); 3 Demderise (9-0, 9); 15 Ran. ½l, 2½l,
3l, ½l, 2½l, sht hd. 1m 13.08s (a 1.28s).
SR: 71/63/56/41/44/28.

May 3, Newmarket, 5f (2-y-o) mdn,
good, £3,249: 1 Zaibaq (USA) (9-0, 3); 2
Sameek (9-0, 1); 3 Mansooj (9-0, 9); 5
GULF KING (9-0, C Asmussen, 6),
chased leading group for 3f (11 to 1
op 6 to 1 tchd 12 to 1 and 14 to 1); 10
Ran. ½l, 1l, 2l, 3l, 1½l, nk, ½l. 1m 0.76s (a
0.96s). SR: 51/48/44/36/24/18.

Probable

(10) GULF KING – P. Kelleway 8.11 C. Asmussen

F.   F.   C.   C.

Prom   (8)   —   D√

★   ★★★   G?

This is an example of a 2 y.o. 6f conditions stakes race for colts and
geldings. This compact field of nine runners included two horses with
previous winning race experience, two others who had prior race
experience, plus five horses making their début on a racecourse. In
assessing the prospects of these contestants, the two prior winners were
the first to be scrutinized. Both were set to carry 5 lb penalties for their
previous victories: JONLEAT winning a maiden race at Leicester and
OLORE MALLE a maiden race at Epsom. This race represented a rise in
class for both these winners who were therefore eliminated from calculations.

Of the two other runners with previous race experience MAKIN
MISCHIEF, who had shown little in its two runs was eliminated; leaving
GULF KING for consideration. GULF KING had run in two prior races
finishing second in its previous race at York, beaten ½ length (receiving
6 lb), from the useful QUEL ESPRIT, but having three other previous
winners behind it in the field of 15 runners. In its first race, a good-class
maiden 2 y.o. race at Newmarket, GULF KING although finishing only
fifth of 10 had a subsequent winner behind it and therefore had the value
of the form in its races strongly endorsed. Of the newcomers, none
were outstanding candidates on breeding, high-priced yearling purchases or from stables noted for their record in winning with 2-year-olds
first time out.

GULF KING was therefore the only probable, and applying the formula made the selection choice.

Result: 1st GULF KING (5–6 fav.) won by 8 lengths.

Form Book No. 788 *SANDOWN 26 May 1986 (good)*

2.00 — (Prefix 2) **MAPPIN & WEBB HENRY II STAKES. £25,000 added (£18,675). 2m**

(10) **STALLS**

1	(3)	1211-41	EASTERN MYSTIC 11 L Cumani 4-9-0	Pat Eddery	73
3	(9)	000-101	BRUNICO 18 R Simpson 4-8-11	C Asmussen ●78	
4	(5)	412124-	I WANT TO BE 197 J Dunlop 4-8-11	B Rouse	63
5	(4)	23/142-6	LONGBOAT 9 (D) W Hern 5-8-11	W Carson	70
7	(2)	122-LL2	SEISMIC WAVE 11 B Hills 5-8-11	B Thomson	74
9	(7)	11361-5	TALE QUALE 11 (D3) H Candy 4-8-11	T Ives	75
10	(8)	15123-4	BOURBON BOY 11 M Stoute 4-8-8	W R Swinburn	72
12	(10)	12209-7	KUBLAI 37 G Lewis 4-8-8	P Waldron	63
13	(1)	2/112L-2	MANGO EXPRESS 9 C Horgan 4-8-8	P Cook	70
14	(6)	5 L0863	PETRIZZO 11 C Brittain 5-8-8	P Robinson	76

Probable S.P.: 5-2 Eastern Mystic, 4 Seismic Wave, 9-2 Longboat, 5 Tale Quale, 6 Brunico, 10 Mango Express, 12 I Want To Be, 16 Bourbon Boy.

FAVOURITES: 1 0 - 1 1 3 0.

1985: Destroyer 4-8-8 (S Whitworth) 9-1 K Brassey. 8 ran.

2.00 Conditions (Gr. 3) 2m

1211-41 EASTERN MYSTIC (4-9-0) b c Elocutionist — Belle Pensee by Ribot. 1985, 1½m good to soft (Newmarket), 1¾m 127yds good (Doncaster), 1m 5f 60yds good to firm (Newbury); 1986, 1¾m good to soft (York). £53,113 (£22,086).

May 15, York, 1¾m good to soft, £22,086: (Group 2) 1 EASTERN MYSTIC (4-8-9, Pat Eddery, 2), **waited with in touch, headway 2f out, ridden and went left approaching final furlong, led and ran on last 50 yards** (9 to 4 fav op 2 to 1); 2 SEISMIC WAVE(USA) (5-8-9, B Thomson, 3), tracked leader, led 4f out, ridden final 2f, headed and not quicken last 50yds (7 to 2 op 2 to 1); 3 PETRIZZO (5-8-9, S Cauthen, 4), always handy , effort and ridden 2f out, stayed on under pressure closing stages (20 to 1 op 16 to 1) ; 4 BOURBON BOY (4-8-9, W R Swinburn , 6), held up in rear, headway final 3f, stayed on final furlong (3 to 1 op 7 to 2 tchd 4 to 1); 5 TALE QUALE (4-8-9, T Ives, 10), chased leaders, every chance over 3f out, on pace last 2f (4 to 1 op 7 to 2) ; 7 Ran. 1½l, ½l, 3l, 6l, 12l. 3m 12.26s (a 15.86s). SR: 42/39/38/32/20/-.

April 30, Ascot, 2m good to soft, £24,388: (Group 3) 1 Valuable Witness(USA) (6-9-0, 1); 2 Ramich John (4-8-5, 10); 3 Spicy

Story(USA) (5-8-11, 5); 4 EASTERN MYSTIC (4-8-8, R Guest, 9), **always prominent, ridden 3f out, soon beaten** (7 to 1 op 5 to 1 tchd 8 to 1); 8 PETRIZZO (5-8-8, P Robinson, 4), led till headed and weakened 4f out (25 to 1); 10 Ran. Sht hd, 4l, 6l, 2½l, 8l. 3m 47.41s (a 21.41s). SR: 30/20/22/13/10/2.

23/142-6 LONGBOAT (5-8-11) b h Welsh Pageant — Pirogue by Reliance II. 1984, 1¼m good to firm (Goodwood), 1¼m 65yds good (Chester), 1m 3f 150yds good (Bath), 1m 3f 30yds good to firm (Kempton); 1985, 2m good (Ascot). £38,729 (—).

May 17, Newbury. See MANGO EXPRESS.

June 20, Ascot, 2¼m good to firm, £42,566: (Group 1) 1 Gildoran (5-9-0 , 11); 2 LONGBOAT (4-9-0 , W Carson , 6), **in touch, headway six out, lost place three out, strong challenge inside final furlong, ran on** (9 to 10 op 8 to 10 tchd 11 to 1) ; 3 Destroyer (4-9-0, 10); 8 PETRIZZO (4-9-0 , S Cauthen , 8), in third place until weakened two out (14 to 1 op 12 to 1); 12 Ran. ½l, ½l, nk, 4l, 1½l, hd. 4m 25.19s (a 3.19s). SR: 49/48/47/46/42/40.

2/1124-2 MANGO EXPRESS (4-8-8) b c
Free State — Polyandrist by Polic. 1985, 1¼m
good (Lingfield), 1m 3f good (Newbury).
£4,193 (---).

May 17, Newbury, 1m 5f 60yds soft,
£8,129: 1 Kaytu (5-8-7, 7); 2 MANGO EX-
PRESS (4-8-7, P Cook, 1), **headway on
inside 4f out, every chance and ridden
inside last, ran on, just failed** (9 to 2 op 3
to 1 tchd 5 to 1); 3 Leading Star (4-8-7, 13);
6 LONGBOAT (5-8-7, B Rouse, 2), prominent, ridden 2f out, soon weakened (13 to
2 op 5 to 1 tchd 7 to 1); 14 Ran. Nk, 2l, ¾l,
hd, 2½l. 3m 3.12s (a 12.82s). SR: 45/44/40/
39/38/33.

Aug 21, York, 1¼m (3-y-o), good to soft,
£30,969: (Group 2) 1D Shardari (8-7 , 6); 1
Damister(USA) (8-11 , 1); 3 Infantry (8-7 ,
2); 4 MANGO EXPRESS (8-7 , P Cook , 4),
**waited with, quickened to challenge enter-
ing straight, weakened well over two furlongs out** (6 to 1 op 8 to 1); 4 Ran. Nk, 6l,
7l. 2m 42.35s (a 12.15s). (Following a stewards' inquiry, Shardari was relegated to
second and the race awarded to Damister).
SR: 21/23/7/-/-/-.

Probables

(1) EASTERN MYSTIC – L. Cumani 4–9.0 P. Eddery
F.   F.   C. C.
Prom (11) — D?
★★   ★★★   G√
            6 lb pen

(4) LONGBOAT – W. Hern 5–8.11 W. Carson
F.   F.   C. C.
Prom (9) — D√
★★   ★★★   G√
            3 lb pen
            trainer√

(13) MANGO EXPRESS – C. Horgan 4–8.8 P. Cook
F.   F.   C. C.
Prom (9) — D?
★★   ★★★   G√

This is an example of a 2m conditions race for 4-year-olds and older horses. The Henry II Stakes is a Group III race that often serves as a preparation race for stayers seeking to challenge for the trilogy of marathon distance cup races (Ascot Gold Cup, Goodwood Cup and Doncaster Cup) which follow later in the season.

On analysis this race resolved to three probables EASTERN MYSTIC, LONGBOAT and MANGO EXPRESS.

EASTERN MYSTIC won the Yorkshire Cup Group II 1¾m in its pre-vious race, beating four other runners in today's race, who were thought unlikely to be able to reverse that form.

The other two probables were LONGBOAT and MANGO EXPRESS, the latter beating the former by just over 5 lengths when the pair made their seasonal débuts in a 1m 5f conditions race at Newbury 9 days earlier. However, this was LONGBOAT's first race since the Ascot Gold Cup of last season where it had been only narrowly beaten by GILDORAN, and was over a distance far too short for it; while MANGO EXPRESS was now set to tackle this 2m distance for the first time.

Applying the selection formula to the three probables these are all rated the same by the star rating scheme, and to decide the issue it is necessary to review the elements of each in the conditions part of the formula. EASTERN MYSTIC was unproven at the distance, having failed to feature in the closing stages of the race when tried at the trip on its seasonal racecourse reappearance, and was penalized 6 lb for a Group II victory. LONGBOAT, in contrast, was proven at the distance and further, and prepared by a master (Dick Hern) at the art of preparing stayers, who had won the corresponding race four times previously (1971–85). MANGO EXPRESS had shown excellent form in its seasonal début race where it easily beat LONGBOAT but was definitely unproven at this longer trip, so it was reasonable to expect reversal of that form.

LONGBOAT was therefore made the selection choice.

Result: 1st LONGBOAT (4–1) won by 2½ lengths.

Form Book No. 799   *SANDOWN 27 May 1986 (good)*

8.55—WHEATSHEAF MAIDEN THREE-YEAR-OLD STAKES.
£3,500 added (£4,046·70.) 1m. 2f. (23)   STALLS

1	(16)	2 BANANAS 45 O Douieb 9-0	R Hills	62
2	(2)	0- BUSTAMENTE 222 B Hills 9-0	M Hills	—
3	(22)	L5-0 CIGAR 10 G Wragg 9-0	Pat Eddery	—
5	(11)	22-54 DANISHGAR 21 M Stoute 9-0	W R Swinburn	●78
7	(15)	DOM STAR J Winter 9-0	Paul Eddery	—
9	(12)	0L FORWARD MOVE 10 D A Wilson 9-0	J Williams	—
10	(13)	0-8 FULL SPEED AHEAD 19 M Smyly 9-0	A Murray	—
11	(17)	007-6 GOD'S PATH 17 D Elsworth 9-0	A McGlone	52
12	(5)	GUESSING G Harwood 9-0	G Starkey	—
15	(14)	LL- LUCKY LAD 361 W Brooks 9-0	G Baxter	—
18	(10)	83 MOEL FAMMAU 15 J Toller 9-0	DOUBTFUL	
19	(19)	00-6L0 NEVER BEE 17 J Bridger 9-0	R Guest	—
22	(20)	0 RISK ANOTHER 8 P Mitchell 9-0	T Ives	—
23	(8)	00-32 SARONICOS 25 (BF) C Brittain 9-0	P Robinson	69
24	(7)	2-9 SILK THREAD 26 W Hern 9-0	W Carson	75
25	(23)	9 STEP IN TIME 26 P Makin 9-0	T Quinn	—
29	(18)	0- WOODLANDS CROWN 213 C Horgan 9-0	P Cook	—
30	(4)	0 BARLEYBREE 12 C Benstead 8-11	B Rouse	—
31	(9)	BARSHAM J Dunlop 8-11	R Fox	—
34	(1)	LOREEF J Dunlop 8-11	J Reid	—
35	(21)	867 NEEDLEWOMAN 14 R Armstrong 8-11	G Sexton	68
36	(6)	STRIKE HOME M Stoute 8-11	A Kimberley	—
38	(3)	L4 KEEPCALM 21 G Wragg 9-0	D Gibson	61

Probable S.P. : 2 Silk Thread. 11-4 Bananas. 4 Danishgar. 7 Saronicos. 8 Guessing. 12 Loreef.   **FAVOURITES** : — — — — — 0.
1985 : Harry's Bar 9-0 (A. Kimberley). 11-1 M. Stoute. 12 ran.

8.55 Maiden
3-y-o 1¼m
(£4,046)

22-54 DANISHGAR (9-0) b c Shergar —
Demia by Abdos.

May 6, Chester, 1½m 65yds (3-y-o), good
to soft, £21,120: (Group 3) 1 Nomrood-
(USA) (8-12, 6); 2 Sirk (8-12, 7); 3 Jumbo
Hirt(USA) (8-8, 3); 4 DANISHGAR (8-8, W
R Swinburn, 4), **led until over 1f out, ran on
same pace** (10 to 1 op 12 to 1 tchd 9 to 1);
7 Ran. Nk, 1l, 1½l, 5l, 1½l. 2m 46.08s (a
7.88s). SR: 38/37/31/30/24/22.

April 30, Ascot, 1⅛m (3-y-o), good to soft,
£8,402: 1 Mashkour(USA) (9-0, 3); 2 Mirage Dancer (8-9, 5); 3 Nisnas (9-0, 6); 5
DANISHGAR (8-9, W R Swinburn, 1), **led
5f out, headed 2f out, soon beaten** (evens
fav op 5 to 4 tchd 5 to 4 on); 6 Ran. 8l, ¾l, 4l,
1l, 30l. 2m 18.70s (a 13.30s). SR: 57/36/39/
26/24/-.

Oct 5, Newmarket, 1m (2-y-o) mdn, good
to firm, £4,623: 1 Nomrood(USA) (9-0 , 5);
2 DANISHGAR (9-0 , W R Swinburn , 3),
**always close up, led one and a half out,
soon ridden, headed inside final furlong,
not quicken** (15 to 8 on op 6 to 4 on); 3
White Reef (9-0 , 12); 13 Ran. 1½l, hd. 1l,
1½l, 2l. 1m 41.03s (a 2.13s). SR: 12/7/6/3/-/

2-0 SILK THREAD (9-0) ch c Relkino —
Silken Way by Shantung.

May 1, Newmarket, 1m 1f (3-y-o), good,
£4,467: 1 Allez Milord(USA) (9-6, 6); 2 All
Haste(USA) (8-7, 5); 3 Verardi (8-7, 10); 9
SILK THREAD (8-7, W Carson, 3), **pulled
hard, chased leaders 7f** (9 to 1 op 6 to 1
tchd 10 to 1); 12 Ran. Hd, 1½l, 1l, nk, sht hd.
1m 54.83s.(a 2.03s). SR: 86/72/67/64/63/
62.

Oct 26, Newbury, 1m (2-y-o), good,
£4,515: 1 El Cuite(USA) (8-11 , 4); 2 SILK
THREAD (8-11 , W Carson , 20), **always
prominent, led over one out, edged left,
soon headed** (11 to 8 fav op 2 to 1 tchd 9 to
4); 3 Prelude (8-9, inc 1lb ow , 14); 12
WOODLANDS CROWN (8-11 , T Williams ,
10), **headway and ridden three out, every
chance two out, soon weakened** (33 to 1);
27 Ran. 3l, 1l, 1½l, 5l, 1l. 1m 43.59s (a
4.89s). SR: 60/51/45/49/25/19.

Probables

(5) DANISHGAR – M. Stoute 9.0 W. Swinburn
F.   F.   C.   C.
Proven (21) dr   D√
★★★   ★★   G√

(24) SILK THREAD – W. Hern 9.0 W. Carson
F.   F.   C.   C.
Prom (26)   —   D?
★★   ★   G√

This is an example of a good-class early summer 3 y.o. maiden race
over the middle distance of 1m 2f. These races at this time in the season
regularly attract large fields of well-bred horses, many of whom have
been previously quite lightly raced and are therefore usually of unproven ability. Some of them will need more time to get their 'racing
act' properly together. Unless there is some 'classic' unraced contestant
who is able to bloom suddenly on its racecourse début, this type of
contest usually readily resolves to those with the clearly identifiable
better form.

Analysis here revealed two form candidates DANISHGAR and SILK
THREAD. DANISHGAR had been a 'talking' horse from his 2 y.o. days
where his reputation had always been much greater than his actual
achievements. However, he had been thought of highly enough by an

213

astute trainer to be pitched against the better horses of its generation in two Classic race trials and having been then found wanting was now lowered in class, here to take on other less well thought of peers.

The other probable, SILK THREAD, had shown promise as a 2 y.o. on its only outing in an end of the season race at Newbury, and had run fairly encouragingly in its reappearance behind a leading Derby candidate ALLEZ MILORD at Newmarket early in May. Applying the selection formula DANISHGAR was made the selection choice.

Result: 1st DANISHGAR (13–8 fav.) won by 1½ lengths.

Form Book No. 815 *CATTERICK 29 May 1986 (firm)*

3.45 — MUKER MAIDEN STAKES. £1,000 (£728·80).
1m. 5f 180yd. (14)   STALLS

1	(1)	39046-0	BILLIDOR 34 N Crump 4-9-9	M Birch	59
2	(8)		BRUNDEAN BREEZE R Juckes 5-9-9	—	—
3	(6)	6024-40	KADESH 2 F Yardley 5-9-9	DOUBTFUL	
5	(7)	32-2	THE PRUDENT PRINCE 12 W Jarvis 4-9-9	R Cochrane	●78
7	(12)		GYPS GIFT J P Smith 4-9-6	M Brennan (7)	- —
8	(14)	0	ONE FOR THE DITCH 50 Mrs C L-Jones 5-9-6 Wendy Jones (7)	—
10	(4)	7-4	GOODTIME HAL 24 J Hindley 3-8-5	M Hills	76
11	(11)	40-	IN DREAMS 201 M Prescott 3-8-5	G Duffield	60
14	(5)	000-0	STORM LORD 8 C Thornton 3-8-5	J Bleasdale	—
16	(9)	640-	FANNY ROBIN 241 Denys Smith 3-8-2	L Charnock	70
17	(3)	00	LINEOUT LADY 47 W Wharton 3-8-2	N Carlisle	—
18	(10)	04L0-68	QUEEN OF SWORDS 3 R Hollinshead 3-8-2	S Perks	74
19	(2)	800-220	SAY SOMETHING 27 J Winter 3-8-2	J Lowe	69
20	(13)		SIANS PET W Mackie 3-8-2	M Wood	—

Probable S.P.: 2 The Prudent Prince, 5-2 Goodtime Hal, 9-2 Say Something, 8 In Dreams, 12 Fanny Robin, 16 Billidor.
FAVOURITES : 1 1 — 1 2 1 0.
1985: Sun Street, 3-8-2 (A. Mackay). 7-1. C. Brittain. 18 ran.

3.45 Maiden 1m 5f 180yds (£728)

32-2 THE PRUDENT PRINCE (4-9-9) b c Grundy — Ragirl by Ragusa.

May 17, Beverley, 1¼m mdn, good, £2,013: 1 Loch Seaforth (3-8-5, 15); 2 THE PRUDENT PRINCE (4-9-7, R Cochrane, 6), **pulled hard, with leader, led approaching straight, headed over 2f out, ridden and kept on** (9 to 1 op 10 to 1 tchd 14 to 1); 3 Call To Honor(USA) (3-8-5, bl, 12); 15 Ran. ¾l, 2½l, hd, ½l, 4l. 2m 40.1s (a 7.3s). SR: 18/22/11/23/9/1.

Aug 5, Ripon, 1½m (3-y-o) mdn, good to soft, £2,327: 1 Teased(USA) (8-11 , 8); 2 THE PRUDENT PRINCE (9-0 , W R Swinburn , 11), **always handy , chased winner final 4f, no impression** (8 to 1 op 7 to 1); 3 Brigadier Troy (9-0 , 9); 10 Ran. 7l, 5l, 1l, 1½l, 1l. 2m 14.2s (a 8.2s). SR: 65/54/44/42/36/37.

April 2 1985, Nottingham, 1½m (3-y-o), soft, £1,328: 1 Cabalistic (9-0, 14); 2 Boom Patrol (9-0, 6); 3 THE PRUDENT PRINCE (9-0, W R Swinburn, 3), **headway 4f out, every chance over 2f out, soon ridden and one pace** (8 to 1 op 6 to 1 tchd 10 to 1); 14 Ran. 8l, 1½l, 3l, 1½l, hd, nk, hd. 2m 25.2s (a 21.2s). SR: 58/42/39/33/30/29.

000-220 SAY SOMETHING (3-8-2) b f
Reform — Sarsgrove by Hornbeam.

May 2, Carlisle, 1¼m good to soft,
£1,179: 1 Mubaaris (3-8-6 , 20); 2 Bantel
Bushy (3-7-10 , 13); 3 Tartan Tailor (5-8-7 ,
7*, 15); 16 SAY SOMETHING (3-7-7 , A
Mackay , 5), **driven up to lead after 2f,
headed and weakened approaching
straight** (5 to 1 op 3 to 1); 20 Ran. ¾l, 8l, 5l,
1¼l, 2l. 2m 40.7s (a 9.4s). SR: 52/41/43/33/
9/26.

April 7, Folkestone, 1¼m (3-y-o), heavy,
£684: 1 Bride (8-11, 2); 2 SAY SOME-
THING (8-11, 7), **led till over 2f,
one pace final 2f** (6 to 4 fav op 5 to 4 tchd 7
to 4); 3 Wrangbrook (8-11, 1); 7 Ran. 4l, 7l,
6l, 10l, 1¾l. 3m 1.4s (a 25.2s). (Flag start).

March 26, Catterick, 1¼m 40yds (3-y-o)
mdn, good to soft, £684: 1 Nimble
Native(USA) (8-11 , 3); 2 SAY SOME-
THING (8-11 , G Duffield , 1), **waited with,
effort approaching straight, every chance 1
¼f out, not quicken** (9 to 4 op 5 to 1); 3
Whittingham Vale (8-11 , 2); 8 Ran. 2l, 4l,
8l, 6l, nk. 2m 59.3s (a 22.1s).

Probables

(5) THE PRUDENT PRINCE – W. Jarvis 4-9.9 R. Cochrane

F.   F.   C.   C.

Proven (12) dr D√

★★★   ★★   G?

(19) SAY SOMETHING – J. Winter 3-8.2 J. Lowe

F.   F.   C.   C.

Prom   (27) — D√

★★   ★   G?

Non-runners: BRUNDEAN BREEZE and DADESH

This is an example of an all-age (3-year-olds+) maiden stayers race where most of the runners can be immediately eliminated from calculation as they have been shown to be singularly lacking in racing ability. Form analysis readily resolved to two probables THE PRUDENT PRINCE and SAY SOMETHING. THE PRUDENT PRINCE, a lightly raced older horse, who had shown, in only two races as a 3 y.o., promising ability, confirmed this impression on his seasonal reappearance by finishing a close second to the useful LOCH SEAFORTH in a Beverley maiden race. SAY SOMETHING, a 3 y.o. filly, had shown she was probably capable of winning a small race from her first two efforts although disappointing on her immediate prior race.

Applying the selection formula THE PRUDENT PRINCE was made the confident choice.

Result: 1st THE PRUDENT PRINCE (11–10 fav.) won by 2 lengths.

Form Book No. 1004 *GOODWOOD 9 June 1986 (good to firm)*

6.15—BBC RADIO KENT STAKES. £3,500 added (£2,998·10).
7f. (9) **STALLS**

4	(1)	026/8-	THREE BELLS 299 M McCourt 4-9-0	R Wernham	—
5	(5)	L24250-	GLIDE BY 250 (D) R Boss 4-8-13	M Miller	65
6	(4)	00-06d†6	DOLLY 11 A Moore 4-8-12	M Wigham	50
7	(7)	84	PERSIAN PERSON 7 G Gracey 4-8-11	N Adams	42
8	(9)	313-421	NATIVE OAK 13 (D) H Cecil 3-8-11	S Cauthen	●78
9	(8)	3-1	GEORGIA RIVER 27 O Douieb 3-8-9	W R Swinburn	59
10	(6)	61-63	FASHADA 24 R Houghton 3-8-7	W Carson	74
12	(3)	216-	ININSKY 228 (D) G Harwood 3-8-1	G Starkey	72
13	(2)	0L00-78	WING BEE (B) 47 J Bridger 3-8-3	T Williams	—

d† — disqualified from 4th place.

Probable S.P. : 6-4 Native Oak, 3 Ininsky, 4 Fashada. 6 Georgia River, 12 Glide
By. **FAVOURITES** : — — — — — 1.
1985 : October, 3-8-6 (W. Carseon). 5-4 fav. R. Armstrong. 11 ran.

6.15 Conditions 7f (£2,998)

313-421 NATIVE OAK (3-8-11) b c Tower Walk — Be Royal by Royal Palm. **1985, 6f good (Yarmouth); 1986, 7f good to firm (Leicester). £4,093 (£2,460).**

May 27, Leicester, 7f (3-y-o), good to firm, £2,460: 1 NATIVE OAK (9-3, S Cauthen, 6), **made virtually all, shaken up final furlong, ran on** (7 to 4 on op 11 to 10 on tchd evens); 2 Riyda (8-10, 12); 3 Bold Admiral (8-11, 4); 19 Ran. ¾l, 4l, 3l, 1¼l, ¾l. 1m 24.3s (b 0.2s). SR: 49/40/29/17/12/13.

May 16, Newbury, 6f (3-y-o), good to soft, £4,971: 1 Governor General (8-9, 5); 2 NATIVE OAK (8-9, S Cauthen, 4), **always chasing leaders, ridden over 1f out, one pace** (9 to 4 fav op 11 to 4 tchd 3 to 1); 3 FASHADA(USA) (8-6, W Carson, 10), **good headway final furlong, not reach leaders** (8 to 1 op 6 to 1); 13 Ran. 5l, 2l, 1l, 1¼l, ¾l. 1m 14.89s (a 1.89s). SR: 77/57/46/45/39/34.

May 3, Newmarket, 7f (3-y-o) h'cap (0-70), good, £9,614: 1 Sylvan Express (7-7, inc 1lb ow , 3*, 2); 2 Fleet Form (8-8 , 3); 3 Mister Wonderful (8-11 , 9); 4 NATIVE OAK (9-2 , S Cauthen , 8), **close up, ridden and edged left over 1f out, stayed on inside final furlong** (7 to 2 eq fav of two op 3 to 1 tchd 11 to 4); 10 Ran. ¾l, ¾l, nk, ¾l, ¾l. 1m 25.44s (b 0.66s). SR: 59/70/71/75/50/75.

216- ININSKY (3-8-7) ch c Niniski(USA) — Buckhurst by Gulf Pearl. **1985, 7f good to firm (Sandown). £2,298 (---).**

Oct 24, Newbury, 7f 60yds good, £24,238: (Group 3) 1 Celtic Heir(USA) (9-0, 12); 2 Hollow Hand (8-9, 6); 3 Hello Ernani(USA) (8-9, 3); 6 ININSKY (9-0, G Starkey, 10), **mid-division, effort and chance two out, not sustain challenge** (7 to 4 fav tchd 2 to 1); 12 Ran. Hd, ¾l, 2l, 1¼l, sht hd. 1m 32.36s (a 3.56s). SR: 52/46/44/43/38/37.

Oct 14, Sandown, 7f (2-y-o) mdn, good to firm, £2,298: 1 ININSKY (9-0, G Starkey, 12), **always prominent, led inside final furlong, easily** (6 to 4 fav tchd 9 to 4); 2 Rhazali (FR) (9-0, 13); 3 Satiapour (9-0, v, 4). 13 Ran. 4l, sht hd, 5l, ½l, 6l. 1m 30.71s (a 2.41s). SR: 53/41/40/25/20/5.

July 13, Salisbury, 7f (2-y-o) mdn, good to firm, £1,697: 1 Atig(FR) (9-0, 17); 2 ININSKY (9-0, G Starkey , 1), **led over 4f out, clear 2f out, headed inside final furlong, finished tired** (2 to 1 on op 5 to 4 on tchd 6 to 4 agst); 3 Sohail(USA) (9-0, 3); 19 Ran. 2½l, 5l, ¾l, nk, nk, 3l, hd. 1m 27.5s (a 1.1s). SR: 37/29/14/12/11/10.

3-1 GEORGIA RIVER(USA) (3-8-9) ch c Irish River — Prize Spot by Little Current. **1986, 1m 50yds good to soft (Nottingham). £3,027 (£3,027).**

May 13, Nottingham, 1m 50yds (3-y-o), good to soft, £3,027: 1 GEORGIA RIVER-(USA) (9-0 , R Hills , 4), **in touch, switched right 2f out, quickened to lead near finish, cleverly** (7 to 2 op 4 to 1 tchd 11 to 2); 2 Picea (9-0 , 1); 3 Al Bashaama(CAN) (9-2 , 15); 15 Ran. 1l, sht hd, 1¼l, 2½l, ¾l. 1m 47.8s (a 5.8s). SR: 57/54/55/48/40/38.

Aug 24, Newmarket, 6f (2-y-o) mdn, good, £3,337: 1 Tanaos (9-0 , 13); 2 Top Guest (9-0 , 4); 3 GEORGIA RIVER(USA) (9-0 , A Lequeux , 8), **always prominent, joined leader 1f out, no extra close home** (7 to 2 op evens); 15 Ran. Sht hd, nk, ¾l, 6l, 2l. 1m 14.91s (a 2.21s). SR: 45/44/43/41/14/8.

Probables

(8) NATIVE OAK – H. Cecil 3-8.11 S. Cauthen
    F.   F.   C. C.
    Prom   (13) — D√
    ★★   ★★★   8 lb pen

(9) GEORGIA RIVER – O. Douieb 3-8.9 W. Swinburn
    F.   F.   C. C.
    Prom   (27) — D
    ★★   ★   6 lb pen

(12) ININSKY – G. Harwood 3-8.7 G. Starkey
    F. ·   F.   C. C.
    Prom   (228) dr D√
    ★★   —   4 lb pen

This is an example of a 7f conditions stakes race for 3-year-olds and 4-year-olds only. It illustrates again how recent winning form plays such a dominant role in pinpointing winners. Analysis revealed three probables NATIVE OAK, GEORGIA RIVER and ININSKY.

ININSKY was making its seasonal reappearance in the race, but had improved sufficiently as a 2 y.o. to finish the season by being allowed to take its chance in the Group III Horris Hill Stakes at Newbury, but where it had been found wanting. NATIVE OAK, by contrast, was having its fourth race of the current campaign having won a not dissimilar contest at Leicester in its previous race. On a rather tenuous collateral form line provided by MISTER WONDERFUL, who also contested the Horris Hill Stakes as a 2 y.o. and had finished third when NATIVE OAK finished fourth in a 3 y.o. 7f handicap at Newmarket, there was little to choose between ININSKY and NATIVE OAK. There was no comparable form line between GEORGIA RIVER and the other two probables, GEORGIA RIVER having won a 1m conditions stakes race for 3-year-olds at Nottingham, beating the useful AL BASHAAMA.

Applying the selection formula, however, NATIVE OAK with a far superior start rating was made the choice.

Result: 1st NATIVE OAK (11–8 fav.) won by 3 lengths.

Form Book No. 1096 *BATH 14 June 1986 (good to firm)*

5.0 — BEDMINSTER MAIDEN STAKES (DIV II) (3-Y-O). £1,200 added (£1,597.60). 1m. 2f. 50yds. (16). STALLS.

2	(6)	87-223	**ASHINGTON GROVE 19** D Murray-Smith 9-0 .... P Cook	75
3	(14)	37	**BASTINADO 11** I Balding 9-0 .... J Matthias	—
4	(11)		**BEDROCK 37** K Bishop 9-0 .... B Procter	—
8	(1)	0	**CELTIC SWORD 33** G Thorner 9-0 .... J Williams	—
16	(12)	·	**GOLD MONOPOLY** K Cunningham-Brown 9-0 .... R Perham (7)	—
17	(10)	09	**GRENDEL 32** P W Harris 9-0 .... R Wernham	—
18	(4)	0	**GUYMYSON 49** M Pipe 9-0 .... R Street	—
21	(9)	87	**KING JACK 19** J Dunlop 9-0 .... S Whitworth	62
23	(7)	5	**LORD IT OVER 16** G Harwood 9-0 .... A Clark	●78
28	(8)	077-90	**ROI DE SOLEIL 12** M Blanshard 9-0 .... DOUBTFUL	—
29	(16)	LL	**SOME GUEST (B) 7** J Roberts 9-0 .... R Weaver	—
33	(5)	986-600	**TOM RUM 33** H Candy 9-0 .... N Adams	—
38	(15)	0	**CALVINETTE 56** B Hills 8-11 .... M Hills	—
45	(2)	00-88	**MIGHTY FLASH 11** D Elsworth 8-11 .... A McGlone·	—
47	(3)	464	**QUEEN'S VISIT 32** P Walwyn 8-11 .... N Howe	77
50	(13)		**SUPER SIHLOUETTE** K Ivory 8-11 .... G Morgan	—

Probable SP: 15-8 Queen's Visit, 4 Ashington Grove, 5 Lord It Over, 7 King Jack, 8 Bastinado, 10 Calvinette, 12 Tom Rum.
FAVOURITES: — — — — — 3
1985: The Footman 9-0 (A McGlone) 9-2 D Elsworth.12 ran.

-30 BASTINADO (9-0) ch g Bustino — Strathspey by Jimmy Reppin.

June 3, Salisbury, 1¼m (3-y-o) mdn, good. £1,837: 1 Almaarad (9-0, 2); 2 Knights Legend(USA) (9-0, 16); 3 Sadeem-(USA) (9-0, 8); 7 BASTINADO (9-0, Pat Eddery, 11), **headway final 3f, kept on inside last** (3 to 1 op 4 to 1); 8 MIGHTY FLASH (8-8, S Dawson, 3*, 10), **well behind until headway 3f out, kept on inside last** (14 to 1 op 12 to 1); 20 Ran. 3l, 4l, 1½l, nk, 5l, ¾l, 1½l. 2m 35.91s (a 1.61s). SR: 60/54/46/40/39/29.

April 29, Bath, 1m 3f 150yds (3-y-o) mdn, good, £1,171: 1 Golden Heights (9-0, 7); 2 Allatum(USA) (8-11, 1); 3 BASTINADO (9-0, J Matthias, 16), **good headway 3f out, every chance over 1f out, stayed on, should improve** (20 to 1 op 12 to 1); 16 Ran. 8l, hd, 1½l, 6l, 1½l, 2l, 6l, ½l. 2m 38.6s (a 10.6s). SR: 52/33/32/29/17/14.

-5 LORD IT OVER(USA) (9-0) b c Best Turn — Idle Hour Princess by Ribot.

May 29, Brighton, 1¼m (3-y-o) mdn, good to firm, £926: 1 Landski (9-0 , 5); 2 Frangnito (9-0 , 12); 3 Admirals All (9-0 , 14); 5 LORD IT OVER(USA) (9-0 , G Starkey , 3), **always prominent, one pace final two furlongs** (5 to 1 op 9 to 4); 17 Ran. ¼l, 6l, ¾l, 1l, 1½l. 2m 2.6s (a 2.6s). SR: 54/53/41/39/37/34.

Probables

(3) BASTINADO – I. Balding 9.0 J. Matthias

F.	F.	C.	C.
Prom	(11)	—	D√
★★	★★★		G√

(23) LORD IT OVER – G. Harwood 9.0 A. Clark

F.	F.	C.	C.
Prom	(16)	—	D
★★	★★		G✓

Non-runner: ROI DE SOLEIL

This is another example of a 3 y.o. maiden race over 1m 2f 50y. In common with many middle-distance 3 y.o. maiden races, this race attracted above the desired minimum number of runners, as many maiden 3-year-olds are entered for this type of event in the faint hope that they might be successful. Therefore, although there are many runners, those with a chance of actually winning are rather few in number. A glance at the form figures of the majority of the field was most unimpressive, and this first impression was confirmed when a deeper study was undertaken. The newcomers were from stables not noted for their first-time exploits with runners and therefore could be disregarded.

ASHINGTON GROVE was perhaps a surprising candidate among those disregarded in the original form review, but was considered to be a typical maiden race performer in its three prior races of similar class, showing commendable form but due to its lack of finishing pace always found a horse or two faster, and therefore at this stage of the season would still succumb to this failing.

QUEEN'S VISIT, a filly, was also perhaps surprisingly disregarded, firstly because as a 3 y.o. filly she would find it difficult to beat colts at this time of the year (fillies do not usually come on to par with colts until late summer or autumn), and although she had shown some commendable form in respectable class this also revealed her limitations.

Form analysis resolved to two probables BASTINADO and LORD IT OVER. BASTINADO had only two previous races, running very encouragingly in the first when finishing third, and the form being endorsed both by the winner and the fourth-placed horse, who subsequently won. In its next race, almost 5 weeks later, BASTINADO never got into the race until late into the proceedings against probably slightly better-class rivals than it was meeting today. LORD IT OVER, meanwhile, had only one previous race (where it had been very easy in the betting market, although opening as favourite, it had drifted out to be returned as third favourite in the starting prices) and finished fifth.

Applying the selection formula, BASTINADO was made the selection choice.

Result: 1st BASTINADO (4–1) won by a neck.

Form Book No. 1150 *ROYAL ASCOT 19 June 1986 (firm)*

3.45—(Prefix 3) **THE GOLD CUP £60,000** added.
(**£44,688·00**). 2m. 4f. (12) **STALLS**

1	(2)	5123-48	**BOURBON BOY** 24 M Stoute 4-9-0		W R Swinburn	69
2	(12)	211-413	**EASTERN MYSTIC** 24 (BF) L Cumani 4-9-0		Pat Eddery	76
3	(8)	214-11	**ERYDAN** 47 Tore Persson (Sweden) 5-9-0		D Persson	—
4	(7)	2209-76	**KUBLAI** 24 G Lewis 4-9-0		P Waldron	69
5	(6)	3142-61	**LONGBOAT** 24 (C) W Hern 5-9-0		W Carson	●78
6	(4)	4224/71	**ORE** 26 (C2) W Musson 8-9-0		M Wigham	60
7	(3)	L08639	**PETRIZZO** 24 C Brittain 5-9-0		C Asmussen	73
8	(9)	00-1431	**RISING** 21 K Prendergast (Ireland) 4-9-0		G Curran	65
9	(10)	22-LL22	**SEISMIC WAVE** 24 B Hills 5-9-0		B Thomson	74
10	(11)	L214-36	**SPICY STORY** 25 I Balding 5-9-0		S Cauthen	71
11	(1)	1361-54	**TALE QUALE** 24 H Candy 4-9-0		T Ives	71
12	(5)	12124-L	**I WANT TO BE** 24 J Dunlop 4-8-11		G Starkey	60

Probable S.P.: 5-2 Longboat, 3 Eastern Mystic, 9-2 Seismic Wave, 6 Spicy Story, 8 Rising, 10 Ore, 12 Kublai, 14 I Want To Be.
FAVOURITES : 2 1 1 1 2 3 1
1985 : Gildoran 5-9-0 (B. Thomson) 5-2 jt.-fav. B. Hills, 12 ran.

3.45 🐎🐎🐎 Gold Cup (Group I) 2½m £44,688

3/142-61 LONGBOAT (5-9-0) b h Welsh Pageant — Pirogue by Reliance II. 1984, 1½m good to firm (Goodwood), 1½m 65yds good (Chester), 1m 3f 150yds good (Bath), 1m 3f 30yds good to firm (Kempton); 1985, 2m good (Ascot); 1986, 2m good (Sandown). £49,404 (£18,675).

May 26, Sandown, 2m good, £18,675: (Group 3) 1 LONGBOAT (5-8-11, W Carson, 4), chased leader till went on well over 2f out, ridden clear below distance, impressive (4 to 1 op 6 to 1); 2 SEISMIC WAVE(USA) (5-8-11, B Thomson, 2), held up, smooth progress 2f out, every chance approaching last, ridden and no extra (5 to 1 op 7 to 2); 3 EASTERN MYSTIC (4-9-0, Pat Eddery, 3), led till well over 2f out, kept on well inside last (7 to 2 fav op 3 to 1); 4 TALE QUALE (4-8-11, T Ives, 7), in touch, lost place 2f out, staying on again finish (10 to 1 op 12 to 1); 6† KUBLAI(USA) (4-8-8, P Waldron, 10), never troubled leaders (50 to 1); 8 BOURBON BOY (4-8-8, W R Swinburn, 8), chased leaders, ridden when not much room over 2f out, faded (11 to 2 tchd 6 to 1); 9 PETRIZZO (5-8-8, P Robinson, 6), in touch till weakened final 3f (14 to 1 op 25 to 1); 10 I WANT TO BE(USA) (4-8-11, B Rouse, 5), always behind (20 to 1); 10 Ran. 2½l, ½l, 1½l, hd, 1l, dd-ht. 3m 37.83s (a 4.93s). SR: 56/53/55/50/46/45.

May 17, Newbury, 1m 5f 60yds soft, £8,129: 1 Kaytu (5-8-7, 7); 2 Mango Express (4-8-7, 1); 3 Leading Star (4-8-7, 13); 6 LONGBOAT (5-8-7, B Rouse, 2), prominent, ridden 2f out, soon weakened (13 to 2 op 5 to 1 tchd 7 to 1); 7 ORE (8-8-7, P Waldron, 4), headway 3f out, stayed on same pace last 2f (16 to 1 op 12 to 1); 14 Ran. Nk, 2l, ½l, hd, 2½l. 3m 3.12s (a 12.82s). SR: 45/44/40/39/38/33.

June 20, Ascot, 2½m good to firm, £42,566: (Group 1) 1 Gildoran (5-9-0 , 11); 2 LONGBOAT (4-9-0 , W Carson , 6), in touch, headway six out, lost place three

out, strong challenge inside final furlong, ran on (9 to 1 op 8 to 1 tchd 11 to 1); 3 Destroyer (4-9-0 , 10); 8 PETRIZZO (4-9-0 , S Cauthen , 8), in third place until weakened two out (14 to 1 op 12 to 1); 12 Ran. ½l, ½l, nk, 4l, 1½l, hd. 4m 25.19s (a 3.19s). SR: 49/48/47/46/42/40.

May 16 1985, York, 1½m good to soft, £18,565: (Group 2) 1 Ilium (4-8-7 , 6); 2 Old Country (6-9-1 , 1); 3 Centroline (7-8-10 , 10); 4 LONGBOAT (4-8-10 , W Carson , 9), driven along after four furlongs, headway entering straight, no impression on leaders (5 to 1 op 7 to 2); 5 PETRIZZO (4-8-7 , J Lowe , 7), outpaced approaching straight, some headway final two furlongs (20 to 1); 9 SPICY STORY(USA) (4-8-7 , Pat Eddery , 8), ridden and outpaced seven out, never dangerous after (7 to 4 fav op 6 to 4 tchd 2 to 1); 10 Ran. 6l, 4l, ½l, 5l, 5l. 3m 5.42s (a 9.2s). SR: 47/47/48/37/29/27.

211-413 EASTERN MYSTIC (4-9-0) b c Elocutionist — Belle Pensee by Ribot. 1985, 1½m good to soft (Newmarket), 1½m 127yds good (Doncaster), 1m 5f 60yds good to firm (Newbury); 1986, 1½m good to soft (York). £53,113 (£22,086).

May 26, Sandown. See LONGBOAT.

May 15, York, 1½m good to soft, £22,086: (Group 2) 1 EASTERN MYSTIC (4-8-9 , Pat Eddery, 2), waited with in touch, headway 2f out, ridden and went left approaching final furlong, led and ran on last 50 yards (9 to 4 fav op 2 to 1); 2 SEISMIC WAVE(USA) (5-8-9, B Thomson, 3), tracked leader, led 4f out, ridden final 2f, headed and not quicken last 50yds (7 to 2 op 2 to 1); 3 PETRIZZO (5-8-9, S Cauthen, 4), always handy , effort and ridden 2f out, stayed on under pressure closing stages (20 to 1 op 16 to 1); 4 BOURBON BOY (4-8-9, W R Swinburn , 6), held up in rear, headway final 3f, stayed on final furlong (3 to 1 op 7 to 2 tchd ‡ to 1); 5 TALE QUALE (4-8-9, T Ives, 10), chased leaders, every chance over 3f out, on pace last 2f (4 to 1 op 7 to 2); 7 Ran. 1¾l, ½l, 3l, 6l, 12l. 3m 12.26s (a 15.86s). SR: 42/39/38/32/20/-.

April 30, Ascot. See SPICY STORY (USA).

Sept 21, Newbury, 1m 5f 60yds h'cap (0-70), good to firm, £10,261: 1 EASTERN MYSTIC (3-9-4, inc 7lb ex , L Piggott , 15), always handy , ridden over 2f out, ran on to lead last 50yards (11 to 2 op 5 to 1); 2 Insular (5-8-7 , 5*, 10); 3 Lundylux (3-7-10, inc 1lb ow , 6); 16 Ran. ½l, 1½l, 6l, 1½l, ¾l. 2m 48.65s (b 1.65s). SR: 94/87/67/63/69/63.

4214-35 SPICY STORY(USA) (5-9-0) b h Blushing Groom(Fr) — Javamine by Nijinsky. 1984, 1m 3f good (Newbury), 2m good to firm (York); 1985, 2¼m good to firm (Doncaster). £31,416 (---).

May 25, Longchamp, 2¼m firm, £30,110: (Group 1) 1 Air De Cour(USA) (4-9-2, 7); 2 Fondouk (5-9-2, 4); 3 Green (5-9-2); 5 SPICY STORY(USA) (9-2 , Pat Eddery . 1), 6 Ran. 1½l, ½l, 1½l. 4m 21.10s

April 30, Ascot, 2m good to soft, £24,388: (Group 3) 1 Valuable Witness(USA) (6-9-0, 1); 2 Ramich John (4-8-5, 10); 3 SPICY STORY(USA) (5-8-11, S Cauthen, 5), al-

ways prominent, led 4f out, headed 1 ¼f out, soon outpaced (5 to 1 op 5 to 2); 4 EASTERN MYSTIC (4-8-8, R Guest, 9), always prominent, ridden 3f out, soon beaten (7 to 1 op 5 to 1 tchd 8 to 1); 8 PETRIZZO (5-8-8, P Robinson, 4), led till headed and weakened 4f out (25 to 1); 10 Ran. Sht hd, 4l, 6l, 2½l, 8l. 3m 47.41s (a 21.41s). SR: 30/20/22/13/10/2.

Oct 3, Newmarket. See TALE QUALE.

Sept 12, Doncaster, 2½m good to firm, £21,246: (Group 3) 1 SPICY STORY(USA) (4-8-9 , S Cauthen , 2), tracked leaders, slight lead approaching 2f out, soon headed, stayed on to lead close home (7 to 4 fav op 6 to 4 tchd 15 to 8); 2 BOURBON BOY (3-7-6 , M L Thomas , 8), waited with, tracked leaders into straight, rapid progress 2f out, headed inside last, kept on (11 to 4 tchd 4 to 1); 3 Bespoke (4-8-5 , 5); 5 PETRIZZO (4-8-5 , T Ives , 4), led after three furlongs till half-way, remained close up until weakened two out (14 to 1 op 12 to 1); 8 Ran. Nk, 4l, 1l, 5l, nk, 2l, ¾l. 3m 56.38s (a 1.38s).

May 16 1985, York. See LONGBOAT.

Probables

(2) EASTERN MYSTIC – L. Cumani 4-9.0 Pat Eddery

F.	F.	C.	C.
Prom	(24)	—	D?
★★	★		C√
			G√

(5) LONGBOAT – W. Hern 5-9.0 W. Carson

F.	F.	C.	C.
Proven	(24)	—	D√
★★★	★		C√
			G√

(10) SPICY STORY – I. Balding 5-5.0 S. Cauthen

F.	F.	C.	C.
Prom	(25)	—	D√
★★	★		C√
			G√

Non-runner: ORE

This is an example of the leading marathon stayers' race where proven top-class form and ability to stay the extreme distance will be the most salient factors.

In this 11-runner race, form analysis revealed three probables, EASTERN MYSTIC, LONGBOAT and SPICY STORY, with all three having raced against each other in earlier encounters. As no runner in the field had raced less than 21 days previously, the incisive influence of very recent form and fitness could play no major role in deciding this race and proven form was considered the most important issue.

On known form LONGBOAT held the other runners, having won its

221

previous race over 2m at Sandown and finishing second to GILDORAN (beaten 1 length) in the corresponding race last season. EASTERN MYSTIC finishing 3¼ lengths behind LONGBOAT in the Group III race at Sandown was not now reopposing the winner on 3 lb better terms and therefore entitled to finish closer. However, the distance of the Gold Cup was 4f further and while LONGBOAT was proven to stay the extreme distance EASTERN MYSTIC had yet to race over any distance in excess of 2m. SPICY STORY, a proven inferior when meeting LONGBOAT in the Yorkshire Cup over a year previously, had last run in the French Gold Cup just over 3 weeks earlier, had been unplaced and had yet to prove that it was capable of winning at this very highest level.

Applying the formula, where LONGBOAT had the proven form (and was proven over the course and distance) LONGBOAT was made the selection choice.

Result: 1st LONGBOAT (evens fav.) won by 5 lengths.

Form Book No. 1154 *ROYAL ASCOT 20 June 1986 (firm)*

2.30—(Prefix 1) **W I N D S O R CASTLE STAKES (2-Y.-O.), £14,000 added (£12,126·80) 5f. (10)   STALLS**

`Formcast`

1	(1)	31232	ALKADI 8 (D) W O'Gorman 9-4	.....T Ives	63
2	(4)	211	CAROL'S TREASURE 11 (D) B Hills 9-4	...B Thomson	●78
5	(10)	43221	QUICK SNAP (B) 6 (D) A Ingham 9-4	...R Curant	61
6	(3)	2211	SINGING STEVEN 18 (D) R Hannon 9-4	...B Rouse	53
11	(5)	33	BATTLEAXE 18 J Toller 8-11	...W Carson	53
12	(8)	32	COPPER RED 6 (BF) P Makin 8-11	...T Quinn	60
13	(7)	322	JOEY BLACK 13 Miss J Morgan (Ireland) 8-11	D Gillespie	65
14	(2)	22	LUCIANAGA 9 P Walwyn 8-11	...Paul Eddery	77
16	(9)	4	NEW MEXICO 11 D Morley 8-11	...S Cauthen	53
19	(6)		MADAM BILLA 32 N Callaghan 8-8	...Pat Eddery	—

Probable S.P.: 2 Carol's Treasure, 3 Lucianaga, 4 Singing Steven, 6 Copper Red, 8 Battleaxe, 10 Alkadi.
FAVOURITES : 3 0 0 1 1 2 0.
1985 : Atall Atall 9-4 (Paul Eddery), 12-1, M. Pipe. 9 ran.

2.30 ★★★	Windsor Castle Stakes (2-y-o) 5f (£12,126)

211 CAROL'S TREASURE (April 24, 13,500gns) (9-4) b c Balidar — Really Sharp by Sharpen Up. **1986, 5f firm (Doncaster), 6f good (Goodwood). £5,452.**

June 9, Goodwood, 6f (2-y-o), good, £3,056: 1 CAROL'S TREASURE (9-1, B Thomson, 1), **held up, led one and a half furlongs out, soon clear, easily** (6 to 5 on op 5 to 4 on); 2 Santella Grey (8-11, 4); 3 Tender Tiff (8-12, 6); 5 Ran. 2½l, 4l, 8l, 1½l. 1m 12.7s (a 1.2s). SR: 53/39/24/-/-/-.

May 26, Doncaster, 5f (2-y-o) mdn, firm, £2,395: 1 CAROL'S TREASURE (9-0, R Street, 7), **chased leaders, led entering final furlong, kept on well** (evens fav op 6 to 4 on); 2 Song N'Jest (9-0, 9); 3 Joint Services (9-0, 11); 9 Ran. 1¼l, 1½l, nk, 3l, hd, 2½l. 1m 00.90s (a 1.4s). SR: 62/56/50/ 49/37/36.

May 17, Newbury, 5f (2-y-o), good to soft, £4,123: 1 Bestplan (9-3, 4); 2 CAROL'S TREASURE (8-11, B Thomson, 2), **headway and not clear run 1 ½f out, ran on and switched inside last, just failed** (20 to 1 op 8 to 1); 3 Mebhil (8-11, 7); 9 Ran. Hd, 1l, 4l, nk, 6l, sht hd. 1m 6.48s (a 5.48s). SR: 31/24/20/4/9/-.

Probable

(2) CAROL'S TREASURE – B. Hills 9.4 B. Thomson

F.	F.	C.	C.
Prom	(11)	up	D√
★★	★★★		G√
			7 lb pen

This is an example of a good-class conditions stakes for 2-year-olds over 5f. The Windsor Castle Stakes is a race held on the final day of Royal Ascot, and although it is usually contested by speedy juveniles they are those considered just below the best of their generation. For most horses this race represents quite a raise in class and therefore favours horses with prior winning form (11 of 12 winners 1974–85 had won at least one prior race) for if a horse was still a maiden before competing here it was hardly likely to lose its non-winning tag in more esteemed company.

Form analysis was therefore centred on the four horses with winning form – three of whom won their previous race. ALKADI, the exception of these, was the first eliminated from calculations as its form seemed moderate having campaigned unsuccessfully around north-country race-tracks and was raised in class here. QUICK SNAP was running commendably and although eventually winning its previous race had shown itself to be below this better class. SINGING STEVEN the winner of its two previous races at Wolverhampton and Bath was another experiencing a rise in the grade. In its last race it had only narrowly beaten two maidens BATTLEAXE and LUCIANAGA whom it reopposed here on the same weight terms. This left CAROL'S TREASURE, a horse probably unfortunate not to have won its three previous races having only just been beaten in its racecourse début against a horse BESTPLAN who had subsequently defeated SIZZLING MELODY the winner of the previous day's Group III Norfolk Stakes at the Royal meeting. CAROL'S TREASURE then won its next two races comfortably, a maiden race at Doncaster and a conditions race at Goodwood over 6f, beating good previous winners. CAROL'S TREASURE was considered the only probable and applying the selection formula was made the selection choice.

Result: 1st CAROL'S TREASURE (6–5 fav.) won by 1½ lengths.

Form Book No. 1186 *AYR 21 June 1986 (good)*

3.00 — EBF ROMAN WARRIOR SHIELD (2-Y-O). £2,000 added (£1,972). 7f. (9). STALLS

1	(8)	759	BEAU BENZ 7 M H Easterby 9-0	M Birch	⚊
2	(9)	0696	BEJANT SKITE (B) 5 C Parker 9-0	T Williams	⚊
3	(4)	8	BE MY PROSPECT 25 Miss I M Bell 9-0	J Quinn (5)	⚊
6	(5)		FRIENDS FOR LIFE N Tinkler 9-0	J Bleasdale	⚊
8	(3)	73	KING BALLADEER 11 G P-Gordon 9-0	G Duffield	77
9	(1)	33	MEBHIL (BF) 21 P Kelleway 9-0	Gay Kelleway (5)	●78
12	(6)	40	SKY CAT 17 J Wilson 9-0	Julie Bowker (7)	65
13	(7)		SOMBRERO GOLD R Whitaker 9-0	K Bradshaw (5)	⚊
14	(2)	3	PINE AWAY 14 J W Watts 8-11	N Connorton	66

Probable SP: 5-2 King Balladeer, 3 Mebhil, 7-2 Pine Away, 5 Sky Cat, 9 Beau Benz, 12 Bejant Skite.

FAVOURITES: ⚊ ⚊ ⚊ ⚊ ⚊ 1
1985: Dancing Zeta 9-0 (E Hide). 4-5 fav. P Kelleway. 7 ran.

3.00 Conditions 2-y-o 7f £1,972

03 KING BALLADEER (Feb 21, 28,000gns) (9-0) b c Dominion — Moonlight Serenade by Crooner.

June 10, Yarmouth, 7f (2-y-o) mdn, good to firm, £964: 1 Midyan(9-0, 2); 2 Bag O'Rhythm (9-0, 1); 3 KING BALLADEER (9-0, G Duffield, 4), **led for 4f, no extra** (16 to 1 op 10 to 1 tchd 20 to 1); 10 Ran. 3l, 2l, 3l, ½l, hd. 1m 13.7s (a 1.1s). SR: 48/36/28/16/14/12.

May 30, Newmarket, 6f (2-y-o) mdn, good to firm, £3,548: 1 Albasar(USA) (9-0, 2); 2 Good Point (9-0, 1); 3 Brave Dancer (9-0, 8); 7 KING BALLADEER (9-0, W Carson, 9), **never dangerous** (20 to 1 op 12 to 1); 11 Ran. 2l, 1½l, 1l, 1l, 1l. 1m 12.83s (a 1.83s). SR: 53/45/39/35/31/27.

33 MEBHIL (May 22, 15,000gns) (9-0) b c Beldale Flutter — Lady Rushen by Dancer's Image.

May 31, Kempton, 6f (2-y-o) good, £2,763: 1 Mister Majestic (9-2, 6); 2 Pensurchin (9-2, 3); 3 MEBHIL (8-11, S Cauthen, 7), **always prominent, ridden 2f out, kept on same pace** final furlong (6 to 5 fav op 11 to 10 tchd 5 to 4 and 11 to 10 on); 9 Ran. 2½l, hd, nk, 7l, 1l, sht hd. 1m 13.68s (a 1.68s). SR: 56/46/40/44/11/7.

May 17, Newbury, 5f (2-y-o), good to soft, £4,123: 1 Bestpian (9-3, 4); 2 Carol's Treasure (8-11, 2); 3 MEBHIL (8-11, S Cauthen, 7), **always prominent, kept on inside last** (12 to 1 op 6 to 1); 9 Ran. Hd, 1l, 4l, nk, 6l, sht hd. 1m 6.48s (a 5.48s). SR: 31/24/20/4/9/-.

3 PINE AWAY (March 26, 96,000gns) (8-11) b f Shirley Heights — Piney Ridge by Native Prince.

June 7, Haydock, 6f (2-y-o) mdn, good to firm, £3,036: 1 Twyla (8-11, 7); 2 Bint Pasha(USA) (8-11, 2); 3 PINE AWAY (8-11, N Connorton, 9), **close up till outpaced approaching final furlong** (12 to 1 op 10 to 1 tchd 14 to 1); 14 Ran. 4l, 4l, sht hd, 2l, 2l, hd. 1m 16.51s (a 3.31s). SR: 49/33/17/16/8/-.

Probables

(8) KING BALLADEER – G. Pritchard-Gordon 9.0 G. Duffield

F.	F.	C.	C.
Prom	(11)	—	D✓
★★	★★★		G✓

Trainer's course record ✓

(9) MEBHIL – P. Kelleway 9.0 Gay Kelleway (5)
F. F. C. C.
Prom (21) — D?
★★ ★★ G√

(14) PINE AWAY – J. W. Watts 8.11 N. Connorton
F. F. C. C.
Prom (14) — D?
★★ ★★★ G√

This is an example of a 7f maiden race for 2-year-olds and shows how good recent form is the strongest influence in deciding races. In the approach to 2 y.o. maiden races one of the first considerations is to view the previously unraced competitors who are making their racecourse début in the event with particular regard to the record of their trainer and breeding. These races will usually take little to win, and the 'dark' unproven horse often can hold sway over the horse already proven in its previous race(s) yet unable to win a race. (In 1985 32.8 per cent of maiden 2 y.o. races were won by horses making their racecourse début.) In this race the newcomers appeared to hold no such threat, being cheaply priced yearlings from stables not noted for their first-time-out record with 2-year-olds.

On analysis the race therefore resolved to three probables, KING BALLADEER, MEBHIL and PINE AWAY. KING BALLADEER had run two previous races. The first appeared as merely an introductory one on its home course at Newmarket where it was never put in the race. Its second run was what appeared a rather 'hot' 7f maiden at Yarmouth won by a smart débutante from H. Cecil's yard. KING BALLADEER had gained needed race experience, being put in the race from the outset only to be found out in the latter part of the race. The second had subsequently confirmed the form by since winning 5 days previously at Windsor.

MEBHIL, the second probable, had also shown promising form, making a very pleasing début in a good 5f stakes race at Newbury behind subsequent winners BESTPLAN and CAROL'S MUSIC, but had been seen as slightly one-paced in its next race when made favourite over 6f at Kempton.

The third candidate was PINE AWAY who had a pleasing introduction although eventually finishing a well-beaten third 2 weeks earlier in a maiden fillies race over 6f at Haydock. She now was tackling a further furlong and against colts who at this time in the season were still likely to be more forward than this filly.

Applying the selection formula, MEBHIL was immediately eliminated and the selection choice rested between KING BALLADEER and PINE AWAY with KING BALLADEER getting the vote by being a proven performer of the distance and being trained by G. Pritchard-Gordon who had such an excellent percentage strike of runners to winners at this Ayr racecourse (28 per cent over a 5-year period).

Result: 1st KING BALLADEER (15–8 fav.) won by 4 lengths.

Form Book No. 1382A CURRAGH 28 June 1986 (good)

3.05 — BUDWEISER IRISH DERBY (3-Y-O). (IR £299,800). 1m 4f. STALLS

1	(2)	1321-23	**BAKHAROFF** 20 G Harwood 9-0 .... G Starkey **74**
			bc The Minstrel—Qui Royalty *(Green, pink sash & cap. white sleeves)*
2	(9)	111-21	**BONHOMIE** 11 (D) H Cecil 9-0 .... Pat Eddery **68**
			bc What A Pleasure—Chatterbox
			(Maroon, white sleeves, maroon cap. white star)
3	(4)	1	**FIGHTING HARD** 20 (D) M Halford 9-0 .... G Curran **40**
			bc Hard Fought—Bunch of Blue *(White, blue stars, red cap)*
4	(8)	111-116	**FLASH OF STEEL** 24 (C3) D K Weld 9-0 .... M J Kinane **72**
			bc Kris—Spark of Fire *(Emerald green, white diamond frame &*
			diamonds on sleeves & quartered cap)
5	(1)	42	**KING RETAIN** 26 L Browne 9-0 .... D J Murphy **41**
			bc Cut Above—De'b Old Fruit
			(Dark blue, mauve spots on body, sleeves and cap)
6	(3)	11-3113	**MASHKOUR** 24 (D) H Cecil 9-0 .... S Cauthen **73**
			ch c Irish River—Sancta Rose
			(Yellow, blue diamonds on body, yellow cap blue spots)
7	(11)	07-4129	**MR JOHN** 24 L Browne 9-0 .... M T Browne **70**
			ch c Northfields—Ashton Amber *(White, emerald green stars,*
			white sleeves, white cap, emerald green spots)
8	(7)	1-370	**OSTENSIBLE** 20 G Harwood 9-0 .... K Butler **40**
			bc Alleged—Proud Pattie *(Green, pink sash & cap, white sleeves)*
9	(8)	0-01713	**PACIFIC DRIFT** 35 (C) B V Kelly 9-0 .... S Craine **53**
			ch c Henbit—Mill's Girl *(Mauve and primrose quarters)*
10	(10)	2-111	**SHAHRASTANI** 24 (D) M Stoute 9-0 .... W R Swinburn **78**
			ch c Nijinsky—Shademah *(Green, red epaulettes)*
11	(6)	05-131	**WORLD COURT** 49 T G Curtin 9-0 .... K Moses **50**
			bc Damascus—My Hollow *(Red, black diamonds, hooped sleeves. red cap)*

Probable SP: 11-10 Shahrastani, 7-2 Mashkour, 4 Bakharoff, 7 Bonhomie, 12 Flash of Steel, 16 Mr John.

1985: Law Society 9-0 (Pat Eddery), 15-8 fav. M V O'Brien. 13 ran.

3.05 Budweiser Irish Derby (Group 1) 1½m (IR£299,800)

2-111 SHAHRASTANI(USA) (9-0) ch c Nijinsky — Shademah by Thatch. **1986, 1½m good (Epsom), 1½m soft (Sandown), 1½m 110yds good (York).** £339,559 (£339,559).

June 4, Epsom, 1½m (3-y-o), good, £239,260: (Group 1) 1 SHAHRASTANI(U-SA) (9-0, W R Swinburn, 10), **well placed, led over 2f out, stayed on close home** (11 to 2 op 4 to 1 tchd 6 to 1); 2 Dancing Brave(USA) (9-0, 6); 3 MASHKOUR(USA) (9-0, S Cauthen, 3), **switched right 3f out, good progress from 2f out, finished well** (12 to 1 op 12 to 1 tchd 13 to 1); 6 FLASH OF STEEL (9-0, M J Kinane, 4), **ran on last 3f, never nearer** (25 to 1 op 33 to 1 tchd 40 to 1); 9 MR JOHN (9-0, T Ives, 2), **started slowly, headway when not clear run 2 ½f out, hampered 1 ½f out, not recover** (50 to 1 op 66 to 1); 17 Ran. ½l, 2½l, hd, sht hd, ¾l. 2m 37.13s (a 2.13s). SR: 97/96/91/90/89/87.

May 14, York, 1½m 110yds (3-y-o), good, £80,454: (Group 2) 1 SHAHRASTANI(U-SA) (9-0, W R Swinburn, 4), **soon tracking leader, led 2f out, edged left and ran on, driven out** (11 to 10 on op evens tchd 6 to 5 agst); 2 Nomrood(USA) (9-0, 2); 3 Sirk (9-0, 1); 7 Ran. 1½l, 1l, 5l, 2½l, hd. 2m 11.75s (a 2.12s). SR: 84/81/79/69/64/63.

April 26, Leopardstown, 1½m (3-y-o), soft, £19,845: (Group 3) 1 SHAHRASTANI(U-SA) (8-7, W R Swinburn, 1), **2nd until led 2 ½f out, driven clear, eased final 100yds** (2 to 1 op evens); 2 BONHOMIE(USA) (8-12, S Cauthen, 3), **led until 2 ½f out, stayed on one pace** (7 to 4 fav op 6 to 4 tchd 2 to 1); 3 Sirk (8-7, 2); 4 Ran. 4l, 5l, dist. 2m 18.77s (a 13.27s). SR: 55/52/37/-/-/-.

Probable

(10) SHAHRASTANI – M. Stoute 9.0 W. R. Swinburn

F.	F.	C.	C.
Proven	(24)	—	D√
★★★	★		G√

This is an example of one of the most important conditions races for 3 y.o. colts over a distance of 1½m. The Irish Derby is a Group I race and ranks only with the English Derby in prestige in the Flat race calendar. It is included here as a fine illustration of how top-class proven form can be reliably depended upon. In this field of 11 runners that included the leading stayers of their generation, form analysis revealed only one probable SHAHRASTANI. SHAHRASTANI the winner of the English Derby was attempting to complete the double of the two premier staying Classics, a feat last achieved by a previous inmate the late SHERGAR (1981).

Approaching selection on an elimination basis, the following horses were immediately discarded:

FIGHTING HARD   a winner of its only race, a Roscommon maiden event was experiencing an enormous rise in class – not good enough.

KING RETAIN   a horse still a maiden was obviously not good enough.

OSTENSIBLE   had been entered to act as a pacemaker for stable companion BAKHAROFF as he did in previous race in the French Derby, not good enough.

PACIFIC DRIFT   unsuccessful in a Group II race at the Curragh over 1¼m in its previous race, was unlikely therefore to win a premier Group I prize.

WORLD COURT   was only handicap class – obviously not capable of winning the Irish Derby.

Of the remaining runners SHAHRASTANI had comfortably defeated MASHKOUR, FLASH OF STEEL and MR JOHN in the English Derby in its previous race, and they would have to improve somewhat to reverse form here – a situation that seldom occurs as the English Derby winner usually proves superior to any rivals it has already defeated in the Epsom race should they ever meet again over the same distance at level weights. Of the two remaining runners BAKHAROFF was held by SHAHRASTANI on a collateral form line with MASHKOUR who had beaten BAKHAROFF ½ length in the Lingfield Derby Trial yet proved no match for SHAHRASTANI in the Derby. The remaining runner BONHOMIE was the candidate that seemed likely to produce the greatest challenge to SHAHRASTANI; although comprehensively beaten 4 lengths by the Epsom Derby winner in the Classic Trial at Sandown when conceding 5 lb it had since won the King Edward VII Stakes Group II 1½m at the

Royal Ascot meeting. However, on a form line with the horse placed third in the Ascot race, NISNAS, who had also finished fifth in the Derby, BONHOMIE would still need to improve at least a length to defeat SHAHRASTANI. Proven form at this level of competition with top-class horses is always likely to be confirmed, and treating this as the major criteria SHAHRASTANI was made the only probable – applying the formula SHAHRASTANI was made the selection choice.

Result: 1st SHAHRASTANI (Evens fav.) won by 8 lengths.

NATIONAL HUNT SEASON 1985–86

Form Book No. 876 *WINDSOR 18 November 1985 (good to firm)*

3.0—TATTERSALLS MARES ONLY NOVICE CHASE (Qualifier).
£2,000 added (£1,503·60). 2m. (8)

1	31LL22	MILANESSA 11 G R Prest 8-11-1	R Dunwoody	65
2	L52-FU4	ESTRALITA 84 (D) R J Hodges 7-10-10	Mr P McEwan (7)	—
3	40PP4-U	EVENING SONG 11 Mrs P Townsley 6-10-10	Mr P Townley	—
4	0U4330-	FIDELIGHT 218 C V Bravery 7-10-10	H Davies	—
7	10/PB-L3	KOHINOOR DIAMOND 11 Miss E Sneyd 5-10-10	B Powell	—
11	745P45	SHIRLEY CREPELLA 11 J J Bridger 5-10-10	M Kinane	—
12	5L3P-23	SWEETCAL 4 (BF) P D Cundell 8-10-10	S Sherwood ●78	
13	72-754	WESTERN KELLY 11 R Parker 8-10-10	P Double	—

Probable S.P. : 13-8 Sweetcal, 11-4 Milanessa, 5 Evening Song, 13-2 Kohinoor Diamond, 8 Estralita.

3.00—TATTERSALLS MARES ONLY NOVICES' CHASE (QUALIFIER)
2m   (£1,503)

316422 MILANESSA (8-11-1) ch m Milan — Ballynavin Money by Even Money. 1985-6, 2½m ch good to firm (Plumpton). £1,131 (£1,131).
Nov 7, Kempton, 2m nov chase, firm, £1,821; 1 Maranzi (7-11-2, 4*); 2 MILANESSA (8-11-1, R Dunwoody), in touch, mistake 8th and 9th, kept on same pace (4 to 1 op 3 to 1); 3 KOHINOOR DIAMOND (5-10-10, B Powell), with leader third, weakened 7th, one pace (12 to 1 op 16 to 1); 4 WESTERN KELLY (8-10-3, Mr T Grantham, 7*), always behind (25 to 1 op 16 to 1); 5 SHIRLEY CREPELLA (5-10-10, Mr L Fogerty), always behind (20 to 1 op 16 to 1); U EVENING SONG (6-11-2, inc 6lb ow, Mr P Townsley), chased leader, second and no chance when blundered and unseated rider last (20 to 1 op 14 to 1); 7 Ran. 8l, 8l, 25l, 4l, dist. 3m 53s (b 1s). SR: 54/41/28/3/-/-.
Oct 29, Plumpton, 3m 1f nov chase, firm, £1,634: 1 Mark Paul(FR) (9-11-5); 2 MILANESSA (8-11-5 , R Dunwoody), always well there, one pace from four out (7 to 1 op 5 to 1 tchd 8 t 1); 3 Armatrist (6-11-5); 5 Ran. 15l, dist. 6m 29.2s (a 15.2s).

Oct 22, Fontwell, 2⅛m 110yds h'cap chase, firm, £1,634: 1 Mood Music (13-10-1, inc 1lb ow, 7*); 2 John Brush(USA) (7-11-3, 7*); 3 Carbury's Kit (10-10-0, inc 9lb ex, 7*); 4 MILANESSA (8-10-0, Mr T Edwards, 7*), no chance from half-way (10 to 1 op 8 to 1 tchd 11 to 1); 9 Ran. Nk, 3l, dist. 4m 35.2s (a 3.2s). SR: 19/35/8/-/-/-.

5630-23 SWEETCAL (8-10-10) b m Caliban — Honey House by Road House II. 1981-2, 2m h Good (Hereford); 1982-3, 2m h good (Ludlow); 1983-4, 2m h good (Ludlow); 1984-5, 2m h good to soft (Nottingham). £5,859 (---).
Nov 14, Uttoxeter, 2m nov chase, good, £1,125: 1 Maid Of Moyode (6-10-12); 2 Little Ginger (6-10-12); 3 SWEETCAL (8-10-12, S Sherwood), always close up, under pressure and every chance when mistake two out, soon beaten (6 to 5 on op 5 to 4 on tchd 11 to 10 agst); 7 Ran. ¾l, 8l, 12l, 4l. 4l. 4m 1s (a 2.3s). SR: 53/52/44/32/28/24.
Nov 2, Chepstow, 2m nov chase, good, £1,740: 1 French Union (7-10-13); 2 SWEETCAL (8-10-8, A Gorman), chased leader, ridden and kept on from two out, no impression (8 to 1 op 7 to 1); 3 Ashlone (6-10-13); 12 Ran. 4l, hd, 15l, 3l, 15l. 4m 6.4s (a 2.9s). SR: 40/31/35/15/17/2.
May 1, Wolverhampton, 2m h'cap hdle, good to firm, £1,035: 1 Brobury (6-10-0 , 4*); 2 Lady Tut (5-11-3); 3 Welsh Oak (5-11-0); 15 SWEETCAL (6-11-7 , A Gorman), soon behind, ridden and lost touch 4th, pulled up before 2 out (14 to 1 op 12 to 1); 15 Ran. 1l, 7l. 4l. 2½l. 2l. 3m 45.5s (Course record). SR: 46/58/48/30/43/38.

Probables

(1) MILANESSA – G. R. Prest 8-11.1 R. Dunwoody

F.	F.	C.	C.
Prom	(11)	—	D?
★★	★★★		G√
			5 lb pen

(12) SWEETCAL – P. D. Cundell 8-10.10 S. Sherwood

F.	F.	C.	C.
Prom	(4)	—	D√
★★	★★★		G√

This 2m novice chase for mares only, serves as a good example of how an experienced handicap hurdler can make a successful early season transition to novice chasing by having the speed element easily to outpace the normal novice chase rivals who are without such known ability.

Analysis of this compact field of eight runners resolved to MILANESSA and SWEETCAL being the only two probables, MILANESSA holding four rivals on their previous race performance at Kempton, and the two other contestants seeming to be completely outclassed.

MILANESSA already had six previous races by this early part of the season, winning a poor-class race at Plumpton on August Bank Holiday and being penalized 5 lb for that success. SWEETCAL by contrast had only two prior races, finishing a very commendable second to FRENCH UNION (a subsequent winner) on her chasing début, but disappointing in her second chasing adventure at Uttoxeter 4 days earlier when beaten by MAID OF MOYODE who had finished well behind her in their initial race at Chepstow. However, with these two experiences behind her and now over these easier fences at Windsor, it was considered SWEET-CAL would reproduce her earlier most promising form. Applying the selection formula SWEETCAL was made the selection choice.

Result: 1st SWEETCAL (2–1 fav.) won by 5 lengths.

Form Book No. 967 *FOLKESTONE 25 November 1985 (good)*

12.45—LE TOUQUET NOVICE HURDLE (Div. 1). £800 (£548). 2m. 5f. (16)

1	0041PL	GARGAMEL 51 W G M Turner 4-10-11	A Jones (4)	66
2	P05255-	AIRBORNE DEAL 270 A Moore 6-10-5	G Moore	●78
4	9	BRUNI BABY 7 J B Sayers 4-10-5	R Rowe	—
5	3523-L3	COLDHARBOUR LAD 27 E L Beever 4-10-5	P Guest	72
6	053P-0	CUMREW (B) 9 N A Vigors 5-10-5	J White	75
11		HIGHLAND CARDINAL J D Davies 6-10-5	R G Hughes	—
12	94	HOWAREYOUGOING 23 S Mellor 6-10-5	G Charles-Jones	—
13	9P-7LPL	MOROCCO BOUND 14 H R Beasley 6-10-5	R Goldstein	76
15	65/0225-	QUAKER LAD 182 B J Wise 9-10-5	E Murphy	69
18	04/	SOBER SAM 643 R Voorspuy 5-10-5	R Rowell	—
20	PF00-	STABLE LAD 254 J A Edwards 6-10-5	P Barton	—
21	P/F0-	STAND FIRM 262 R S Gow 5-10-5	A Webber	—
22	9P-	TRUE PROPHET 333 P D Haynes 4-10-5	A Webb	—
24	946P0P-	WORDEL 265 Mrs R Murdoch 7-10-5	Miss C Moore (7)	64
25		OWENELLEN A R Davison 7-10-0	G McCourt	—
26	0P0-	RUSHOISE 223 Mrs B Dukes 5-10-0	V MvKevitt	—

Probable S.P.: 11-4 Howareyougoing, 7-2 Cumrew, 9-2 Coldharbour Lane, 6 Gargamel, 8 Airborne Deal, 10 Stable Lad, 12 Quaker lad.

FAVOURITES : No corresponding race.
1984 : Abandoned—Course Waterlogged.

12.45 —LE TOUQUET NOVICES' HURDLE (DIV I) 2m 5f £548)

053P-0 CUMREW (5-10-5) b g Gunner B — Almadena by Dairialatan.
Nov 16, Huntingdon, 2½m nov h'cap hdle, good, to firm, £1,334: 1 Kalooki Bert (4-10-12); 2 Dunvegan Castle (6-10-3, inc 2lb ow); 3 Sandyla (4-10-0, 4*, bl); 10 CUMREW (5-11-7, J White), in touch to 8th (7 to 1 op 4 to 1); 11 Ran. Nk, ¾l, 5l, 3l, 5l. 4m 48.9s (b 2.6s). SR: 40/28/30/31/34/26.
March 1, Newbury, 2½m 120yds nov h'cap hdle, soft, £1,742: 1 The Liquidator (5-10-5); 2 Edenspring (6-10-0); 3 Master Cone (8-10-7); P CUMREW (5-10-0, B de Haan), behind when pulled up before last (20 to 1 op 16 to 1); 22 Ran. 15l, ¾l, 15l, ¾l, 5l. 5m 27.8s (a 25.8s). SR: 45/25/31/16/15/10.
Jan 3, Lingfield, 2m nov hdle, soft, £668: 1 Larry-O (5-11-3); 2 Taylorstown (5-10-10, 7*); 3 CUMREW (5-11-3, J White), headway 5th, led two out to last, one pace (11 to 1 op 7 to 1 tchd 12 to 1); 10 Ran. 2l, 3l, 2l, 5l, 1l. 4m 17.4s (a 26 9s).

3031-04 HOWAREYOUGOING (6-10-5) ch g Bargello — Grangeclare Lady by Menelek.
1984-5, 2m 5f soft (Mallow). £828 (---).
Nov 2, Chepstow, 2m nov hdle, good, £1,233: 1 Cottage Run (5-11-0); 2 Kamadee (5-11-0); 3 Sidab (5-11-8); 4 HOWAREYOUGOING (6-11-0, G Charles-Jones), never nearer (14 to 1 op 10 to 1); 17 Ran. 3l, hd, 20l, 5l, 1½l. 4m 6.1s (a 12.5s).
Oct 12, Uttoxeter, 2m nov hdle, good, £548: 1 hotkole (4-10-11); 2 Granville Park (4-11-4); 3 Rovigo (4-10-11); 9 HOWAREYOUGOING (6-10-12 , G Charles-Jones), led to 5th, steadily weakened (7 to 1 op 7 to 2); 15 Ran. Hd, 12l, 1¾l, 1l, 7l. 3m 50.2s (a 2.7s).
April 6, Mallow, 2m 5f (Flat), soft, £828: 1 HOWAREYOUGOING (6-11-7, P Dempsey, 7*). (7 to 1); 2 Kool Look (6-11-7, 7*); 3 Coddie Hill (6-11-7, 7*); 25 Ran. 1¾l, 12l, 10l, 3l, 1l. 5m 21.9s.

Probables

(6) CUMREW – N. A. Vigors 5-10.5 J. White

F.	F.	C.	C.
Prom	(9)	dr	D
★★	★★★	GV	
		BLV	

(12) HOWAREYOUGOING – S. Mellor 6-10.5 G. Charles-Jones

F.	F.	C.	C.
Prom	(23)	—	DV
★★	★	G?	

This is an example of a longer distance, all-age novice hurdle, and in common with most novice hurdles having above the desired size of field. However, also in common with many novice hurdles, the outcome of the race readily resolved to only a couple of probables, with many of the runners being quickly eliminated as no-hopers.

Of the runners which had a semblance of form, AIRBORNE DEAL and QUAKER LAD were both making their seasonal début for the National Hunt season, and their fitness had to be taken very much on trust, especially as neither had been given any preparation with a Flat race outing. COLDHARBOUR LAD, although with a form figure of being placed third in its previous race, was in fact beaten by a distance and therefore could be seen to be hardly good enough. This left two probables CUMREW and HOWAREYOUGOING both with some aspirations of form.

HOWAREYOUGOING had won a National Flat race in Ireland over a distance of 2m 5f on its final appearance last season, and since joining the English stable of Stan Mellor had shown encouraging form in its two novice hurdle races over distances of 2m which seemed likely to be inadequate for this horse.

CUMREW was a candidate whose abilities had been endorsed by the rating of the official handicapper who had given this horse top weight in its previous race, a novice handicap hurdle at Huntingdon. However, CUMREW was now meeting rivals at basically level weights (age and sex allowance taken into consideration) and was therefore at a weight advantage to inferior rivals. CUMREW had two Flat race outings in the previous months and after a seasonal reappearance for a hurdle campaign 9 days earlier was thought to be likely to be reaching peak race fitness. A further pointer to be taken into account was that blinkers were being fitted to CUMREW for the first time in a hurdle race although previously they had been worn when competing in Flat races.

Applying the selection formula CUMREW was made the selection choice.

Result: 1st CUMREW (7–1) won by 10 lengths.

Form Book No. 1011 *PLUMPTON 27 November 1985 (good to firm)*

1.30—ASTAIRE STOCKBROKER NOVICE CHASE. £2,500
added (£1,983·50). 2m. 4f. (9)

1	PPP/PL1	CHOICE OF CRITICS 16 (C) R Akehurst 9-11-8	R Rowe	●78
2		CASTLE TALBOT J Long 8-11-3	R Rowell	—
4	00000/3	DRIVE EASY 13 R Parker 7-11-3	P Double	—
10	00/000-0	MASSABIELLE 9 J Ffitch-Heyes 5-11-3 ...Miss P Ffitch-Heyes (7)		—
11	16-F8F6	RISING SOVEREIGN (V) 29 P Butler 7-11-3	M Furlong	—
12	1P98L-8	ROBAND 9 W M Perrin 5-11-3	K Burke (4)	—
13	27P6P-5	WATERHEAD 22 T M Jones 5-11-3	G McCourt	—
14	007PPF/	LUCYS WILLING 931 H Beasley 11-10-12	D Murphy (4)	—
15	52-754P	WESTERN KELLY 9 R Parker 8-10-12	M T Grantham (4)	—

Probable S.P. : 10-11 Choice of Critics, 7-2 Rising Sovereign, 9-2 Waterhead,
7 Roband, Drive Easy.
FAVOURITES : 1 3 1 0 — 1 2.
1984 : Notre Cheval, 5-11-13 (M. Perrett) 2-1. S. Mellor. 9 ran.

1.30 —ASTAIRE STOCKBROKER NOVICES' CHASE
2½m   (£1,983)

PPP/P61 CHOICE OF CRITICS (9-11-8) b g
Prince Hansel — Marjo by Le Dieu d'Or.
1985-6, 3m 1f ch good to firm (Plumpton).
£2,022 (£2,022).

Nov 11, Plumpton, 3m 1f nov chase, good
to firm, £2,022: 1 CHOICE OF CRITICS
(9-11-0, H Davies), led to second, led 4th to
6th, almost unseated rider 8th, soon
recovered, stayed on well from four out to
lead run-in (20 to 1 op 14 to 1 tchd 25 to 1); 2
Wait For Me (7-10-9); 3 Golden Minstrel
(6-11-0); 4 Ran. 5l, ½l. 6m 41.8s (a 27.8s).

Sept 23, Plumpton, 2½m nov chase, firm,
£1,501: 1 Middle-Mark (7-11-1 , 4*); 2 Taffy
Jones (6-11-10); 3 Mark Paul(FR) (9-11-5);
6 CHOICE OF CRITICS (9-11-5 , H
Davies), never reached leaders (33 to 1 op
16 to 1 tchd 50 to 1); 7 Ran. 2l, 10l, 2l, 8l, 6l.
5m 17.2s (a 19.9s).

Sept 7, Stratford, 2¾m nov chase, good to
firm, £1,264: 1 Ayle Hero (6-11-6); 2
Master of Fun (8-11-6); 3 Langton Cross
(8-11-0); P CHOICE OF CRITICS (9-11-0
, H Davies), tailed off 13th, pulled up
before 15th (50 to 1); 11 Ran. 1½l, 12l, 1l, 3l,
dist. 5m 42.2s (b 0.1s).

Probable

(1) CHOICE OF CRITICS – R. Akehurst 9–11.8 R. Rowe

F.	F.	C.	C.
Proven	(16)	—	C√
★★★	★★		D√
			G√
			5 lb pen?

This is an example of a 2½m novice chase and serves to illustrate how jumping ability (best confirmed by winning form) is always a basic requirement to win over the larger obstacles. In what was a very moderate race where most of the runners were no better than selling-class ability, CHOICE OF CRITICS was the only candidate with such credentials, having won a 3m+ novice chase over the same course 16 days previously. This was a vast improvement on all its previous form, and while at first sight this might have seemed no more than a fluke, there was evidence to suggest this not to be the case. For in beating only three other opponents in what was its first ever victory, CHOICE OF CRITICS had beaten one horse which was a previous winner, while the two other defeated horses both won their subsequent races, to endorse the value of the form.

CHOICE OF CRITICS was made the selection choice after applying the formula.

Result: 1st CHOICE OF CRITICS (7–4 fav.) won by 8 lengths.

Form Book No. 1206 *HAYDOCK 11 December 1985 (soft)*

2.0—TOMMY WHITTLE 'CHASE. £8,000 added (£5,554). 3m. (4)

1 21211-1 **FORGIVE'N FORGET 21 (C&D D2)** J G FitzGerald 8-11-10 **M Dwyer** 76
2 281-1U3 **WAYWARD LAD 11 (C&D CD5)** Mrs M Dickinson 10-11-6 **G Bradley** 73
4 315F1/L **JUST FOR THE CRACK 11** K C Bailey 7-11-2 .... **P Croucher** —
6 D1132-L **EARLS BRIG 39 (C & D D3)** W Hamilton 10-10-12 .... **P Tuck** ●78

Probable S.P. : 4-5 Forgive 'N Forget, 2 Wayward Lad, 4 Earls Brig, 14 Just For The Crack. **FAVOURITES : — — — — 2 0 1.**

1984 : Gaye Chance, 9-10-12 (S. Morshead), 7-4 fav. Mrs M. Rimell. **6** ran.

2.00—TOMMY WHITTLE CHASE 3m (£5,554)

11132-3 EARLS BRIG (10-10-12) br g New Brig — Naughty Tara by Black Tarquin. **1981-2, 3m ch good (Kelso), 3m 110yds ch good to soft (Ayr), 3m 110yds ch soft (Ayr); 1982-3, 3m ch good to soft (Kelso); 1983-4, 3½m ch good to soft (Kelso), 3m 100yds ch good (Wetherby), 3m 300yds ch good (Catterick); 1984-5, 3m ch good (Newcastle), 3m ch good to soft (Haydock), 3m 100yds ch good to soft (Wetherby), 3m 110yds ch good (Ayr). £33,047 (---).**

Nov 2, Wetherby. See WAYWARD LAD.

March 28, Liverpool. See WAYWARD LAD.

March 14, Cheltenham. See FORGIVE 'N FORGET.

21211-1 FORGIVE 'N FORGET (8-11-10) ch g Precipice Wood — Tackienne by Hard Tack. **1981-2, 2m h heavy (Leopardstown); 1982-3, 2¾m h good to soft (Stratford), 2¾m h soft (Ayr), 3m 1f h good to soft (Cheltenham), 3m 300yds h good (Catterick); 1983-4, 2½m ch good (Haydock), 3m 100yds ch soft (Wetherby); 1984-5, 2½m ch good to soft (Haydock), 2¾m ch good to soft (Kelso), 3¼m ch good (Cheltenham), 3m 100yds ch good (Wetherby); 1985-6, 3m ch good (Haydock). £113,092 (£8,908).**

Nov 20, Haydock, 3m h'cap chase, good, £8,908: 1 FORGIVE 'N FORGET (8-12-0, M Dwyer), always going easily, led after last, unchallenged (2 to 1 op 6 to 4 tchd 5 to 2); 2 Richdee (9-10-7); U WAYWARD LAD (10-12-0, inc 1lb ex, G Bradley), tracked leader, jumped left 5th, hit rails and unseated rider (6 to 4 on op 13 to 8 on); 3 Ran. 8l. 6m 23s (a 11.8s). SR: 90/61/-/-/-/-.

March 14, Cheltenham, 3¼m chase (G1), good, £52,560: 1 FORGIVE 'N FORGET (8-12-0, M Dwyer), held up, hit 9th, headway 18th, led last, ran on (7 to 1 tchd 8 to 1); 2 Righthand Man (8-12-0); 3 EARLS BRIG (10-12-0, P Tuck), with leaders, every chance 18th, stayed on same pace (13 to 2 op 6 to 1 tchd 7 to 1); 8 WAYWARD LAD (10-12-0, R Earnshaw), never near leaders (8 to 1 op 7 to 1 tchd 10 to 1); 15 Ran. 1½l, 2½l, 4l, 3l, 1½l. 6m 48.3s (a 8.6s). SR: 105/103/100/96/93/91.

March 2, Haydock, 2½m chase (listed), good to soft, £11,200: 1 FORGIVE 'N FORGET (8-11-8, M Dwyer), waited with, closed up 4 out, challenged from 2 out, mistake last, led run-in, ridden out (7 to 4 on op 6 to 4 on); 2 By The Way (7-11-4); 3 Golden Friend (7-10-10); 7 Ran. 1½l, 30l, 7l, 4l. 5m 12.1s (a 6.1s). SR: 93/86/48/45/34/30.

201-1U3 WAYWARD LAD (10-11-6) b or br g Royal Highway — Loughanmore by Bargello. **1979-80, 2½m h heavy (Chepstow), 2¾m h heavy (Nottingham), 2m h good (Haydock), 2m h good (Leicester), 2m 5½f h soft (Liverpool), 2m 5f h heavy (Warwick); 1980-1, 2½m ch firm (Chepstow), 2½m ch good to soft (Ayr), 2½m ch good to soft (Sedgefield), 3m 300yds ch soft (Catterick); 1981-2, 2½m ch good (Ascot, twice, 2½m ch good (Chepstow), 2½m ch good (Huntingdon), 2½m ch good to soft (Haydock), 2½m 100yds ch good (Wetherby); 1982-3, 2½m ch good (Worcester), 3m ch good to soft (Kempton); 1983-4, 2½m ch good to firm (Huntingdon), 3m ch good (Kempton), 3m 100yds ch good to firm (Wetherby), 3m 122yds ch good to firm (Doncaster); 1984-5, 2m 5f ch good to firm (Wincanton), 3m ch good to soft (Haydock), 3m 1f ch good (Liverpool); 1985-6, 3m 100yds ch firm (Wetherby). £182,261 (£9,572).**

Nov 30, Chepstow, 3m chase (listed), good to soft, £4,409: 1 Burrough Hill Lad (9-11-12); 2 West Tip (8-11-4); 3 WAYWARD LAD (10-11-8, G Bradley), held up, headway three out, hard ridden and no impression approaching last (7 to 4 op 6 to 4); 5 JUST FOR THE CRACK (7-11-0, P Croucher), prominent to 15th, weakened and mistake next (66 to 1 op 50 to 1); 5 Ran. ¾l, 2½l, dist, 1l. ().

Nov 20, Haydock. See FORGIVE 'N FORGET.

Nov 2, Wetherby, 3m 100yds chase, firm, £9,572: 1 WAYWARD LAD (10-11-6, G Bradley), jumped well, waited with, progress four out, led on landing last, ran on strongly (evens fav op 4 to 5); 2 Allerlea (7-11-2); 3 EARLS BRIG (10-11-2, P Tuck), with leader till ridden and weakened four out (15 to 8 op 5 to 4); 4 Ran. 2½l, 20l. 6m 19s (b 5.4s). SR: 86/79/59/-/-/-.

March 28, Liverpool, 3m 1f chase, good, £7,180: 1 WAYWARD LAD (10-11-5, J Francome), held up, ran on 15th, led last, quickened run-in (6 to 1 op 5 to 1 tchd 13 to 2); 2 EARLS BRIG (10-11-5, P Tuck), chased leader until led 12th, headed 2 out, stayed on again from last (11 to 4 op 9 to 4); 3 Half Free (9-11-5); 6 Ran. 3l, ½l, 8l, 4l, 4l. 6m 02s (b 5.8s). SR: 88/85/84/76/72/68.

March 14, Cheltenham. See FORGIVE 'N FORGET.

Probables

(1) FORGIVE 'N FORGET – J. G. FitzGerald 8-11.10 M. Dwyer

F.	F.	C.	C.
Prom	(21)	dr	C√
★★	★★		D√
			G√
			12 lb pen

(2) WAYWARD LAD – Mrs M. Dickinson 10-11.6 G. Bradley

F.	F.	C.	C.
Prom	(11)	—	C√
★★	★★★		D√
			G√
			8 lb pen

(6) EARLS BRIG – W. Hamilton 10-10.12 P. Tuck

F.	F.	C.	C.
Proven	(39)	—	C√
★★★	—		D√
			G√

This is an example of a 3m conditions chase involving the very top-class staying chasers, and demonstrates how, with other factors being equal, the value of top-class form can never be disregarded, endorsing the maxim, 'Form beats everything'.

Here, in this small field of four runners, only one contestant, JUST FOR THE CRACK, could be safely disregarded. Therefore the other three runners emerged as equal probables. Each had at least one prior race already this season, FORGIVE 'N FORGET having won a handicap chase over the same course and distance 21 days earlier in a three-horse race where one of the other probables, WAYWARD LAD, had the unfortunate experience of colliding with the running rail and unseating its jockey. WAYWARD LAD had had a race since then, being beaten 3 lengths by BURROUGH HILL LAD (conceding 4 lb) and finishing third in a 3m chase at Chepstow. Earlier WAYWARD LAD had comprehensively beaten the third probable in this race, EARLS BRIG (receiving 4 lb), by 22½ lengths when they both made their seasonal début in a 3m 100yd chase at Wetherby.

On this form WAYWARD LAD would seem clearly superior. However, when last season's form is taken into account, when our three probables were all at the height of their form and fitness, it can be seen there is little to separate them. In the Gold Cup at Cheltenham over 3¼m FORGIVE 'N FORGET had beaten EARLS BRIG (at level weights) by 4 lengths with WAYWARD LAD (level weights) trailing in arrears by over 14 lengths. While at Liverpool on the fast, tight-turning Mildmay Course a fortnight later, WAYWARD LAD had reversed this form, beating EARLS BRIG (level weights) in a 3m chase by 3 lengths. Therefore the margin between these three runners at level weights was obviously likely to be quite small.

However, the entry conditions of this race prescribed that EARLS BRIG should receive a weight concession of 12 lb and 8 lb from FORGIVE 'N FORGET and WAYWARD LAD respectively. This turnaround in the weights (with ½ lb a length being the allowance for 3m chases) meant that if EARLS BRIG produced form of the consistency it had shown in the final two races of last season it would just have the measure of its two main rivals here. EARLS BRIG was therefore made the selection choice irrespective of the application of the formula because the value of its proven form could not be lightly dismissed.

Result: 1st EARLS BRIG (3–1) won by ½ length.

Form Book No. 1215 *HAYDOCK 12 December 1985 (soft)*

3.30—GOLBORNE NOVICE HURDLE (3-Y.-O.). £850 added (£1,170). 2m. (18)

4	41	STRING PLAYER 5 (D) F H Lee 11-0	C Hawkins	●78
5		APRICATE Miss C Caroe 10-7	M Barnes	—
6		BABSLAD G G Morgan 10-7	S Johnson	—
7	85	BRONZE EFFIGY 21 M Henriques 10-7	G McCourt	64
9	8	DENSTONE WANDERER 54 T H Caldwell 10-7	P Caldwell (7)	—
10	389	EMPIRE SANDS (B) 16 B E Wilkinson 10-7	M Dwyer	60
11	0	GET AWAY 20 R G Frost 10-7	J Frost	—
13	0	HICKLING SQUIRES 7 W Wharton 10-7	S J O'Neill	—
14	FP	HUMPHREY THYME 8 M W Eckley 10-7	A O'Hagen	—
17	0	RAISABILLION 22 Capt J Wilson 10-7	Mrs G Rees	—
19	4	SENOR RAMOS 5 Ron Thompson 10-7	Jayne Thompson (7)	68
20		SMART IN BLACK G W Richards 10-7	D Coakley	—
21	F	SNOW BABU 16 D Moffatt 10-7	B Storey	—
22	5	TARTAN TOMAHAWK 19 G W Richards 10-7	N Doughty	—
24		TWO COUNTIES D J Moorhead 10-7	D Condell (7)	—
25	0	ABSANNE 68 D J Moorhead 10-2	C Grant	—
26	OL	CHERRYWOOD ROSE 15 H O'Neill 10-2	S McCrystall (7)	—
28	08	SWEETWATER LASS 3 M W Eckley 10-2	J J O'Neill	—

Probable S.P. : 2 String Player, 7-2 Senor Ramos, 9-2 Tartan Tomahawk, 6 Smart In Black, 8 Bronze Effigy, 12 Empire Sands, 14 Absanne.
FAVOURITES : — — — 0 1 2.
1984 : Life Guard, 11-0 (J. Frost), 3-1. S. Harris. 16 ran.

3.30—GOLDBORNE NOVICES' HURDLE
(3-y-o) 2m (£1,170)

41 STRING PLAYER (11-0) ch c Orchestra — Ghanas Daughter by Sallust. 1985-6, 2m h soft (Wetherby). £548 (£548).
Dec 7, Wetherby, 2m (3-y-o) nov hdle. soft, £548: 1 STRING PLAYER (10-7, C Hawkins), tracked leaders, disputed lead third, led three out, stayed on strongly (9 to 4 op 2 to 1 tchd 7 to 4); 2 Syrinx (10-2); 3 Commander Robert (11-0); 12 Ran. 8l, sht hd, 15l, 5l, 4l. 4m 8.7s (a 19.2s).
Nov 20, Haydock, 2m (3-y-o) nov hdle. good, £1,243: 1 Northern Ruler (11-0); 2 Commander Robert (11-0); 3 Hobournes (11-0); 4 STRING PLAYER (11-0, S Holland), pulled hard, headway 6th, ridden and no extra from last (7 to 2 eq fav of three tchd 9 to 2); 0 RAISABILLION (11-0, Mr R Cottan), (33 to 1); 20 Ran. 1½l, 6l, hd, 2¼l. 4l. 3m 55.8s (a 6.2s). SR: 48/46/40/39/36/32.

Probable

(4) STRING PLAYER – F. H. Lee 3-11.0 C. Hawkins

F.	F.	C.	C.
Proven	(S)		D√
★★★	★★★		C√
			G√
			7 lb pen
			J√

This is an example of a 3 y.o. novice hurdle and demonstrates how the horse with experience in this type of race and good recent form is likely to hold the key. In this race which is common with most novice hurdles had more than the desired maximum number of runners, form analysis quickly suggested only one probable, STRING PLAYER.

This fair staying handicapper on the Flat seemed to have adapted well to its new hurdle career, having won comfortably in its second race over hurdles 5 days previously. This was an improvement on its initial outing when it was promoted to equal favourite to make a successful début (over this course and distance) only to pull too hard early in the race and consequently able to finish only fourth. A change of jockey, who was continuing the partnership today, may have helped to resolve the initial failure, for STRING PLAYER reversed this form with previous conqueror COMMANDER ROBERT (who itself had won before their re-encounter and therefore endorsed the value of the form). Applying the formula STRING PLAYER was made the selection choice.

Result: 1st STRING PLAYER (5–4 fav.) won by 5 lengths.

Form Book No. 1715 *TOWCHESTER 17 January 1986 (good to soft)*

3.45—SHOT GUN NOVICE HURDLE (Div. II). £1,000
(£874·70). 2m. (18)

2	P	ALDINGTON MANOR 41 P R Hedger 6-11-3	J Lovejoy	—
3		BARGE POLE T Forster 5-11-3	R Dunwoody	—
6	0	CANTORIAL 30 R C Armytage 5-11-3	A Webber	—
7	117	CLEARLY BUST 8 (D2) C Holmes 6-11-3	C Mann	●78
14		JOCKSER J Webber 6-11-3	G Mernagh	—
15	536	MORAL VICTORY 8 G B Balding 5-11-3	Pleach	65
16	349	MYNAH KEY 16 R A Perkins 5-11-3	Dai Williams	51
17	0	NO SCORE 59 R Parker 7-11-3	P Richards	—
18	94	PROVERITY 34 J A Edwards 5-11-3	P Barton	57
19		RODDY D'OR A James 5-11-3	G Jones	—
24		SINGING BOY A Hide 5-11-3	J Barlow	—
27	45	WHARRY BURN 30 I M Dudgeon 5-11-3	K Mooney	63
29		MELISSA GOLD J A Old 5-10-12	—	—
32		SINGWELL D Jeffries 7-10-12	—	—
33		TRUE BLOSSOM J Webber 5-10-12	—	—
38	P	LOVER COVER 15 J S King 4-10-5	S McNeill	—
43	F	DOMVONY 29 J A George 4-10-0	—	—
44	0	HALLOWED 29 P A Pritchard 4-10-0	—	—

Probable S.P: 9-4 Clearly Bust, 7-2 Moral Victory, 4 Barge Pole, 11-2 Proverity, 6 Wharry Burn, 12 Mynah Key.

FAVOURITES: — — — — — 2 —.

3.45 —SHOT GUN NOVICES' HURDLE (DIV II) 2m (£874)

-110 CLEARLY BUST (6-11-3) ch b Busted — Crystal Light by Never Say Die. 1985-6, 2m h good (Southwell), 2m h soft (Southwell). £1,199 (£1,199).

Jan 9, Wincanton, 2m nov hdle, soft. £993: 1 Fort Rupert (4-10-8); 2 Kitto (6-11-13); 3 Vital Boy (5-11-6 , bl); 7 CLEARLY BUST (6-10-13 , D Hood , 7*), prominent, weakened approaching two out (3 to 1 op 2 to 1 tchd 4 to 1); 23 Ran. 4l, 2l, ½l, 1½l, 1½l. 3m 58.4s (a 14.4s). SR: 16/31/22/21/19/5.

Dec 12, Southwell, 2m c/j nov hdle, soft. £651: 1 CLEARLY BUST (5-11-10, D Hood), headway fourth, led and hung left last, soon headed, led again close home (8 to 1 op 7 to 2 tchd 10 to 1); 2 Asswan (5-11-0); 3 Magnifica (4-10-6); 13 Ran. Hd, 2½l, 6l, 2½l, 6l. 4m 4.3s (a 15.3s). SR: 55/44/33/27/32/23.

Nov 25, Southwell, 2m c/j nov hdle, good, £548: 1 CLEARLY BUST (5-11-0, D Hood), in touch, ran on from two out, quickened to lead near finish (6 to 1 op 3 to 1); 2 Saint Acton(FR) (4-10-11); 3 Relkisha (4-10-1, 5*); 5 MORAL VICTORY (4-10-11, R Guest), stayed on from three out, never nearer (12 to 1 op 7 to 1); 14 Ran. ½l, 2½l, 2½l, 20l, ½l. 4m 1.5s (a 12.5s). SR: 25/21/13/16/-/-.

56-536 MORAL VICTORY (5-11-3) gr g Sweet Revenge — Princess Modesty by Lord Gayle.

Jan 9, Wincanton, 2m nov hdle, soft. £966: 1 Riva Rose (5-11-9, 4*); 2 Parang (5-11-6); 3 Pegwell Bay (5-11-6); 6 MORAL VICTORY (5-11-6, B Reilly), headway three out, one pace from next (20 to 1 op 12 to 1); 21 Ran. 15l, 1½l, 1½l, 2l, 2l. 3m 55.6s (a 11.6s). SR: 63/41/39/37/43/34.

Dec 14, Towcester, 2m nov hdle, good to soft, £1,014: 1 Tenzing (5-10-11); 2 Upham Gamble (4-10-11); 3 MORAL VICTORY (4-10-4, R Guest, 7*), tracked leaders to fourth, outpaced halfway, ran on again from three out, not quicken approaching last (20 to 1 op 10 to 1); 18 Ran. 4l, 3l, 8l, nk, hd. 3m 58.3s (a 6.6s). SR: 49/45/42/34/33/32.

Nov 25, Southwell. See CLEARLY BUST.

March 21, Towcester, 2m N H flat, good to soft, £529: 1 Hasty Gamble (5-11-3, 7*); 2 Timely Star (4-10-12, 4*); 3 Upham Gamble (4-10-9, 7*); 5 MORAL VICTORY (4-10-9, P McDermott, 7*), headway final 3f, never nearer (25 to 1); 7 PROVERITY (4-11-2, A J Wilson), no chance final 3f (25 to 1); 17 Ran. 2½l, 2l, 10l, 3l, 8l. 3m 57.7s.

0-245 WHARRY BURN (5-11-3) b g Gunner B — Sarum Lady by Floribunda.

Dec 18, Worcester, 2m nov hdle, soft, £882: 1 Atrabates (5-11-5); 2 Observer Corps (4-11-0); 3 Indian Range (5-11-0); 5 WHARRY BURN (4-11-0, M Richards), always prominent, ridden three out, weakened after two out (3 to 1 op 9 to 4); 14 CANTORIAL (4-11-0, A Webber), (25 to 1 op 14 to 1); 21 Ran. 2½l, 1½l, 4l, 2½l, 1l. 4m 11s (a 27.4s).

Nov 28, Warwick, 2m nov hdle, good, £693: 1 Ten Plus (5-10-10); 2 Timely Star (4-10-6 , 4*); 3 Prince Ramboro (4-11-3); 4 WHARRY BURN (4-10-10 , M Richards), behind till good headway from sixth, ran on (33 to 1); 9 PROVERITY (4-10-10 , P Barton), some late headway, never dangerous (33 to 1); 20 Ran. 12l, 3l, 2½l, 3l, 2½l. 3m 45.6s (a 4.6s). SR: 68/56/60/50/47/44.

Sept 21, Warwick, 2m N H flat, firm, £896: 1 Spend Easy (5-10-9 , 7*); 2 WHARRY BURN (5-10-7 , 7*), progress half-way, every chance 2f out, not quicken (12 to 1 op 8 to 1); 3 Sweet Rascal (6-10-4 , 7*); 13 Ran. 5l, 2½l, 8l, 5l, 3l. 3m 32.8s.

Probables

(7) CLEARLY BUST — C. Holmes 6-11.3 D. Hood (7) (substitute for declared jockey)

F.	F.	C.	C.
Prov	(8)	—	D√
★★★	★★★		G√

(15) MORAL VICTORY — G. Balding 5-11.3 P. Leach

F.	F.	C.	C.
Prom	(8)	—	G√
★★	★★★		C√

(27) WHARRY BURN – I. M. Dudgeon 5-11.3 K. Mooney

F.	F.	C.	C.
Prom	(30)	—	D√
★★	—	G√	

This is an example of an all-age novice hurdle which in common with the majority of such events had more than the desired number of runners. Analysis, however, quickly revealed only three probables CLEARLY BUST, MORAL VICTORY and WHARRY BURN.

CLEARLY BUST immediately appeared to have the strongest credentials, having won two novice hurdles already and in doing so beating three horses in the second of these successes who had all since been subsequent winners to endorse the value of this form. On its racecourse début in the winter sport, CLEARLY BUST had easily accounted for its present rival MORAL VICTORY, beating it by 25½ lengths, and whom it was now meeting on better weight terms. This was because CLEARLY BUST's two victories had been gained in conditional jockey races which like their Flat race counterpart (apprentice races) enable winners to compete in their next race(s) without incurring a penalty. The only doubt shed on CLEARLY BUST's superiority over MORAL VICTORY was due to both competing 8 days previously in two different divisions of a novice hurdle at Wincanton where MORAL VICTORY had finished in further place order in a faster time than CLEARLY BUST had in its race.

The explanation for this was that while MORAL VICTORY's race was the first race on the card, CLEARLY BUST's was the final race of the day. This usually accounts for the second division of the equivalent races being run slower than the first due to the race-track cutting up more on soft going. CLEARLY BUST's rather listless display may also have been accounted for by the fact that it had made numerous fruitless journeys to racecourses in the fortnight preceding this race only for the meeting to be abandoned *en route* or on arrival.

Applying the selection formula to the three probables WHARRY BURN immediately fell below the prescribed standard while CLEARLY BUST, with the considerable margin of proven form over MORAL VICTORY, was made the selection choice.

Result: 1st CLEARLY BUST (7–4 fav.) won by 1½ lengths.

Form Book No. 1779 *NEWCASTLE 22 January 1986 (heavy)*

3.0—**CRESTED GREBE HURDLE.** £2,500 added (£2,005). 3m.
(6)

2	132-0L2	CHETEL 34 (C & D2 C D) R Brewis 12-11-11	P A Farrell (4)	76
4	142604	TAELOS 11 (C) A Scott 5-11-11	C Hawkins	●78
6	L743	BLUE RAVINE 11 W G Reed 7-11-5	Mr T Reed (4)	50
8	6-54274	GAMESMANSHIP 11 P Monteith 5-11-5	D Nolan	48
9	05-6658	CALIRA 4 (C) Miss M J Benson 7-11-3	D Condell (7)	65
10	749L2-5	CHEENY'S BRIG 37 B Mactaggart 6-11-0	P Tuck	40

Probable S.P. : 7-4 Chetel, 5-2 Taelos, 4 Blue Ravine, 6 Calira, 10 Gamesmanship, 12 Cheeny's Brig.
FAVOURITES : — — 2 1 3 — —.

238

3.00 —CRESTED GLEBE
HURDLE 3m (£2,005)

21142604 TAELOS (5-11-11) gr g Godswalk — Quality Blake by Blakeney. 1984-5, 2m h good (Sedgefield), 2m h good to soft (Kelso), 2m h heavy (Kelso), 2m 120yds h firm (Newcastle); 1985-6, 2½m h soft (Ayr), 2m 330yds h good (Carlisle). £6,406 (£3,538).

Jan 11, Leopardstown, 2m h'cap hdle (Grade 1), soft, £24,426: 1 Bonalma (6-10-13); 2 Cats Eyes (6-11-4); 3 Chrysaor (8-11-5); 4 TAELOS (5-10-4, C Hawkins), (20 to 1); 22 Ran. 6l, 2½l, 1l, 3l, hd. 3m 59.6s

Dec 14, Doncaster, 2½m h'cap hdle, good to firm, £4,103: 1 Peter Martin (4-10-0, v); 2 Tamino (4-10-0); 3 Model Pupil (5-10-7); 11 TAELOS (4-11-1, C Grant), progress half-way, soon prominent and ridden, weakened three out (14 to 1); 17 Ran. 3l, ½l, ¾l, 5l, 2l. 4m 39.4s (b 4.4s). SR: 66/63/69/67/55/68.

Dec 7, Wetherby, 2m h'cap hdle, soft, £8,103: 1 Tancred Walk (6-10-1); 2 Peter Martin (4-10-0, inc 5lb ex, v); 3 Chipped Metal (6-10-10, 7*); 6 TAELOS (4-11-2, R Lamb), behind and shaken up four out, some late headway (16 to 1 op 14 to 1); 14 Ran. 4l, 1l, 3l, 3l. 3l. 4m 0.6s (a 11.1s). SR: 66/61/70/78/60/65.

Probable

(4) TAELOS – A. Scott 5-11.11 C. Hawkins

F.	F.	C.	C.
Proven	(11)	dr	D?
★★★	★★★	C✓	
		G✓	
		6 lb pen	

This 3m condition hurdle was an example of how good-class form beats everything. It was a race of a small field of six runners, where half the field as yet were still to win a race, and could be disregarded, while of the others CALIRA was a mare meeting TAELOS and CHETEL at much worse terms than in a handicap. CHETEL as a 12 y.o. was a senior dual-purpose performer experienced over both fences and hurdles, racing over the larger obstacles in two prior races this season. This left TAELOS clearly the superior hurdler who had contested the prestigious and very competitive Irish Sweeps Handicaps Hurdle at Leopardstown 11 days earlier, finishing a most creditable fourth, beaten 10½ lengths.

TAELOS here was experiencing a huge drop in class, facing inferior rivals at basically level weights. The only doubts to winning this race appeared to be the distance, over which TAELOS was previously untried. However, finishing second in a 2¾m handicap at Ayr earlier in the season suggested that the extra 2f should not be beyond it.

Applying the selection formula TAELOS was made the selection choice.

Result: 1st TAELOS (11–8 jt. fav.) won by 1 length.

Form Book No. 1835 *CHELTENHAM 25 January 1986 (good to soft)*

2.45—BISHOPS CLEEVE HURDLE. £6,000 added
(£4,542). 2m. 4f. (8)

401	147-664	BAJAN SUNSHINE (B) 7 M Tate 7-12-0	....	J J O'Neill	70
402	5111-11	CORPORAL CLINGER 23 (C & D2 C) M C Pipe 7-12-0	.	P Leach	●78
403	53/1322-	CRIMSON EMBERS (B) 297 (C) F Walwyn 11-12-0	.	S Shilston	65
404	61-11L2	GALA'S IMAGE 23 (C) Mrs M Rimell 6-12-0	....	H Davies	71
406	11111/	SABIN DU LOIR 1021 (C & D) D M-Smith 7-12-0	...	G Bradley	—
408	4307-54	MEISTER 29 (C & D BF) J A Old 6-11-8	....	Mr C Llewellyn	40
409	00/UPOO-	ANIECE 264 (D) Mrs G Jones 8-11-5	....	J Suthern	—
410	329-464	STANS PRIDE 7 G Price 9-11-5	....	R Beggan	69

Probable S.P. : 7-4 Corporal Clinger, 5-2 Crimson Embers, 5 Gala's Image, 7 Bajan Sunshine, 10 Stans Pride, Sabindu Loir. **FAVOURITES :** 0 3 3 2 1 2.

1985 : Rose Ravine, 6-11-5 (R. Pusey), 100-30. F. Walwyn. 9 ran.

2.45 —BISHOPS CLEEVE HURDLE 2½m (£4,542)

5111-11 CORPORAL CLINGER (7-12-0) ch g Bruni — Penny Candy by Tamerlane. 1983-4, 2m h good to firm (Hereford), 2m h good to soft (Haydock); 1984-5, 2½m h soft (Cheltenham), 2m h good (Haydock), 2m 30yds h soft (Windsor); 1985-6, 2½m h soft (Cheltenham), 2m h soft (Cheltenham). £42,765 (£14,657).

Jan 2, Cheltenham, 2½m hdle (listed), soft, £4,737: 1 CORPORAL CLINGER (7-11-12, P Leach), always prominent, led approaching last, ran on well (6 to 1 tchd 7 to 1); 2 GALA'S IMAGE (6-11-8, G Bradley), headway three out, challenged last, ran on (20 to 1); 3 First Bash (5-11-12); 6 BAJAN SUNSHINE (7-11-12, P Scudamore), raced wide, led to fifth, weakened two out (14 to 1 op 12 to 1tchd 16 to 1); 9 Ran. 2½l, 7l, 10l, ½l, 3l. 5m 41.5s (a 45.4s).

Dec 7, Cheltenham, 2m hdle (Grade 2), soft, £9,920: 1 CORPORAL CLINGER (6-11-2, P Leach), led after three out till approaching last, led again run-in, ran on well (20 to 1 tchd 33 to 1); 2 Kesslin (5-10-12); 3 Gaye Brief (8-11-10); 9 Ran. 2l, 2½l, 3l, nk, 1½l. 4m 22.5s (a 31s).

May 6, Haydock, 2m h'cap hdle, good, £21,397: 1 CORPORAL CLINGER (6-10-3, inc 3lb ow , P Leach), always prominent, closed up 2 out, disputed lead next, ran on under pressure to lead run-in, all out (11 to 2 eq fav of 2 op 7 to 1 tchd 8 to 1); 2 Statesmanship(USA) (5-10-3); 3 Dicks folly (6-9-11, inc 1lb ow , 4*); 9 STANS PRIDE (8-11-1 , N Coleman , 4), (14 to 1 op 12 to 1 to 1); 21 Ran. ¾l, 10l, ½l, 2½l, 1l. 3m 48.2s (b 1.4s). SR: 89/88/75/74/69/68.

320-464 STANS PRIDE (9-11-5) b m Celtic Cone — Columba by Star Gazer. 1981-2, 2m 80yds h soft (Bangor); 1982-3, 2m h good (Wolverhampton), 2m h good to soft (Wincanton), 2m h soft (Leicester), 2m h soft (Ludlow), 2m h soft (Wincanton); 1983-4, 2½m h good to firm (Worcester), 2m h good (Wincanton); 1984-5, 2½m h good to soft (Cheltenham). £17,828 (—).

Jan 18, Haydock, 2m hdle (Grade II), heavy, £11,095: 1 Humberside Lady (5-11-6); 2 Asir (6-12-0); 3 Robin Wonder (8-11-8); 4 STANS PRIDE (9-11-6 , R Rowe), held up, ran on from two out, nearest finish (9 to 1 op 7 to 1 tchd 10 to 1); 7 Ran. 2l, 2l, ½l, 12l, 10l. 4m 18.8s (a 29.2s). SR: 8/14/6/3/-/-.

Jan 10, Ascot, 2m h'cap hdle, good to soft, £3,288: 1 Kesslin (6-11-9); 2 Sailor's Dance (6-11-0); 3 French Captain (10-10-0); 6 STANS PRIDE (9-11-8, H Davies), held up, headway 5th, weakened two out (7 to 2 op 3 to 1 tchd 4 to 1); 7 Ran. 1½l, 25l, 1½l, ½l, ½l. 4m 2.6s (a 10.9s). SR: 58/57/8/18/20/26.

Jan 1, Windsor, 2m 30yds hdle (listed), soft, £7,349: 1 Southernair (6-11-4); 2 Ra Nova (7-11-7); 3 Sailor's Dance (6-11-7); 4 STANS PRIDE (9-11-2, H Davies), good headway approaching three out, soon every chance, beaten two out (11 to 1 op 6 to 1 tchd 12 to 1); 5 Ran. 2½l, 5l, ½l, 2l. 3m 49.5s (b 2.0s). SR: 86/86/81/75/75/-.

May 6, Haydock. See CORPORAL CLINGER.

Probables

(2) CORPORAL CLINGER – M. Pipe 7-12.0 P. Leach

F.	F.	C.	C.
Prom	(23)	—	D√
★★	★		C√
			G√

(10) STANS PRIDE – G. Price 9-11.5 R. Beggan

F.	F.	C.	C.
Prom	(7)	—	D√
★★	★★★		C√
			G√

This condition race hurdle over 2½m is an interesting example which demonstrates how the obvious does not always apply in racing and how a detached and questioning viewpoint can sometimes heartily reward the diligent backer. Analysis of this race with a nicely compact field of eight runners revealed two probables CORPORAL CLINGER and STANS PRIDE.

Two of the field, MEISTER and ANIECE, were clearly outclassed. Of the others CRIMSON EMBERS was definitely more suited to a longer distance and was making its seasonal reappearance, while SABIN DUE LOIR was making a return to racing after injury and an absence of almost 3 years. BAJAN SUNSHINE and GALA'S IMAGE were clearly held by CORPORAL CLINGER on their latest running over the course and distance in their previous race, and there seemed no reason to suggest they were capable of reversing this form.

Of the two remaining candidates CORPORAL CLINGER had shown much improved form this season graduating from a handicapper to being a contender for top condition race honours; while STANS PRIDE a proven performer in top company appeared to be gradually coming into form after three races within the past 25 days, the last one being a promising performance 7 days earlier at Haydock. The only comparable form line between these two probables was in their final appearance of the previous season at Haydock where CORPORAL CLINGER (receiving 12 lb) had beaten STANS PRIDE by over 15 lengths. Today CORPORAL CLINGER was set to concede STANS PRIDE 9 lb, a turnaround in the weights of 21 lb. This had to place the horses very close to one another today, other things being equal, with STANS PRIDE likely to be more favoured by this track and the distance of the race than in their meeting at Haydock. Applying the selection formula, with a strong dependence being placed on the fact that top-class horses will reproduce their known form, STANS PRIDE was made the selection choice.

Result: 1st STANS PRIDE (15–2) won by 5 lengths.
2nd CORPORAL CLINGER (4–6 fav.)

Form Book No. 2594 *BANGOR-ON-DEE 22 March 1986 (good)*

5.0—GRUNWICK NH FLAT RACE. £600 added (£1,152·00). 2m. 80yd. (18)

4		CHERRY BRAVE R Francis 5-11-10	—
9		MR GIBSON A J Wilson 6-11-10	Mr B Dowling
10	4	PHAROAH'S LAEN 113 J Francome 5-11-10	—
12	63	PROFESSIONAL VIEW 12 P Charlton 5-11-10	—
16		MUSKCAT RAMBLER W Clay 5-11-5	Diane Clay (7)
17		RYMERSTAR B Palling 5-11-5	C Evans (7)
23		CHARTER HARDWARE Mrs J Pitman 4-11-2	S Selby (7)
24		CHEDDLETON WHIFF E Wheeler 4-11-2	A Leese (7)
29		MASTER OF LYRIC D McCain 4-11-2	A Murphy (7)
30		MR REX Mrs J Pitman 4-11-2	P Plumb (7)
34		RED FESCUE C Thornton 4-11-2	
38	6	TARNSIDE LAD 12 C Parker 4-11-2	S Turner (7)
39		BELA ANGEL R Hollinshead 4-10-11	—
40		DOLEILAS BOUNTE D McCain 4-10-11	—
43	0	FILLABUMPER 17 R Hollinshead 4-10-11	—
44		GYPS GIFT J P Smith 4-10-11	N Fearn (7)
45		MODEL LADY O O'Neill 4-10-11	T Williams (7)
48		SCALE MODEL Mrs S Oliver 4-10-11	Miss Sophie Oliver (7)

Probable S.P. : 2 Pharoah's Laen, 3 Professional View, 4 Charter Hardware, 6 Mr Gibson, 12 Mr Rex.
FAVOURITES : — — — — — 1.

5.00 —GRUNWICK STAKES NATIONAL HUNT FLAT RACE (4, 5 and 6-y-o) 2m 80yds (£1,152)

-4 PHAROAH'S LAEN (5-11-10) b g Laen — Pharoah's Lady by Pharoah's Hophra.

Nov 29, Sandown, 2m N H flat, good to firm, £1,872: 1 Vale of Secrecy (4-11-2 , 7*); 2 The Sunken Road (4-10-9 , 7*); 3 Up Cooke (4-10-4 , 7*); 4 PHAROAH'S LAEN (4-11-2 , Mr T Thomson Jones), **headway half-way, every chance 2f out, weakened final furlong** (10 to 1 op 6 to 1 tchd 5 to 1); 22 Ran. 1l, sht hd, 8l, ¾l, 12l. 3m 58.2s

-63 PROFESSIONAL VIEW (5-11-10) b g Mandamus — Trade View by Khalkis.

March 10, Ayr, 2m N H flat, good, £875: 1 The Demon Barber (4-10-7 , 7*); 2 Border Peril (4-11-0, inc 4lb ow , 4*); 3 PROFESSIONAL VIEW (5-11-1 , A Charlton , 7*), **close up till lost place six furlongs out, headway on inside three out, ran on** (5 to 1); 6 TARNSIDE LAD (4-10-7 , S Turner , 7*), **progress half-way, challenged three furlongs out, weakened well over one out** (33 to 1); 24 Ran. ¾l, 3l, 2½l, 2l, hd. 3m 57.4s.

Probables

(10) PHAROAH'S LAEN – J. Francome 5-11.10 T. Thomson Jones

F.	F.	C.	C.
Prom	(113)—	D✓	
★★	—	G	

(12) PROFESSIONAL VIEW – P. Charlton 5-11.10 A. Charlton (7)

F.	F.	C.	C.
Prom	(13) —	D✓	
★★	★★★	G✓	
		C✓	

This is an example of a National Hunt Flat race, which normally attracts more than the desired number of runners and which is restricted to horses that have not previously run in a Flat race, to be ridden by conditional jockeys or amateur riders only. The nature of these races is therefore one of inexperienced horses being ridden usually by inexperienced jockeys and serving both as a learning stage in the early part of their racing careers. In the Grunwick Stakes all the horses were very inexperienced with the majority making their début on a race-track, and it would not necessarily take a particularly outstanding performance on the part of a newcomer to succeed. The most likely indication of a smart débutant emerging is by a strong market move for such a newcomer. However, this situation did not materialize and was therefore not a consideration to counter the earlier appraisal of the race where analysis had produced two probables – PHAROAH'S LAEN and PROFESSIONAL VIEW.

Both horses made their racing débuts before the midwinter freeze-up in February 1986, PHAROAH'S LAEN at Sandown late November 1985 where it finished an encouraging fourth, while PROFESSIONAL VIEW made its course début here at Bangor in early December, finishing sixth. Both these horses had been beaten by an experienced horse in terms of National Hunt Flat racing, VALE OF SECRECY, who was gaining its second consecutive victory at Sandown and third consecutive victory at Bangor, beating PHAROAH'S LAEN and PROFESSIONAL VIEW 9 lengths and 25 lengths respectively. Strictly on this running, using the collateral yardstick of VALE OF SECRECY, PHAROAH'S LAEN should have the beating of PROFESSIONAL VIEW. However, looking at the three wins of VALE OF SECRECY it seemed that its best performances had been when there had been softer going encountered, on its début performance at Ayr (won by 25 lengths) and final National Flat race at Bangor (won by 10 lengths), while at Sandown the going was only good to firm, and therefore possibly misleading.

Meanwhile PROFESSIONAL VIEW had a second outing since the midwinter freeze-up, finishing a very promising third at Ayr; with another horse, LAST GRAIN, who had finished 4½ lengths behind it, having since reappeared to win a similar contest at Kelso and endorse the value of this form. In contrast, the Sandown race PHAROAH'S LAEN contested had produced no subsequent National Hunt Flat race winners, apart from VALE OF SECRECY, completing a hat-trick. Therefore with PHAROAH'S LAEN's long absence (113 days) from racing shedding doubt as to its fitness, especially in respect of the month's freeze-up suffered throughout the country, selection formula was applied and PROFESSIONAL VIEW made the selection choice.

Result: 1st PROFESSIONAL VIEW (4–1) won by 2½ lengths.

Form Book No. 2836 *SOUTHWELL 10 April 1986 (soft)*

5.30—BROMLEY ARMS NOVICE 'CHASE (Div. II). £1,600
(£1,024). 3m. 100yd. (13)

3	P-65P61	SWIFT MESSENGER (B) 12 (C & D) D Williams 7-11-7	
			G Williams ●78
7	BPOFF	AUTUMN SHOW 29 Mrs S Oliver 7-11-3 ....J Duggan	—
10	1063/P-L	CAMP DUNPHY 15 G Hubbard 8-11-3 ....R Fahey (7)	—
16	4-2PFLL	FRENCH LIEUTENANT 24 N Stevens 9-11-3 ....R Crank	70
19	P0-B80L	HIGHLAND CHATTER (B) 20 T Bulgin 7-11-3 ....W Newton	—
21	44968P	HOWAREYOUGOING 12 S Mellor 7-11-3 ....G Charles Jones	—
26	00063/F4	RUKOTSO 6 H Wharton 7-11-3	—
28	92L9P-P	SATANTILLER 14 H Dale 7-11-3 ....S Youlden (4)	—
29	P9P77-L	SIT AND WAIT 23 G Lee 9-11-3 ....G Davies	—
33	000	THE STEEL ERECTOR 80 T Bill 7-11-3 ....J A Harris	—
36	FP	TRUDY'S LOVE 136 B Cambidge 6-11-3 ....R Crank	—
41	LL	COOMBE VALLEY 24 S Christian 9-10-12 ....R Hatfield (7)	—
42	OLFP	GILLOGUE BRIDGE (B) 19 J George 6-10-12 ......K Mooney	—

See Div. I.

Probable S.P. : 7-4 Rukutso, 3 Autumn Show, 7-2 Swift Messenger,˙ 6 French Lieutenant, 12 Highland Chatter.

P-65P61 SWIFT MESSENGER (7- 11-7)
b m Giolla Mear — Homewrecker by
Wrekin Rambler. 1982-3, 2m 1f h heavy
(Gowran Park); 1985-6, 3m 110yds ch
soft (Southwell). £2,238 (£1,272).

March 29, Southwell, 3m 110yds
h'cap chase, soft, £1,272: 1 SWIFT
MESSENGER (7-10-0, G Williams,
bl), **well placed, led to tenth, clear
from 13th, jumped right next, stayed
on comfortably** (10 to 1 tchd 8 to 1
and 12 to 1); 2 Jupiter's Gem (8-10-0);
3 Western Border (10-10-0); 13 Ran.
Dist, 10l, dist, 4l. 6m 59.9s (a 51.9s).

Jan 17, Towcester, 3m nov h'cap
chase, good to soft, £1,616: 1 Ronalds
Carole (6-10-8); 2 Country Agent (8-10-
6); 3 Royal Gambit (6-10-7); 6 SWIFT
MESSENGER (7-10-9, Dai Williams,
bl), **chased leaders to 15th** (25 to 1 op
16 to 1 tchd 40 to 1); 9 FRENCH
LIEUTENANT (9-9-11, inc 3lb ow, Mr
A Orkney, 7*), **in touch to 13th, tailed
off** (20 to 1 op 14 to 1); 16 Ran. 5l, 25l,
2l, 6l, 2l. 6m 33.4s (a 12.8s). SR: 52/45/
21/15/16/12.

Jan 1, Cheltenham, 3m 1f c/j h'cap
chase, soft, £3,635: 1 Broomy Bank
(11-11-10); 2 Lisboney Hill (10-10-2, inc
2lb ow); 3 St Alezan (9-10-0); P SWIFT
MESSENGER (7-10-2, inc 2lb ow, K
Burke), **prominent to 13th, soon behind, pulled up before two out** (50 to
1 op 33 to 1); 8 Ran. 15l, 15l, 20l, dist.
7m 3.4s (a 40.8s). SR: 38/-/-/-/-/-.

Probable

(3) SWIFT MESSENGER – D. Williams 7-11.7 G. Williams

F.	F.	C.	C.
Proven	(12)	—	C√
★★★	★★★		D√
			G√
			9 lb pen

This is an example of a 3m novice chase. It demonstrates how jumping
ability is essential to win long–distance novice chases, where in many of
these races more than half the runners fail to complete the course. An

immediate impression of this novice chase, where 5 of the 13 runners failed to complete the course in their previous race, and 5 others had finished last, was that it was hardly necessary to require any great performance in order to win.

Form analysis of the 13 runners readily revealed only one probable, SWIFT MESSENGER, a horse who won a novice handicap chase over the same course and distance and on the same going 12 days previously. This was a considerable improvement on the horse's prior form and suggested that the horse had now adapted effectively to the business of novice chasing, winning its previous race by no less than a distance (this means by over 30 lengths). Applying the selection formula SWIFT MESSENGER was made the selection choice.

Result: 1st SWIFT MESSENGER (9–4 fav.) won by 30 lengths.

Form Book No. 2900 *CHELTENHAM 17 April 1986 (heavy)*

5.10—CHELTENHAM JUVENILE NOVICE HURDLE (4-Y.-O.). £2,000 added (£2,211·50). 2m. (14)

3	911	SUPER REGAL 27 (D2) Mrs M Rimell 11-7	G McCourt	50
4	165	YALE 13 (D) J Gifford 11-7	R Rowe	69
8	4L73	BENDICKS 27 A Moore 11-0	G Moore	40
9	854444	BRONZE EFFIGY 15 M Henriques 11-0	Mr B Dowling (7)	40
10	00	CLERMONT LANE 27 M Tate 11-0	C Smith	—
12	3	DONAVAN'S CHOICE 17 (BF) F Winter 11-0	P Scudamore	40
15	845	GALTERIO 27 A J Wilson 11-0	P Richards	40
16	0520	GET AWAY 40 R Frost 11-0	C Hopwood (7)	41
19	6	LYSANDER 34 M Tate 11-0	R Crank	—
22	0P7	SAILORS REWARD 27 J King 11-0	S McNeill	—
25		SOUTHERN REAPER T Casey 11-0	E Buckley (7)	—
26	U14	STERNE 13 (D) S Mellor 11-0	M Harrington	●78
28	6	BARDO 225 Mrs D Onions 10-9	K Mooney	—
29	5	LIZZY LONGSTOCKING 14 Mrs J Wonnacott 10-9	D Wonnacott (7)	—

Probable S.P. : 5-4 Sterne, 5-2 Yale, 6 Super Regal, 8 Donavan's Choice, 14 Get Away, Bendicks, 20 Galterio, Bronze Effigy.
FAVOURITES & 1985 : No corresponding race.

U14 STERNE(FR) (11-0) b c Arctic Tern — Cesarine by Royal Palace. 1985-6, 2m h good to soft (Lingfield). £685 (£685).

April 4, Liverpool, 2m (4-y-o) hdle, good, £19,275: 1 Dark Raven (11-0); 2 Raretylo (11-0); 3 Brunico (11-0); 4 STERNE(FR) (11-0, G Charles-Jones), **leading group , disputed lead approaching last** (17 to 2 op 7 to 1 tchd 9 to 1); 5 YALE (11-0, R Rowe), **led to third, lost place three out, ran on from last** (15 to 1 op 14 to 1 tchd 16 to 1); 16 Ran. 4l, 12l, 4l, 12l. 4m 3.2s (a 11.2s). SR: 38/34/22/18/9/6.

March 14, Lingfield, 2m (4-y-o) nov hdle, good to soft, £685: 1 STERNE(FR) (11-0 , M Harrington), **always prominent, led 6th, soon clear, ran on well** (5 to 2 fav tchd 5 to 1); 2 Owen's Pride (11-0); 3 Arnhall (11-0); P SAILORS REWARD (11-0 , C Brown), **tailed off when pulled up after 6th** (20 to 1 op 10 to 1); 19 Ran. 8l, 3l, 8l, hd, 14l. 4m 1.2s (a 10.7s). SR: 51/43/40/ 32/31/19.

Jan 25, Cheltenham, 2m (4-y-o) hdle, good to soft, £7,692: 1 Tangognat (11-7); 2 Prime Oats (11-0); 3 Troy Fair (11-0); U STERNE(FR) (11-0, G Charles Jones), **blundered and unseated rider third** (20 to 1 op 14 to 1); 11 Ran. ¾l, ½l, 2l, 20l, 2¼l. 4m 21.4s (a 29.9s).

165 YALE (11-7) ch c Orchestra — Treasure Boat by Hook Money. 1985-6, 2m h soft (Chepstow). £2,810 (£2,810).

April 4, Liverpool. See STERNE(FR).

March 13, Cheltenham, 2m (4-y-o) hdle (Grade 1), good, £24,335: 1 Solar Cloud (11-0); 2 Brunico (11-0); 3 Son Of Ivor(USA) (11-0); 6 YALE (11-0 , R Rowe), **with leaders until weakened after 6th** (12 to 1 tchd 14 to 1); 28 Ran. ¾l, sht hd, 10l, 1½l, 1½l. 4m 3.1s (a 11.6s). SR: 58/57/56/46/44/42.

March 8, Chepstow, 2m (4-y-o) hdle, soft, £2,810: 1 YALE (11-3 , Peter Hobbs), **always prominent, led approaching two out, soon clear, easily** (10 to 1 op 8 to 1 tchd 12 to 1); 2 Stanwood Boy (11-3); 3 Santella Boy (11-3); 14 GET AWAY (11-3 , J Frost), (33 to 1); 21 Ran. 15l, 4l, ¾l, 4l, 3l. 4m 19.1s (a 25.5s). SR: 66/51/47/46/37/39.

Probables

(4) YALE – J. Gifford 11.7 R. Rowe

F.	F.	C.	C.
Prom	(13)	dr	D√
★★	★★★		C√
			G√
			7 lb pen

(26) STERNE – S. Mellor 11.0 M. Harrington

F.	F.	C.	C.
Proven	(13)	dr	D
★★★	★★★		C
			G

This is an example of a first season novice hurdle for 4-year-olds and demonstrates how recent top-class form can be reliably depended upon. Form analysis quickly resolved to just two probables, YALE and STERNE. Both were lightly raced having only three previous races since joining new trainers from successful 3 y.o. Flat race careers.

YALE, after comprehensively winning its début over hurdles, had been pitched into the very top class in its next race, finishing a respectable sixth in Cheltenham's Triumph Hurdle. STERNE meanwhile had made a slower start, having unseated its rider over the course and distance in its hurdle début, but went on to win comfortably its subsequent race at Lingfield.

The pair then met each other in what was the next 4 y.o. hurdle race of the season at the Liverpool Festival meeting 13 days earlier, with STERNE finishing fourth and 4 lengths in front of YALE (level weights) who finished fifth. Today the pair reopposed each other with YALE now having to concede 7 lb to STERNE although already defeated by this horse. Applying the selection formula, STERNE was made the selection choice.

Result: 1st STERNE (11–8 fav.) won by 20 lengths.

Form Book No. 2989 *TAUNTON 24 April 1986 (soft)*

3.30 — MELODY MAN CUP HURDLE. £4,000 added. 2m. 1f. (10)

3	01-0200	CATS EYES (B) M C Pipe 6-11-12 ......P Leach
5	100030	KAMAG D Holly 8-11-12 .... C Seward
6	211F22	PANTO PRINCE L G Kennard 5-11-12 ...B Powell
7	1114PF	RHYTHMIC PASTIMES J R Jenkins 6-11-12 S Smith Eccles
8	233200	SAILOR'S DANCE F T Winter 6-11-12 ...J Duggan
9	1000BP/	HIT THE ROAD Miss A Lingard 8-11-8
11	403003	ROBIN WONDER D R Elsworth 8-11-8 .. G Bradley Miss V Williams
12	0-40410	STANS PRIDE G Price 9-11-7 ....P Scudamore
16		HONEY GAMBLE P Wakely 7-10-13 George Knight
17	40F/P00	MIDINETTE Mrs E Scott 9-10-13 ....Peter Hobbs

Probable S.P. : 5-2 Panto Prince, 7-2 Stan's Pride, 4 Robin Wonder, 5 Cats Eyes, 13-2 Kamag, Rhythmic Pastimes.

01-6205 CATS EYES (6-11-12) b g
Sparkler — Le Chat by Burglar. 1984-5,
2½m h soft (Fontwell), 2m h good
(Liverpool), 2m 150yds h soft (Newton
Abbot), 2m 1f h heavy (Devon and Exeter, twice, 2m 1f h soft (Devon and Exeter). £21,977 (—).

April 3, Liverpool, 2m 5f 110yds
h'cap hdle, good, £5,524: 1 Ishkomann
(7-10-9); 2 Celtic Time (9-9-10 , 4*); 3
Indamelody (8-10-3, inc 2lb ow); 5
CATS EYES (6-11-4 , S Sherwood , bl),
**led 3rd until approaching 2 out, kept
on same pace** (7 to 1 op 6 to 1); 13
SAILOR'S DANCE (6-11-5 , J Duggan
), **led to 3rd, well placed until
weakened approaching 3 out** (6 to 1
eq fav of two tchd 13 to 2); 14 Ran. 6l,
5l, 1l, nk, 6l, sht hd. 5m 8.5s (a 2.5s).
SR: 77/62/60/71/73/49.

March 13, Cheltenham, 2m h'cap
hdle (listed), good, £11,314: 1 Jobroke
(6-10-3); 2 Taelos (5-10-6); 3 Marshell
Key (8-10-10); 8 CATS EYES (6-11-2 ,
J Lower , 7*, bl), **pressed leaders till
approaching 2 out** (10 to 1 op 8 to 1
tchd 11 to 1); 29 Ran. 3l, ½l, 2l, 7l, ½l, 1½l,
hd, ¾l. 4m (a 8.5s). SR: 78/78/79/69/75/
59.

Jan 11, Leopardstown, 2m h'cap
hdle (Grade 1), soft, £24,426: 1 Bonalma (6-10-13); 2 CATS EYES (6-11-4, P
Leech), (16 to 1); 3 Chrysaor (8-11-5);
22 Ran. 6l, 2½l, 1l, 3l, hd. 3m 59.6s.

0-46410 STANS PRIDE (9-11-7) b m
Celtic Cone — Columba by Star Gazer.
1981-2, 2m 80yds h soft (Bangor); 1982-3,
2m h good (Wolverhampton), 2m h
good to good (Wincanton), 2m h soft
(Leicester), 2m h soft (Ludlow), 2m h
soft (Wincanton); 1983-4, 2½m h good to
firm (Worcester), 2m h good (Wincanton); 1984-5, 2½m h good to soft (Cheltenham); 1985-6, 2½m h good to soft
(Cheltenham). £22,370 (£4,542).

March 11, Cheltenham. See ROBIN
WONDER.

Jan 25, Cheltenham, 2½m hdle, good
to soft, £4,542: 1 STANS PRIDE (9-11-
5, R J Beggan), **held up, led on bit
last, ran on well run-in** (17 to 2 op 6
to 1 tchd 9 to 1); 2 Corporal Clinger (7-
12-0); 3 Gala's Image (6-12-0); 8 Ran.
5l, ½l, 15l, 1½l, 25l. 5m 32.4s (a 36.3s). SR:
18/22/21/6/4/-.

Jan 18, Haydock. See ROBIN
WONDER.

4403053 ROBIN WONDER (8-11-8) b g
Dawn Review — Rainbow Wonder by
Runnymede. 1981-2, 2m h soft (Wincanton), 2m 1f h heavy (Devon and Exeter);
1982-3, 2½m h soft (Lingfield), 2m h
good to good (Cheltenham), 2m h good
to soft (Hereford), 2m 5f 110yds h heavy
(Newton Abbot); 1983-4, 2½m h good to
soft (Cheltenham); 1984-5, 2m h soft
(Cheltenham). £28,613 (—).

April 12, Ascot, 2m h'cap hdle,
good, £4,337: 1 Jobroke (6-10-11); 2
Admiral's Ruler (6-10-1, inc 1lb ow); 3
ROBIN WONDER (8-11-8, P Holley,
7), **ran on from rear fifth, every
chance from two out, one pace run-in**
(12 to 1 op 10 to 1 tchd 14 to 1); 6
SAILOR'S DANCE (6-11-5, J
Duggan), **tracked leaders, every
chance two out, no impression on
winner from last** (11 to 2 op 4 to 1
tchd 13 to 2); 11 Ran. 3l, 1½l, 3l, ½l, 3l. 3m
58.8s (a 7.1s).

April 5, Liverpool, 2m 5f 110yds
hdle (Grade II), good to soft, £13,705:
1 Aonoch (7-11-9); 2 See You Then (6-
11-11); 3 Sheer Gold (6-11-1); 5 ROBIN
WONDER (8-11-6, C Brown). **mid-division, no progress from 9th** (25 to 1
op 20 to 1); 9 Ran. 1l, 15l, 15l, 1l. 5m
25.9s (a 19.9s). SR: 68/69/44/29/23/-.

March 11, Cheltenham, 2m hdle
(Grade I), good to soft, £41,435: 1 See
You Then (6-12-0); 2 Gaye Brief (9-12-
0); 3 Nohalmdun (5-12-0); 3 ROBIN
WONDER (8-12-0 , G Bradley), **well
in touch, every chance 6th, lost place
next** (66 to 1 op 50 to 1); 21 STANS
PRIDE (9-11-9 , R Rowe), **always
rear, tailed off** (25 to 1 tchd 28 to 1);
23 Ran. 7l, 1½l, nk, 2½l, hd, 2l, ½l. 3m 53.3s
(a 1.8s). SR: 90/83/81/80/77/76.

Jan 18, Haydock, 2m hdle (Grade 2),
heavy, £11,095: 1 Humberside Lady
(5-11-6); 2 Asir (6-12-0); 3 ROBIN
WONDER (8-11-8 , C Brown), **chased
leader, every chance from three out,
outpaced after next** (7 to 2 op 11 to 4
); 4 STANS PRIDE (9-11-6 , R Rowe),
**held up, ran on from two out, nearest
finish** (9 to 1 op 7 to 1 tchd 10 to 1); 7
Ran. 2l, 2l, ¾l, 12l, 10l. 4m 18.8s (a
29.2s). SR: 8/14/6/3/-/-.

Probables

(3) CATS EYES – M. Pipe 6-11.12 P. Leach

F.	F.	C.	C.
Prom	(21)	dr	D✓
★★			G✓
			8 lb pen
			BL✓

(11) ROBIN WONDER – D. Elsworth 8-11.8 G. Bradley

F.	F.	C.	C.
Prom	(12)	dr	D✓
★★	★★★		G✓
			4 lb pen

(12) STANS PRIDE – G. Price 9-11.7 P. Scudamore

F.	F.	C.	C.
Prom	(44)	dr	D?
★★	—	GV	
		8 lb pen	

This 2m 1f condition hurdle race is a fine example of how good-class form can be relied upon and how experienced hurdlers can be expected faithfully to reproduce their known form. The entry conditions of this race stated that winners of a previous race above a prescribed value should carry a weight penalty, and except for an allowance for maidens, and sex, all horses, irrespective of ability, were to carry level weights.

Analysis resolved readily for three probables, CATS EYES, ROBIN WONDER and STANS PRIDE who had all been contesting more valuable prizes than this in their prior races. Comparison of immediate form showed that ROBIN WONDER comfortably held STANS PRIDE on their Champion Hurdle form, but there was little between them on their earlier meeting in a race at Haydock. There was no such straight comparison between ROBIN WONDER and CATS EYES, but by using a collateral form line with the reliable JOBROKE, winner of three consecutive races, there seemed little between the pair. CATS EYES had been beaten approximately 13 lengths by JOBROKE (received 13 lb) in the County Hurdle at Cheltenham, while ROBIN WONDER had been beaten 4½ lengths by JOBROKE (received 3 lb) at Ascot. However, conditions of this race required CATS EYES to concede 4 lb to ROBIN WONDER and this was considered the balancing factor. Applying the selection formula, ROBIN WONDER was made the selection choice.

Result: 1st ROBIN WONDER (5–2) won by 2 lengths.

HANDICAPS

A practical example of a handicap treated by the elimination approach, beginning at the top weight and working down the list of runners, is included here to demonstrate the technique.

It must be added that the selection decision was made before the race was run and the result known. The example chosen may seem surprising in the light of some observations and directions given elsewhere in this book, but the example of the 1986 Grand National has been included because of its immediate public familiarity, and to show how the method may be successfully employed even in what may first appear as a very daunting challenge.

The first major objection to this race obviously is the size of the field of runners, 40 horses, the now maximum safety limit for the Grand National. However, while the larger the number of runners the greater the mathematical possibilities of the result, it can be immediately stated that a large number of runners in this race have no chance of winning. In the six Grand Nationals from 1980 to 1985 75 per cent of the bottom-weighted horses failed to complete the course.

Statistically, this would suggest that the bottom-weighted horses may be immediately disregarded; and in this contest of 1986 it would include over half the runners, from ANOTHER DUKE downwards. In the original long handicap for the race all these competitors were allotted less weight than the minimum 10 st which they were required to carry in the race; ANOTHER DUKE (9 st 13 lb) was 1 lb out of the handicap, while the very bottom weight MOUNT OLIVER (8 st 10 lb) was required to carry 18 lb more than its original weight!

By beginning at the top weight in the handicap, and then utilizing the expert assessment of the official handicapper, the following horses were eliminated:

3.20 SEAGRAM GRAND NATIONAL CHASE (HANDICAP) (Listed Race), four miles and a half; £70,000 added to stakes; distributed in accordance with rule 194 (iv)(a); (Includes a fourth prize); **for six yrs old and upwards which, before Jan 12, 1986, and since July 1, 1983, have won a chase or which have been placed first, second or third in the Maryland Hunt Cup**; £50 to enter; £60 ex unless forfeit dec by Feb 11th; £60 ex unless forfeit dec by Mar 18th; £120 ex if dec to run. (No penalties after the publication of the weights). The Horserace Betting Levy Board Prize Money Scheme provides for the inclusion of £15,000 in the added money subscribed for this race. SEAGRAM LTD have generously given £54,000 towards the prize money for this race, which includes a trophy value £1,500 plus a Challenge Trophy to be returned to the racecourse by Mar 10th, 1987. In addition, they will present the trainer of the winner with a trophy value £500 and the rider of the winner with a trophy value £500. In addition, the stable employee in charge of the winner will receive £100 plus a carriage clock value £100. The stable employee in charge of the best turned out horse will receive £100 plus a carriage clock value £100. THERE WILL BE A PARADE FOR THIS RACE. (Total ent 109, 8 pay £50, 17 pay £110, 41 pay £170)—Closed Jan 15.

Weights raised 3lb

1	21112F	**ESSEX(HUN)** (Josef Cuba) Vaclav Chaloupka, in Czechoslovakia	8 12	0	Mr V Chaloupka
2	000412	**CORBIERE** --cse wnr 4½m ch - (B R H Burrough) .... Mrs J Pitman	11 11	7	B de Haan
3	P-00020	**DRUMLARGAN** (Mrs G Webb Bronfman) E J O'Grady, in Ireland	12 11	6	T J Ryan
4	023220	**KILKILOWEN** --btn fav h'cap ch- (Exors of the late Mrs S W N Collen) J Dreaper, in Ireland	10 11	3	K Morgan
5	12P1-11	**LAST SUSPECT** --cse wnr 4½m ch - (Anne, Duchess of Westminster) ..T A Forster	12 11	2	H Davies
6	31F233	**DOOR LATCH** --btn fav h'cap ch- (H J Joel) .... J T Gifford	8 11	0	R Rowe
7	0-132P0	**ACARINE** (Mrs P W Harris) .... P W Harris	10 10 13		R Stronge
8	220001	**WEST TIP** (Peter Luff) .... M Oliver	9 10 11		R Dunwoody
9	23P130	**GREASEPAINT** (Michael W J Smurfit) D K Weld, in Ireland	11 10	9	T Carmody
10	032310	**BALLINACURRA LAD** --cse wnr 2m 5f 110yds hdle - (Mrs A Moynihan) ... M C Pipe	11 10	8	G Bradley
11	0F-2241	**HALLO DANDY** --cse wnr 4½m ch - (Richard Shaw) .... G Richards	12 10	8	N Doughty
12	12-PP02	**MR SNUGFIT** --btn fav h'cap ch- (T P Ramsden) .... M W Easterby	9 10	7	P Tuck
13	024021	**THE TSAREVICH** (Major I C Straker) N J Henderson	10 10	7	J White

14 3212-F0 **LANTERN LODGE** (Mrs M Farrell)
P Mullins, in Ireland **9 10 7** .... **A Mullins**
15 1/30-4PP **TRACYS SPECIAL** (L A H Ames)
Andrew Turnell **9 10 6** .... **S C Knight**
16 0-10100 **BROOMY BANK** (Capt J M G Lumsden)
J A C Edwards **11 10 3** ....**P Scudamore**
17 130-000 **CLASSIFIED** (Cheveley Park Stud)
N J Henderson **10 10 3** .... **S Smith Eccles**
18 12111/3 **GAYLE WARNING** --cse wnr 2¾m ch - (J
G Dudgeon) .... J G Dudgeon **12 10 3** ....**Mr A Dudgeon**
19 142003 **WHY FORGET** (P Piller)..... W A Stephenson **10 10 3** .... **R Lamb**
20 00400-2 **ANOTHER DUKE** (Des Lynam) .... P Davis **13 10 0** .... **P Nicholls**
21 214/040 **PLUNDERING** --btn fav h'cap ch- (Mrs
Miles Valentine) .... F T Winter **9 10 0** .... **S Sherwood**
22 40F-0PP **TACROY** (A J Duffield) .... G A Calvert **12 10 0** ....**A Stringer**
23 234P00 **IMPERIAL BLACK** (T Webster)..... D McCain **10 10 0** .... **R Crank**
24 4030-00 **RUPERTINO** (Lord Kenyon)... E H Owen, jun **11 10 0** ...... **G Charles Jones**
25 23-0100 **SOMMELIER** (David Wates).......... R S Gow **8 10 0** .... **T J Taaffe**
26 4FP020 **YOUNG DRIVER** (J B Russell) ..... J S Wilson **9 10 0** .... **C Grant**
27 001141 **MONANORE** (J Meagher)
W Harney, in Ireland **9 10 0** .... **T Morgan**
28 P00440 **DUDIE** (J Halewood) .... P Mullins **8 10 0** ....
29 20-0411 **KNOCK HILL** (Peter S Thompson) .J Webber **10 10 0** .... **M Dwyer**
30 F-23P01 **BALLYMILAN** --cse wnr 2½m ch - (Felix
Sheridan) .... F Sheridan **9 10 0** .... **C Hawkins**
31 213224 **FETHARD FRIEND** --btn fav h'cap ch- (K
Al-Said) .... J A C Edwards **11 10 0** .... **P Barton**
32 PF030F **LATE NIGHT EXTRA** (Lt-Col E C Phillips)
K C Bailey **10 10 0** . **Mr T Thomson Jones**
33 304-444 **MASTER TERCEL** (B P Monkhouse)
D T Thom **10 10 0** ....
34 320320 **ST ALEZAN** (Lord Coventry) .... M Tate **9 10 0** ....
35 2P-0322 **PORT ASKAIG** (Lord Chelsea).... T A Forster **11 10 0** .... **G McCourt**
36 3-PP201 **LITTLE POLVEIR** (M L Shone)
J A C Edwards **9 10 0** .... **C Brown**
37 P4-P400 **DOUBLEUAGAIN** (B Clark) .... C Holmes **12 10 0** .... **C Mann**
38 1111-0U **TEN CHERRIES** --btn fav ch- (Michael Bell)
Mrs M Rimell **11 10 0** .... **A Sharpe**
39 002321 **NORTHERN BAY** (Cheveley Park Stud)
T T Bill **10 10 0** .... **Philip Hobbs**
40 0P3043 **MOUNT OLIVER** (D A Smith). M Scudamore **8 10 0** .... **J Bryan**

Adjusted long handicap weights: Another Duke 9-13, Plundering 9-13, Tacroy 9-12, Imperial Black 9-10, Rupertino 9-9, Sommelier 9-9, Young Driver 9-6, Monanore 9-6, Dudie 9-5, Knock Hill 9-5, Ballymilan 9-4, Fethard Friend 9-3, Late Night Extra 9-2, Master Tercel 9-1, St Alezan 9-1, Port Askaig 9-1, Little Polveir 9-0, Doubleuagain 8-11, Ten Cherries 8-11, Northern Bay 8-10, Mount Oliver 8-10.

LAST YEAR.—LAST SUSPECT 11-10-5 H Davies 50-1 (T Forster) 40 ran

1. ESSEX 8–12.0   the Czechoslovakian representative received top weight not because of its ability but because he was unable to be assessed by the Jockey Club handicapper, and therefore was automatically given the highest weight.

2. CORBIERE 11–11.7   a winner in 1983, and though placed third in two subsequent Grand Nationals, considered past his best and set to carry 3 lb more than on the earlier victory.

3. DRUMLARGAN 12-11.6   pulled up in 1985 Grand National, now set to carry 2 lb less but now also past its best.

4. KILKILOWEN 10-11.3   third in 1985 in a 2¾m race over the Grand National course and fences but not guaranteed to last out this extreme distance, and had showed best form on heavy going.

5. LAST SUSPECT 12-11.2   the winner in 1985 but now expected to carry 11 lb more than when successful, and as a 12 y.o. hardly likely to improve that amount. (Even the famous RED RUM who won the race as a 12 y.o. for the third time, had his weight reduced from the second occasion when he won, and from the year previously when second.)

6. DOOR LATCH 8-11.0   the most promising newcomer to the race, but as an 8 y.o. still somewhat immature. Only one 8 y.o. had won in the preceding 11 years 1975–85.

7. ACARINE 10-10.13   Held readily by DOOR LATCH when they had met in their same previous race 28 days earlier at Sandown Park, and therefore considered not good enough.

This left the next horse in the handicap WEST TIP 9-10.11, whose form credentials gave it the most promising prospects.

In its previous race 14 days earlier at Newbury in a 3m handicap chase, WEST TIP, conceding 11 lb, had beaten BEAU RANGER by 2½ lengths. The value of this form was supported in the best possible fashion by BEAU RANGER, who 2 days before the Grand National won a 3m 1f chase over the Mildmay Course at Liverpool, beating WAYWARD LAD (conceding 8 lb) by 1½ lengths, and DAWN RUN who was a first fence faller.

Since the previous year's Grand National, when WEST TIP had fallen at Bechers Brook while leading on the second circuit, this year's race had always been the horse's major objective. Therefore, having now reached the peak of its form in a race a fortnight before Aintree, WEST TIP seemed to have the strongest form credentials, especially as a winner receives no penalty after the publication of the Grand National weights.

The elimination process therefore stopped, and WEST TIP was made the selection choice, with the remaining horses in the handicap not needing to be considered as these competitors had already been assessed by the handicapper to be inferior.

Applying the selection formula to our selection choice:

WEST TIP	Form	Fitness	Class	Conditions
	★★★	14 days ★★	—	Going √
				Course √
				Distance √

with a five star rating WEST TIP could be seen to conform almost to the highest standard in the formula's rating criteria.

WEST TIP (15–2) was the winner of 1986 Grand National

Form Book No. 989 *HUNTINGDON 26 November 1985 (good)*

3.0 — HUNTINGDON SPONSORS' & TRADERS' HANDICAP 'CHASE. £3,000 added (£2,372·40). 3m. 100yd. (3)

1 31P45-1 GREENWOOD LAD (7lb ex) 10 (C D3) J Gifford 8-12-3
 Mr T Grantham (7) 76
3 2511F-L BROWN TRIX 13 (BF) F Winter 7-10-7 .... B de Haan 69
5 F35-248 HILL OF SLANE 6 (D2) A Jarvis 9-10-3 .... T Jarvis (4) ●78
 Probable S.P. : 11-10 Greenwood Lad, 13-8 Brown Trix, 3 Hill Of Slane.
 FAVOURITES : — 2 2 2 — 0 2.

3.00 —HUNTINGDON SPONSORS AND TRADERS' HANDICAP CHASE 3m 100yds (£2,372)

31P45-1 **GREENWOOD LAD** (8-12-3) b g Menelek — Rathcolman by Royal Buck. 1982-3, 2m ch heavy (Warwick), 2m ch heavy (Waterford & Tramore), 2m ch soft (Worcester); 1984-5, 3m ch good (Ascot), 3m 118yds ch good to soft (Sandown); 1985-6, 3m ch good to firm (Huntingdon). £24,594 (£3,526).

Nov 16, Huntingdon, 3m h'cap chase, good to firm, £3,526: 1 GREENWOOD LAD (8-11-2, Mr T Grantham, 7*), chased leader until left in clear lead 13th, unchallenged (5 to 4 on op 6 to 4 on tchd evens); 2 Ebony Bill (10-10-4, inc 4lb ow); 3 Ran. 20l. 6m 20.1s (a 10.1s).

April 10, Cheltenham, 3¼m h'cap chase, soft, £12,887: 1 Aces Wild (7-10-5, 4*); 2 Charter Party (7-10-11, inc 4lb ex); 3 Scot Lane (12-10-12); 5 GREENWOOD LAD (8-11-0, T Grantham, 7*), headway 16th, every chance 18th, weakened three out (20 to 1 op 16 to 1); 10 Ran. 2l, 6l, 3l, 15l, 12l. 7m 19s (a 39.3s). SR: 78/78/73/67/64/42.

March 23, Newbury, 3m h'cap chase, soft, £3,778: 1 Charter Party (7-10-7); 1D Solid Rock(NZ) (9-10-3, inc 5lb ex); 3 Areus (7-9-12, inc 2lb ow, 4*); 4 GREENWOOD LAD (8-11-7, R Rowe), chased leaders till weakened 3 out (5 to 1 op 4 to 1 tchd 11 to 2); 6 Ran. Sht hd, 25l, 8l, 10l, 5l. 6m 24.6s (a 26.1s). (Solid Rock(NZ) finished 1st and Charter Party 2nd, but following a stewards' inquiry the placings were reversed). SR: 69/66/37/50/25/33.

Probable

(1) GREENWOOD LAD – J. Gifford 8-12.3 Mr T. Grantham (7)

F.	F.	C.	C.
Proven	(10)	dr	C√
★★★	★★★		D√
			G√
			7 lb pen?

This is an example of a 3m handicap chase with a small field of three runners, where the work has already been done for the selector by the handicapper.

A glance at the form of the top-weighted and best horse GREENWOOD LAD showed it to be in top form and currently at the peak of its fitness. The only problem was whether (its jockey's allowance notwithstanding) it might be able to concede 24 lb and 28 lb respectively to its two rivals.

A close look at the form credentials of these two runners revealed BROWN TRIX to be unproven at this distance, and finishing last of four runners in its seasonal début over this distance 13 days earlier at Newbury. The form of HILL OF SLANE, although only a 9 y.o. suggested that his better days were behind him, having not won a race since the 1982–83 season, and in a previous race only 6 days earlier finishing eighth out of 14 runners, beaten by over 34 lengths.

Applying the selection formula, GREENWOOD LAD was made the selection choice.

Result: 1st GREENWOOD LAD (11-10 jt fav.) won by 3 lengths.

(*NB*. The bookmakers' margin in this small field was only 7.5 per cent making the odds most attractive to the backer and not so good for the layer.)

Form Book No. 1145 *CHELTENHAM 7 December 1985 (soft)*

2.50—GEORGE STEVENS HANDICAP 'CHASE. £5,500 added (£4,318·60). 2m. (3)

502	1116L-2	ROMANY NIGHTSHADE 14 (D4) T Forster 9-11-7	...R Dunwoody	●78
503	1F211/L	NORTON CROSS 14 (D3) M H Easterby 7-11-2	.........A Brown	71
505	L0321-2	JO COLOMBO 7 (C & D D9) Mrs W Sykes 10-10-13	...P Warner	76

Probable S.P. : 5-4 Romany Uightshade, 6-4 Norton Cross, 5-2 Jo Colombo.

FAVOURITES : 0 0 2 — 0 0 1.

1984 : Romany Nigthshade, 8-11-1 (H. Davies), 9-4 fav. T. Forster. 7 ran.

2.50—GEORGE STEVENS HANDICAP CHASE 2m (£4,318)

00321-2 JO COLOMBO (10-10-13) b g Tycoon II — Dellas Year by Coronation Year. 1980-1, 2½m ch heavy (Doncaster), 2m ch good to soft (Stratford), 2m ch soft (Ludlow); 1981-2, 2m ch good (Wolverhampton), 2m ch heavy (Warwick); 1982-3, 2m ch good (Wolverhampton), 2m ch heavy (Chepstow), 2m ch soft (Worcester); 1984-5, 2m ch good (Haydock), 2m ch soft (Cheltenham), 2m ch soft (Hereford). £19,699 (—).

Nov 30, Chepstow, 2m h'cap chase, good to soft, £1,870: 1 Troilena (9-10-0); 2 JO COLOMBO (10-11-9, P Warner), every chance three out, ran on (9 to 1 op 9 to 2 tchd 10 to 1); 3 Midnight Song (10-10-11); 9 Ran. 5l, 1½l, 1½l, 20l, 2l. (Time not taken).

April 10, Cheltenham, 2m h'cap chase, soft, £4,292: 1 JO COLOMBO (10-10-7, P Warner), chased leader till went on three out, driven out (7 to 2 tchd 4 to 1); 2 Toirdealbhach (11-11-0); 3D Lulav (7-10-4); 3 Midnight Song (10-10-5); 7 ROMANY NIGHTSHADE (9-11-11, H Davies), led to three out (6 to 1 op 7 to 1); 7 Ran. 6l, 3l, 1½l, 7l, 15l. 4m 25s (a 25.5s). (Lulav was later disqualified. Midnight Song was placed third and Dennis Auburn fourth). SR: 64/65/52/51/39/37.

11160-2 **ROMANY NIGHTSHADE** (9-11-7) b
g Deadly Nightshade — Romany Queen by
Romany Air. 1983-4, 2¼m ch **soft** (Ludlow),
2m ch **good** (Ludlow), 2m 160yds ch **good**
(Newbury), 2m 40yds ch **good to firm**
(Windsor); 1984-5, 2m ch **good** (Ascot), 2m ch
good to soft (Cheltenham), 2m 160yds ch **soft**
(Newbury). £19,334 (---).
　　Nov 23, Newbury, 2m 160yds h'cap
chase, good to firm, £3,648: 1 Admiral's
Cup　　(7-10-0); 2 ROMANY
NIGHTSHADE (9-11-1, H Davies), led
until headed two out, hard ridden run-in,
rallied near finish, just failed (11 to 2 op 5 to
1 tchd 6 to 1); 3 Ragafan (8-10-0); 7 Ran.
Hd, 12l, 1¼l, 15l. 4m 7.3s (b 1.20s). SR:
45/59/32/24/29/7.
　　April 10, Cheltenham. See JO
COLOMBO.

Probables

(2) ROMANY NIGHTSHADE – T. Forster 9-11.7 R. Dunwoody

F.	F.	C.	C.
Proven	(14)	—	D√
★★	★★★		C√
			G√

(5) JO COLOMBO – Mrs W. Sykes 10-10.13 P. Warner

F.	F.	C.	C.
Proven	(7)	—	D√
★★★	★★★		C√
			G√
			Trainer form√

This is an example of a 2m handicap chase involving a small field of only three runners and illustrates the good opportunities that always exist when the mathematical possibilities of the result are extremely few, and how in terms of odds this should favour the backer.

Assessing the race in terms of selecting the winner, each runner deserved some consideration. NORTON CROSS was the first to be eliminated having only its second race since an 18-month lay-off due to injury. It was competing here against two very experienced handicappers while only having its second race since graduating from novice company. Therefore the race seemed set to resolve between two probables, ROMANY NIGHTSHADE and JO COLOMBO.

Both were appearing in only their second race of the season, each having been placed second in their reappearances 14 days and 7 days earlier respectively. Previously the two had met in their final race of last season over the same course and distance on the same going, with JO COLOMBO winning and ROMANY NIGHTSHADE beaten over 32½ lengths and finishing last. Today the two opposed each other again on terms 10 lb better in ROMANY NIGHTSHADE's favour, but at the estimated 2 lb per length allowance (considered as the yardstick for this distance), JO COLOMBO was still favoured.

The form of JO COLOMBO had also been endorsed at Chepstow 7 days previously with the winner TROILENE subsequently appearing and defying a penalty to win again. The stable at which JO COLOMBO was trained, although modest in size, had also hit a purple patch, with three winners in the preceding 12 days – suggesting all was well with the yard.

Applying the selection formula, JO COLOMBO was made the selection choice.

Result: 1st JO COLOMBO (7–4) won by 7 lengths.

(The bookmakers' margin in this three-runner field was only just over 9 per cent – a favourable margin from the backer's viewpoint endorsing the 'value' of betting in small fields.)

Form Book No. 1582 *CHEPSTOW 6 January 1986 (soft)*

4.0—DUCK CONDITIONAL JOCKEYS HANDICAP HURDLE
£850 added (£918·80). 2m. (21)

2	101/02	VANTAGE 3 Mrs J Pitman 7-12-7	S Selby (8)	—
3	0213-U0	COUNTY PLAYER 10 (D) Mrs S Oliver 9-11-10	Jacqui Oliver (4)	69
5	10-006L	EAMONS OWEN 157 (D) Mrs S Oliver 7-11-0	D Darling (8)	70
6	12-2711	RIBOBELLE (7lb ex) 3 (D2) M Pipe 5-11-1	J Lower	71
7	24F-112	CAWARRA LAD 20 (D2) C James 7-11-0	E Murphy	●78
9	P11-55	INLANDER 11 (D) J D J Davies 5-10-10	G Heaver (4)	65
11	9614-21	SEASON'S DELIGHT (7lb ex) 25 (D) R Holder 7-10-8	A Dicks (4)	62
12	31-12F0	RETSEL 10 (D) C Popham 7-10-8		—
13	70P9-37	BALLYWEST 16 (D) R Hodges 8-10-8	W Irvine (8)	68
14	431-00	CELTIC BOB 53 O O'Neill 6-10-8	T Williams (8)	60
15	44-1421	ASMID (B) 28 (D) F Winter 7-10-8	N Fearn	61
18	246325-	PANTO PRINCE 229 L Kennard 5-10-8	D Mustow (8)	60
19	8-21337	CHEMIST BROKER 26 P D Haynes 6-10-8	P Corrigan	60
23	2-LL776	LUIGI'S GLORY 16 G H Yardley 6-10-8	W McFarland (8)	55
24	440540-	KILSYTH 222 E Wheeler 7-10-8	M Bowlby	62
25	F1P-070	MIAMI HOLIDAY 11 (D) M Castell 5-10-8	K Traylor (8)	60
27	6P3L-10	DERWENT KING 24 (D) Mrs J Croft 9-10-8	W Humphreys (4)	55
28	433747	WEE WILLIAM 32 (D5) B Hicks 9-10-8	C Evans	58
29	60500/8	JUBILEE LIGHTS 19 P Pritchard 9-10-8	D Chinn	—
31	338/0P2-	SHANNIE 371 O O'Neill 7-10-8		—
32	50FR2/6-	HUMBER PRINCE 450 G E Jones 10-10-8	C Warren	—

Probable S.P. : 11-4 Ribobelle, 4 Cawarra Lad, 5 Asmid, 8 Vantage, 9 Season's Delight, 10 Inlander, 12 Chemist Broker, 14 Eamons Owen.
FAVOURITES : 2 — 1 — 0 0 —.

4.00—DUCK CONDITIONAL JOCKEYS' HANDICAP HURDLE 2m (£918.80)

24F-112 CAWARRA LAD (7-11-0) b h Sovereign Spitfire — Spanish Coin by Matador. 1983-4, 2m 200yds h good (Huntingdon); 1985-6, 2m h good (Towcester), 2m 30yds h good (Windsor). £3,392 (£2,485).

Dec 17, Ludlow, 2m h'cap hdle, good, £1,248: 1 Merry Jane (4-10-12, inc 5lb ex, 4*); 2 CAWARRA LAD (6-11-1, inc 5lb ex, C Cox, 7*), well behind, steady, headway after sixth, strong run from two out, ran on, not reach winner (11 to 2 op 4 to 1 tchd 6 to 1); 3 Baton Match (5-10-3, 7*); 20 Ran. ½l, 8l, 8l, 4l, nk. 3m 50.5s (a 10.5s). SR: 55/60/40/41/23/35.

Nov 30, Towcester, 2m h'cap hdle, good, £1,153: 1 CAWARRA LAD (6-10-3, C Cox, 7*), held up, steady headway from two out to lead run-in, pushed out (9 to 4 fav op 5 to 2 tchd 11 to 4 and 2 to 1); 2 Wearmouth (9-10-3); 3 Desert Hero (11-11-7, 7*); 9 Ran. 3l, 2l, 2l, 1l, 2l. 4m 4.3s (a 12.6s).

Nov 18, Windsor, 2m 30yds h'cap hdle, good, £1,332: 1 CAWARRA LAD (6-10-4, C Cox, 7*), headway three out, strong run to lead run-in, soon clear (14 to 1 tchd 16 to 1); 2 Braunston Brook (7-11-7); 3 Pip (5-10-2, inc 2lb ow); 19 Ran. 5l, ½l, 2l, 2l, 2½l. 3m 45.5s (b 6s). SR: 55/60/40/52/42/36.

12-2011 RIBOBELLE (5-11-1) b m Riboboy — Belle Royale by Right Royal V. **1984-5, 2m h good to soft (Wetherby), 2m 1f h firm (Devon and Exeter), 2m 1f h hard (Taunton); 1985-6, 2½m h good (Ascot), 2m h soft (Haydock). £5,800 (£4,064).**

Jan 3, Haydock, 2m c/j h'cap hdle, soft, £1,383: 1 RIBOBELLE (5-11-7, J Lower, 7*), led after third, clear from three out, easily (13 to 8 fav op 2 to 1); 2 VANTAGE(FR) (7-12-0, S Selby, 7*), well behind till ran on from two out, stayed on run-in (16 to 1 op 12 to 1 tchd 20 to 1); 3 Lulav (8-11-3, 7*); 7 Ran. 20l, 5l, 5l, 25l. 4m 7.8s (a 18.2s). SR: 62/49/33/17/-/-.

Dec 14, Ascot, 2½m h'cap hdle, good, £2,680: 1 RIBOBELLE (4-10-5, Miss H Handel, 7*), in touch, led approaching two out, driven out (10 to 1 tchd 14 to 1); 2 Ray Prosser (9-9-7, 7*); 3 Windbreaker (7-9-12, 7*); 28 Ran. ½l, 5l, ¾l, 2½l, nk. 4m 55.2s (a 5.2s). SR: 42/29/33/34/46/36.

Oct 10, Cheltenham, 2½m c/j h'cap hdle, good, £1,459: 1 Zircon's Sun (6-10-0); 2 Billilov (4-9-9, 5*); 3 Our Fun (8-11-0, 5*); 7 RIBOBELLE (4-10-2, J Lower, 5*), led 4th to two out, still every chance flat, not quicken (5 to 2 fav tchd 3 to 1); 13 CELTIC BOB (5-10-5, T Williams, 5*), started slowly, always behind (14 to 1 op 16 to 1); 16 Ran. 2l, hd, ¾l, ½l, 1½l, sht hd, nk. 5m 5.1s (a 9s).

Probables

(6) RIBOBELLE – M. Pipe 5-11.1 J. Lower

F.	F.	C.	C.
Prom	(3)	dr	D√
★★	★★★		G√
			J√
			7 lb

(7) CAWARRA LAD – C. James 7-11.0 E. Murphy

F.	F.	C.	C.
Prom	(20)	dr	D√
★★	★★		J√
			G?

This is an example of a 2m handicap hurdle for conditional jockeys which with its large field of 21 runners may seem an unlikely race to consider for selection. However, upon closer inspection the race may be viewed in a more favourable light, holding definite possibilities for the astute selector.

Conditional jockey races tend to be some of the easiest races for a horse to win, being only just above selling grade in terms of class, and therefore requiring little ability to win. The entry conditions here stipulated the minimum weight any horse should carry was to be 10 st 8 lb. This therefore meant that 15 of the 21 runners had to carry more weight than in the original long handicap for the race. This ranged from SEASON'S DELIGHT carrying 3 lb overweight to the lowest-rated horse in the handicap, HUMBER PRINCE, being required to carry 2 st 6 lb more than its original weight. These 15 horses could be ruled out of calculations leaving only the top 6 horses to be subjected to an elimination process.

The top-weighted horse, VANTAGE, could be immediately disregarded, having been beaten by 20 lengths by RIBOBELLE who it now had to reoppose on worse terms in weight. COUNTY PLAYER had yet to show any form that had given it this position in handicap in two prior races, while EAMONS OWEN was an Irish import yet to race in Great Britain and could also be disregarded.

This left the next weighted horse RIBOBELLE, a winner in slightly better class of her two previous races, having easily trounced a field of seven horses by 20 lengths in her last race at Haydock only 3 days previously. She was penalized 7 lb for that victory, which meant her weight was raised from her original handicap assessment. Therefore it was necessary to consider the next weighted, CAWARRA LAD, who had won two of its three races this season, being raised in the handicap in the process, and encountering soft going conditions for which he was unproven.

INLANDER, the next horse in the handicap, also needed to be considered as it too originally was assessed higher than RIBOBELLE. INLANDER, a long-distance stayer on the Flat, appeared from its two race performances in this National Hunt campaign to need further than this minimum 2m distance and was therefore eliminated from the calculation. Applying the selection formula to the two probables, RIBOBELLE was made the selection choice.

Result: 1st RIBOBELLE (7–4 fav.) won by 2 lengths.

Form Book No. 1736 *KEMPTON 18 January 1986 (good)*

2.15—FULWELL HANDICAP 'CHASE. £6,000 added (£4,721·40). 2m. 4f. (5) **C 4**

301 152/1-13 **FIFTY DOLLARS MORE 9** (C D7) F T Winter 11-12-0 **B de Haan** 60
302 625-132 **ACARINE 8** (C&D D2) P W Harris 10-11-5 .... **R Stronge** 77
303 2-17246 **THE TSAREVICH 7** (C&D C2 D3) N Henderson 10-11-5 **J White** 76
307 3-3L411 **RYEMAN** (8lb ex) 7 (D2) (B) M H Easterby 9-10-6 **J J O'Neill** ●78
308 F1/LU2P **JUST FOR THE CRACK 7** (D) K C Bailey 8-10-0 .. **S Sherwood** —

Probable S.P.: 9-4 Ryeman, 11-4 Acarine, 7-2 Fifty Dollars More, 4 The Tsarevich, 16 Just For The Crack.

FAVOURITES: No corresponding race.

2.15—FULWELL HANDICAP CHASE 2½m (£4,721)

3-34411 RYEMAN (9-10-6) b g Andrea Mantegna — Enniris by Ennis. 1981-2, 2½m h good (Wolverhampton), 2m h good (Ayr), 2m h good (Haydock), 2m h good to firm (Sedgefield); 1982-3, 2m ch good (Catterick), 2m ch good to soft (Cheltenham), 2m ch heavy (Warwick), 2m ch soft (Liverpool); 1984-5, 2m 50yds ch good (Wetherby); 1985-6, 2½m ch good to soft (Ascot), 2½m ch soft (Cheltenham). £47,268 (£12,064).

Jan 11, Ascot, 2½m h'cap chase, good to soft, £7,164: 1 RYEMAN (9-10-4, inc 4lb ex, M Dwyer), led, left clear ninth, ridden and ran on well flat (5 to 1 tchd 9 to 2 and 11 to 2); 2 Ballinacurra Lad (11-11-1, 4*); 3 Misty Fort (9-11-7); 6 THE TSAREVICH (10-11-7, J White), with winner until bad mistake ninth, not recover (13 to 2 op 5 to 1 tchd 7 to 1); P JUST FOR THE CRACK (8-10-5, A Webber), hit sixth, soon behind, tailed off when pulled up before last (33 to 1 op 20 to 1); 10 Ran. 3l, 20l, 10l, 1½l, 15l. 4m 51.5s (b 1s). SR: 76/88/50/60/37/43.

Jan 1, Cheltenham, 2½m h'cap chase (Listed), soft, £4,900: 1 RYEMAN (9-10-4, J J O'Neill), made virtually all, ridden out (2 to 1 tchd 9 to 4); 2 The County Stone (9-10-0); 3 Kathies Lad (9-11-7); 6 Ran. ¾l, ¾l, 8l, 5l, 30l. 5m 32.7s (a 28.7s). SR: 69/64/84/55/50/26.

Dec 14, Doncaster, 2m 150yds h'cap chase, good, £10,016: 1 Somerled (6-10-7); 2 Itsgottabealright (8-10-7); 3 Kathies Lad (8-11-10, 4*); 4 RYEMAN (8-10-11, A Brown, bl), chased leaders, headway when mistake six out, soon outpaced, ran on towards finish (8 to 1 op 6 to 1); 10 Ran. 20l, 2½l, ½l, 2½l, 15l. 3m 54.6s (b 10.3s). (Course record). SR: 78/58/76/58/51/36.

Probable

(7) RYEMAN – M. H. Easterby 9-10.6 (8 lb ex) J. J. O'Neill

F.	F.	C.	C.
Prom	(7)	dr	D√
★★	★★★		G√
			8 lb pen

This is an example of a 2½m handicap chase with a small field of only five runners where all the runners were of almost equal fitness (all having run within the previous 9 days), and therefore simply resolving on to which was the best horse on current form.

In a field of this size it requires no great endeavour to make a thorough examination of each runner. Beginning at the top weight, FIFTY DOLLARS MORE was a top-class 2½m chaser in its prime, who had won the Mackeson Gold Cup as a 7 y.o. and the Kennedy Construction Gold Cup as an 8 y.o. at Cheltenham, but who now had, due to injury, only raced three times in the past 15 months, and who, although no longer the force of the past, was still heavily burdened with top weight of 12 st.

ACARINE, the second top-weighted horse, was these days possibly more suited by a distance of 3m and therefore likely to find this trip shorter than it required, having raced over the longer distance in all its races this season and showing a tendency in two of these to be outpaced in the final stage.

This left, of the three remaining runners, RYEMAN clearly the superior, having beaten THE TSAREVICH (conceding 17 lb) by almost 50 lengths, and JUST FOR THE CRACK (conceding 1 lb) who was pulled up in an encounter at Ascot 7 days earlier. RYEMAN also had won a 2½m handicap chase at Cheltenham only 10 days before and was now obviously at the peak of its form and fitness. The only doubts to halt its winning run seemed to be the 8 lb penalty it was required to carry, but to balance this concern, RYEMAN was set to carry just 10 st 6 lb in this race, only 2 lb more than when it was successful in a higher-class race at Ascot.

Applying the formula, RYEMAN was made the selection choice.

Result: 1st RYEMAN (6–5 fav.) won by 15 lengths.

Form Book No. 2766 *FONTWELL 2 April 1986 (heavy)*

4.30 — ROBERT GORE MEMORIAL CHALLENGE CUP (HANDICAP 'CHASE). £3,000 added (£2,599·20).
3m. 2f. 110yd. (11)

3	1-4P4PP	DON'T TOUCH 4 (C2 D) G G Gracey 12-11-7 ....C Cox	70
6	111F3-P	DR PEPPER 18 (C & D2) P D Hayes 9-10-12 ....C Rowe	70
7	3L23-32	LAURENCE RAMBLER (B) 8 (D2) S Mellor 12-10-11 Mr T Mitchell (7)	77
9	8954L2	STAR GAZETTE 18 J D Roberts 10-10-9 ....R Earnshaw	74
11	64-L31†	GRAIGUENAMANAGH 4 (C2) Miss L Bower 11-10-5 .. R Rowell	74
12	1242F2	GOLDEN HORNET 6 K W Dunn 8-10-4 ....R Stronge	●78
13	PP-5PL4	KNIGHT OF LOVE 4 (D) B Stevens 11-10-1 ..J H Davies (7)	60
14	14PPB-P	MONKTON RILL 14 (C & D) P Dufosee 7-10-0 ....R Dunwoody	65
15	3431.6/P	SPINNING REEL 12 (C & D) Miss P Barnes 10-10-0 .. M Bastard	—
16	L-24L56	BALLYDONAGH 6 (D2) D H Nugent 13-10-0 ...Mr L Harvey (7)	65
17	4PL3P/P-	SERVILIA 361 D W Browning 10-10-0 ....J Akehurst	—

Probable S.P.: 9-4 Star Gazette, 3 Laurence Rambler. 4 Graiguemanagh, 6 Golden Hornet. 8 Dr Pepper.   FAVOURITES : — — — 0 2 0 2.
1985 : Navajo Brave 7-10-9 (R. Goldstein), 9-2, J. F-Heyes. 16 ran.

4.30 —ROBERT GORE MEMORIAL CHALLENGE CUP (HANDICAP CHASE) 3¼m 110yds (£2,599)

1242F2 GOLDEN HORNET (8-10-4) ch m Golden Love — Petite Madam by Vulgan. 1983-4, 2½m h heavy (Hereford); 1984-5, 2m 1f ch heavy (Devon and Exeter); 1985-6, 3m 1f ch soft (Plumpton). £3,891 (£1,637).

March 27, Ludlow, 3m h'cap chase, soft, £1,786: 1 Little Polveir (9-11-9); 2 GOLDEN HORNET (8-10-1, inc 1lb ow , R Stronge), led to 3rd, led 8th to 11th, then 12th till after 15th, led again 2 out, headed run-in, ran on well (8 to 1 op 7 to 1); 6 BALLYDONAGH (13-9-7 , Mr L Harvey , 7*), led third, hit seventh, headed next, led 11th to 12th, weakened three out (25 to 1 op 14 to 1); 11 Ran. Hd, 12l, sht hd, 1l, 20l. 6m 17s (a 16.5s). SR: 62/39/28/44/35/4.

March 12, Newton Abbot, 3½m 100yds h'cap chase, good to soft, £3,282: 1 Broadheath (9-11-10); 2 Easter Carnival (10-10-7); 3 Bay Forest (8-10-7); F GOLDEN HORNET (8-10-7 , S May), close fourth when fell 9th (14 to 1 op 10 to 1); 14 Ran. 1l, 20l, 10l, 8l, 8l, 7l. 6m 57.1s (a 24.1s). SR: 40/22/2/ 9/-/-.

Jan 9, Wincanton, 3m 1f h'cap chase, soft, £2,066: 1 Macoliver (8-10-5, bl); 2 GOLDEN HORNET (8-10-2, inc 2lb ow, R Stronge), led 5th to 17th, every chance four out, soon beaten (16 to 1 op 12 to 1); 3 Greenore Pride (9-10-6, inc 6lb ow); 16 Ran. 15l, hd, 12l, 2½l, hd. 6m 50.9s (a 36.9s).

0005432 STAR GAZETTE (10-10-9) ch g Stubbs Gazette — Staresca by Escart III. 1981-2, 2m h soft (Roscommon), 3m ch good (Clonmel); 1983-4, 2½m ch firm (Killarney). £2,831 (—).

March 15, Uttoxeter, 3½m h'cap chase, good to soft, £2,348: 1 Covent Garden(USA) (8-10-8); 2 STAR GAZETTE (10-10-2, inc 2lb ow , R Earnshaw), good headway 13th, ridden and every chance last, ran on (14 to 1 tchd 16 to 1); 3 King Ba Ba (11-11-10); 15 Ran. ¾l, nk, 1½l, 5l, 5l. 7m 1.0s (a 28.3s).

Jan 24, Wincanton, 3m 1f h'cap chase, good to soft, £1,808: 1 Royscar (9-10-0); 2 Macoliver (8-10-10, bl); 3 STAR GAZETTE (10-10-2, inc 2lb ow, C Brown), always handy , every chance from three out, weakened between last two (20 to 1 op 12 to 1); 10 Ran. 4l, 12l. 6m 56.8s (a 42.8s)

Jan 17, Kempton, 3m c/j h'cap chase, good, £2,427: 1 Castle Warden (9-11-10); 2 Co Member (10-10-6); 3 Membridge (11-10-0); 4 STAR GAZETTE (10-10-0, M Bowlby), in touch until weakened 16th (25 to 1 op 20 to 1); 8 Ran. 2½l, 2½l, 8l, 4l, 4l. 6m 21.6s (a 21.1s).

Probables

(9) STAR GAZETTE – J. D. Roberts 10-10.9 R. Earnshaw
F.   F.   C.   C.
Prom   (18) — D√
★★   ★★   G?

(12) GOLDEN HORNET – K. W. Dunn 8-10.4 R. Stronge

F.	F.	C.	C.
Prom	(6)	—	D√
★★	★★★		G√

This is an example of a long-distance handicap chase where recent form and fitness are likely to hold the key to selecting the winner. In this 10-runner field by using the assessment of the handicapper the 4 bottom-weighted horses, all of which were carrying more than their original handicap weight, could be eliminated leaving the remaining 6 runners to be subject to individual scrutiny.

Beginning at the head of the handicap DON'T TOUCH, who had failed to complete the course in three of its previous four races, was an obvious candidate to eliminate. DR PEPPER similarly failed to complete the course in its seasonal reappearance after over a 12-month lay-off and therefore seemed likely still to need a further outing. LAURENCE RAMBLER seemed high in the handicap for a horse which had not won a race under National Hunt rules for five seasons and now was more suited to slower hunter chases in which it had been respectably competing. STAR GAZETTE, having run encouragingly in its three previous races, had to be made a probable along with GOLDEN HORNET who had similar encouraging performances in its three prior races. With GRAIGUENAMANAGH also to be discounted after failing to complete the course in its previous race, the issue rested between these two probables.

On a form line with MACOLIVER who had beaten both horses at level weights there should be little to choose between these two horses, but with STAR GAZETTE having to concede 5 lb to GOLDEN HORNET the advantage seemed to lie with the latter, especially as GOLDEN HORNET had run such a good race at Ludlow only 6 days previously and was a confirmed heavy ground specialist, which STAR GAZETTE was not.

Applying the selection formula GOLDEN HORNET was made the selection choice.

Result: 1st GOLDEN HORNET (2–1 fav.) won by 6 lengths.

Form Book No. 2854 *ASCOT 12 April 1986 (good)*

3.50—(PREFIX 4) **TRILLIUM HANDICAP HURDLE. £5,000 added (£4,337·50). 2m. (12)**

2	44730L **ROBIN WONDER** 7 (D4) D Elsworth 8-11-7 ....**P Holley** (7)	76
3	1-2332L **SAILOR'S DANCE** 9 (D4 BF) F Winter 6-11-5 ....**J Duggan** ●78
7	46-0411 **JOBROKE** (4lb ex) 7 (D6) M H Easterby 6-10-11 ......**J J O'Neill**	74
8	3105-10 **YOUNG NICHOLAS** 30 (D) N Henderson 5-10-9 ......**S Smith Eccles**	67
10	0-90F33 **MARSHELL KEY** 22 (D BF) Mrs J Pitman 8-10-7 ....**M Pitman**	70
11	5L3-114 **LANNYDROCKKK** 107 (D2) O Sherwood 5-10-6 ....**S Sherwood**	66
12	123020 **ACE OF SPIES** 35 (D3) L Kennard 5-10-6 ....**B Powell**	76
14	F-23125 **RUSTSTONE** 9 (D) R L Brown 6-10-5 ....**J Brown** (7)	71
17	6513-PL **ANYTHING ELSE** 84 (D) J Fox 5-10-0 ....**S Moore**	67
18	B56-302 **ADMIRAL'S RULER** 12 (D3 BF) F Walwyn 6-10-0 ....—	73
19	09P-123 **CIMABUE** 73 (D) C Read 5-10-0 ....—	47
24	26-31W†5 **WARILY** 138 (D) G Enright 8-10-0 ....**C Cox** (4)	47

W†—walked over

Probable S.P. : 9-4 Jobroke, 3 Sailor's Dance, 7-2 Ruststone, 11-2 Lanydrock,
7 Robin Wonder, 8 Admiral's Ruler.

FAVOURITES : 3 1 3 1 3 2 1.
1985 : Comedy Fair, 5-10-5, (J. J. O'Neill), 7-4 fav., M. H. Easterby. 8 ran.

46-0411 **JOBROKE** (6-10-11) b g Busted
— Joey by Salvo. 1983-4, 2m h good to
soft (Wetherby); 1984-5, 2m h good
(Wetherby), 2m h soft (Catterick), 2m h
soft (Sedgefield); 1985-6, 2m h good
(Cheltenham), 2m h good to soft (Liverpool). £22,358 (£16,753).

April 5, Liverpool, 2m h'cap hdle,
good to soft, £5,439: 1 JOBROKE (6-
11-8, Mr L Wyer), **headway 6th, joined
leader three out, led last, ridden
clear** (4 to 1 fav op 7 to 2 tchd 5 to 1); 2
Bold Illusion (8-10-6); 3 Chipped Metal (7-10-9, 7*); 19 Ran. 6l, 5l, 3l, 2l, ¼l. 4m
10.2s (a 18.2s). SR: 40/18/23/11/13/9.

March 13, Cheltenham, 2m h'cap
hdle (listed), good, £11,314: 1 JOB-
ROKE (6-10-3 , J J O'Neill), **progress
6th, quickened to lead run-in** (6 to 1
fav tchd 8 to 1); 2 Taelos (5-10-6); 3
MARSHELL KEY (8-10-10 , M Dwyer
), **progress 6th, led approaching last,
headed and not quicken run-in** (33 to
1 op 16 to 1 tchd 40 to 1); 0 YOUNG
NICHOLAS (5-11-1 , H Davies), **well
in touch to 5th** (8 to 1 op 7 to 1 tchd 10
to 1); 0 ADMIRAL'S RULER (6-9-12 ,
R Chapman , 4*), **joined leaders 5th,
every chance approaching last no extra** (12 to 1 op 14 to 1); 29 Ran. 3l, ¼l,
2l, 7l, ¼l, 1¼l, hd, ¾l. 4m (a 8.5s). SR: 78/78/
79/69/75/59.

Jan 24, Doncaster, 2m 150yds h'cap
hdle, good, £1,164: 1 Apple Wine (9-10-
3); 2 Vulrory's Clown (8-10-0); 3 Nice
One Andy (5-10-0); 4 JOBROKE (6-
11-10 , A Brown), **headway half-way,
every chance three out, not quicken
from next** (11 to 2 op 3 to 1); 15 Ran.
Nk, 5l, 2l, 2½l, ¾l. 3m 52.9s (b 1.9s). SR:
52/48/43/65/38/66.

Probable

(7) JOBROKE – M. H. Easterby 6-10.11 J. J. O'Neill

F.	F.	C.	C.
Proven	(7)	dr	D√
★★★	★★★		G√
			4lb pen?

This is an example of a 2m handicap hurdle showing how good recent form and fitness play such an important role in deciding what might initially seem to be a quite competitive race. However, by using the assessment of the official handicapper it was possible to eliminate many of the runners in this 11-runner handicap, beginning with the 4 horses allotted bottom weight of 10 st each. (All had been given less in the original long handicap and therefore were now required to carry over-weight ranging from 4 lb to 22 lb.)

The elimination process then proceded from the top of the handicap. ROBIN WONDER, a horse without a win in the current season had been competing in the very best class condition hurdle races including the Champion Hurdle, at the Liverpool Festival meeting 7 days previously, where it was well beaten and so appeared to be too high in the handicap.

SAILOR'S DANCE, the second top weight, also raced at the Liverpool Festival meeting, but in a handicap hurdle finishing a disappointing thirteenth of 14 runners. It was also from the stable of F. Winter which was under a cloud at this time.

This brought us to the third top-weighted horse JOBROKE who, having won its two previous races was seeking a hat-trick of successes here. Having won the County Hurdle (a very competitive handicap) at the Cheltenham Festival, and 7 days previously an amateur riders' handicap hurdle at Liverpool, it seemed the horse in top form and the one which all the others had to beat.

It had defeated three other rivals here in the County Hurdle at Cheltenham but reopposed them all on much worse terms – MARSHELL KEY was 11 lb better off for a 3½-length defeat, YOUNG NICHOLAS 14 lb better for over a 15½-length defeat and ADMIRAL'S RULER 6 lb better off for over a 15½-lengths defeat. MARSHELL KEY, if repeating its Cheltenham form, was entitled on these weight conditions to reverse form; however, in a race since this encounter it had disappointed somewhat, finishing third in a conditional jockeys handicap hurdle at Newbury. In contrast JOBROKE had continued to improve, winning a handicap at Liverpool carrying 11 st 8 lb. The elimination process therefore stopped with JOBROKE who in the opinion of the handicapper was the best horse. Applying the selection formula, JOBROKE was made the selection choice.

Result: 1st JOBROKE (7–4 fav.) won by 3 lengths.

Form Book No. 1190 *AYR 21 June 1986 (good)*

5.0—BELMONT HANDICAP (3-Y-O). £2,200 added
(£1,887.60). 1m. 2f. (6)   STALLS

1	(3)	30-3123 **TAYLORMADE BOY** 28 (BF) Denys Smith 9-7 .... D Leadbitter (5)	71
3	(2)	504-562 **FLEET FOOTED** (B) 19 G P-Gordon 9-2 .... G Duffield	77
6	(6)	08-1236 **CRAMMING** 15 W Musson 9-1 .... M Wigham	75
10	(1)	908-41 **HARD AS IRON** (D) 5 (5lb ex) P Haslam 8-9 .... T Williams ●78·
12	(4)	459-705 **ULTRESSA** 14 S Norton 8-2 .... J Quinn (5)	71
13	(5)	900-01 **SPRING FLIGHT** 25 A Jarvis 8-2 .... R Hills	74

Probable SP: 2 Hard As Iron, **7-2** Taylormade Boy, **5** Spring Flight, Cramming, **7** Fleet
'Footed, **8** Ultressa.
FAVOURITES: 1 1 0 2 3 0 0
1985: Kelro 9-3 (T Ives). 8-1, B Honbury. 8 ran.

5.00 Handicap
(0-35) 1¼m
£1,887

000-41 HARD AS IRON (8-9) b g Ardoon
— Prancer by Santa Claus. **1986,** 1½m firm
(Nottingham). £1,625 (£1,625).

June 16, Nottingham, 1½m h'cap (0-35),
firm, £1,625: 1 HARD AS IRON (3-8-3, T
Williams, 5), **well in touch, quickened to
lead 1 ½f out, soon clear** (9 to 1 op 8 to 1
tchd 12 to 1); 2 Primrose Way (4-8-4, 2); 3
Minus Man (8-7-13, 5*, 10); 19 Ran. 5l, 1½l,
1l, ½l, 5l, 2l, 2l. 2m 3.8s (b 0.2s). SR: 41/32/
29/44/35/26.

May 19, Windsor, 1m 70yds (3 and 4-y-o)
sell h'cap (0-25), good to firm, £966: 1
Snake River (4-9-5, 7); 2 Angel Drummer
(3-7-10, 3*, 14); 3 Ostentatious (4-8-13, 4);
4 HARD AS IRON (3-8-7, G French, 17),
ran on final 2f, never nearer (14 to 1 tchd
16 to 1); 21 Ran. 4l, ½l, 2l, 1½l, 2l, 1l, sht hd.
1m 43.2s (a 0.4s). SR: 45/13/25/14/21/13.

Nov 9, Doncaster, 1½m 50yds (2-y-o),
soft, £1,376: 1 Bonshamile (8-8, 3); 2 Al
Salite (9-1, 8); 3 HARD
AS IRON (8-11, T Williams, 2), **in touch till
weakened three out** (33 to 1); 16 Ran. Hd,
1½l, 7l, 2½l, nk. 2m 23.19s (a 14.69s). SR:
22/28/18/7/1/-.

00-1236 CRAMMING (9-1) b g Viking —
Damaring by Saidam. **1986,** 1m 1f soft (Ripon). £1,380 (£1,380).

June 6. Epsom, 1½m (3-y-o) h'cap (0-50),
good, £3,908: 1 Emrys (8-4, ,1); 2 Swift
Trooper (9-7, bl, 6); 3 Washaan(USA) (9-3,
inc 5lb ex, 8); 6 CRAMMING (8-0, P Robinson, 4), **behind till headway and switched
right one and 'a half furlongs out, not a
danger** (8 to 1 op 7 to 1 tchd 10 to 1); 10
Ran. Nk, 1½l, nk, nk, nk. 2m 6.07s (a 4.07s).
SR: 45/61/54/43/38/34.

May 27, Leicester, 1½m (3-y-o) h'cap (0-
50), good to firm, £2,687: 1 Modena Reef
(9-7, 6); 2 Al Zumurrud (9-5, inc 5lb ex, 10);
3 CRAMMING (9-2, M Wigham, 5), **progress 3f out, ridden and not much room 1f
out, ran on** (7 to 1 op 4 to 1); 10 Ran.
Sht hd, 2l, 6l, 1½l, 2l. 2m 6.4s (a 1.0s). SR:
42/39/32/29/12/4.

May 19, Wolverhampton, 1m (3-y-o)
h'cap (0-35), good, £2,404: 1 Al Zumurrud
(9-0, 16); 2 CRAMMING (9-2, P Waldron,
14), **led after 2f till well inside final furlong, no extra** (7 to 2 eq fav of two tchd 5 to
1); 3 Lady Bishop (8-10, bl, 4); 19 Ran. 1½l,
1l, hd, nk, 3l, sht hd, nk, 2l. 1m 43.2s (a
3.9s). SR· 53/50/43/42/33/29

Probables

(6) CRAMMING – W. Musson 3-9.1 M. Wigham
    F.   F.   C. C.
    Prom (15) dr D√
    ★★   ★★   G

(10) HARD AS IRON – P. Haslam 3-8.9 (5x) T. Williams
    F.   F.   C. C.
    Prom (5) — D√
    ★★   ★★★   G√
                        5 lb pen?

This is an example of a 3 y.o. handicap for horses graded 0–35 over a distance of 1m 2f. This race has been included to show how many handicaps may sometimes be considered fruitful betting mediums. This race has a small field of only six runners and therefore with it the possibility of assessing each runner thoroughly. The spread in the handicap was 19 lb between top weight and bottom weight.

In considering each runner these were the conclusions drawn: TAYLORMADE BOY, top of the handicap and in the handicapper's view the best horse, appeared somewhat harshly treated for its one success in a 1m maiden at Edinburgh earlier in the season, and although having raced over this distance was not guaranteed to stay 1¼m. FLEET FOOTED, a horse who had shown its best form of the season in its previous race at Folkestone, but was now fitted with blinkers for the first time (the statistical record of horses winning with blinkers for the first time is so poor that such horses should be avoided). CRAMMING was the next horse and received due consideration – having won its initial race of the season, a selling event at Ripon, but had shown itself to be better than plating class, graduating to 0.50 races where it had run respectably without being good enough to win – and was obviously a probable for this race. HARD AS IRON was the horse in form, having impressively accounted for a large field of older horses in its previous race 5 days earlier at Nottingham, which was a vast improvement on a prior performance in a selling handicap and appeared the one all had to beat. The two other runners ULTRESSA and SPRING FLIGHT appeared no more than selling-class performers.

Applying the formula to the two probables, CRAMMING and HARD AS IRON, the latter was made the selection choice having a higher star rating.

Result: 1st HARD AS IRON (85–40 fav.) won by a head.

13 CONCLUSION

The conclusion to the selection is the race result. This is the moment of truth when the opinion of selection is tested against the actual outcome of the race. It is an encounter that will provide indisputable proof of a selector's ability to apply the selection formula. And gives rise to the post-race questions: 'How' and 'Why' did the horse win the race?

The question 'How' may be quickly answered; it is always because on the day at the time of the race the horse was the first to reach the winning-post. The question 'Why', however, requires a fuller explanation, especially when selection is formulated on the understanding that all events are the subject of cause and effect.

The reasons why a horse may have won the race vary and can range from the almost inexplicable through to causes less incomprehensible but extremely rare – freak occurrences which border the edges of possibility. In the majority of instances, however, the reasons for a horse winning will be found contained within the bounds of reasoned probability.

This, therefore, allows a developing understanding to be achieved by closely referring race results to the factors that constitute the selection formula. The elements of the selection formula consistently can be identified, combined or singly, as the salient factors responsible for affecting the results of races.

The power of reasoning probabilities is therefore seen to play a commanding role in the successful prediction of race results, and such realization sweeps aside the bafflement and mystery which can surround the outcome of events. The selector is then placed in the favourable position of being able, by using the selection formula, to assess objectively the issues pertaining to past and future races.

Although there are numerous ways of making a selection it is only by the constant use of a truly objective method that the backer can hope to remain detached when partaking in the act of betting. It is essential in the understanding of success and failure for the backer to retain an unemotional detachment which will allow the selection process to be observed from a viewpoint of balance and calm.

Intuitive powers and inspiration can undoubtedly play a part in the acts of selection and betting, but they can never reliably replace the solid power of logical reasoning. The qualities of intuitive prediction should not be regarded lightly, but their value realized for what it is – the spontaneous response to situations. The initial clear intuitive insight quickly becomes clouded in the mundane chase for financial reward.

Successful betting, the profit-motivated exploitation of selection, has then always to be approached in a cool calculated objective fashion and its aims are best achieved by the use of the objective selection method provided in the selection formula.

The selection formula, although packaged to display only the cold abstracted facts of the situation, can with imaginative translation be the embodiment of the living events and acts it has represented – the flesh and blood issues it has encapsulated in names, numbers and symbols.

SUMMARY

Here are 10 commandments for the backer to obey:

1. NEVER BET WITH MONEY YOU CANNOT AFFORD TO LOSE.
2. NEVER BELIEVE BETTING IS SOMETHING FOR NOTHING.
3. NEVER RETAIN AN OPINION WHEN NEW EVIDENCE DEMANDS YOU CHANGE IT.
4. ALWAYS BET ON THE BEST – the best horses, jockeys and trainers.
5. ALWAYS BET WINNERS – winners win again.
6. ALWAYS BET ON RECENT FORM – this has the greatest bearing on results.
7. NEVER GET GREEDY WHEN YOU WIN – playing up winnings usually loses them.
8. NEVER CHASE LOSSES WHEN YOU LOSE – bookmakers depend upon punters trying to get their money back and losing more in the process.
9. NEVER LOSE YOUR CONFIDENCE – whatever else you might lose.
10. ALWAYS HAVE THE COURAGE TO BACK YOUR CONVICTIONS – yet if in doubt – don't bet.

    REMEMBER THERE'S ALWAYS ANOTHER RACE TOMORROW

You might break these rules some of the time and remain unscathed, but once you make a habit of doing so it can be guaranteed you will quickly end up wearing no shoes or socks.

REFERENCES

Daily Mail: daily – national newspaper recommended by the author for racing coverage. (Associated Newspapers Group, Carmelite House, London EC4Y OJA. Tel. 01 353 6000.)

Directory of the Turf: biannual – biographical backgrounds of trainers, jockeys, owners, etc. (Pacemaker Publications Limited, P.O. Box 90, 642 Kings Road, London SW6 2DF. Tel. 01 731 4404; postal subscriptions and orders to 20 Oxford Road, Newbury, Berks RG13 1PA.)

Raceform Up-to-Date: weekly – official form book; Flat-racing edition and National Hunt edition. (Raceform Limited, 19 Clarges Street, London W1Y 7PG. Tel. 01 499 4391; postal subscriptions and orders to 2 York Road, Battersea, London SW11.)

Raceform Up-to-Date Flat and National Hunt Annual: annually. (Published by Raceform Limited – see above.)

Racing Post: daily – national daily racing paper. (Cannon House, 120 Coombe Lane, Raynes Park, London SW20 0BA. Tel. 01 879 3377.)

The Sporting Life: daily – national daily racing paper. (Mirror Group Newspapers Limited, Alexander House, 81/89 Farringdon Road, London EC1M 3LH. Tel. 01 831 1969.)

The Sporting Life Annual Form Books: Flat Results in Full 19—, National Hunt Results in Full 19—. (Published by Macdonald/Queen Anne Press, Maxwell House, 74 Worship Street, London EC2A 2EN.)

Timeform ('Black book'): weekly. (Timeform Publications, Timeform House, Northgate, Halifax, West Yorks HX1 1XE. Tel. 0422 63322.)

Timeform Racecards (Flat and National Hunt meetings): daily. (Published by Timeform Limited – see above.)

Racehorses of 19– (Flat): annually, March. (Published by Timeform Limited – see above.)

Chasers and Hurdlers (National Hunt): annually, October. (Published by Timeform Limited – see above.)

Trainers Record: annually – annual analysis of trainers' records, Flat and National Hunt edition. (Trainers Record, Melplash Farmhouse, Melplash, Bridport, Dorset DT6 3UH. Tel. 030888 383.)

FURTHER READING

Pacemaker: monthly racing magazine. (Pacemaker Publications Limited, P.O. Box 90, 642 Kings Road, London SW6 2DF. Tel. 01 731 4404; postal subscriptions and orders to 20 Oxford Road, Newbury, Berks RG13 1PA.)

Racing Calendar: weekly – official Jockey Club record of entries; Stewards report; horses' official handicap rating, etc. (Weatherbys, Sanders Road, Wellingborough, Northants NN8 4BX. Tel. 0933 76241.)

Statistical Record: annual – details of sires' and dams' performances. (Published by Weatherbys – see above.)

The European Racehorse: quarterly racing publication. (Raceform Limited, 19 Clarges Street, London W1Y 7PG. Tel. 01 499 4391.)

INDEX

The numerals in **bold** type refer to the illustrations